A Moral Critique of Development

D1472020

In the twenty-first century, the ideology of development is no longer secure. Vitriolic critiques of international development practice, affecting some of the West's most prestigious and best-supported aid organisations, have attacked the motives of those heading the 'monolithic machine' of global development, suggesting that development intervention is in reality just too politically complex for good to come of it. But, despite the genuine need for critical appraisal of development work, any anti-development backlash appears to lead towards a moral impasse. Is it worth engaging with countries and people in need, given the risk of potentially corrupt and harmful involvements? On the other hand, can we morally legitimise any withdrawal of aid from those whose livelihoods depend on it?

A Moral Critique of Development is a pragmatic and sometimes prophetic moral response to this crisis. Featuring sophisticated perspectives from workers and consultants in the development industry, the book draws practical lessons from actual projects – successful and otherwise – to propose a novel ethical solution to a very modern problem. Arguing that moral understanding of development intervention cannot successfully be generalised, it instead proposes a theory of 'emergent ethics': that local moral responses to specific projects must give the basis for a way forward. Restoring both practical, political and scholarly agendas for development, the book is an invaluable commentary on how and where international development might once again become a visionary project.

Philip Quarles van Ufford teaches Cultural Anthropology and Non-Western Sociology at the Free University in Amsterdam. **Ananta Kumar Giri** teaches at the Madras Institute of Development Studies, Chennai.

A Moral Critique
of Development

In search of global responsibilities

Edited by
Philip Quarles van Ufford
and Ananta Kumar Giri

EIDOS

Routledge
Taylor & Francis Group
LONDON AND NEW YORK

First published 2003
by Routledge
11 New Fetter Lane, London EC4P 4EE

Simultaneously published in the USA and Canada
by Routledge
29 West 35th Street, New York, NY 10001

Routledge is an imprint of the Taylor & Francis Group

Typeset in Times by Taylor & Francis Books Ltd
Printed and bound in Great Britain by MPG Books Ltd, Bodmin

British Library Cataloguing in Publication Data
A catalogue record for this book is available from the British
Library

Library of Congress Cataloging in Publication Data
A catalog record for this book has been requested

ISBN 0–415–27625–X (hbk)
ISBN 0–415–27626–8 (pbk)

Contents

Contributors

Albert E. Alejo, SJ, was director of the Archdiocese of Manila Labour Centre and an author of books on philosophy and poetry in Filipino, before he took his doctorate in social anthropology at the School of Oriental and African Studies, University of London. His book *Generating Energies in Mount Apo: Cultural Politics in a Contested Environment* (Ateneo de Manila University Press, 2000) describes a tribal people's cultural energies in the face of a controversial power development project. He teaches social science and philosophy at the graduate school of Ateneo de Davao University, where he heads the Research and Publication Office and 'Mindanawon Initiatives for Cultural Dialogue'. Alejo is involved in putting up a graduate programme in anthropology, as well as in encouraging indigenous peoples towards greater participation in the Mindanao peace process.

Des Gasper is an economist who has studied in Cambridge and East Anglia. He is attached to the Institute of Social Studies in The Hague. He specialises on issues of public policy and administration and development ethics. He has been convenor to the development ethics study group. He has published widely in the domains of development ethics. His regional interests are South Asia and Southern Africa.

Ananta Kumar Giri is currently on the faculty of the Madras Institute of Development Studies, Chennai, India and has an abiding interest in contemporary social theory and cultural movements. Dr Giri is the author of *Global Transformations: Postmodernity and Beyond* (1998), *Values, Ethics and Business: Challenges for Education and Management* (1998), *Building in the Margins of Shacks: the Vision and Projects of Habitat for Humanity* (2001) and *Conversations and Transformations: Towards a New Ethics of Self and Society* (2002). He has recently edited *Rethinking Social Transformation: Criticism and Creativity at the Turn of the Millennium* (2001). He also writes in Oriya, in which he has written five books.

Elizabeth Harrison is a Lecturer in Social Anthropology at the University of Sussex. She has undertaken research in Southern Africa, Ethiopia, and Sri Lanka. Her research has focused on the anthropology of development, with a particular interest in gender and development. She is the co-author of *Whose Development? An Ethnography of Aid* (Zed Books, 1998). This book examines the gap between policy and practice in the development process, and is based on ethnographic material from Zambia and Sri Lanka. Recent research projects, both funded by DFID, have examined policies of participation and institutional aspects of aid.

David Mosse is a lecturer in Social Anthropology at the School of Oriental and African Studies, University of London, specialising in the anthropology of development. He has undertaken ethnographic and historical work in south India on common property water resources, popular religion and missions, and *dalit* social life. He worked as an Oxfam Representative in south India for several years and as a consultant in participatory rural development throughout the South Asian region.

Peter Penz is Director of York University's Centre for Refugee Studies, and Associate Professor in the Faculty of Environmental Studies. He is principal investigator for two team projects on the ethics of development-induced displacement, one in partnership with the Centre for the Study of Regional Development at the Jawaharlal Nehru University in New Delhi. His publications include *Consumer Sovereignty and Human Interests* (Cambridge University Press, 1986), *The Real Poverty Report* (co-authored, Hurtig, Canada, 1971), the edited volumes *Political Ecology: Global and Local* (Routledge, 1998) and *Global Justice, Global Democracy* (Fernwood, Canada, 1997), a monograph on structural unemployment, and chapters and articles on atrocities policing, development ethics, state sovereignty and international justice, power and justice in international relations, land-rights mobilisation in India, and the colonisation of tribal lands in Bangladesh and Indonesia.

Philip Quarles van Ufford is attached to the department of anthropology of the Free University, Amsterdam. He has published various essays and volumes specialising on development policy practices, and the international linkages between private and governmental development agencies. He has also published a number of studies on Indonesian churches, especially in Central Java. His regional interest is Southeast Asia, particularly Indonesia. He has been active in various managerial and advisory capacities in development agencies. He is currently preparing two studies, the first entitled 'Christianity as a Javanese religion (1860–2000)', the second 'Contradictions and contingencies of development policy practice'.

Alan Rew is an anthropologist who, very early in his career, became interested in the institutional and moral dilemmas of planned development.

His detailed research into street-level bureaucracy and urban poverty in Papua New Guinea and the Philippines and the social life within formal institutions led him to reflect on the institutional encounters experienced by villagers and slum-dwellers as they seek to build livelihoods and adapt to new social circumstances. This led him to undertake research and advisory work on international development, especially on the morally tense 'institutional connection' between individuals and communities and the organisation of planned development through state, private sector and civil society agencies. He has often been engaged in the social analysis of the livelihood and ethical consequences of displacement and re-settlement. In addition to the case study reported in this volume, he has carried out research and advisory work on population dislocation and re-settlement in Sri Lanka, Orissa and West Bengal, Zimbabwe and Ethiopia. His other current research interests include livelihood diversification and poverty reduction, 'process' and impact indicators, forest sector policy, and state and society in Orissa, India. He can be contacted by email at alan_rew@bigfoot.com. He is currently Professor of Development Policy and Planning and Director of the Centre for Development Studies at the University of Wales, Swansea.

Dik Roth currently works as a researcher and lecturer at the Law and Governance Group of Wageningen University, the Netherlands. His teachings focus on socio-legal studies, the role of law in development intervention processes, and the use and management of natural resources. He has worked as a consultant on land reform and farmer settlement in the Pompengan Integrated Area Development Project, an irrigation and rural development project in Luwu District, South Sulawesi, Indonesia. In the framework of his PhD research he has carried out extensive research in the same region on migration and transmigration, land reform and irrigation development, and local irrigation management among Balinese settlers. He is currently engaged in a research programme in India and Nepal, covering the technical, socio-legal and institutional aspects of irrigation.

Oscar Salemink is a lecturer of cultural anthropology and development sociology at the Free University in Amsterdam. He studied anthropology and history and received his doctoral degree from the University of Amsterdam with a study of the highland minorities of Vietnam. From 1996 to 2001 he worked for the Ford Foundation as a programme officer for social sciences and humanities in Vietnam. His publications include 'Colonial Ethnographies', a special issue of *History and Anthropology* (co-edited with Peter Pels, 1994); *Colonial Subjects: Essays on the Practical History of Anthropology* (co-edited with Peter Pels, University of Michigan Press, 1999); *The Ethnography of Vietnam's Central Highlanders: a Historical Contextualization, 1850–1990* (Curzon

Press/University of Hawaii Press, 2000); and *Viet Nam's Cultural Diversity: Approaches to Preservation* (UNESCO, 2001).

Els Scholte studied business communication in Utrecht and cultural anthropology at the Free University in Amsterdam. She has worked as a communication officer for Kerken in Aktie, the development agency of the Dutch Protestant Churches, from 1997 to 2001. In April 1999 she worked as a spokesperson for Kerken in Aktie in Macedonia. Currently she is working as a communications officer for the WHO/PAHO in Surinam. She has one daughter.

George Ulrich holds an MA in social anthropology, and an MA and PhD in philosophy. He is currently employed as senior researcher at the Danish Centre for Human Rights. He has previously worked extensively in the area of research ethics, in particular in the areas of medicine and social science, and in connection with donor-sponsored research in developing countries. He is now engaged in various projects concerning the philosophy of human rights, the relationship between bio-ethics and human rights, and the interpretation and implementation of the right to health. Recent publications include: *Globally Speaking: On the Ethics of Research in Developing Countries*, report prepared for the Danish Council for Development Research, Copenhagen, 1999 (under revision); 'What we are talking about when we talk about ethics: towards an integrated approach to the ethics of development and development research' in *FAU Seminar 2000: the Politics and the Ethics of North–South Relations*, The Association of Development Researchers in Denmark, Copenhagen, 2000; 'Universal Human Rights: An unfinished project' in *Human Rights on Common Grounds: The Question of Universality*, Pluto Press, 2001.

Preface

Development is a global moral engagement. This conviction is central to this book. We set ourselves the task of regaining a morally meaningful perspective on development. Studies of development should once again become clearly expressive of a sense of responsibility. For that reason, in every chapter an effort is made to link debates in the domains of development anthropology with contesting points of view in moral philosophy. Development practices imply both empirical and moral narratives. Learning to fuse the two is important, for we do not yet know how this should be done. Let us therefore first seek to make sense of the ambiguous relations between the two genres. This may lead to reasoned moral judgement and, as these emerging moral views become part of a disciplinary debate, to new modes of learning. At the same time the academic standards of a critical empirical narrative describing and analysing the relationship between various kinds of actors need to be upheld. Taking up the two tasks simultaneously may help us go beyond the impasse in which the latest traditions of deconstruction and post-structuralism in development anthropology have seduced us. This volume, then, is an explorative moral critique of development practices. This may – we hope – pave the way towards greater awareness that development is a shared responsibility.

How shall we link the tasks of understanding and responsibility? We propose a multi-dimensional view of development – as hope, as politics (and administration), and as critical reflection. These have in the past stealthily grown apart. Would not acknowledging each of these three domains of practice, so that they can be taken up into a broader moral view of development, be a step forward? Much is to be gained when we allow space for a search for new linkages between them. This is why we here also mean to address politicians and administrators. They too should allow themselves to rethink development relations as a moral problem, and open the door for an engagement in development which goes beyond the accustomed routines of development agencies, policies and programmes. The gradual locking of the doors of development institutions to a wider public has first of all harmed the work of the professionals inside.

The core of the volume consists in case studies. The contributors reflect critically on their wide practical experiences in development institutions and policies. This results in something of a panorama of development practices. The authors look for morally meaningful linkages between micro practices analysed in the case studies and the notion of a global moral responsibility in development.

We propose an approach to development ethics at the hub of which are notions of contingency, disjuncture and emergence. We cannot place either facts or values first and come away unscathed. Ultimately, therefore, we intend to articulate the disjuncture within development ethics in terms of an uncertain relationship between two moral engagements: an ethical concern as 'care for the other' on the one hand, and an aesthetic 'care of the self' on the other. While development ethics has been seen as expressive of responsibility to the other, aesthetic development prepares the self for undertaking such responsibilities. In this way we propose some transformation of more conventional approaches in which the care of the self did not gain an appropriate place. This broadening of the agenda of development ethics would skirt the pitfalls of an 'either or' approach of ethics or aesthetics and points the way to moral engagement which is attentive to both responsibility to the other and responsibility to self. This morally inclusive view indeed allows development to become a shared global concern. In an afterword Ananta Kumar Giri adds some further comments. He makes a strong plea for a 'transcivilisational understanding' of the notion of development, and to go beyond development as a primarily Western-induced practice.

The idea of a moral critique of development was conceived within the EIDOS group, a network of German, English and Dutch anthropologists. It was the last part of a research project called: 'Development, a Retreat from the Real'. We acknowledge with gratitude the efforts of the people and institutions who made the volume possible. We are deeply appreciative of the Ministry of Foreign Affairs of the Netherlands, especially to Rob D. Van den Berg and his successor Dr Leen Boer as head of the Ministry's department of research. They graciously gave the EIDOS project a chance even when its practical uses may have been somewhat unclear. For their willingness to make room for and devote time to this endeavour we are deeply grateful. We wish to thank also the Netherlands Organisation for Scientific Research (NWO), and the International Institute for Asian Studies (IIAS) in Leiden for their support. The Faculty of Social Cultural Sciences of the Vrije Universiteit, Amsterdam, and the Madras Institute of Development Studies, Chennai, also graciously allowed us to spend the time needed for our common endeavour, for which we thank them.

We owe much to a great many colleagues and friends, both academics and practitioners in diverse fields of development. There is a large reservoir of open mindedness, commitment and, at times, courage to engage in critical questioning, from which we were allowed to nurture ourselves. We mention Hans-Dieter Evers, Heiko Schrader, Rüdiger Korff and Mark Hobart and Oscar Salemink from the EIDOS group. We are especially happy that David Mosse who recently joined the EIDOS core group was willing to join us in co-authoring the first chapter. We greatly benefited from his contribution as well as from the remarks of various anonymous reviewers. Many people from development agencies shared with us their deep and invaluable insights into the practical spaces for manoeuvring in institutional and spiritual terms. We are well advised to listen and learn as much as we can from good administrators, whose daily business it is to cope with the contingencies of development. Academic and practical insights fused in marvellous ways, often blurring the different backgrounds and allowing for a space for learning. We only mention a few of those from whom we greatly, and gratefully, benefited over many years: Wil Erath, Pim Verhallen, Wiebe Nauta, Pieter van Dijk, Pim Schoorl, Pradjarta. Ds., C.T. Kurien and Felix Wilfred.

Amsterdam/Chennai
May 2002

Part I

Evolving a new approach

'critical understanding'; some disjunctures are between different kinds of actors – between the state, the market and NGOs; some are between values and practices of application; some between action and reflection, between development's advocates and its critics, between coping with the future and understanding the past. We suggest that because there is a loss of meaningful linkage between development intervention on the one hand, and reflective understanding on the other, between the dynamics of 'doing' and critical understanding, between common global responsibilities for the future and understanding the history of experience, the crisis has a moral nature. Part of the problem is a prevailing tendency to ignore disjuncture and to press for coherence and closure, to assert one or another *a priori* logic of development – the logic of the state or of the market, of management or criticism. We suggest an alternative perspective in which the understanding of our past experiences with the enterprise of 'applied development' in the last fifty years and the search for new global concerns and responsibilities can come together in a meaningful way.

The chapters of this book will explore development's disjunctures and their implications in an empirical way. The purpose of this introduction is to provide a schematic view of transformations in international development action and reflection over fifty years, necessarily simplifying and developing 'ideal-type' representations, as a basis for defining the way forward. We will suggest firstly that, in the world of action, there has been a broad transition (since the 1980s) from a situation in which development interventions were an expression of specific *political* responsibilities to one in which *manageability* takes central stage. The focus of moral and political reasoning has shifted from goals to results. Secondly, in the world of reflection, we see a shift from a modernist faith in development as 'applied enlightenment' towards the post-modern de-constructive critique of development as domination. These two transitions have gradually widened the gap between action and reflection.

As we see it, the reinvigoration of development requires efforts to reconnect the worlds of action and reflection, to build bridges and cross borders, keeping pace with or even anticipating changes in the nature of criticism and reconstruction of development. Above all, this reinvigoration – conceptual, practical and moral – requires that we unravel generalising and universalising models of all kinds (managerial, critical, moral) and take disjuncture seriously, acknowledging the historicity of development, and the contingent nature of action and ethics. Here we will need to take clues from moral philosophy in order to develop a language of development as *global responsibility* in the light of new problems of risk – of environment, conflict or terror – adding this to the ethics of rights and justice inherited from the early modern revolutions (political and industrial) (cf. Strydom 2000). And finally, we suggest that the politics and ethics of development shift from a conception of the problem as the 'care of the other', to include 'care of the self' in both a societal and personal (and spiritual) sense (Beck 2000; Giri 2002a, 2002b). We suggest a move from development's 'othering' (even orientalising) discourses of poverty or livelihoods towards perspectives which place the developers and the developed, self and other, within a common framework. These, then, are the themes explored in this chapter.

A moral critique of development: our contemporary predicament

The shift from 'must do' to 'can do': changing definitions of manageability and the new cult of accountability

The first dimension of the contemporary crisis concerns the macro level, the level at which the rules for development interventions are defined. Here, we suggest that the primacy of global political responsibility for planned change is evaporating. The very notion of development as a project of political engagement and responsibility is increasingly seen as anachronistic. Confidence came to be placed in the *market* as a harbinger of development, and in the role of free enterprise and free trade in the quest for development (although today the market is increasingly seen as need regulation by state institutions). As Michael Edwards puts it, 'The market is the only proven mechanism of economic integration since no other can respond to the constant signalling that complex systems demand' (1999: 8–9).

This shift to the market is much more encompassing than it seems. It aims at transforming society as a whole into a 'market society'. The metaphor of the market deeply penetrates the conventions of steering, understanding and justifying modes of operation within the non-market sector also, public and private. Government departments, NGOs and private organisations active in the domains of development are required to operate as if they are businesses. As Max van den Berg, until recently the director of NOVIB, a major Dutch NGO, describes the changing *modus operandi* of his agency, '[s/he] who speaks of the market, must take into account "suppliers" of development as well as customers, a product and a buyer' (van den Berg 1998: 132).

The implications of this view are many. For one thing the new discourse gives rise to an a-historical morality. General criteria and rules for judging and steering interventions in development arise irrespective of historical context. This development regime has formed a new class of management experts without political responsibility, who defend interventions with reference to results rather than political goals. A new ethics emerges focussed on the capacity of professionals and agencies to manage outcomes and actually deliver promised results. Notions of 'can do' (management) rather than 'must do' (responsibility) are increasingly dominant in definitions of the problems of development.

The quest for new definitions of manageability evolved from an awareness of the many failures of experiments of political planning or 'high modernism' in the hands of political actors (Scott 1998; Crewe and Harrison 1998). By the end of the 1980s the facade of development as a political agenda collapsed, giving rise to an explosion of reports and books calling for 'effectiveness', and impact (e.g., Cassen and Associates 1986; Hoebink 1988).[1] The shift started in the developing world in the early 1980s and overwhelmed western donor agencies at the end of that decade. One set of general moral assumptions concerning the nature of good policy was replaced by another equally universalising set of rules. Manageability and the delivery of results became the ends, leading to a drastically new definition of good policy, with 'accountability' the cornerstone of a new doctrine, and 'participation' its paradoxical means (cf. Giri 2000; Strathern 2000; Turner and Hulme 1997; Quarles van Ufford et al. 1998).

Two further recent trends within the managerialist approach are detectable. The first is a narrowing of development goals, which for several agencies now focus on a set of internationally agreed development targets for the reduction of poverty, ill-health and illiteracy[2] (e.g., 'a reduction by one-half in the proportion of people living in extreme poverty by 2015, universal primary education in all countries by 2015, a reduction by two-thirds in infant and under-five mortality rates and by three-quarters in maternal mortality by 2015').[3] The second trend, is a widening and proliferation of the *means* to achieve these goals (beyond narrow market mechanisms) – prudent financial policy, political pluralism, vibrant civil society, participation, or democracy. At the extreme, nothing short of the reorganisation of government and society is required to deliver on these development targets. Developing countries become conceptualised as giant corporations which require not only financial restructuring (through structural adjustment programmes) but also better-trained top management ('good governance') and corporate culture (strong civil society). Through concepts of 'social capital' and the organisation of 'civil society', current models extend the field of intervention and management from the technical and economic realm (defined in terms of incentives to maximise material returns) to the social and cultural. Announcing the World Development Report 2002/3, the World Bank President James Wolfensohn concludes that 'overall ... the greater challenge for the future is to modify social institutions and behavioural incentives so individuals and communities can better manage *human, social, physical, and natural assets* over longer time periods' (World Bank 2002; emphasis in original).

The confidence in rational design and social engineering has never been greater, and the policy concepts applied reflect a growing sophistication of management which is able to absorb and deflect challenges. Bottom-up, and 'participatory' development approaches, which spread within mainstream development agencies in tandem with 'results-oriented management', often serve the instrumental needs of programme delivery rather than reviving a critical politics of development. As a growing critical literature attests, participatory approaches rarely provide a radical challenge to existing power structures, professional positions and knowledge systems, but on the contrary prove compatible with top-down planning and management systems (Cooke and Kothari 2001; Chapter 2 in this volume). Since James Ferguson first used the phrase, international development has become an ever more sophisticated 'anti-politics machine'.

With its clearly defined development 'bottom line' (i.e., income-poverty reduction), and sophisticated managerial instruments, international development is arguably entering a new phase of 'high managerialism' analogous to, but the reverse of, its earlier phase of 'high modernism' (cf. Scott 1998). Today's narrowly defined development *ends* and broadly defined *means* precisely contrast the modernisation models of the 1950s and 1960s in which broadly defined and radically future-oriented development *ends* – the transition to modernity – were to be accomplished through narrowly defined *means*, namely technology-led growth (roads, seeds or architecture).

This transition to 'management-by-results' and its new goals and accountabilities has infiltrated the views, practices and organisational cultures of development agencies, reverberating through their internal organisations. In some cases the thematic and regional experience and expertise of staff become a liability almost overnight. In the past, the 'corporate identity' of development institutions was constituted of a specific political awareness and loyalty to international thematic and policy networks. As this changed in the early 1990s, sometimes harsh measures were used to transform development agencies into 'businesses of commitment'. Staff were simultaneously sacked and invited to reapply for their jobs under new contractual arrangements as malleable managerial players. Some resigned, having experienced a dispiriting transformation and broken commitment. As a senior member of one Dutch development NGO remarked on resigning,

> Now that it has become clear that my agency is starting to seriously stress the 'quality' of development projects, it is better for me to go. The knowledge of the region I have gained in the last twenty years and the many friendships I have built up in the course of my work clearly have become an obstacle.

His board had hired management consultants to 'modernise' the agency. Policy, he was informed, was now something different. The shared substantive responsibility with his counterparts in other countries was too slippery a process. These relations were too personalised; such 'policy' did not meet new requirements of accountability. Policy now meant a 'document' to be written once every four years, with concrete targets for action – perhaps a logical framework. In the future his secretary could easily consult the agency's checklist of priorities whenever an application for funding was received. His wider input had become superfluous. Longer-term perspectives had given way to more limited time frames. The shift from 'goals' to 'targets' turned professional actors inwards. Any notion of historical process which went beyond the cycles of the development institution became irrelevant. The 'information' collected in order to allow for judging interventions also reflected the new priority of such agencies. Indeed a new 'audit culture' created its own specific body of 'information', a new virtual reality of development (Baudrillard 1993, 1995). We thus witness the constitution of a myopia within the new regime of accountability. This myopia is quite comparable to the distortions of knowledge gathered in an earlier phase.[4]

But there is no reason to 'romanticise' the past when criticising the present. An earlier stage of development as applied politics, as 'high modernism', had its own costs. As James Scott (1998) shows in his *Seeing Like a State*, high ideals and maintaining the purity of political goals and ideologies of development could engender ignorance and marginalise concerns with practical (social and economic) effects (cf. Quarles van Ufford 1988; Hobart 1993). The new creed of market- and result-orientation is no less universal and hegemonic in its aspirations, but it has emptied itself of the earlier historical awareness of development as an initiative in global responsibility first expressed in the agenda of global development which emerged towards the end of the Second World War (1944–1947) (Sardar 1998).

The persisting smile of Icarus: the continuance of excessive optimism

Despite transformations in the discourse and practice of development there is a remarkable continuity of optimism about the possibility of transforming society through organised interventions. The first wave of critical reactions to development – the 'age of unintended consequences' – paradoxically invigorated the sense of manageability, and with it optimism about producing desired results, although the locus of optimism shifted. Primacy was no longer given to political actors but to managers who controlled an expanding range of instruments (of policy, management and field method) to conceptualise a world in which social and economic relations could be engineered to deliver desired outcomes. As the focus on results sharpened, the scale of aid operations increased in many agencies. Above all, development impacts have now to be visible at the national level. As a result, many international development agencies have made a decisive shift away from 'micro-managed' projects and have begun to direct aid in the form of 'programme' or budgetary support to regional or national governments. This does not return development to an engagement with politics, but rather expands the field of management (from project to state) .

At first sight the ideology of the marketplace stressing the role of subject-less social forces and managerialist optimism are a strange couple. The stress on the market as the 'hidden' arbiter of progress, and high expectations concerning the management of desired results, are clearly in contradiction. Indeed it is efforts to overcome (or disguise) such contradictions that have driven recent innovations in the theory and practice of development, including the rise of social capital theory and institutional perspectives on markets which are characteristic of what – distinguishing it from the earlier anti-state free-market orientation – has sometimes been called the 'post-Washington' consensus (cf. Dasgupta and Serageldin 2000; Putnam *et al.* 1993; Fine 1999). This is the theory that frames the extension of managerial optimism from the project to state, from economy to society.

How can we understand the amazing continuity of development optimism? We take the view that there is continuity because some of the core assumptions have remained the same. Principal among these is the implicit and under-explored relationship between development goals and outcomes which are linked only through the logic of the concealing 'black box'. When we speak of a transformation of political goals to managed ends, we see a change not in the nature of this black box, but only in the direction of reasoning: first forwards from interventions to rational political goals; then backwards from results to development mechanisms. But the black box of administration of interventions remains the same. And as the ambitions of international development shift again from localised projects (back) to state-level, or 'sector-wide approaches', the black box separating inputs and outputs/effect is drawn larger and larger, hiding more and further blurring the links between goals and their effects.[5] The instrumentalities of interventions, the praxis of projects, the contingencies of programmes all disappear between proclamations of high level development partnerships on the one hand, and the national/regional statistical record on poverty, illiteracy, morbidity (etc.) on the other. In a sense 'high managerialism' firmly privileges policy over action. Donor advisers and specialists are involved in a scramble 'upstream' away from the localised triviality of 'neo-colonial' projects into the offices of national planning. Meanings and opportunities in international development appear increasingly centrally generated. Action at the periphery (in field level programmes) depends upon its ability to contribute to sustaining consensus in policy frameworks (see Chapter 2, for example). Those that fail to do so lose their reality and 'fail'.

The ambition to manage more and more and have macro impacts may have the effect of creating a world in which, in fact, less is manageable; one in which there is a palpable growth of ignorance and uncertainty. One of the effects of uncertainty and reduced control is a focus on knowledge. Today, it is the framing and re-framing of policy that links interventions and outcomes, rather than the practical testing of implementation modalities. The former is a conceptual exercise. Of course aid organisations still have to disburse money – indeed today's foreign policy dictates that aid budgets should grow. But the old models linking spending and results have lost credibility. There is a constant need for new theory in order to disburse money meaningfully, and to link old instrumentalities of development which disburse money efficiently (e.g., investment in infrastructure, or budgetary support) to new policy goals. And this is the task of increasing numbers of knowledge workers in aid agency head offices, producing policy papers which explain, justify, make coherent, and create meaning out of uncertainty. Meanwhile, the dynamics of policy making are more weakly linked to development practices than ever. Questions of implementability are downstream problems that belong to someone else. Despite the growth of its own 'audit culture', development's 'high managerialism' is more and more the management of the conceptual space of meaning and legitimacy, 'success' and 'failure'.

The morality based on the belief in the 'black box' condemns us to artificial optimism. But stories from the field suggest that the instruments of understanding at the centre are insecure, the judgements of success and failure are unreliable, and the 'downstream' effects of new policy consensuses are unknowable. Models for managing social change are revealed as culturally weighted and as having specific political effects. For example, David Abramson's anthropological study of the use of the policy model of 'civil society' by donor-supported Uzbek national NGOs shows that the model is far from politically neutral, but 'foster[s] a particular hegemony in which "civility" is opposed to accommodating an Islamic political culture' (1999: 247). The denial of Islam as an organising framework for Uzbekistan alienates the poorer sections of society and intensifies conflicts between different social groups.

'Up-stream' development managerialism sits on the edge of a crisis – a policy machine increasingly isolated from the 'local' or 'vernacular', to which it remains materially connected (through fund flows and action), is unable to understand its own effects. We suggest here that the issue of excessive optimism about the manageability of events has to be confronted as a moral problem, if we are to move beyond the impasse of development after more than fifty years of application.

From unbounded optimism to unrestricted criticism: contemporary critiques of development as love affair in the guise of a confrontation

Another relatively recent and major shift against the primacy of politics must be noted. It has taken place not in the domain of politics or administration but in that of academic research in development (Booth 1994; Nederveen Pieterse 2000; Schuurman 1993). Halfway into the 1980s a poststructuralist tradition in development studies expressed a deeply anti-political turn (Ferguson 1990; Escobar 1995; Gasper 1997; Grillo and Stirrat 1997). Previously development sociologists and anthropologists had stressed the importance of their academic research to improving development interventions. Academic analysis had always been understood as a source of knowledge useful for practical purposes. But now critical scholars tended to focus on analysing the hegemonic relations which development entailed. In this way academic research became confrontational rather than 'constructive' in its analysis of development interventions. If any political value could be deduced from discourse analysis as it emerged over the last fifteen years, it was in a destructive (or deconstructive) rather than a practical sense: systematic pessimism challenged excessive optimism (cf. Putnam 2001). But the insights of critical understanding have been bought at a price.

Critical understanding entailed a process of social closure from the wider context. Post-structuralist critiques looked 'inwards' and moved in ever smaller circles producing a kind of mirror image of the development practices they studied. Indeed, the managers' development optimism and the post-structuralist rejection of development were inter-related. The confrontation was total; a struggle between two sets of equally generalising, yet deeply antagonistic points of view (e.g., Sachs 1992; Escobar 1995) that drove a wedge between policy makers and their critics. As antagonists they not only confront each other, they are linked as the two sides of the same coin. They remind us of the couple portrayed by Edward Albee in his play *Who's Afraid of Virginia Woolf?*: the two are antagonistic to be sure, yet in their antagonism they are deeply dependent upon one another. The excessive optimism over managed development and the systematic pessimism about hegemonic regimes both 'black boxed' the complex agency and the contingency of development.

We feel that the overall antagonism between critical academic analysis and political and administrative practice is one of the main problems we are currently facing in development. These two worlds have drifted apart; their limited interactions are characterised by accusation and confrontation. Confrontation may produce an ironic satisfaction among students of development when dismantling yet another intervention in a sweepingly coherent way, or confirm the 'pragmatically inclined' manager of the irrelevance of critical research, whose academic authors can be safely stored away in advisory boards and committees. But it provides no way forward.

Van Middelaar (1999) has recently called attention to – as he sees it – the French philosophical inclination (from Kojeve to Sartre and Foucault) for a full course of intellectual collision with any political elites that be. He calls this an intellectual effort to actually 'murder' the very idea of politics as a meaningful engagement. It is a case of 'politicide'. Yet, as he adds, the price which is being paid for this attempted murder is high indeed. The preference for confrontation has left us without the sensitivity – van Middelaar argues –

to discern real possibilities for transformation and improvement. The post-structuralist tradition of studying development as a hegemonic engagement has itself turned into a hegemonic exercise, insufficiently attentive to the responsibility of initiating dialogue across the borderlands of action and reflection. Important insights into the limitations of development interventions has not allowed openings for processes of learning in modest and incremental ways. The task before a morally sensitive development anthropology is to move beyond the post-structuralist critique of development and to strive for ways in which critical analysis can allow space for a new moral and political understanding of development.

Towards an alternative genealogy of development

In this chapter we argue that it is possible to have a history of development which is not presented as the march of a continuous hegemony, but one which begins instead with moments of hope. Here we build on both Kant and Foucault to explore the pathways of an alternative genealogy of development. As is well known, Kant posed three questions as being central to our human condition in general and to the Enlightenment project in particular: what can we *know*, what can we *do* and what can we *hope for*? Using these Kantian distinctions of hope, politics and critical understanding, we can distinguish three historical settings of our post-war tryst with development. In each, priority is given to one specific kind of knowledge: development as hope in the early post-war years; development as politics and administration in the subsequent decades; and most recently development as critical understanding. These are really overlapping 'ideal-type' phases. In each the moral nature of development has been defined in a different and distinctive way.

To this genealogical exploration we also bring the late Foucault's concern with ethics, namely the challenge of responsibility and the cultivation of virtues for the holders of power and, we can add, for the critics of power (Foucault 1986; Chapter 12 of this volume). Foucault's later concern with ethics is a turning point as it enables us to go beyond a simplistic agenda of reducing all knowledge to power, and to explore the ontological challenge of self-cultivation that any project of development faces whether hegemonic or participatory.[6]

Development as work of hope (1944–1947)

Development constituted a new moral universe for international relations emerging at the end of the Second World War. The concept was first used in Los Angeles in 1944 in one of the subcommittees preparing for the setting up of the United Nations (Van Soest 1978). The idea of development became the carrier of an almost exclusive preoccupation with the global future. Various people have commented on the lack of historicity of the concept. It has often been said that 'development has no history' (e.g. Van Schendel 1989). Indeed a remarkable historical emptiness and an intense focus on the future together are important constitutive dimensions of the concept. In development, the future is declared to begin *now*. It is opposed to the past and must in fact be 'rescued' from it.

The emphasis on a new beginning at the expense of historical depth deserves special notice. This idea of a future severed from the past allows us to see the constitution of development more clearly as a work of hope. The future must be saved from a past of cataclysmic experiences of the Second World War. These are almost too horrible to contemplate. Hope became important precisely because of that. In Los Angeles in 1944 during the constitution of the UN, the past was strongly defined as 'over and done with'. Since the legitimacy of colonial empires was declared dead too, development also became the carrier for the concurrent process of decolonisation (Van Soest 1978; Locher 1978). The almost exclusive focus on the future derived from an acknowledgement of extreme crisis (cf. Wolf 1999). From this perspective the very emptiness of the concept of development and its almost obsessive concern with redefining the past from the perspective of development can be understood. These so-called 'a-historical' elements constitute practices of hope. They are not a-historical at all. They express the acknowledgement as well as a first mode of coping with extreme global crises in a specific historical way (e.g., van den Berg and Bosma 1994: 9–23).

Michael Ignatieff (1999) has called our attention to two specific characteristics of the context. He speaks of the political arena around 1946 and 1947. His remarks help us to see how practices of hope could assert themselves for some time. Ignatieff writes about the constitution of *The Declaration of Human Rights* in a way that is pertinent to understanding the birth of the idea of development. He speaks of a certain stillness, of a short period in which the arms of war and global power struggles were laid to rest. In 1946/7 the Cold War had not yet fully come to predominate the political agenda. The struggle for global hegemony had not yet asserted itself in the domains of the United Nations. Thus the shock of the terrible past still allowed for some space to articulate a commonly defined hope for a better future. There was a certain moment of stillness between political ebbs and flows of war, hot and cold.

This 'armistice' allowed for atonement, contemplation and a dream of common global responsibility and human rights to be articulated. Ignatieff makes a further point: the Universal Declaration was possible because the articles made no reference to *modes of enforcement* of human rights. The Declaration did not come with concrete political programmes. It did not address politics directly, but provided the contours of a new moral universe. The statement was clearly a response to the holocaust. But it was a moral and not a political statement. The universal acceptance of the articles of human rights by all governments was possible because it transcended the domains of the political. As a practice of hope, the Declaration thus did not pose a concrete threat to any government in the short run. Similarly, and more or less simultaneously, the articulation of development as hope on a global scale and the emergence of a new moral universe was possible because in the beginning it too was divorced from concrete modes of 'enforcement' or implementation. The 'practice of charisma, of hope' was allotted some time and space divorced from politics.

This reading of the birth of the idea development is corroborated by two influential commentators of our time: Ralf Dahrendorf and Jürgen Habermas. Dahrendorf (1968) was one of the first to link the idea of development with the crisis of the past and war. Almost thirty years later Habermas (1998a, 1998b) calls our attention again to the links between deep cataclysmic transformations and the shaping of a new moral perspective of development. He mentions specifically the year 1945 in which colonial empires were collapsing, the war had ended and the shock over the holocaust was there to remain for a considerable time. This year 'has set free energies and finally, even insights' (Habermas 1998b: 312). Cataclysmic events led to important universal moral insights. A new sense of direction and true hope emerged in the acknowledgement of crisis. The very universality of the insights must be seen as an expression of deep moral urgency. Indeed, in another important essay, 'Coping with contingencies', Habermas (1996) urges us to understand social theories in general not as abstract models but as coping mechanisms – to see specific forms of knowledge as modes of coping with important historical problems.

Development as practices of politics and administration (1949–)

Following the universal call for development as hope – the 'never again' – a second phase called for modes of *doing* development. Development here entered the domain of politics, application and administration. The key questions became, who will take the lead; which actors should be given primacy in shaping and putting into practice the goals of development? The answer to the question of agency has varied over the years: while at first the emphasis was on the state and benevolent international donors, the initiative passed to non-governmental organisations and the market, and then back to the state with a concern with governance. As one commentator put it recently:

> in the 1960s, newly independent governments in a hurry displace the private sector (donor-supported National plans, Government-led industrialisation ...); in the 1970s donors in a hurry displace govern-

ment (donor-driven projects with their own management structures ...); in the 1980s governments return ownership to the private sector (structural adjustment, privatisation); in the 1990s donors begin to return ownership to governments (sector-wide programmes, direct budget support ...), and in the 2000s agencies emphasise accountability to domestic institutions (governance, participation, Poverty Reduction Strategy Papers ...).

(paraphrasing Barry Ireton, cited in Foster 2000: 7)

Each of these trajectories evinces a characteristic emphasis on doing. In the earlier years of 'doing', political action retained some connection with dreaming and hoping. The *magnum opus* of Gunnar Myrdal (1968), *Asian Drama: An Enquiry into the Poverty of Nations*, written in the early 1960s, is a telling case in point. Myrdal makes explicit reference to the new values which provided a frame of reference for action. But it was not yet clear what kind of practical political agenda would come from these values. Myrdal asks himself the questions, which course of action, which practical problems of development must be given priority over and against others? Is priority to be given to the strengthening of weak states and their capacity for national planning? Or is a direct attack on poverty more advisable? His three[7] volumes allow us to discern clearly the intellectual and political struggle of translating new general and universal values and dreams into distinctive international political agendas.

This struggle did not last. After some time the enterprise of development became divorced from such encumberments. The machinery of various political creeds each entailing its distinctive planning, policy formulation and application of development became increasingly self-contained. A social, moral and intellectual closure set in. While in the early 1960s Gunnar Myrdal was concerned with making an honest choice between a number of contrasting political and intellectual agendas, this did not last long. As 'development' transformed into specific political discourses a process of compartmentalisation set in. Each discourse provided not only political priorities, but also a 'theory' of development specific to the interests of multiplying national development institutions. Development turned into a set of competing agendas, theories and sets of organisations. Rapidly rising (inter)national budgets transformed the development agenda into a preoccupation with political and administrative action, on actually 'doing' something. And each new political agenda and 'scientific' paradigm of development was accompanied by a preoccupation with a new beginning. Each time development was invented again, each time in confrontation with the other paradigms and families of development institutions that come with it. The marketplace of development became increasingly segmented as brand names – theories and agencies – started to exert themselves (to such an extent that in order to gain a legitimate position in the arena of development it was sufficient to say that one was not a governmental agency; the very emptiness of the concept of NGO, non-governmental organisation, became an asset, not a liability).

At the end of the seventies the segmentation of development as political and administrative action had intensified to such an extent that in his overview of the competing theories and definitions of development, Foster-Carter (1976) could question

> the extent to which a common concern with development is a sufficient condition for a scientific community to say meaningful things to each other despite paradigm differences.
>
> (Foster-Carter 1976: 177)

The broad perspective of a new beginning to development in the 1940s narrowed down to a process of Balkanisation between competing political and administrative agendas, not only between but also *within* development agencies themselves. Quarles van Ufford (1988) provided an early case study of the harsh in-fighting between staff members of Dutch NGOs responsible for monitoring and evaluation and the staff members assigned to spend money on specific topics or within certain areas. The agencies and the policies that these agencies carried out were increasingly conceived of as 'battlefields' (Long and Long 1992). Administrative processes were increasingly seen as divorced from wider political agendas and more dependent on the shifting balances of power between staff members and the changing demands of the environments to which development agencies were accountable (see note 2). The erratic nature of 'doing' has been described as 'pathological' (Rew 1997; Quarles van Ufford 1999), with growth serving no visible purpose any longer. In the last decade we have witnessed an endless series of reorganisations, shifts, new directions, increasing ignorance and segmentation, loss and destruction of a sense of purpose, disheartening to people, destruction of their motivation, increasing cynicism, impression management, and high declarations of a new more market-oriented sense of purpose, of 'effectiveness now'.

The shift from 'ideological orthodoxy' to 'doing' is part of the new legitimation of development, namely expediency (cf. Habermas 1996). In so far as this does not conclusively lead to more responsible and transformational developmental practice on the ground, development as 'doing', when left to itself, appears as a dead end. Moreover, the emphasis on 'doing' gave rise to its own 'development ethics', narrowed to the technical and professional domains and captured in 'mission statements', development agency identities, or certifications of good practice (cf. Goulet 1995; Gasper 1999; Hamelink 1997). Moral issues increasingly obtained an instrumental significance and an a-historical and uncritical preoccupation with so-called 'relevance'. But a preoccupation with relevance, dissociated from development as hope and critical understanding, makes the practice of development bereft of meaning (cf. Baudrillard 1993). Moral choices become important political assets of specific agencies, constituting their 'symbolic capital' in the marketplace (cf. Hoebink 1988; Chapter 2, this volume).

Development as critical understanding (1990–)

About fifteen years ago, critical students began to disengage themselves from the political and administrative concerns of development. They felt that the high walls built around the multinational development agencies had to be demolished. Knowledge about 'doing' suddenly became dangerous. For the critical students hegemony was the buzzword. Development was no longer *a priori* a must; rather, it was a mess. The romanticism of a bunch of young and energetic missionaries doing their very best for the wretched of the earth was replaced with another image: the spectre of a chaotic multinational enterprise experiencing great difficulty and open to all-out critique. It seemed as if the core of development, its moral and political perspectives, were part and parcel of the mess. Instead of being young and energetic, development now confronted the pangs of midlife crisis. Trusted discourses, goals and mission statements, and defensive parameters of various sorts, now looked like artificial statements of optimism.

Development as critical understanding is vital to reconstituting development as a global responsibility, especially as it makes us aware of hegemonic intentions and relationships parading in the name of global solidarity, but in itself it is not enough. The hermeneutics of suspicion (of development interventions) leads to an impasse if it is not supplemented by a hermeneutics of recovery and reconstruction (Giri 2002a). To put it in the words of David Harvey, critics have to be 'insurgent architects' with a desire to 'translate political aspirations across the incredible variety and heterogeneity of socio-ecological and political-economic conditions' (Harvey 2000: 246). But this is not possible if critics are wedded to an essential logic of pessimism, that no learning and improvement are possible in society and history. As Hilary Putnam argues, it is important for post-structuralist critics to realise that although great crimes have been committed in history in the name of progress and development, 'there have been learning processes in history and there can be further learning in the future' (Putnam 2001: 27; see also Mohanty 1998).

Towards an alternative ontology of development

Development as hope, as politics/administration, and as critical understanding, do not only (or primarily) constitute historical phases, they also constitute domains in which distinct but interconnected knowledges and actions arise. There is no historical teleology here. Instead of a logic of succession or the *a priori* privileging of one (domain) over another, we have to think of development as hope, politics/administration and critical understanding as presupposing each other – existing as intersecting circles (cf. Afterword to this volume; Mohanty 2000; Uberoi 2002).[8] Creative and critical action can begin from any one domain, and actors in development – from the sectors of state, market, private/NGO or within social movements – inhabit in a significant manner one or two of the domains.

Practitioners in specific domains have a responsibility to be 'mutually interpretative'. There are dangers in the self-assertion of one category of thought/action. There are, for instance, dangers in the assertion of the state as a hegemonic actor through interventionist models of development. In this form, state action has often been challenged by the creative and critical work of NGOs and social movements (for example the anti-dam, or anti-mining struggles in India (Kothari 1988; Mohanty *et al.* 1998)). But then such social movements – and even scholars who see them as harbingers of new beginnings in the world of development – need to cultivate within themselves a self-critique of the telos of power so that a politics of empowerment does not become an end unto itself and does not degenerate into another system of exclusion and oppression (cf. Laclau 1992; Giri 2001). The simultaneous attention to ethics and politics in the turn to social movements in contemporary deconstructive development anthropology is sadly missing.[9]

In the intersecting and interacting field of development there is a moral problem when categories and actors exist or are allowed to exist as pure categories. By implication, instead of a stable conception of development we suggest an 'emergent ontology' which sees development as a heterogeneous field of action and imagination, and as a dynamic process of learning and mutual transformation (cf. Dallmayr 2001; Vattimo 1999). There is a problem in looking for coherence, or assuming that translation between the different domains of development is always possible. Academic critics of development are mistaken if they believe that in development good administration and politics is possible, if only meticulous use was made of their research insights.[10] This assumes an unproblematic whole to the knowledge of development. But in reality we cannot expect an administratively applicable insight 'logically' to emerge from our studies. Equally, there is no foolproof way of letting the hope of a better world determine the political and administrative efforts to bring it about (Nuijten 1998); and neither can administrative rationality be attributed centre place in the development enterprise over and against the critical understanding and the practices of hope. Knowledge of development arises in different contexts and serves quite different purposes. We have to confront the issue of incompatibility. Failure to accept this constitutes a core moral problem in our daily routines of development. In this volume through our theoretical reflections as well as our ethnographic case studies we show that there is no reason to assume that 'more' or better in one domain will be beneficial to the other. T.S. Eliot, anthropologist as well, helps us phrase this problem: 'Where is the wisdom we have lost in knowledge? Where is the knowledge we have lost in information?' (Eliot 1969: 147).

The agenda of the volume

This volume contributes to remaking development anthropology as a morally sensitive as well as a critical empirical practice. As anthropologists of development practice we not only have to describe the moral choices that actors make, study the rules of legitimation to which they refer, and the modes of dealing with constraints, contradictions and dilemmas, but also try to add our own emerging judgements about these moral practices. Here we have a two-fold engagement: first, ethnographic enquiry is informed by moral issues embedded in practice as well as broader frames of moral reflection; and second, modes of moral reasoning are informed by the empirical study of concrete practices. For this, anthropology can no longer be a study of bounded groups and themes, but has to be an open-ended enquiry into pathways and flows, including those between different kinds of knowledge, actors and practices – the roots and routines of both ethnographic and moral encounter.[11] In such an anthropology of encounter, the moral and the empirical are mutually transformed.

Equally fundamental to this volume is a conception of development as daily rout and relationships that cope with disjunctures. The notion of coping with disjunctures underpins our moral critique of development practices. We reject a view of development as the production and manageability of order. The notion of order arises out of a confrontation with extreme situations.[12] Hope is often proclaimed as a new order. But in this volume we study daily routines of development, not extreme situations, routines which need to be perceived as specific modes of coping with disjunctures. In all the case studies which follow this view is evident: some study the problematic relationship between goals and outcomes; the incompatibility of processes of administration and critical learning, the slippery nature of authentic communication, the management of inescapable tensions between the self interest of institutions and care for the other as expressed in development discourse. We comment on the findings of these contributions below.

On the question of coming to terms and coping with disjunctures, we are enriched by the work of thinkers such as Michel Foucault and Frank Ankersmit. In his reflections on Kant, Foucault (1984a) endorses Kant's distinction between three domains of knowledge (knowledge related to political action, knowledge related to critical reflection, and knowledge related to hope) as constitutive of Enlightenment but urges us to acknowledge the lack of fit between them. Foucault gives importance to hope, but his emphasis on hope is not based on an uncritical universalising plan; rather it arises out of acknowledgement of the difficulty of putting theory into practice both in the past and present.[13]

As we shall argue more fully later in the volume, Foucault makes an important ethical step forward in his search for a practice of hope, which is non-hegemonic. He indicates the great ethical importance of a 'care of the self', that is a willingness of the powerful to practise restraint and ascesis *vis-à-vis* the other, rather than involving oneself (more) closely with the life of the other through all kinds of concrete activities and interventions. This moral concern with the self may have many important consequences for development too. Foucault stresses the care of the self as a form of restraint and self control, and consequently as a restraint in involving oneself directly with the life of others. This may indeed create new spaces for hope, as this restraint does not lead to the manifold hegemonic consequences of more conventional involvement in the life of the others (cf. Chapter 12 in this volume).

In his brilliant meditation on our contemporary predicament, Dutch historian and philosopher Frank R. Ankersmit also urges us to be aware of the role of contingencies in generalising and unifying formulations about the human condition and its betterment. Both Foucault (1984a, 1984b) and Ankersmit (1996) problematise assumptions about the possibility of a coherent body of knowledge and provide new directions in the search for meaningful interrelationships between bodies of knowledge. For Ankersmit there are no prerogatives to start with. We must see how in specific historical contexts one domain of understanding may be predominant over another, and how the balance changes again. As the relationship changes over time, so may our moral views and knowledge of development. Ankersmit (1996: 5–7) warns against universalistically defined moral views such as those of Rawls. Moral problems are not abstract. We do not concern ourselves with a search for 'some underlying basis of philosophical and moral agreement' (Rawls 2001: 2). Rather, as Ankersmit suggests, history is 'lived' by men 'with their unpredictable mixture of egoism and altruism, rationality and irrationality'. We share his view. Our moral views of development cannot be seen as universal in an unproblematic way. We must accept not only disjunctures in relationships and the contingent nature of our bodies of knowledge of development, but also the contingent nature of our moral views. We do not know of a core idea of development, deep down, which may constitute the basis for a moral view. On the contrary. As Ankersmit remarks we must do our best to save politics and understanding from an ethics which claims universal relevance. Moral views must not be seen just as universal guidelines for action. The history of the development enterprise as well as the field of development needs to be looked at *as a contingent struggle between different kinds of knowledge*, including the moral.

Turn to contingency: modes of acknowledgement and modes of coping

So, in this volume we propose a turn away from an a-historical and general-ising mode of thinking about ethics and development towards appreciation of the significance of contingency. This not only helps us understand our own situatedness in place, in time, and in webs of relationships, but also the situatedness of our perspective. As David Harvey argues, 'contingency does not imply, however, that as opposed to the designer ideal, the actual archi-tecture is secondary and constantly in danger of collapse. Rather, contingency ensures that no architect is able to determine a design free from the relationship with the "other" – the client, staff, and other factors relevant to the design process' (Harvey 2000: 230). And as Habermas tells us, contin-gency arises from a historical consciousness.

> Until the eighteenth century, history had served as a repository for exemplary stories which supposedly can tell us something about the recurring features of human affairs. ... [But with the rise of historical consciousness] ... the focus of attention shifts from the exemplary to the individual ... this historical consciousness gave birth to an evermore intense awareness of evermore widely spreading contingencies.
>
> (Habermas 1996: 7)

To be aware of contingency is to realise that history is not only a story of progress but also a story of 'shattered expectations' (Habermas 1998b: 13) – a mode of understanding that reminds us of Foucault's genealogical approach which does not confuse history 'with a quest for origins', but seeks to 'cultivate the details and accidents that accompany every beginning' and avoids 'thinking of emergence as the final term of an historical develop-ment' (Foucault 1977: 148).

We suggest, then, that development can only be properly understood as a contingent narrative, both moral and empirical. After all, it was the concrete historical context of deep crisis that led to the birth of development as a 'moralising discourse' in the first place (cf. Wolf 1999).[14] The turn away from generalising, and the critique of universalistic claims – in short the abandonment of the view that development is a case of 'applied Enlightenment' (*Angewandte Aufklarung*, cf. Dahrendorf 1968) – has profound practical consequences. It does not make the efforts of dreaming, or of hoping for a better world irrelevant, but gives them a specific historical context and frees us from alluring and false promises of progress, and from creeds which promise certainty and eternal meaning. It enables us to have a humbler view of progress and development, to adopt a 'fallibilistic concep-tion of knowledge' (Putnam 2001) and to respond creatively to uncertainty, and to abandon the habitual clinging to order and stability (van Staveren 1999; Toulmin 2001).[15]

But are we not losing sight of a whole, with each practice 'encapsulated' as it were within a specific historical context? We think not. The notion of contingency does not imply relativism. On the contrary, the understanding of contingency may well become a stepping stone for shared responsibility. Acknowledging different ways of coping with the very concrete problems at hand may help us to learn and move beyond our specific contexts. For example, claiming universality for the notion of development and human rights in the 1940s must be understood as a highly appropriate mode of coping with a particular crisis. And more generally, clues for development practice come from the historically specific context, event and relationship, rather than from the generalised model. Contingency and universality have to be interrelated in the sense that universal significance may well emerge from the response to a specific development situation. The challenge is to learn to distinguish in a sensitive way between various possible responses to concrete contingent situations. Some may be irrelevant, other modes of coping may have universal significance.

The notion of 'contingency' is not to be confused with 'accidentality'. These two notions are not the same. In fact it is an integral part of an awareness of contingency that concrete practices, as well as discourses and history, could have been different. As social theorist Nancy Weiss Hanrahan reminds us, 'the outcomes of social processes are always contingent in that things could turn out otherwise' (Hanrahan 2000: 35; Walker 1998). An awareness of contingency while making us attentive to the historicity of development action and perspective does not make us prisoners of history or absolve us from specific responsibilities; rather, it enables us to discover creative and less absolutist ways of overcoming the limitations of a particular situatedness.

Acknowledgement of contingency is only a first step. The second is to examine how people cope with the contingency of their development practices. At one extreme development managerialism ignores contingency and reasserts optimism. At the other extreme, ironic responses produce political and moral relativism. An anthropology of development needs to study cultural and institutional 'modes of acknowledgement' and 'modes of coping' with contingency and the 'regimes of development' that produce them.

Emergent ethics: border crossing between facts and values

What do we mean by ethics in development? We are *not* primarily preoccupied with ethics as a domain of rules and regulations, 'correct' motivations or the application of values in development policy.[16] As Gasper (1999: 54) tells us, such a preoccupation hides 'the tendency still to seek security and certainty through detailed pre-set plans and conditions'. Development ethics involves not generalising universal principles, but our contingent responsibilities. We have suggested a new mode of 'emergent ethics' seeing how people deal with the dilemmas they encounter in concrete situations, and how they realise justice. In so doing we can build on moral philosophical work on virtue ethics, virtue epistemology and care (Nussbaum 1993; Goulet 1995). The emphasis on contingency implies a linking of moral views to a wider historical analysis, and points to the need for *Fingerspitzengefuhl*, a kind of practical moral sensitivity. This is missing in the 'justice' approach to morality. As G.A. Cohen points out, 'In the case of Rawlsian doctrine, the relevant life is not mine in particular, but people's life as such ... egalitarian justice is not only, as Rawlsian liberalism teaches, a matter of the rules that define the structure of society, but also a matter of personal attitude and choice' (Cohen 2000: 3).

We do not secure development ethics on the firm ground of ideological and political certainties, those 'ruthless abstractions from history' (Ankersmit 1996: 2).[17] Rather, 'emergent ethics' first arises from a confrontation with that past of development. It implies that we cannot make a new beginning as if from a clean slate, but have to engage with the best possible data on the experience of more than fifty years of application of ideological regimes, be they Marxist, populist, or neo-liberal. Emergent ethics in development also implies attentiveness to different points of view especially the narratives of suffering arising from development's own 'monological' interventions – for which big dams and mines are tropes (cf. Giri 2002a).

The notion of emergent ethics also calls for a morally engaged ethnography (Newton 1997) in which our anthropological narratives are told in ways that are morally as well as empirically sensitive, and that facilitate learning in both subjects and objects.[18] This in turn calls for border crossing between anthropology and moral philosophy,[19] building on fertile traditions from both (cf. Geertz 2000; Strathern 1988; Hobart 1993; Sen 1999; Nussbaum 2000).[20] Correspondingly, we need to find new kinds of links between the domains of 'hope', 'politics' and 'critical understanding' that help to break the processes of social closure which have encapsulated each of the three domains, based on a hard look at the kinds of present compartmentalisation.

Finally, the notion of 'emergent ethics' involves recognition of the tensions between two sides of development: the ethical and the aesthetic. Development as a shared global responsibility entails two concerns: the ethical concern with 'care of the other' and the aesthetic 'care of the self' (see Chapter 12 of this volume). We suggest that development ethics must deal with these two at the same time, as well as acknowledging that links between them are problematic. Gradually over the last fifty years development can be seen as having transformed from the *shared* concern of our global selves into an ethics of care for *the other* (the Third World poor). Development's discourses of poverty or livelihoods, for example, focus on the problems and conditions of 'others'. In mainstream development institutions such concerns have been separated from the conditions and problems of ourselves, the rich. We can propose here a shift from a focus on poverty and under-development – which explicitly or implicitly takes 'Western' industrial living as normative, as did old evolutionist models of modernisation – towards a perspective which places the developers and the developed, self and other, within a common framework. One way to do this is to focus on consumption and lifestyles instead of 'poverty'. How are valued lifestyles produced? What and how do people consume? What are the social and environmental effects? A focus on 'lifestyles' enables the driving forces of high levels of consumption in 'the West' to be considered in the same frame as 'poverty'. An anthropology of development is as much about Texas as Nepal. After all, consumption is a matter of reproducing lifestyles, and goods (as Mary Douglas pointed out) are for mobilising people, for connecting through things to other people.

There are signs already with mainstream policy that managerial views of development as 'care of the other' are beginning to be seen as breakdown in a globalised world. The language of development's 'high managerialism' deploys concepts of universal prescription (e.g., social capital, civil society, governance) which focus on the institutional deficiencies of underdeveloped places. But the universalising development agenda of 'getting institutions right' ('how the poor countries can help themselves get richer by fixing their institutions') (e.g., World Bank 2002) is challenged by irreducible inequality and institutional difference. Whether spurred by the events of 11 September 2001 or by a multitude of smaller signs of the failure of global management, there are some signs that policy debate can no longer ignore the issue of global inequality and difference.[21] Such themes have a new profile in present discussions around the World Development Report 2003 and the World Summit on Sustainable Development in Johannesburg 2002. Of course the destabilising threat of social and political crisis that inequality in a globalising world presents is not new, and there is no certainty that fear of 'crisis' will sustain shared global responsibilities (e.g., in debates on 'over-consumption in a globalised world'). In the past such threats have often led to self-protecting political and economic strategies, and there is plenty of evidence (from the political mood in Europe and America in 2002) that they continue to do so today.[22] Nonetheless, the challenge of an 'emergent ethics' in global development is to dislodge the 'othering' perspectives of development's 'orientalist ethics'.

So an 'emergent ethics' for development firstly questions the naive and unproblematic universalisation of values lying behind managerialist development policies by opening these to a trans-cultural and trans-civilisational interrogation and dialogue.[23] (For example, the Afterword to this volume subjects the underpinning values of the Enlightenment model of human development, which give primacy to rationality and economic development, to such interrogation by setting them against other values of development such as self-cultivation, and authentic humanisation/divinisation from within Europe, as well as from India and China.) Secondly, an emergent ethics defines the moral concerns of development in a double way: as a 'care of the other', which means that we must look at the need to intervene in the domains of the other; and as a form of self-constraint and 'care of the self' which means that we need to be sensitive to the necessity of non-involvement.

Ethical issues and the contributions to the present volume

The contributors to this volume present concrete anthropological case studies where moral questioning of the development enterprise is linked to empirical analyses of specific interventions. The intention is not further deconstruction *per se*. We aim at more. We ask ourselves what kind of judgement emerges from these case studies. These can be seen as 'ethical narratives' (Newton 1997: 8). In their presentation the authors analyse the nature of the 'reciprocity between narrative and ethics'. In each case study the authors make an effort to come to terms with the need for a judgement as well as a critical understanding of the interventions. We assume no fit between the two, however. The case studies all acknowledge 'uncertainty' when dealing with empirical data as well as with a search for moral views.

Each author offers specific suggestions for charting the territory of development as a political and moral engagement. All contributions except two originated from an EIDOS conference held in London at SOAS in 1998, on the ambiguous relationship between power and morality. But this does not mean that these efforts to link concrete analyses of empirical data and moral reasoning are, as it were, 'applications' of a common view expressive of a new orthodoxy.

Broadly speaking, there are four sections to the volume. Following the present reflection on the crisis of development and an emerging moral critique, the second section presents case studies of local/regional development programmes informed by this thinking. The third section contains case studies analysing the problematic nature, and practical implications, of scientific and political knowledge of development. The final section evolves a new approach to development and global responsibility.

The second section begins with an extensive case study of a development programme in western India presented by David Mosse. From his detailed historical analysis of the rural development project a surprising conclusion emerges. Mosse is not sure after ten years of involvement whether the programme is a 'success' or a 'failure'. In all these years, collaboration between all kinds of actors at the international, national, regional and local level developed shared parameters, a model, with which to interpret and judge the dynamics and outcomes of the programme; but the relationship between these parameters and events became highly uncertain. There are several good reasons to consider the programme a failure. Participatory goals have not clearly been met, for example. Yet Mosse does not stop there. It would be too easy to add yet another case to the long list of so-called failed interventions. Instead he presents a line of argument to the contrary: the project has not failed; it is only fallible parameters that make it appear so. Why? Mosse argues that 'success' or 'failure' are not the only modes of arriving at a judgement. He clarifies the inherent ambiguity of the project 'data' by distinguishing the project as a system of representations, as well as an operational practice. The project should not be judged on the basis of its system of official representations alone, but also on its actual operations. And while these two representations must be distinguished they cannot be separated from each other. In this detailed analysis Mosse identifies the inherent uncertainty of *coherent* representations of a project and the judgements that they generate. Neither a naive trust in the empirical, nor any adherence to official norms and goals, provides a reliable basis for judgement. The narrative of his case study involves a confrontation with various lines of moral argument. Is it a success? The two answers, 'yes' and 'no', must be carefully brought together.

In the third chapter a similar problem arises. Quarles van Ufford and Roth confront two narratives of ten years of integrated rural development in Sulawesi, Indonesia. The first is an official evaluation report, written by the first author together with a team of experts. It provided insight into the history of the integrated regional development project in Sulawesi, Indonesia, as well as a number of concrete recommendations concerning the next phase. The report about the project's past and problems faced at the time was the outcome of an official evaluation; it was, that is, an exercise of administrative learning routinely carried out by the Dutch and Indonesian governments involving the engineering bureau, responsible for the project's implementation, as well as the project's staff. The second author was a member of the project's staff at the time. In this chapter the two authors look back at the same project: what happened in the project? They make an effort here to write the project's longer-term history, including that of the administrative machinery of which it was a part. They take a rather different – much more critical – look at the project, and at their own roles as evaluators and staff members. They contrast their earlier 'administrative optimism' about the project's future with a more critical and distanced present point of view. The 'cyclical surge of optimism' in the evaluation exercise now becomes a topic on which they reflect – with some dismay perhaps. The chapter confronts us with two stories, each providing a historical analysis, each coming to a different view of its problems. The two stories are clearly incompatible. How must one deal with the problem? The *problematique* of the volume as a whole is reflected in this question. The contingency of the two stories becomes evident. Administrative knowledge and learning as well as critically detached analyses are important and worthwhile. But how can one deal with the clear disjuncture between the two? What are morally acceptable ways of dealing with the problem of incompatible bodies of knowledge which cannot simply be ignored?

Harrison (Chapter 4) analyses a relatively small development project in Zambia. Her questioning of the project resembles that of Mosse to some extent. She questions various official assumptions underlying the planning and execution of development projects. She touches upon problems and issues such as the apparent disparity between the kind of assumptions and goals as constituted by those politically responsible for the programme (the project as a system of representation by officials) and her own observations in the field as a researcher concerning the actual *modus operandi*. She highlights the gap between the two representations. The official assumptions concerning the local context as 'community', and also the process of administering the project, do not apply at all. Harrison notes the prolific use of notions of integration, coherence and system. The administration seems not to be able to cope with more open and flexible conceptualisations of planning and the execution of local projects. Harrison provides us with a detailed account of all kinds of biases fusing into a monolithic whole. What are the consequences of all this? It would be absurd to give in to a 'quietist' conclusion and start 'smiling ironically' for want of a political purpose. Harrison therefore explores the possibilities of small-scale endeavours in which tensions between the various life-worlds of 'the locals' and the government and NGOs would be less awesome. Acknowledging the problem, she concludes, would be a vital first step.

In his case study of an integrated area and rural development programme in Sarawak, Alan Rew (Chapter 5) raises some fundamental questions concerning ethical issues inherent in the dynamics of the implementation of a large and complex development scheme. His analysis of the programme clearly indicates that the idea of a black box, with its neat distinctions between goals, implementation and outcomes, poses serious questions: the programme's goals are much more ambiguous than expressed in the project's administrative language. While there may be a sense of duty and political obligation involved as far as the national government is concerned, this does not mean that programme goals are primarily of an operational nature. They are not. A gap arises between the practices of planning and of implementation. If such a gap should be understood as indicating failure, this was built in from the beginning – at which, as Rew himself writes, 'the welfare of indigenous people was seriously compromised in a way that almost everyone was guilty in part and yet no category of stakeholder could be held wholly responsible'. Rew considers this, as an outcome of such interventionist projects, to be a black box – but despite his critical engagement, he is still wedded to it. He talks about 'preventable factors' which created 'major discontent among the Iban', but in his moral narrative there is no story of indigenous people whose lives were uprooted as a result of the hydro-electric project. We do not see any face of the violated person nor do we hear any voice. This shows the limits of contemporary critiques of interventionist models of development and, as one of us argues in the Afterword to this volume, this in itself now poses a great moral challenge.

In the six case studies which follow, attention shifts from the analysis of interventions to a questioning of the different and competing knowledges of various actors involved, and the moral and empirical arguments inscribed in them. What roles do these play? In what ways do they compete with and transform each other? We begin with contributions by Penz, Ulrich and Salemink (Chapters Six, Seven and Eight) each of which points to the fact that development interventions do not comprise a well-informed machinery, and make this the starting-point for further questioning.

Penz's contribution to the volume deals with the very urgent moral problems associated with the forced removal of large numbers of people as a result of the building of big dams. He discusses the rationalities, the moral justifications and perspectives of some of the actors involved. Each of the normative and judgemental lines of reasoning are carefully put forward and distinguished from one another. This leads Penz to present and discuss contrasting normative and moral frameworks and 'theories' – ranging from Kantian perspectives on duty to consequentialists' theories stressing the outcomes. His overview and discussion of the preferences of particular categories of actors – international donors, national donors, NGOs and local communities – for specific lines of moral argument is very instructive. It leads Penz to search for the limitations and contingencies of each normative framework. This debate is not an abstract exercise at all. We gain insight into the question 'Whose moral views, whose moral reasoning and rationality are involved?' in relation to the great issues at stake in the context of building large dams and the complex displacements involved. The analysis of the various contesting moral views thus reaches an empirical common ground for allowing the testing of each.

In his contribution Ulrich also provides us with an overview of different moral views and claims, this time concerning recent studies of peri-natal HIV transmission in Africa and Asia. From the point of view of the ethics of research in developing countries, this is one of the most important issues in recent years, if for no other reason than it calls widespread international attention to the difficulties of articulating and upholding universal ethical standards in a context of extreme inequity. In the heated and often politically aggressive debates that Ulrich analyses it becomes evident that both the arguments in favour of universal scientific standards and the case made for a more equitable access to available medical resources are put forward exclusively by *Western* spokespersons. Indeed, the contradiction between proponents of a situated ethics and of a more universal scientific duty is not

only artificial, but involves a high-sounding moral debate which systematically excludes those whose lives are most affected. Ulrich makes a plea for
establishing procedures which allow for a more genuinely situated moral
contestation involving those who carry the brunt of the risks identified in
different arguments. He gives primacy to this *procedural* line of argument
above the dilemma between a so-called universalistic or a quasi-situated
moral point of view.

While most of the chapters concentrate on the moral dimensions of interventions in the practices of application, Salemink's (Chapter 8) focuses on
the emergence of specific political and moral views. The core of this chapter
concerns itself with the debate in the 1960s between two contrasting lines of
thought in the USA about Southeast Asian (Vietnamese) peasant society:
the 'moral economy' and the 'rational peasant' perspectives. Given the
significant fact that these debates took place within the US military and
scientific community, Salemink's interest is in what this tells us about the
nature of the relationship between the scientific and political communities in
the USA. Salemink's subtle overview of the debates and their context points
to an important moral dimension of all political *and* scientific behaviour.

Gasper's contribution (Chapter 9) can be clearly distinguished from those
of both Penz and Salemink. In these chapters empirical data provide the
basis for a discussion of various contesting points of views. Empirical data
serve as 'evidence', deployed by authors with specific expertise on a local
situation (or on the corridors of power), in reaching a judgement. Gasper
stands this line of reasoning on its head. His main point is that the kinds of
empirical data and evidence that are used to arrive at a political or moral
judgement themselves arise from such judgements. Gasper's chapter
provides clear evidence that specific kinds of actors – inside and outside the
enterprise of development – have their own selective preference for certain
kinds of data and evidence (and reject others), whether thick or thin description, extended case analysis or quantitative surveys of various kinds, or data
gathered at various levels of aggregation. Gasper makes us aware of the
contingency of 'empirical' data and evidence, which are as contingent as the
moral views which may have given rise to them. There is no firm, undis-
puted, privileged evidence to be had. The lesson is clear: do not trust the
experts when they claim a privileged position in our relation to the empirical
world. Such claims of expertise are just as problematic and quasi-priestly as
the explicitly moral claims encountered elsewhere. There is no way around
contingency. The question is how do we deal with it? What modes of coping
can we discern and how do we judge these?

Els Scholte and Albert Alejo present the last case studies in the volume.
These provide perhaps the first points of reference for a new agenda in
analysing development practices in an empirically as well as a morally
sensitive manner. Both move beyond the (artificial) opposition of norms
and facts. Alejo's contribution presents us with a clear view of some of the

disjunctures inherent to acquiring knowledge about development. He analyses his experience of collecting data in the Philippines for his PhD, showing us how his insights into the dynamics of change among those he studied were revealed through the negotiations in which he himself was involved as a researcher with his informants. Specifically, he argues that the quality and reliability of his data depended to a large extent upon people coming to a judgement about him (his role as priest and researcher) and his authenticity. Good and reliable knowledge about the development programmes now reflect a moral judgement, not so much by the researcher on a project, but by the people on the researcher. The point is that the empirical data to which Alejo gained access contain a deep moral dimension. Research is inevitably a moral practice in which the researcher is required to allow his respondents access into his own history and background. The disjuncture in the relationship becomes a concern for both researcher and his respondents. Good knowledge is the outcome of a dual coping with the disjunctures inherent to research relationships. It involves dimensions of power, certainly; for example, Alejo's access to institutions in the outer world, but also judgements about authenticity. In Alejo's sensitive description of his case the notion of trustworthiness regains its two inherent dimensions: the moral as well as the empirical.

In Scholte's chapter it again becomes clear that discussion of the moral dimensions of interventions in development cannot focus on outcomes or results, but must give first place to understanding the moral, political and cognitive nature of the relations involved. Scholte deals with the everyday world of Western public relations associated with development interventions and the pressures to create and sustain specific images which have an almost accidental or contradictory relation to practice. The daily routines of public relations management in NGOs challenge the authenticity of moral or political convictions or scientific claims to understanding in the field of development interventions. The question is 'How to remain authentic as a person, confronted with all the claims and interests that seem to eat away the meaning of that which has become dear to you?' Along with Alejo's, this chapter, then, presents the moral issue in development as one of authenticity.

Expanding and deepening the meaning and practice of development interventions

In this book we use the term 'development intervention' and present an ethnographically attuned moral engagement with several projects of development interventions. These projects of interventions are initiated by either the external donor agencies or the state. But development interventions are not the sole prerogatives of state or donor agencies or even market; local communities, voluntary organisations and people's movements have also undertaken significant development activities. While the notion and practice of development intervention has the contemporary connotation of a process of working from the outside, the later initiatives in development help to broaden and deepen the meaning of development intervention as an autonomous and endogenous activity, as an aspect of self-initiated programmes of well-being. In the afterword to this volume, one of us undertakes a more elaborate discussion on the way people's movements' have interrogated, broadened and deepened the meaning and practice of development interventions and seek to make development *autopoietic* (cf. Maturana 1980).

Such broadening and deepening of the meaning of intervention helps us to recover its original connotation as a process of 'coming in between', that is, between the self and the other, agents of development interventions and their interlocutors, the developing society and the developed and vice versa, and between cultures. What is important to note is that 'to come in between' involves much more than 'doing'; it also involves love, care and good will. In the contemporary discourse of development intervention, we have bound the meaning of intervention exclusively to projects of doing, and for the most part initiated from the outside. In this context, there is an epochal need now to recover the original meaning of development intervention as a process of *intervenire*, and to reconstitute development as a relational field of sharing and contestation where coming in between involves establishing an appropriate relationship between the care of the self and care of the other, between attentiveness to self-cultivation and attentiveness to the other, between the aesthetic and ethical dimensions of our modes of engagement. Passing through the ethical narratives of the following case studies, the journey of this reconstruction and reconstitution awaits us in the last two chapters. Here we devote ourselves to evolving a new approach to ethics and development. In Chapter 12, we continue our efforts in reconstituting the vision and practice of development as a shared responsibility. We argue that we need to rethink ethics and responsibility as involving not only care of the other but also care of self. But we go beyond an either/or approach to this issue and call for an interpenetration of ethics and aesthetics. Going beyond Foucault and Levinas we strive to reconstitute ethics and development from the vision and perspective of integral self-development. In the following chapter, the afterword, one of us carries this task of border crossing further by bringing the challenge of trans-civilisational dialogue and global justice in going beyond the interventionist models of development and in reconstituting development as a shared responsibility.

Notes

1 The isolation of the political process preceding interventions in development from the domains of outcomes of intervention has been well documented in the report 'Evaluation and Monitoring' prepared by the Policy Evaluation and

Review Unit of the Ministry of Foreign Affairs in The Hague (Ministry of Foreign Affairs of the Netherlands/IOB 1993). The report concluded that evaluation had not impacted policy making in any discernible way. The conclusion was made on the basis of a relatively large number of case studies. For Dutch NGOs a similar conclusion concerning the relative isolation of policy making from the domains of outcome was made earlier (cf. Quarles van Ufford 1988). It was interesting to note how helpless the agencies were in amending the situation. More was apparently at stake than a 'technical' administrative problem.

2 OECD (1996) *Shaping the 21st Century: the Contribution of Development Cooperation*, Development Assistance Committee, Paris: OECD.

3 DFID (Department for International Development) (1997) *Eliminating World Poverty: a Challenge for the 21st Century*, Government White Paper on International Development, Cm 3789, London: Department for International Development.

4 The Policy and Operations Evaluation Department of the Ministry of Foreign Affairs of the Netherlands recently called attention to serious flaws in the assessment of 'result-oriented development intervention'. Reliable empirical data for making a judgement were absent. While available data allowed for financial accountability 'more data are needed for policy evaluations' (Ministry of Foreign Affairs of the Netherlands/IOB 2000: 1). The complaints may well indicate the problematic nature of the empiricist assumptions involved (see Hobart 1993 and Gasper in this volume). The 'prices' of transforming public organisations into business-like operations have been analysed by Mintzberg (1989). See also Jacobs (1992); Quarles van Ufford *et al.* (1998).

5 From 1997, UK's DFID, for example, prioritised support to state governments with pro-poor policies to develop their own strategies for poverty reduction on a large scale, with the provision of budgetary support in the short term, on condition that fiscal and other reforms were put in place (DFID 1997, 2000).

6 Post-structuralist critics of development make great use of Foucault's formulations about knowledge and power but they do not explore a possible alternative trajectory to which Foucault's self-critical questions about politics and power point. Consider the following lines of Foucault:

> In fact, I have especially wanted to question politics, and to bring to light in the political field, as in the field of historical and philosophical interrogation, some problems that had not been recognized there before. I mean that the questions I am trying to ask are not determined by a pre-established political outlook and do not tend to the realization of some definite political project.
>
> (Foucault 1984b: 376)

In his *Care of the Self*, what Foucault writes about Emperor Antonius of Antiquity may be taken note of by Foucauldian critics of development such as Arturo Escobar in being aware of our responsibility as holders and critics of power:

> By avoiding useless outbursts, satisfactions of vanity, transports of anger and violent displays, by eschewing everything in the way of vindictiveness and suspicion, by keeping flatterers away and giving access only to wise and frank counselors, Antonius showed how he rejected the 'Caesarian' mode of being. Through his practice of self-restraint (whether it was a matter of food, clothes, sleep, or boys), through the moderate use he made of the comforts of life, through the absence of agitation and the equanimity of his

soul, and through the cultivation of friendship without inconstancy or passion, he trained himself in the art of sufficing himself without losing his serenity. … A whole elaboration of the self by oneself was necessary for these tasks, which would be accomplished all the better because one did not identify in an ostentatious way with the trappings of power.

(Foucault 1986: 90)

7 This process of social closure has been well documented. Quarles van Ufford *et al.* (1988), building on the seminal work of Mintzberg (1979), show how in the 1980s the spending staff in some Dutch NGOs gained the upper hand over those responsible for learning through monitoring and evaluation. Another study of the learning capacity of government institutions came to a similar conclusion. A study of actual impact of evaluation on wider policy processes by the Dutch government demonstrated that norms and rules guiding the administrative machinery tend to become a world unto themselves, and that learning tends to have a limited role to play in the policy processes. Actual implementation is also cut off from the very people on whose support it depends. So donor spaces of hope, commitment and caring become increasingly self-contained. See Els Scholte's contribution in this volume.

8 Mohanty (2000) helps us understand the link between multi-valued logic and the idea of shared contents: 'Different "worlds" have shared contents' (Mohanty 2000: 24). And we can similarly say: Different worlds of development have shared content. Mohanty's pathway of multi-valued logic finds an inspiring companion in Uberoi's recent effort to go beyond the dualist logic of European modernity, building as he does on the Hermetic traditions of Europe, and his plea for a 'four-valued logic of truth and method in place of the restricted two-valued logic of dualism' (Uberoi 2002: 118).

9 Escobar's (1995) work here is a case in point. His angry study rejecting organised development was prepared along with another study presenting local social movements as alternatives. But his turn to social movements lacks an ethical critique of the logic of preoccupation with power on the part of movements themselves.

10 This view may come forward in many guises of policy-supportive traditions. It is also alive in more recent traditions of post-modern research on development which put much emphasis on the acknowledgement of a great diversity of life worlds. One of the post-modern interlocutors in the field of development studies, Long, urges us to see the scientific as well as practical benefits of acknowledging the almost limitless diversity encountered in field research. He writes: 'we argue that an actor-oriented perspective entails recognizing the "multiple realities" and diverse social practices of various actors, and requires … to get to grips with these different and often incompatible social worlds' (Long and Long 1992: 5). It remains unclear, however, how we might be 'getting to grips' in a practical way. We must acknowledge specific constraints set to political and administrative actors. Any generalised call to heed the great diversity of life worlds of other subjects of development thus remains problematic.

11 Our path of development anthropology departs from many scholars who in their ethnography of development practice confine themselves to bounded groups. For example, in their ethnography of aid, Crewe and Harrison write: 'Our description and analysis is ethnographic in the sense that we are presenting our interpretation of patterned social relations within a conceptually bounded group of people' (Crewe and Harrison 1998: 6). The path we plead for is more border-crossing but in this we do not sacrifice the logic of place to a logic of flows, or what Clifford Geertz warns: too quickly leaving roots 'in favor of routes'.

12 In this context, it is helpful to take note of Norbert Elias's argument that the distinction between order and anomie as proposed by Robert Merton is artificial and morally dubious (Elias and Scotson 1994).

13 The allowing for hope to assume its place implies a willingness to confront the makings of crisis in the past. As Kekes (1992: 12) remarks: 'True hope can follow only after we have faced evil, while false hope is fuelled by a denial of evil.'

14 Eric Wolf tells us of the inherently generalising nature of perspectives and ideologies that arise out of situations of crisis. What Wolf says about the situation of the Kwakitul helps us understand the link between crisis and generalising perspectives. These moralising discourses did not merely advertise norms of proper conduct, but projected the hegemonic values that governed a whole cultural world (Wolf 1999: 278).

15 Stephen Toulmin makes this calling clear for us: 'The world as we understand it at present may be the same world as it always was, but we no longer look to Physics to understand the Myth of Stability, and provide the same comforts as before. The claims of contemporary sciences, both natural and human, are a good deal more modest, seeking neither to deny nor to explain away the contingency of things' (Toulmin 2001: 209–210). The concluding lines of *Return to Reason*, in which Toulmin makes an inspiring distinction between reason and reasonableness and shows us how passionate development workers cultivate our gardens rather than shout slogans of Reason, deserve our careful attention:

> Our first intellectual obligation is to abandon the Myth of Stability that played so large a part in the Modern Age: only thus can we heal the wounds inflicted on the Reason by the seventeenth-century obsession with Rationality, and give back to Reasonableness the equal treatment of which it was for so long deprived. The future belongs not so much to the pure thinkers who are content – at best – with optimistic or pessimistic slogans; it is a province, rather, for reflective practitioners who are ready to act on their ideals. ... The ideals of practical thinkers are more realistic than the optimistic daydreams of simple-minded calculators, who ignore the complexities of real life, or the pessimistic nightmares of their critics, who find these complexities a source of despair.
>
> (Toulmin 2001: 214)

16 For Goulet, development ethics is the 'cement that binds together multiple diagnoses of problems with their policy implications through an explicit ... study of values' (Goulet 1995: 27). This has led many scholars in the field to be concerned with the study and care of the application of certain developmental values. In this way ethics comes to be linked to a large extent with the quest for certain rules and regulations.

17 Ankersmit's attack on Rawls and on the liberal ethical tradition which he represents must be noted especially (Ankersmit 1996: 2–6). It is interesting to note that Ankersmit pleads for a historically situated universalist perspective. He distinguishes between Rawls's abstract a-historical reasoning and the moral philosophies of others such as Hobbes and Montesquieu whose 'quasi universalist argument ... was always intended to some well defined, concrete and urgent political problem'. A similar rejection of abstract moral argument, especially in the liberal tradition, has been put forward by Kekes (1998).

18 In much of critical development anthropology there seems to be a naive assumption that if anthropologists assemble empirical facts systematically and with the right critical attitude, this itself would lead to learning on the part of the policy

makers. But here critical anthropologists leave the problematic task of learning to others – politicians, policy makers and people – while excluding themselves from this process.

19 In proceeding with the act of border-crossing, the following thoughts offered by Mae G. Henderson on this process are helpful: 'What we are proposing is border crossing with a difference – as an act of creation rather than one of violation. ... In methodological terms, remapping the border between disciplines contributes to the larger intellectual project of rethinking culture, canon, and disciplinarity. ... Border crossing yields what W.E.B. Du Bois calls "double vision" – it expands our field of vision without being expansionist; it includes without consuming; it appreciates without appropriating and it seeks to temper politics with ethics' (Henderson 1995: 27).

20 Other notable contributors in nurturing such fertile traditions of dialogue from anthropology and moral philosophy are: Veena Das (1995a, 1995b, 1999), Hilary Putnam (2001), Stephen Toulmin (2001), John Kekes (1998).

21 World Bank Group website, World Development Report 2003.

22 As William Robinson (1996) shows, in the post-war period US foreign policy can be seen as oriented towards *sustaining* global economic differences and preserving affluent lifestyles. The disrupting threats of inequality, he suggests, have been dealt with either militarily (military support for right-wing pro-US regimes) or through promoting democracy ('low intensity democracy'). There is an obvious relevance to present-day international political and development policy (Robinson 1996).

23 In this context what anthropologist and social theorist Martin Fuchs writes deserves our careful attention:

> What seems necessary is a concept of universalism which does not take it as stable, fixed order, as something once and for all achieved and secured, and as something that others can be confronted with. Universalism has again to be understood as what it strictly speaking had always been, an objective. And it must be seen in relation to social actors who practically and interpretively confront the world. Both considerations imply not only a processual notion of universalism, they also imply that universalism can be seen as something shared, a common ground, a *common achievement*.
>
> (Fuchs 2000: 18)

References

Abramson, David (1999) 'A critical look at NGOs and civil society as means to an end in Uzbekistan', *Human Organisation* 58 (3): 240–250.

Ankersmit, F.R. (1996) *Aesthetic Politics: Political Philosophy beyond Fact and Value*, Stanford: Stanford University Press.

Baudrillard, J. (1993) *The Transparency of Evil: Essays on Extreme Phenomena*, London: Verso Press.

—— (1995) 'The map precedes the territory', in W. Truatt Anderson (ed.) *The Truth about the Truth: De-confusing and Re-constructing the Postmodern World*, New York: P.G. Putnam's Sons, pp. 79–82.

Beck, Ulrich (2000) *The Brave New World of Work*, Cambridge: Polity Press.

Booth, D. (ed.) (1994) *Rethinking Social Development: Theory, Research and Practice*, Harlow: Longman Group.

Cassen, R. and Associates (1986) *Does Aid Work?* report to an intergovernmental Task Force, Oxford: Clarendon Press.

Cohen, G.A. (2000) *If You're an Egalitarian, How Come You're So Rich?*, Cambridge, MA: Harvard University Press.

Cooke, Bill and Uma Kothari (2001) *Participation, the New Tyranny?*, London: Zed Books.

Crewe, E. and E. Harrison (eds) (1998) *Whose Development? An Ethnography of Aid*, New York: Zed Books.

Dahrendorf, Ralf (1968) 'Der Geist der Aufklaring: die machbare Welt und ihre Grenzen', in *Die angewandte Aufklarung*, Munchen: Fischer Bucherei.

Dallmayr, Fred (2001) 'Homecoming/homelessness: Heidegger on the road', manuscript, University of Notre Dame.

Das, Veena (1995a) 'Voice as birth of culture', *Ethnos* 60 (3–4): 159–179.

—— (1995b) *Critical Events: Anthropological Perspectives on Contemporary India*, Delhi: Oxford University Press.

—— (1999) 'Wittgenstein and anthropology', *Annual Review of Anthropology* 27: 171–195.

Dasgupta, Partha and Ismail Serageldin (eds) (2000) *Social Capital: a Multifaceted Perspective*, Washington, DC: World Bank.

DFID (Department for International Development) (1997) *Eliminating World Poverty: a Challenge for the 21st Century*, Government White Paper on International Development, Cm. 3789, London: Department for International Development.

—— (2000) *Eliminating World Poverty: Making Globalisation Work for the Poor*, White Paper on International Development, London: Department for International Development.

Edwards, Michael (1999) *Future Positive: International Cooperation in the 21st Century*, London: Earthscan Publications.

Elias N. and Scotson, J.L. (1994) *The Established and the Outsiders: a Sociological Enquiry into Community Problems*, London: Sage.

Eliot, T.S. (1969) 'The Rock', in *The Complete Poems and Plays of T.S. Eliot*, London: Faber and Faber, pp. 14–17.

Escobar, Arturo (1995) *Encountering Development: the Making and the Unmaking of the Third World*, Princeton: Princeton University Press.

Ferguson, James (1990) *The Anti-politics Machine: 'Development', Depoliticization and Bureaucratic Power in Lesotho*. Cambridge: Cambridge University Press.

Fine, Ben (1999) 'The development state is dead – long live social capital!', *Development and Change* 30 (1): 1–19.

Foster, Mick (2000) 'New approaches to development co-operation: what can we learn from experience with implementing sector-wide approaches?', *ODI Working Paper 140*, London: Overseas Development Administration.

Foster-Carter, A. (1976) 'From Rostow to Gunder Frank: conflicting paradigms in the analysis of development', *World Development* 4 (3): 167–180.

Foucault, Michel (1977) 'Nietzsche, genealogy, history', in Donald F. Bouchard (ed.) *Language, Counter-Memory, Practice: Selected Essays and Interviews*, Oxford: Basil Blackwell.

—— (1984a) 'What is enlightenment?', in P. Rabinow, *The Foucault Reader*, New York: Pantheon Books.

—— (1984b) 'Politics and ethics: an interview', in P. Rabinow, *The Foucault Reader*, New York: Pantheon Books.

—— (1986) *The Care of the Self*, New York: Pantheon.

Fuchs, Martin (2000) 'The universality of culture: reflection, integration and the logic of identity', *Thesis Eleven* 60: 11–22.

Gasper, Des (1997) 'Development ethics – an emergent field? A look at scope and structure with special reference to the ethics of aid', in C.J. Hamelink (ed.) *Ethics and Development: on Making Moral Choices in Development Cooperation*, Kampen: Kok.

—— (1999) 'Ethics and the conduct of international development aid: charity and obligation', *Forum for Development Studies* 1.

Geertz, C. (2000) *Available Light*, Princeton: Princeton University Press.

Giri, Ananta K. (2000) 'Audited accountability and the imperative of responsibility: beyond the primacy of the political', in Marilyn Strathern (ed.) *Audit Cultures: Anthropological Studies in Accountability, Ethics and the Academy*, London: Routledge, pp. 173–195.

—— (ed.) (2001) *Rethinking Social Transformation: Criticism and Creativity at the Turn of the Millennium*, Jaipur: Rawat Publications.

—— (2002a) *Conversations and Transformations: Towards a New Ethics of Self and Society*, Lanham, MD: Lexington Books and Rowman and Littlefield .

—— (2002b) 'Towards a new mode of embodiment of responsibility: Swadhyaya and the spiritual regeneration of social capital', *Gandhi Marg*.

Goulet, Denis (1995) *Development Ethics*, London: Zed Books.

Grillo, R.D. and R.L. Stirrat (1997) *Discourses of Development: Anthropological Perspectives*, Oxford: Berg.

Habermas, Jürgen (1996) 'Coping with contingencies: the return of historicism', in Jozef Niznik and J.T. Sandes (eds) *Debating the State of Philosophy: Habermas, Rorty, and Kolakowsky*, Westport, CT: Praeger, pp. 1–30.

—— (1998a) 'Learning by disaster? A diagnostic look back on the short 20th century', *Constellations* 5 (3): 307–320.

—— (1998b) 'Can we learn from history?', in Jürgen Habermas *The Berlin Republic*, Cambridge: Polity Press.

Hamelink, C. (1997) 'Making moral choices in development cooperation', in C.J. Hamelink (ed.) *Ethics and Development: on Making Moral Choices in Development Cooperation*, Kampen: Kok, pp. 11–25.

Hanrahan, Nancy W. (2000) *Difference in Time: a Critical Theory of Culture*, Westport, CT: Praeger.

Harvey, David (2000) *Spaces of Hope*, Edinburgh: University of Edinburgh Press.

Henderson, Mae G. (1995) 'Introduction: borders, boundaries and frameworks', in M.G. Henderson (ed.) *Borders, Boundaries and Frames: Cultural Criticism and Cultural Studies*, New York: Routledge, pp. 1–27.

Hobart, Mark (ed.) (1993) *Anthropological Critique of Development: the Growth of Ignorance*, London: Routledge.

Hoebink, P. (1988) *Geven is Nemen: de Nederlandse Ontwikkelingshulp aan Tanzania en Sri Lanka*, Nijmegen: Stichting Derde Wereldcentrum.

Ignatieff, Michael (1999) 'Human rights: the midlife crisis', *New York Review of Books*, 20 May, pp. 58–62.

Jacobs, J. (1992) *Systems of Survival: a Dialogue on the Moral Foundations of Commerce and Politics*, New York: Random House.

Kekes, J. (1992) *Facing Evil*, Princeton: Princeton University Press.

—— (1998) *A Case for Facing Evil Conservatism*, Ithaca: Cornell University Press.

Kothari, Rajni (1988) *Transformation and Survival*, Delhi: Ajanta.

Laclau, Ernesto (1992) 'Beyond emancipation', in Jan Nederveen Pieterse (ed.) *Emancipations, Modern and Postmodern*, London: Sage.

Locher, G.W. (1978) *Transformation and Tradition; and Other Essays*, The Hague: Nijhoff.

Long, A. and N. Long (eds) (1992) *Battlefields of Knowledge: the Interlocking of Theory and Practice in Social Research and Development*, London: Routledge.

Maturana, Humberto (1980) 'Introduction', in Humberto Maturana and F. Varela (eds) *Autopoiesis and Cognition: the Realization of Living*, Dordrecht: D. Reidel.

Melucci, Alberto (1996) *The Playing Self: Person and Meaning in the Planetary Society*, Cambridge: Cambridge University Press.

Ministry of Foreign Affairs of the Netherlands/IOB (1993) *Evaluatie en Monitoring: de rol van projectevalutaties en monitoring in de bilaterale hulp*.

—— (2000) *Yearly Report 2000*.

Mintzberg, Henry (1979) *The Structuring of Organizations*, Englewood Cliffs, NJ: Prentice-Hall.

—— (1989) *Mintzberg on Management: Inside Our Strange World of Organizations*, New York: The Free Press.

Mohanty, J.N. (2000) *Self and Other: Philosophical Essays*, Delhi: Oxford University Press.

Mohanty, Manoranjan and Partha Nath Mukherji with Olle Tornquist (eds) (1998) *People's Rights: Social Movements and the State in the Third World*, New Delhi: Sage.

Mohanty, Satya (1998) *Literary Theory and the Claims of History*, Delhi: Oxford University Press.

Myrdal, G. (1968) *Asian Drama: an Inquiry into the Poverty of Nations* (3 vols), Harmondsworth: Penguin Books.

Nederveen Pieterse, J. (2000) 'Futures of development', mimeograph.

Newton, A.Z. (1997) *Narrative Ethics*, Cambridge, MA: Harvard University Press.

Nuijten, M. (1998) 'In the name of the land: organization, transnationalism and the culture of the state in a Mexican ejido', unpublished PhD, Wageningen University.

Nussbaum, Martha (1993) 'Non-relative virtues', in: M.C. Nussbaum and Amartya Sen *The Quality of Life*, Oxford: Clarendon Press.

—— (2000) *Women and Human Development*, New Delhi: Kali for Women.

Putnam, Hilary (2001) *Enlightenment and Pragmatism*, Spinoza Lectures, Assen: Koninklijke van Gorcum.

Putnam, Robert with Robert Leonardi and Raffaella Y. Nanetti (1993) *Making Democracy Work: Civic Traditions in Modern Italy*, Princeton: Princeton University Press.

Quarles van Ufford, Philip (1988) 'The myth of rational development policy: evaluation versus policy-making in Dutch Protestant donor agencies', in Philip Quarles van Ufford, D. Kruyt and Th. Downing (eds) *The Hidden Crisis in Development:*

Development Bureaucracies, Tokyo/Amsterdam: United Nations University Press/Free University Press, pp. 75–99.

—— (1999) 'The organisation of development as an illness: about the metastasis of good intentions', in John Campbell and Alan Rew (eds) *Identity and Affect: Experiences of Identity in a Globalising World*, London: Pluto, pp. 275–93.

Quarles van Ufford, Philip, F. Thomése and B. Verbeek (eds) (1998) *De ideologie van de markt: de koopman tussen staat en burger*, Bussum: Coutinho.

Rawls, J. (2001) *Justice as Fairness: a Restatement*, Cambridge, MA: Harvard University Press.

Rew, A. (1997) 'The donors' discourse: official social development knowledge in the 1980s', in R.D. Grillo and R.L. Stirrat (eds) *Opus Citatus*, Oxford: Berg.

Robinson, W. (1996) *Promoting Polyarchy: Globalisation, US Intervention, and Hegemony*, Cambridge: Cambridge University Press.

Sachs, Wolfgang (ed.) (1992) *Development Dictionary: a Guide to Knowledge and Power*, London: Zed Books.

Sardar, Z. (1998) *Postmodernism and the Other*, London: Pluto Press.

Schuurman, F. (ed.) (1993) *Beyond the Impasse: New Directions in Development Theory*, London: Zed Books

Scott, James. C. (1998) *Seeing Like a State: How Certain Schemes to Improve the Human Condition Have Failed*, New Haven: Yale University Press.

Sen, A. (1999) *Development as Freedom*, Oxford: Oxford University Press.

Strathern, Marilyn (1988) *Gender of the Gift*, Berkeley: University of California Press.

—— (2000) 'New accountabilities: anthropological studies in audit, ethics and the academy', introduction to Marilyn Strathern (ed.) *Audit Cultures*, London: Routledge, pp. 1–18.

Strydom, Piet (2000) *Discourse and Knowledge: the Making of Enlightenment Sociology*, Liverpool: Liverpool University Press.

Toulmin, S. (2001) *Return to Reason*, Cambridge, MA: Harvard University Press.

Turner, M. and David Hulme (1997) *Governance, Administration and Development: Making the State Work*, London: Macmillan.

Uberoi, J.P.S. (2002) *The European Modernity: Truth, Science and Method*, Delhi: Oxford University Press.

Van den Berg, M. (1998) 'Ontwikkelingssamenwerking: de Markt van de Geëngageerde Zakelijkheid', in Ph. Quarles van Ufford, F. Thomése and B. Verbeek (eds) *De ideologie van de markt: de koopman tussen staat en burger*, Bussum: Coutinho.

Van den Berg, R. and U. Bosma (1994) 'The historical dimension of change and conflict: between local history and grand theories', in R. van den Berg and U. Bosma (eds) *Poverty and Development: Historical Approach to Processes of Change in the South*, Amsterdam: Drukkerij Randstad.

Van Middelaar, L. (1999) *Politicid, de moord op de politiek in de franse filosofie*, Amsterdam: van Gennep.

Van Schendel, Willem (1989) *Terug naar de Toekomst: Het verleden in ontwikkeling*, inaugural address, Rotterdam.

Van Soest, J. (1978) *Het Begin van de Ontwikkelingshulp in de Verenigde Naties en in Nederland 1945–1955*, Assen: van Gorcum

Van Staveren, Irene (1999) *Caring for Economics: an Aristotelian Perspective*, Delft: Eburon.

Vattimo, Giani (1999) *Belief*, Cambridge: Polity Press.

Walker, Ralph C.S. (1998) 'Contingency', in Edward Craig (ed.) *Routledge Encyclopaedia of Philosophy*, Volume 2, London: Routledge.

Wolf, Eric (1999) *Envisioning Power: Ideologies of Dominance and Crisis*, Berkeley: University of California Press.

World Bank (2002) *World Development Report 2002: Building Institutions for Markets*, New York: Oxford University Press (published for the World Bank).

Part II

Coping with ethical challenges

Development programmes and projects

Chapter 2

The making and marketing of participatory development[1]

David Mosse

Introduction

Why are there so many failures and disappointments in development? Why have development goals been so unattainable? For those working within aid agencies perhaps the most common response is to say that past approaches have been misguided, and if only aid agencies had better theory, the results of development would be more positive. Certainly, development agencies of all kinds promote a constant search for better theory, clearer goals, new paradigms, and alternative frameworks. They have little loyalty to their ideas: community development is abandoned in favour of micro-credit, farming systems development gives way to sustainable rural livelihoods (cf. Edwards 1999: 122). But, then, for others the problem is not theory, but the gap between theory and practice, and the real question is how can the gap between intention and results be explained and reduced? How can plans be more effectively implemented?

These are the questions commonly asked of development projects, both by their dedicated practitioners and by their most virulent critics. This chapter provides a different perspective. For one thing, I will suggest, that despite appearances, development interventions are not driven by theory, but rather by practices. It is not policy ideas or project models but the institutional realities of development funding and 'cooperation' that determine what happens in development. For another, it is not the failure of development projects that needs to be explained, but rather their remarkable success; not the gap between intention and results, but its absence; not the unforeseen nature of consequences, but the production of predictable results. To be more specific, my focus is not on the way in which policy theory is implemented in practice, but rather on the manner in which development practices produce and reaffirm theory and models of development. The chapter will illustrate this by showing how project practices institute and protect sets of representations, which in turn serve to interpret activities, measure performance and define success. Even where they do not direct action, it is essential that policy theory and project models be sustained as legitimising ideas. A concomitant of this is the peculiar capacity of development theory of all kinds (policies, programmes and projects, from macro-level structural adjustment policy based on economic theory,[2] to small-scale community projects) to isolate itself from the empirical.

Conceptualising development policy and projects

Later I will develop these themes through case material; but I need first to provide an appropriate conception of the development policy and project reality that I want to describe. Understanding the relationship between policy discourse and field practices has been hampered by the dominance of two opposing views on policy. These can be caricatured as follows. On the one hand there is an *instrumental view* of policy as problem solving – directly shaping the way in which development is done. On the other hand there is a *critical view* that sees policy as a rationalising discourse concealing hidden purposes of bureaucratic power or dominance, in which the true political intent of development is hidden behind a cloak of rational planning (e.g., Ferguson 1990; Escobar 1995; cf. Shore and Wright 1997). Neither of these views does justice to the complexity of policy making and its relationship to project practice, or to the creativity and skill involved in negotiating development. While simple planning models use outmoded mechanical input–output models, critical analysis assumes a political intentionality and unity of interest which simply cannot be assumed to exist. Both seriously distort the work of agents of international development.

From an instrumental view, the usual concern is how to implement policy, how to realise programme designs in practice, how (as the questions that began this chapter ask) to reduce the gap between theory and practice? My question, as already indicated, is the reverse. How do project practices sustain and protect models (i.e., from contradiction by events)? Development practitioners (including anthropologist consultants such as myself) are not so much agents of policy implementation, as members of 'interpretive communities' (Porter 1995) creating and sustaining policy models that reveal, conceal or give meaning to local activities and events. Practices affirm policy theory and models of change. And these frames are in turn crucial to the measurement of performance and the definition of success, as well as more broadly to the justification of a particular allocation of resources by donors or governments. Of course, failure as much as success can re-confirm theory and its models. As Apthorpe notes, even if projects fail as practice they may nonetheless succeed as code or policy argument in the wider arena (1997: 45).[3]

Such a view of policy departs markedly from the simple input–output models, and even from more sophisticated process perspectives on policy (Brinkerhoff 1996).[4] Rather than programmatic statements oriented towards (or responsive to) action, project models can be understood as primarily concerned to retain the impression (the myth?) of project rationality; the impression that is of causal linkage and manageability in the face of its absence, and the self-representation of project community members as decision-making implementers of policy. Now this may appear to be a critique of project rationality as deception. It is not. In fact it is clear that all development projects not only need legitimising representations, but also require that these be distinct from practice. As I will show, projects may work even while declaring themselves failures.

But if the 'instrumental view' of policy is naive, the 'critical view' is also problematic. To point out the inadequacy of the simple assumptions of development policy as a rational problem-solving instrument (Shore and Wright 1997: 5) is not very difficult. Moreover, it is self-evident that policy and planning are political instruments through which, as Arun Agrawal puts it, 'power manifests itself as the cunning of reason' (1996: 470; cf. Shore and Wright 1997: 8). But it does not follow from this – as some deployments of a crude form of Foucauldian analysis imply – that development policy is a blind instrument of external (Western) power, a kind of agent-less 'space age juggernaut on auto-pilot' (Sivaramakrishnan and Agrawal, forthcoming); or even merely an elaborate media event, a kind of Baudrillardian simulacra, free-floating in its own hyper-reality. Such perspectives divert attention from the complexity of policy as institutional practice. Policy goals and their project instruments never encode a unity of interests. They are the result of complex negotiations over meaning, and as such are very much part of the wider social life and politics of development organisations that need to be explored ethnographically. And this points, perhaps all too obviously, to the need to pay more attention to the development projects, organisations and professionals which frame and control policy ideas (cf. Craig and Porter 1997), and for a more grounded interpretation of policy and project processes.

It is from this perspective that it is possible to see an oblique relationship between the rationality of policy and the world of practice; how projects and programmes shape as well as implement policy; how the language of policy is co-opted from below as much as imposed from above; how there is never a singular voice, or a harmonious consensus around projects; and how power in development is multi-centred, and practices indeterminate and adaptive. The boundary between the makers and consumers of 'development' becomes blurred. As the detail of project practice makes clear, the 'beneficiaries' of development are equally the makers and manipulators of policy. Escobar overstates and overdemarcates the power of aid agency discourse when he writes: 'a textually mediated discourse substitutes for the actual relations and practices of the "beneficiaries", burying the latter's experience in the matrix that organizes the institution's representation' (1995).

What this overlooks is, first, the fact that no project can retain coherence independent of its beneficiaries, and second, that these beneficiaries themselves constitute and manipulate project discourse in managing their own relationships with external patrons and donors. In other words the 'relations and practices of the "beneficiaries"' are constitutive of development texts and project models. In the following pages I will address both of these issues.

In order to deal with this complex inter-face world we need a clear conception of projects and programmes themselves. Both the normative and critical literature on rural development has had a tendency to reify 'the project' as a unified source of intention and power, and attribute to it an agency in the re-shaping of social and productive relations.[5] In order to avoid this misplaced concreteness, it may be useful to draw a distinction between projects and programmes as, on the one hand, 'systems of representations' – sets of key ideas, models, organisational designs and strategies, and as, on the other, 'operational systems' (to borrow from Baudrillard, via Hobart 1995). Of course, this is not the same as the distinction between planning and action in that there is no assumption that project representations – models, goals, objectives – are primarily operational (cf. Quarles van Ufford 1993: 143). Rather, they are constructs invested with the power to interpret and give coherence to activities and events. Project designs are 'official models', in Bourdieu's (1977) sense, themselves maintained through 'officialising strategies' that translate the messiness of reality into authorised categories. Project models have the purpose of conveying precisely the impression of manageability, coherence and rationality that is absent in practice. And as such their orientation is more often upwards (or 'outwards') to validate higher policy goals or justify the allocation of resources, than downwards to orientate action.

As representations, project models provide a mask or a framework of interpretation, revealing and concealing, labelling and giving significance. It is only by means of the model that chaotic practices are stabilised and validated, and that progress is measured and success proclaimed. Models have important work to do – to explain, to justify, to mobilise political support, to track and instantiate new development policy trends, and to enrol the often very different interests and agendas of project 'stakeholders'. These themes will be illustrated below. But projects as systems of representations are never independent from actions. Even though they are not in any straightforward way generated by them, I will show how practices are essential to sustain project models. Project failure may not be a failure to turn designs into reality; but it *is* the consequence of a certain disarticulation between practices, their rationalising models and overarching policy frameworks.

Before taking this argument further, let me introduce the project case through which I want to explore the making and maintenance of rural development as a set of representations, focussing here on the key policy concept of 'participation'.

Making a participatory rural development project

Significant for what I have to say here about this project – as a system of both representations and operations – is the fact that I am myself a part of it. I find no position from which to analyse the circuitry of project-policy processes, that does not place me within it. As both development project practitioner and ethnographer critic I remain part of this 'interpretive community'. And in consequence my own analysis is subject to critical appraisal. If the project is a community of which I am a member, then this is at least partly anthropology from the inside in which one may, as Geof Wood puts it, speak of the methodological category of 'participant comprehension' (1998: 55, citing Mikkelsen).

In fact, I need to reflect on two different roles or positions which stand in tension. The first is my 'constructive role' in the framing of development policy and project discourse, its signs and representations. Here I operate within what Quarles van Ufford calls a 'system model' of the project, where there is a necessary assumption (or fiction) of coherence, integration and manageability. This provides a framework within which development policy and project design are bargained often by individuals from different disciplinary backgrounds or employing different criteria of relevance (concerning people, places, resources). The second of my roles involves not the making of project myths and symbols, but their 'participant deconstruction', the dislodging of certainties (Shore and Wright 1997: 16–17). Here a 'sceptical model' (Quarles van Ufford 1993) applies in which there is no assumption of order and coherence – but rather there are competing interests and contradictory strategies. Here I try to locate pragmatic rules of project behaviour, rather than argue over normative ones.[6] This places me at the margins of the project 'community' – perhaps re-incorporated as a means for self-critical learning, but also at risk of being excluded as an irrelevant, not to say disruptive, academic outsider.

These roles create separate analytical sites, in what has to be a *multi-positioned* as well as multi-sited (Marcus 1995) ethnography of development – taking place in donor policy-making forums, consultant design teams, project meetings, amidst village-level events, in the 'emancipatory reading' of texts (Apthorpe 1997), and the reflective interstices of development practice. Such a research endeavour necessarily abandons the outmoded conception of its objects of study as localised and separate from the researcher – 'the field' separate from 'home' (Gupta and Ferguson 1997). Indeed, I want to explore rather than conceal the personal connections and affinities that tie me as an anthropologist to my object of study (Marcus 1998: 16). And this means exploring a new kind of anthropology, one which situates the production of knowledge about other people, and places it explicitly within the framework of international relations, analysing rather than concealing the political and historical relations or power, and the systems of values which shape representations.[7] Moreover it does so in a way that places the anthropologist within this frame, and turns a self-critical lens onto the anthropologist-actor as member of a transnational development community, speaking from within and in the first person.

The different subject positions of consultant and researcher, and the constructive and deconstructive analytics involved, produce different forms of knowledge; and of course there are others (those of donor officers, project staff, technical colleagues and more). Moreover, since the interpretive account that is 'anthropological' always 'coexists with other forms of knowledge', 'the political task [is] not "sharing" knowledge with those who lack it, but as forging links between different knowledges that are possible from different locations' (Gupta and Ferguson 1997: 39). Indeed anthropological insights have themselves to be relativised in giving space to contending representations. Research relationships and identities based on unsupportable claims to authority need to be re-thought (cf. Marcus 1998: 17).

In Chaper 1 of this volume, Quarles van Ufford *et al.,* suggest that *hope, politics* and *critical understanding* provide alternative frames for development. It follows that this insider analysis of project processes suggested here should involve a moral and a strategic-administrative (i.e., political) as well as a critical perspective, and will be judged from these viewpoints. Hope, politics and critical understanding are co-present perspectives. However, the personal shifts in working within a project community tend to bring one or other frame to the fore at different moments in the life of a project. Thus initially, while being formulated and negotiated, and when staff and supporters were being enrolled, the project discussed below was, collectively and personally, a set of moral choices; a design of hope. Goals were also moral responsibilities (e.g., to focus on the needs of the poorest, of women, to promote democratic processes). Characteristically, hope involved the re-definition of the past and present in terms of an imagined future. But project formulation, design and textualisation were also contexts for political engagement. The project was about coalition building and influence. It aimed to challenge a particular structure of power and certain dominating knowledge. Project work and the knowledge generated were not independent of social position; and project design, implementation and review were always political agency of a kind. But this political–administrative involvement itself gave rise to a need for a critical understanding of the development project itself; a perspective which gradually became more central to my own work over a 10-year period. As I will show towards the end of this piece, while writing here analytically, I am also forced to bring moral and political–administrative judgements to bear, to ask again, what are my responsibilities?

In 1990, while working for the British NGO Oxfam in south India, I was invited to join an ODA (Overseas Development Administration, now Department for International Development, or DFID) 'mission' of expatriate consultants to design a new agriculture development project in 'tribal' western India, the Indo-British Rainfed Farming Project (IBRFP). This was a fairly typical consultancy which brought together a group of professionals from different disciplines (economics, soil science, plant genetics and social anthropology) into a 'transitory knowledge building community' (Wood 1998)[8] around an ambitious donor 'Terms of Reference': 'to review all available information which may be relevant to the formulation of the approach and technical content [of the project] ... and to produce a detailed proposal for ... a fully participatory and poverty focused rainfed farming project.' Typically ignorant of local and historical detail, our team was attributed high status as international experts, given access to top people, and mobility through the five Indian states and the capital. Working to tight time-frames, the team relied on working assumptions, guesswork, borrowed ideas or past experience to put together a coherent project idea, a viable design and a convincing argument to justify the investment of public money by the donor (cf. Wood 1998). Complex worlds and local histories had to be pressed into the service of current policy debates. And in this case upland *adivasi* ('tribal') communities and regional institutions to be rendered comprehensible and responsive to planned project inputs in predictable ways – within six weeks. That indeed is what development consultants are well paid to do; to come up with models that reduce disorder and allow rational sense to be made of programme inputs. This sort of 'project design mission' is itself an important subject of ethnographic enquiry. However, here I want to press on to consider the *output* of this consultancy – the project model – rather than the process. What sort of representation was 'the project' and what interests were involved? A few key points: .

First, as James Ferguson (1990) argued for World Bank project discourse in Lesotho, the IBRFP project document represented places and people as embodiments of those development problems which are amenable to the donor's currently favoured 'technical' solutions. Two solutions stand out: the first was 'the introduction of improved agricultural *technology*' and the second 'enhancement of farmer capacities through *participation*'. The initial technical design document described the farming system of the project area as an arena of almost unlimited possibilities for increased production through the introduction of agricultural technologies – improved cultivars, crop husbandry, livestock improvement, soil and water conservation techniques, etc. – an inventory extended and detailed by a series of (always hopeful) UK consultants.

But, while the project area quickly became known as the environmentally degraded home to a catalogue of deficiencies in existing practice (reduced fallows, cultivation on steep slopes, low inputs, limited knowledge, livestock disease, etc.), development problems could *not* legitimately be traced to farmer ignorance and traditional agriculture. This was a project in the new 'Farmer First' policy mould. Problems pointed instead to the mistaken priorities and procedures of the Indian agricultural research and extension establishment, which in common with most, or even all, national agricultural research systems, had failed to develop and deliver technology appropriate to the complex, diverse and risk-prone agricultural environment of upland tribal farmers (Witcombe *et al.* 1998). And one of the root causes of this was the failure to involve farmers in technology development, testing and popularisation.

This leads, then, to the second 'solution', namely 'participation'. Farmer participation would ensure that more appropriate technologies would be developed and delivered. But this was only one aspect of participation. In a much broader sense our documentation conceived of the project districts as an *area without participation*, meaning, among other things, that they were remote from government administration and services, agricultural technology and inputs, institutional credit, and markets. Indeed, in writing the project design I (and my consultant colleagues) found it possible to re-frame a variety of political, economic and technical issues in terms of the 'master metaphor',[9] *participation*. The beauty of this idea (as I will explain below) was that while it had been made into a powerful interpretive device – not least by my own writing – which legitimised and amplified the meaning of project action,[10] it could at the same time, in *operational* terms, involve a restricted and eminently manageable set of project activities (village level meetings, PRAs, workplans, etc.), formalised and 'manualised' as the 'IBRFP Participatory Planning Approach to Farming Systems Development', which I also helped to draft.[11]

Having established a 'people in need of participation' (as much as in need of better technology) our project design then invoked a 'model of change' – that is a simplified set of problem–solution linkages *causally* connecting activities and objectives, inputs and outputs. These established, for example: the relationship between farmer-managed trials, widening cultivar choice and crop yield increases; soil and water conservation and yield stability; or farmer organisations and access to credit and reduced debt. Above all, the project was defined by a 'theory of participation'. This asserted that persisting poverty and isolation and inappropriate and unsustainable development programmes were the consequence of 'top-down' planning and the non-involvement of farmers in the process of need identification and programme design. Correspondingly, maximising farmer participation (including the specific involvement of women) would result in better designed, more effective and sustainable programmes. And, to quote the project document, '*The basic premise is that sustainable development can only be achieved by enhancing local self-reliance through institutional and community development*'. Ultimately, participation was about the transfer of power.

The project design was synthesised into the currently dominant project formulation model – the Logical Framework (or LogFrame) which conveyed to outside decision makers the idea of manageability based upon the existence of logically and causally related activities and objectives, an ordered sequence of events, the functional integration of different components and institutional actors (donors, implementing agencies, field staff and villagers) within a single knowledge system (cf. Quarles van Ufford 1993: 139). The logical relations of the model of change were in fact clarified through successive re-working of the LogFrame, which was the point of reference to validate approaches, report achievements, and negotiate changes in strategy as the project went along. The LogFrame was itself part of a carefully negotiated and drafted Project Document which stood for the project and justified it in prescribed form (through separate annexes dealing with economic cost–benefits, technical viability, institutional viability, and social policy acceptability – in terms of poverty, equity and gender criteria). Once its elements – approaches, roles, expected outputs, categories of activities – were present in the text, the project existed in our minds and in our conversations, regardless of the actuality of events.

But the project text was only partly and imperfectly written for internal coherence; it was also a container for wider policy argument, both within the donor agency and externally. For example, farmer participation in plant breeding and varietal selection (a core project innovation) was explicitly a challenge to the prevailing regulatory frameworks and bureaucratic practice in the Indian agricultural research establishment (cf. Witcombe *et al.* 1998). The emphasis on farmer agency and indigenous knowledge was a critique of monolithic top-down modernist approaches to agricultural development directed at collaborating Indian bureaucrats, while 'sustainability' through self-reliance and farmer control was intended as a critique of subsidy-driven government programmes, and to restrain the dominance of technical agendas over social ones within donor and project agencies. Finally, participation and the poverty focus were aimed at answering public criticism of the British aid programme from NGOs and media in the UK and in India. Indeed, in the early 1990s the project was intended to mark and advertise a major departure from earlier practice. The project design was a policy argument, a discourse of persuasion (Apthorpe 1997).

The project text was both the outcome of social processes of persuasion and enrolment, and a point of reference anticipating future policy arguments. And these were not confined narrowly to project actors. Through regional networks, the nascent project would also serve as a vehicle for other interests, for example, Indian and international NGOs lobbying donors and government. I was myself deputed by Oxfam to connect the emerging official aid agenda with that of Indian NGOs, to exert policy influence and re-orientate a public-sector implementing agency. Projects are rarely bounded entities.

Local planning, open-ended design, a focus on the needs of the poorest and women, and prioritisation of the protection of subsistence cropping through low-risk, low-cost technologies over investment for commercial agriculture – these were clearly political choices. But they were advanced as technical decisions, concomitants of the paradoxical universal rationality of 'participation', a globally valid development approach endorsed by international donors, the work of NGOs and valorised 'local' knowledge. By reference to this discourse we foreign consultants could effectively de-author potentially threatening change, making it the impersonal demands of the 'system' (i.e., the participatory approach) (cf. Porter 1995: 79). We stood as guarantors of the universal technical validity of changes that still had to be negotiated within a large bureaucratic public sector project agency.

So, this project design – and its emphasis on 'participation' – was, like most others, a bid for political support, a site for institutional politics (around the competing agendas of technical and 'social' donor advisers, donor and project agency and project management and field staff). Against Ferguson, such institutional politics is as much about coalition building in order to *restrict* bureaucratic and technical power as about its extension.[12] But in order to advance policy arguments at any level, and so acquire and retain political support, project ideas have to meet other criteria.

Firstly, a project has to be *consequential*; it has to be ambitious and have big effects. IBRFP 'aimed to improve the long-term livelihoods of poor farmers in a drought prone region … and promote a replicable participatory poverty-focussed [and environmentally benign] approach to farming systems development elsewhere'. Programme discourse requires such over-ambition. Relatedly, a development project has to be *innovative*. It needs the quality of novelty, and has to mark a new beginning. This theme reverberates through IBRFP's initial documentation.

Secondly, the designed interventions have to be seen to be *technical*. The political nature of the project's participation goals and its critique of existing state policy and programmes are concealed behind the technical expertise of international consultants. As a 'Participation Specialist' my own 'technical' annexes were able to stand alongside with those relating to seed technology or soil conservation methods, rendering regional social analysis in terms of the apolitical organising development idea of 'participation'. More broadly, the language of international development consensus (and ultimately legal and inter-governmental agreement) is always technical and never political. And this is what gives Logical Frameworks such an important position in the formal negotiation of development. The project had to be represented *as if* it had no political or institutional context.

Finally, project formulations including objectives have to have a high degree of *ambiguity*, which in project discourse (as in cultural systems, see Osella and Osella 1996) facilitates and helps maintain consensus by allowing the multiplication of criteria of success (see below). As an interpretive device, the project model should function so as to enable a variety of actors and institutions to isolate and claim credit for desirable change. Importantly, the ambiguity of the project idea also allows it to absorb and give expression to shifting agendas. Over its first ten years, the IBRFP project would bear the imprint of successive international development fashions. By 1993–1994 watershed development had gained primacy over rainfed farming technologies and 'farmer first' approaches; by 1995 trends towards micro-finance and 'self-help' groups were strongly mirrored in the project, while from 1998 the project was to exemplify DFID's new Sustainable Rural Livelihoods (SRL) framework. Again one of the key roles of external consultants is to ensure effective re-interpretation of project models in terms of shifting policy trends. Indeed, the project model was characteristically more permeable to such policy trends than to its own constantly re-interpreted field experience.[13]

Donors and their consultants were without doubt the dominant voice in the design and (re-)formulation of this project and its language of legitimacy, even though donor power and imposed designs had to be veiled behind a rhetoric of partnership and rituals of collaboration, including carefully orchestrated 'joint' planning workshops.[14] But, in order to gain acceptance, donor-imposed designs have to appear to reflect national policies, or to draw on the emerging aims/approaches of implementing agencies (which are flatteringly cited in project documents).[15] At the same time, the work of international consultants, feasibility reports or studies of various kinds accumulate data that serve to symbolise the rationality of decisions (cf. Alvesson 1993).

Donor project designs, including that of the IBRFP project, however, only have to *appear* to be hegemonic. For this project to work at all, its model had to be porous to the interests of a range of actors and institutions. There *had* to be a *single* project model – given privilege in the text – but there were always several readings of it, several shadow or subordinate models and rationalities validating action from different points of view or operational positions (i.e., of fieldworkers, managers, consultants, etc.). Indeed, the purpose of the singular, technical–rational, politically acceptable, ambitious and *ambiguous* project model is often precisely to provide a vehicle for very different interests beyond the donor, including (in this case) those of central/state government, a para-statal agency, agro-research centres, among others. Like an international regime (on, say, trade), the project model with its ambiguous metaphor of participation was able to facilitate cooperation between different institutional interests.[16] Moreover, once a vehicle for the different interests of various 'stakeholders', the representations of the official model find many supporters and so acquire greater stability and protection from failure. In this case, the IBRFP project model, at one level an unstable operating consensus, was secured on diverse institutional interests, which were uniquely underpinned and symbolised by the ambiguous concept of 'participation' itself. What is characteristic of 'successful' projects is a high degree of convergence of disparate interests and priorities onto a single validating and interpretive model; and therefore a shared interest in reaffirming and protecting it. And successful project ideas are those that provide an interpretive framework (official objectives and measures of progress) broad enough to contain and stabilise the various interests involved. Successful models (and their architects) are those that 'assist in the critical process of creating certainty, of turning arbitrariness into givenness and actuality' (Porter 1995: 74). 'Success' in development is an institutional process, not an objective fact.

In order to illustrate the way in which 'participation' as part of a consensual project model was linked to quite distinct institutional concerns, I want to turn in more substantial detail to the IBRFP project, and begin by exploring the alternative interpretations of the project goal held by two key actors: the donor and the host agency. Between these two was the 'project management unit' or project unit itself.[17]

'Participation' as symbolic capital and commodity

Donor concerns

In the late 1980s, there was mounting public criticism from NGOs, the media and even the national audit office directed at the UK Overseas Development Administration (ODA)'s India country programme and its natural resources (forestry and agriculture) projects in particular.[18] As a Regional Representative for Oxfam in India, I was part of this critique which pointed to a major failure of official aid projects implemented through government machinery to meet the needs of poor men and women. At a senior policy level the donor's mandate was being re-oriented towards a poverty-reduction agenda, but there were precious few projects that could demonstrate this new priority. ODA clearly needed, and its management were prepared to support, a convincingly participatory and poverty-focussed project which would signal departure from old-style 1970s bureaucratic top-down planning, and simplified package approaches to agricultural development based on 'transfer of technology', *but* which could do so while still delivering on established production enhancement objectives. The new IBRFP project idea promised to contribute the requisite symbolic capital, and in so doing to incorporate and reflect the conflicting objectives of the donor's technical and social development advisors, emphasising respectively technology adoption leading to increased production, and enhanced community capacity leading to equitable gains.

The late 1980s development goals also brought an added emphasis on political pluralism and the private sector, and encouraged a search for alternative project agencies, NGOs and para-statal organisations, beyond the traditional partnerships with line departments (forestry, agriculture, etc.) in state government. The host agency, KBCL, was one such partner. This organisation was a large national cooperative sector agro-input manufacturing and marketing agency promising, from ODA's point of view, to combine flexible independence from the bureaucratic constraints of a government department with a scale of operation and a national network which no NGO could match. Whether a large bureaucratic marketing organisation (KBCL) had the necessary capability to implement a 'state-of-the art' participatory project (as defined by the donor) was a matter on which there was little consensus. But at the project's design stage, donor concerns for *internal coherence* and *support* for the project gave little space to discussion of such 'organisational constraints'. Such issues were edited from the record, and buried in laudatory commentary on KBCL's qualities and efficiencies.

The new project brought together key late-1980s policy concerns, namely poverty reduction and support to the non-state sector. A strong conception of the new project as path-breaking suppressed concerns about its institutional viability. One might have expected this blindness to institutional realities to be the preface to a tale of project failure, bureaucratic inflexibility, top-down planning and another failure of development to reach the poor. Few observers of bilateral aid would have been surprised. But, on the contrary, what was surprising was not the failure, but the overwhelming *success* of the KBCL host agency in promoting ODA's participatory development project. This itself requires some explanation.

Making and marketing participation

The project began work in July 1992. By the end of 1995, a small highly committed project team was working in a handful of the poorest tribal villages in a remote corner of western India. They had earned local credibility slowly over three years, by helping farmers identify and test improved rice and maize varieties for poor upland soils with few inputs, providing them with credit, in some places establishing low-cost soil and water conservation structures, deepening wells, providing tree seedlings, vegetable seeds and improved breeds of goats and chickens. They had begun by using PRA to identify people's needs and priorities, while exposing local people to new ideas, technologies and options; regularly taking men and women to distant research centres, or bringing government experts and administrators to their doorsteps. Staff worked hard to build relationships with groups of poor farmers, meeting again and again, sitting, discussing, explaining ideas, initiating activities and delivering a range of schemes. This was an approach to development understood and increasingly favoured among donors and NGOs, but what did it mean to the KBCL project host?

KBCL was a leading national commercial organisation involved in the production and marketing of fertiliser, with a firm commitment to agricultural development through 'scientific management' and the 'transfer of modern technology' through its own demonstrations and promotional campaigns aimed at expanding its capacity to deliver agricultural inputs and services. Its nation-wide marketing operations were concentrated in the same broad region as the project, although its clients were not the poor farming communities that were to be the project's focus. The question is how could KBCL's strong marketing agenda and its understanding that input supply was the principal constraint to agriculture and that low input demand was a constraint to market development be reconciled with a project model which stressed low/no-cost low-input technology and response to the demands of very poor farming communities (with negligible demand for fertiliser)? How could a fertiliser company, with staffing and procedures evolved to meet the considerable logistical demands of transporting and supplying 1.5 million tonnes of fertiliser (yearly) to a precise schedule, manage to respond to the range and complexity of needs of small tribal farming communities? How could a company with tight systems of control and accountability allow tribal farmers to develop their own development responses? Why would KBCL sign up to the external donor-driven development agenda anyway? What interests did it have in a participatory poverty-focussed project, and how was it to make this project a successful part of its own organisational agenda?

In order to answer these questions, a little more needs to be known about KBCL itself. In its marketing operations, KBCL had only one legitimate channel of distribution, namely local cooperative societies, 2,000 of which from different parts of the country were its members. KBCL marketed its government-allocated quota of fertiliser through apex cooperative societies or directly to lower-level societies at fixed prices. Its marketing strategy could only be geared towards increasing its market share of cooperative sales by gaining and retaining farmer loyalty. But the only difference between KBCL urea and that of its competitors was the 'KBCL' name and logo printed on the bags. There was therefore a fundamental organisational imperative to promote itself and its brand name and to do so through serving the wider interests of farmers as its shareholders and its market. For this reason various farmer services (ranging from warehousing to soil testing) and educational and welfare activities were central to its broader marketing strategy; and these included a network of client-service centres and local input supply nodes, as well as an expanding 'village adoption' welfare programme. Finally, along with promoting its name in relation to its farmer clients, KBCL had the equally important need to preserve and enhance its profile in relation to the government (at both state and central level) which controlled the allocation of fertiliser quotas and other commercial projects in which KBCL would be interested.

In short, KBCL senior management could give meaning to the project in terms of its own enduring concerns with advancing its profile to its client base, extending its capacity to deliver agro-inputs and services, enhancing its link with government and the national goal of increasing agricultural production, as well as straightforward fertiliser marketing. Initially, they were also hopeful of opportunities to exploit additional commercial/marketing possibilities, for example, through large-scale wasteland development and social forestry plantations, or the marketing of agricultural seeds or produce. Indeed, KBCL was far more interested in the value of the project as a high-profile, high-prestige internationally funded venture able to promote its image and relationship with government and other external observers, and to expand its broad patronage role in relation to its farming community clients, than with any potential it had in establishing a (very low value) local market for fertiliser. What was unexpected was that it was the rhetoric and practice of 'participation' that proved most effective in pursuing these promotional and patronage objectives.

So, why was a *participation* agenda so compatible with the self-promotional goals of a fertiliser company? From one point of view the answer is that the project was able, very effectively, to turn 'participation' into a *commodity*, which, like urea, could be bagged with KBCL's own label on it. This was made possible by the high profile accorded to the project by the donor, and by a rising demand for skills in 'participatory' approaches and a 'package of methods' (mostly PRA) by large-scale state-led development programmes such as the National Watershed Development Programme within India, and the project's ability to deliver these. Through skilful public relations the project management succeeded in establishing 'participation' as a technique/commodity and itself as the primary local source and supplier, and reaped the rewards of high-profile visibility, and reputation. This 'commodification' of participation was inadvertently helped by the efforts of myself and other consultants working with the project team to systematise the processes of village-level planning. And this systematisation was itself a means both to validate community-based approaches (within the team) and to deal with considerable pressure to press ahead quickly with the implementation of physical works. But what it meant was that participation (ultimately a matter of shifting relations of power) could be formatted, printed, wrapped (sometimes quite literally in coloured tissue paper) and delivered as a gift.

But if the project was able to advance the marketing agenda of its parent organisation, it was also clear that it would be under considerable pressure to conform to this organisation's systems and procedures, to respect its hierarchy, observe its rules, and to deliver progress in its terms – that is as quantified outputs in compliance with pre-defined categories – however inconsistent these demands might be with the donor's principles of participatory development. At the level of the IBRFP project unit, considerable management energy was devoted to handling these demands, negotiating flexibility and protecting the project's work and culture from external pressure. Often this meant trying to pursue exploratory approaches at village level, while remaining upwardly accountable and delivering against specified expectations; translating the realities of project experience into categories that would be meaningful to senior marketing and accounts managers. Through its routine monitoring and progress reports, and in its presentations to official visitors, the project constructed a 'plans–targets–output' version of itself in order to satisfy external audit, while preserving an autonomy for its own practices. Indeed, the creativity of the new project could only be protected if key people within it were willing to engage with the bureaucratic culture of the parent organisation on its own terms; people who could act as buffers and manager–brokers of organisational culture, who were bilingual in the discourse of KBCL bureaucracy and donor policy.

But ultimately it was impossible for the project to resist external control, and its buffers and brokers were also conduits for external institutional demands. Those who interpreted the project and made it meaningful to the marketing agency also brought back expectations; personalised mediation brought personal obligations to control the process and deliver the result. Conflicting demands – the commitment to participation, and its opposite, the imperative to control – appeared to make the project unmanageable; *except* that paradoxically the notion of 'participation' itself brought these incompatible agendas together. The 'participation' framework preserved integrity and made an unmanageable project manageable. How?

Well, as a set of practices 'participation' proved eminently *manageable*. Practically, 'participation' produced not (as might be expected) a diverse and locally variable development programme, but the strong convergence of activities into a fixed set – crop trials, soil and water conservation, agroforestry and input supply credit and a range of *ad hoc* welfare programmes. There is no question that these interventions were important, shaped by project staff's sincere interactions with villagers and pursued with commitment; but choices were also constrained to comply with prevailing organisational systems and procedures (budget categories and time-frames, procedures for approval and sanctioning, rules for costing, fund disbursement and procurement, etc.). Over time, it was inevitable that priority would be given to familiar, conventional programmes over innovative initiatives where approval might be uncertain or delayed. At the same time, the institutional need to maintain relationships with local government, senior management, research institutions or donor advisers, each with distinct development agendas, required the introduction of a stream of other (frequently flawed or inappropriate) schemes for which farmers had little input – the promotion of new winter crops, drip irrigation, grain banks, compost pits, farm machinery, mushroom cultivation, women's handicraft, or first aid kits.

The point is that the participation framework enabled all of these to be widely perceived as a direct response to 'local needs'. In ways that I have explored elsewhere (Mosse 1996, 2001), participatory techniques allowed the development priorities conveyed by the project (or demanded by its systems) to be mirrored back to them; in fact this was unavoidable. Self-interested villagers would of course collude with project staff in endorsing external assumptions and programme priorities where this guaranteed benefits; the disincentives to innovate or to challenge prevailing preconceptions were shared by staff *and* villagers. And as villagers shaped their needs and priorities to match the project's schemes and administrative realities – validating imposed schemes with local knowledge and requesting only what was most easily delivered – the wider institutional interests of the project (including those of host and donor organisations) became built into community perspectives and project decisions became perfectly 'participatory'. The shift from a relatively open and exploratory system towards a closed one was not intentional but a side effect of institutional factors (including the effects of my own systematising documentation) that were not perceived by project actors themselves, or even by external observers. Indeed, project actors had become caught up in a system that was increasingly closed and controllable – increasingly impervious to variable local needs, re-enforcing preconceptions and narrowing options – but which was, at the time, being widely acclaimed for its participatory processes and the sophistication of its methods.

Once in place, moreover, the 'participation' framework provided a uniquely strong basis for defining programme success. As a normative framework and an ordered set of field techniques (from 'village entry' and PRAs to 'workplans') participation became embedded in the project's practices, increasingly routinised but providing ready measures of achievement. The publicised record of village meetings, attendance, PRAs, trainings, etc., provided an unassailable quantitative record of the project's participatory performance. Participation goals were supremely ambiguous – generating multiple criteria by which the project could claim success with authority in ways that did not depend upon field-level verification. Through the discursive practices of the project – notably the reports of its consultants (including myself) – 'participation' had come to represent a range of desired social transformations (people's empowerment, control, voice, awareness, etc.) which could symbolically be invoked by the trivial and routine practice of PRA. My own exhortations on the importance of pursuing 'genuinely' participatory approaches served further to thicken the meaning of 'thin' development practice.

On the basis of its 'participation' methodology, KBCL's IBRFP project was given a reputation (by the donor) that generated a steady stream of international visitors. The project found that it could advertise its participatory achievements while (of necessity) retaining control over an increasingly standard set of project activities, reproduced through conservatism and convenience, the risk aversion of both villagers and staff, and administrative pressure from the parent organisation. Among donor staff, the project was already a front-runner, a flagship, 'the jewel in the India aid programme crown', and a compelling advertisement for the new face of British aid.

As a model of participation the project served both to enhance the 'symbolic capital' of a donor agency and its new policy agenda, and to provide a new 'commodity' to promote the profile and reputation of a marketing agency. While neither of these organisational concerns was directly encoded in the 'official' project objectives, the ambiguity of these provided a vehicle for both, as well as the basis for strong overt consensus around this successful participatory project. Moreover, the discourse of 'participation' had also made it possible to manage the conflicting pressures on the project implied by these different agendas. Only self-proclaimed participatory development success could marry KBCL bureaucratic pressures and donor policy expectations, rendering an unmanageable project manageable. The satisfaction of key institutional interests of the donor and host agencies had raised the profile of this project; but it had also raised the stakes. The project was trapped in 'success'.

A core contradiction? Participation and the delivery of development

Well-promoted activities in the area of 'participation' – PRAs, village workplans, meetings, trainings, villager events – were not, however, in themselves sufficient to secure visible and recognised success. What validated the project was the donor-supported *theory* that linked 'participation' on the one hand, and better (more effective/sustainable) physical programmes of soil and water conservation, forestry, minor irrigation and so forth, on the other. Success depended crucially upon the timely implementation of measurable quantities of high-quality development schemes that would hold the attention of outside observers, political bosses and paymasters (and continue to secure 'participation' from villagers). But the timely delivery of programme outputs – the construction of kilometres of soil conservation structures, the planting of trees, deepening of wells, purchase of pumps, or the supply of input credit – had become far too important to be left to *participatory* (i.e., farmer-managed) processes. External pressures were translated into unofficial systems of rewards and punishments which encouraged a strong vertical control of programme activities and implementation, as well as the export of participation 'commodities' (e.g., PRA training, presentations, workshops, manuals). With measures of performance and 'efficiency' linked to the speed and extent of programme completion, staff who tried to be *too participatory* – spending too much time investigating 'real needs', or women's needs, or working at a pace that would ensure local control and the mobilisation of local resources – would soon be seen as under-performing by both project and community.

Field staff not only took direct control of programme implementation (in some instances), but also recruited, trained and paid male and female 'village volunteers' or *jankars*. While crucial to the project's delivery system, *jankars* were also key indicators of 'participation'. The operational system of the project demanded quality and quantity: on the one hand, quality control and upward accountability, and on the other, a constant stream of new activities and commitments to 'keep up momentum'. This in turn ensured expanding networks of patronage locally. Field staff found themselves acting as local patrons and benefactors – a role underlined by the high public profile KBCL gave to its welfare activities. Indeed, the identity and credibility of the project locally became consolidated around its role as benefactor, source of technology, inputs, or credit. Rather than making subsidies redundant, village workers were the means to acquire subsidies. In a region where tribal farmers were historically predisposed to engage with outsiders as clients – whether labour contractors, traders, money lenders or development projects – this may be less than surprising.

This then was the operational logic of the project which resulted from the tension between internal participatory development goals and external institutional demands. The need for close control over works schedules, fixed budget calendars, purchasing and expenditure norms, and reporting formats emphasised upward accountability, the proper use of funds, and the planning and delivery of high-quality programmes against quantitative targets. The project system was simply not capable of transferring power to communities or dealing with the uncertainty that would result from allowing Bhil farmers to develop their own ways of doing things, making their own decisions, taking risks and making mistakes. But, when interpreted through the assumptions of the project model, the impressive landscape of well-laid-out soil and water conservation bunds, improved varieties, newly planted woodlots, deepened wells and operating pumpsets, could nonetheless be read as demonstrating the success of the donor goals of people's participation and farmer-managed development and self-reliance. Both *participation* and its *denial in practice* were necessary to the management of reputation and the marketing of success.

By its second and third year the project management (including consultants) became increasingly oriented towards the management of what could be read as a profound internal contradiction: high profile 'participation' on the one hand, and the strong control over programme delivery and expanding patronage on the other. Now the key point is that the core validating project model established *ideologically* precisely the link between 'participatory processes' and efficient implementation that was weak or absent in practice. Indeed this is precisely why the core model was constantly repeated and invoked in meetings, workshops and during donor review visits. Through ritualised expression the model allowed the interpretation of events and landscapes (smartly bundled) that confirmed its presuppositions. We consultants were officiants at these rituals. As with many projects, donor review visits often served as occasions to *explicate* project assumptions, rather than to examine their practices in any detail.[19]

And a good deal of management, donor and consultant effort (through monitoring and reviews, project workshops, etc.) went into the re-articulation of
the participatory project model. Not only reports, but also video films and
manuals reaffirmed the model – indeed by the third year of the project, *the
model* had become so important that it had been restated *as the* key project
Purpose. Which now read as establishing a 'replicable, participatory … FSD
approach – i.e., a model' (Revised LogFrame, 1995) (rather than sustainable
increases in production, etc.). The project had developed a dissemination
strategy and defined a 'Replication programme' as a key Output (including
production of manuals, national/regional seminars/workshops, audio-visual
productions, training for NGOs and GOs on the now systematised
Participatory Approach).

As a goal, *replication* further underlined the coherence of the project as
model or simulation, emphasising coherence and generality (cf. Fairhead
2000: 101) in a way that strengthened the position of the project in the
policy circles (donor, government, international) where it sought to
command attention. It effectively denied the contingency of project
processes and the strong influence of particular institutional interests.
Similarly, the emphasis on outward dissemination and upward policy influence underlined the project design as a legitimising representation rather
than an operational model. The effect of the discourse of replication,
dissemination and policy influence was further to blur distinction between
the normative and the descriptive, event and representation, so that planning
manuals could be cited and reproduced in donor texts and elsewhere as
project experience.

Now, it is important to stress that there is absolutely no suggestion here
of deception or a cover-up on the part of the project. The project's own
reporting (its monthly progress reports) itemised the number of 'participation' activities (participants, meetings, PRAs, trainings, etc.) undertaken and
the physical programmes implemented with strikingly little interpretive justification of the project model (instead it met the requirements of upward
accountability within a management hierarchy). In fact the project did not
itself need to provide such analysis since its data were produced within a
powerful interpretative community constituted by the wider circle of consultants, donor representatives, technical experts or KBCL senior management
– all firmly committed to the project's participatory model and the meanings
it imposed in one way or another. Most visitors remained ignorant of the
contradictions of the project or unable to criticise the dominant interpretations offered. Every new engagement with the project, including my own
critical monitoring of progress in 'participation', served only to add
resilience to the model and its core assumptions. Nobody assumed that
participation was easy or the project faultless. Critical writing on the project
could be routinely included in information packs, mildly raising eyebrows,
but mostly adding extra endorsement to the model by demonstrating open-

ness to criticism. Success was stable, and in the context of donor policy commitments to poverty and participation, rare. Very few senior donor administrators were not taken to this flagship project. In the UK, the project manager was honoured, and in India the project was invited by government to advise on the design of a new large-scale national watershed development programme.

At the same time the project model derived support 'from below'. The Bhil tribal members of the project's selected villages were not passive victims of imposed development that failed to meet their needs. Rather they participated in and concurred with project representations of their needs and their role as 'participants', because only by so doing could they make legitimate claims on project resources, gain access to important benefits (low-interest credit, agro-inputs, pumps, tree nurseries, wage labour, etc.) and win locally influential project patrons. Field staff, by delivering desirable goods, schemes and work, won support from locals – who agreed to 'participate', attend meetings, train as volunteers, host visitors, to save and make contributions, do things for the poor, willingly to participate in the hosting of the project visits, donor monitoring missions, or evaluation studies, and in other ways to validate both the wider project and staff performance within it. The 'participatory' goals of self-help, local control, low subsidies, local contributions and cost recovery may have been far from self-evident development ideals to villagers accustomed to maximising gains from high-subsidy state programmes. But then villages in their dealing with local staff had little need to engage with the ideals of the project's participatory 'high culture' – the language of representation rather than operation.

But there was a cost to success, a cost which those 'too participatory' staff who resisted organisational imperatives towards patronage believe that they bore in seeking to resolve the contradictions of participation. While these project workers also endorsed the model, they spoke to me of the frustration and disillusionment experienced within the operational system of the project. Resented by the project as poor implementers, and by villagers as weak patrons, such staff did not then have the luxury of my own type of back-seat critical commentary. Several claim that they resigned from the project out of frustration. Several took the project model with them, set up independent NGOs and began working locally towards participatory development; although often in practice this meant substituting the constraints of IBRFP with those of the government watershed programmes that they were now funded to implement. Anyway, within the project, resignations, internal appointments, and a prevailing insecurity of tenure conspired to produce a project team better able to mediate the core contradictions and win the rewards derived from sustained uncritical support from the donor, the project agency and a remote international community, while at the same time institutionalising a fear of failure.

This is not to imply the culpability of management. Indeed, the project manager perhaps had to work hardest of all to secure the relationships and mediate the contradictory organisational demands necessary to conjure success. He had the near impossible task of satisfying immediate and urgent demands for short-term quantified outputs (schemes of all kinds) from his bosses whose high publicity visits had regularly to be hosted, while at the same time delivering on the donor's agenda of sustainable self-reliance, as well as dealing with a multitude of technical recommendations from authorised and unauthorised visiting experts and consultants. He was expected to manage processes of decentralised development while complying with institutional procedures – especially in the areas of personnel and finance – which practically speaking made this impossible. He was expected to allow and facilitate devolved power, when he himself was granted very little. He not only had to manage representations, but also constantly to manage his managers, to be a hidden hand in boardroom battles between the donor/consultants and management, and in other ways to act as a buffer-mediator between a participatory project, a fertiliser company and an international donor. In short, the project manager was a critical broker of organisational cultures; his was a personally demanding task requiring social sensitivity and managerial talent, made all the more difficult because of his own relatively junior position in the company hierarchy.

A particular institutional nexus made the marketing of success and the fear of failure a necessary management style. Success is perhaps always experienced as fragile (even though it may not be) and praise is reassuring. It is not at all surprising therefore that in its expanding network of links, project management emphasised those with more distant appreciative government officials, donor representatives and international institutions over peer NGOs, especially those working in the region and grappling with the same difficult dilemmas of participatory development, some of whom had the disconcerting confidence to say that 'if we are really honest we have to admit that even after thirty years of work in tribal villages we have failed to achieve our goal of participatory development'.

Impact – a crisis is representation?

The apparently secure foundation of the IBRFP project success was, itself, challenged in 1995 when the project faced its *mid-term evaluation*. The report of the independent evaluation study was most striking in its refusal to accept the prevailing criterion of success – namely the concept of 'participation' itself – or to accept the assumptions of the model, namely that more participation equals better programmes and impact. Indeed, the report criticised the project for having *too much* participation and too little impact. The evaluation team was struck by the strong normative stress on participation as the principal project idea and objective, but the isolation of this from concern with people's livelihoods about which the project simply lacked adequate information. The team was perceptive, and the first outsiders to pick up on the self-referring nature of the project's discourse of participation.

Their report coincided with new indications (in the mid-1990s) of donor disenchantment with 'participation', a re-evaluation of the benefits and cost-effectiveness of participation rather than what was coined as the alternative 'investment approach', and criteria of accountability that stressed impact. Participation was regarded by some as human resource intensive, time consuming, limited in scale, non-replicable and expensive. It was clear that the project had become the site for a contest between different development models. But it had to protect itself against the eroding impact of the new critique that assailed its core participation model. The main instrument for this would be information, and particularly a series of impact studies through which it would re-establish and reaffirm the relationship between participatory processes and impact on livelihoods, and, importantly, justify donor decisions in favour of a second phase.

As well as economic surveys of benefits from new crop varieties and soil and water conservation, a remarkably sustained and detailed set of village 'livelihood impact' studies were undertaken. These focussed not on indicators of performance, but on what people ('the beneficiaries') had to say about changes they had experienced during the period of the project. Of course these were influenced by hopes for the future, but they were far from wholly structured by project concerns, and there were plenty of critical comments. Among other things, a view of livelihoods emerged which departed from the dominant model, for example, in the centrality it gave to wage labour, debt and seasonal migration (as against low agricultural productivity) in local livelihood strategies.[20] These studies also drew attention to the extremely restricted nature of routine project monitoring, geared as it was to self-reporting success in participation and programme delivery.

Given my own rising sense of the project as a self-referring discourse, I was at the time surprised (and relieved) to find that overwhelmingly the village studies suggested that the project *was* perceived as important and having a significant *positive impact* in the villages in which it was working, even though the distribution of project benefits was uneven.[21] Moreover, programme impacts were not always those expected. For instance, villagers – men and women – emphasised the importance of savings and credit groups set up in hamlets, while the results of impact from new crop varieties or SWC were more ambiguous.[22] Some impacts were entirely unanticipated; for example several groups of women valued the savings groups for their effect of reducing men's drinking and consequently domestic violence. A great deal was at stake in the findings of these studies. Not surprisingly, a fair amount of controversy over methodology and interpretation, and the demand for follow-up studies, arose where findings were not in line with project assumptions. For the present, the point that I want to make is that despite a complex and conflicting body of information, the impact assessment studies not only affirmed project impact, but also did so in such a way as to realign the project with a new donor framework which emphasised livelihoods and impact instead of agricultural productivity and participation.[23]

But while these studies confirmed the 'success' of the project, significantly they did not directly validate the participatory model, or investigate the relationship between project practices and the model (i.e., they could not distinguish impacts from patronage and programme delivery from those of 'self-determined change'). Indeed, by this omission, the central contradiction of the project could be evaded and project assumptions could be confirmed. This, indeed, was the case. As the project was re-formulated for a second, greatly expanded phase, its 'participatory' success appeared almost unassailable. The new project text endorsed project assumptions, smoothed out blemishes, and made contradictions invisible. As Dik Roth and Quarles van Ufford note (in this volume), the administrative discourse of the 'project cycle' allows the recovery of optimism. Failure can be relegated to the past, hope reserved for the future.

Conclusions

What can be concluded here? Several rather obvious things: it can be said that participation is a politically desirable development idea to which institutions will sign up for different reasons; that its ambiguities allow contradictory objectives to persist within projects; that some of these contradictions make 'participation' an unimplementable idea; that participation can be made into a commodity and marketed; that it is not difficult to manufacture success; that 'local knowledge' is relational, produced by the interactions between project patrons and villager clients; and more. Above all I have suggested that 'participation' (and the participatory project) is primarily a form of representation oriented towards concerns that are external to the location. Such representations do not speak directly to local practice and provide little clue to implementation.

Critical engagement with institutional processes of development is always difficult, and any analytical overview will be perceived as ignoring reality from certain points of view: 'this is very one-sided', 'this is unfair', 'you have not reflected our dedication and hardwork'. Even though I have engaged with many points of view, ultimately this chapter provides my own perspective and not another's. When first aired, the chapter's analysis provoked a stormy response from my managerial and technical colleagues (although it equally won support from others). At one level it was mis-read as a critique of the project, an accusation of duplicity levelled at its management. But the critique implied here is above all levelled at my own efforts, as the consultant providing advice on how to turn 'participation' from policy text into meaningful practices. I certainly attempted, and to a degree succeeded, in negotiating practices from project theory, and frequently invoked the project's participatory model in arguments over practical matters such as staffing arrangements (the employment of women, village residence, pay scales), work schedules, or development strategies (against subsidies, etc.). But ultimately I was more concerned to impose a normative model and to protect it from the eroding effects of project reality, than to engage with that reality itself.

In fact, after two or three years, events on the ground related less and less to the normative rules I was purveying. I would have been less surprised and a good deal less frustrated had it been clearer to me then that the project designs on participation *could not* primarily serve as guides for action. There were too many other pressing institutional needs and agendas to be met. I would have been less surprised that team agreements were rarely reached or implemented, that consensus on future action was deferred as key decision makers (having to reconcile too many conflicting demands) adopted the tactic of absenting themselves from key meetings, that consultant recommendations were fully acknowledged but largely ignored; acknowledged that is as interpretive *framework*, ignored as a guide to *action*. Consultant and donor engagements with the project regularly re-articulated the project rationale but rarely had any effect on practices. Major donor reviews, mid-term evaluations and visits appeared to have even less. My reports, workshops and discussions contributed to project representations and self-representation. They helped to establish valid categories for reporting and the interpretation (or representation) of events. But what they routinely did not do was orientate action. The more critical and ardent I personally became in engaging with the apparent gaps between the 'participatory development' model and practices, the more ineffective my contributions became. Clearly I was misunderstanding something fundamental.

What I was missing, of course, was an understanding of the project's 'participation' goals as a model for representation rather than implementation; indeed, the fundamental *unimplementability* and practical meaninglessness of the community self-reliance ideal. Moreover, my re-articulation of the normative goals of participatory development – my contribution of a rhetorically useful, but practically useless discourse – had made me complicit in this unimplementability. Let me illustrate this.

Central to the project was the idea of '*enhancing community self-reliance through institutional development*'. This came to mean establishing self-help farmer *groups* capable of independently organising local development: managing financial resources (savings and credit), supplying agro-inputs (seed and fertiliser supply) or managing natural resources (e.g., irrigation and forest user groups) so that the project would *withdraw* its services from given villages and areas (Mosse *et al.* 1996). This concept, based on a model adopted from the wider objectives of NGOs in South Asia, became a core principle around which the project's social development strategy revolved. It was also a 'position' in an on-going argument about the primacy of 'capacity building' objectives over 'programme and patronage' approaches; a means to contain the technical enthusiasms of colleagues and to challenge the patronage–welfare approach of the project agency. But what it sought to challenge was far too fundamental to budge.

After all, the project's reputation, the validation of the myth of participation, the performance of local field staff, indeed the core rationale of the project from KBCL's point of view, were all based on its network of patronage and welfare, largesse and the delivery of an expanding range of high-quality programmes, increasingly through village 'volunteers' (jankars) who operated as the lower orders of the project delivery mechanism. The whole venture required the retention and extension of project power, not its transfer to people. This carefully controlled and intensively managed system was simply not going to be abandoned for the grave risks of allowing independent decisions and financial responsibility, local autonomy and the withdrawal of the project. Why would the KBCL project want to get rid of its best customers; and villagers of a serviceable patron? Even assuming it wanted to promote farmer capacities, the project was part of an organisation whose hierarchy and system of accountability was not able to take the risks necessary to devolve power to communities.

To be sure the effect of many of the project activities was to expand knowledge, increase confidence, develop new skills, and release a 'spirit of experimentation', but the idea of a systematic devolution of power and responsibility to tribal farmers involved an unreal image of the project as a flexible risk-taking agent, a facilitating presence, rather than a unit of a politically intelligent, strategically operating marketing organisation, determined to retain a firm grip on the development process. The project idea of sustainable community development was initially forged (by myself among others) to underpin key negotiating positions in development policy arguments, and as a critique of dominating agrarian modernism. However, this bore little relationship to the institutional possibilities of this project structure, at this time, in this place. Examined critically, the self-reliance model involved a neo-orientalist delegitimising of all forms of external dependence – subsidies, money lenders, migration, agro-inputs, or the marketing of commercial crops – as deviation from the primacy of local control, and the protection of low-risk subsistence livelihoods.

Much to the frustration of many (including myself) the group-based capacity model (or some version of it) was (during my association with the project, i.e., up to 1998) never procedurally internalised in the project; although it remained a key element in the project's Phase II, newly underscored by a DFID Sustainable Rural Livelihoods model, with the language of 'social capital'. But as is becoming clear, it was quite unreasonable to expect this development goal to have been operationalised (at least within the prevailing institutional arrangement) since it was fundamentally at odds with what was driving the project – namely, marketing-oriented networks of patronage.[24]

So the way in which I (and others) constructed project 'failure' was just as ideological as the representation of 'success'; both in fact endorsed the same model and privileged it over practices. This produced ignorance of project impacts. So what if the model (or my version of it) fails? The project can still succeed. Indeed, a more pragmatic appraisal of circumstances – less shaped by ideological debates, or middle-class NGO intellectual distaste for Indian industrialist perspectives in general, let alone those of a fertiliser company[25] – would have seen new avenues of patronage as advantageous in a remote tribal area, providing new input lines for improved technology, marketing possibilities, and a consistency between local needs and the organisational imperatives of KBCL, rather than the failure to meet objectives. These are, indeed, the very things happening – even as the project purveys images of participation and is represented/represents itself (at least to some observers) as either success or failure in terms of this validating paradigm of 'participation'.

Preoccupation with the elevated principles of self-determined change also ignores perhaps the project's most remarkable achievement, namely its identification and development of improved rice and maize varieties through a careful process of consultation and farmer-managed trials. Scientists and farmers jointly bred, tested and popularised seeds which out-performed both local and officially recommended varieties in poor soil and low-input conditions by farmer-relevant parameters (early maturity, taste, cooking quality, and price as well as grain yield). The official release of a maize variety GDRM-187 developed in a project-initiated partnership with Gujarat Agricultural University was a major victory. This crop programme did not depend upon independent farmer action, the creation of self-sustaining institutions or the resolution of complex collective action problems, although the appellation 'participatory' (i.e., *participatory* varietal selection (PVS) and *participatory* plant breeding (PPB)) may yet invite misplaced claims about farmer control of technology development or unwarranted judgements on the role of scientists, project staff or consultants in its design and execution. In practice this programme of client-oriented technology development was a sophisticated form of market research – albeit focussed on the subsistence needs of the most marginal farmers and drawing on their capacities to experiment – but consistent nonetheless with the institutional rationale of KBCL.

The project benefits of improved seed inputs, assisted seed distribution and storage, and mediated links to national and international agricultural research agendas have been highly significant – at least to the individuals or groups who have been lucky enough to receive project patronage. Arguably they depended upon the permanent and expanding presence of the KBCL project as a para-statal extension service – offering better technology and more affordable inputs to remote tribal villages rather than autonomy and independence. This may or may not be 'participation' or 'sustainable development'; it is certainly a subversion of some currently dominant international development ideas of 'farmer-managed development'. But then 'subversion' wrongly implies both a coherence of dominant policy, and the intent to undermine it. On the contrary, IBRFP project practice constantly aspired to be represented in the most legitimate policy terms. Far from celebrating a diversity of approaches or the multiplicity of rationalities and values (cf. Arce and Long 2000), policy discourse in international donors struggles to ensure that practices are rendered coherent in terms of a single overarching framework.

In order to work, programme designs and policy models have to be transformed in practice, but they also have to be reproduced as stable representations. The impact of the IBRFP project would not have been achieved without an international validating framework, whether participatory development or 'sustainable rural livelihoods'; but at the same time in this form it would/could not have been implemented. The legitimacy, political support and continued funding of the project depended upon maintaining this model. From one point of view, the first phase of the IBRFP project worked and deserved the praise that it received, because it engaged creatively with donor policy process, both preserving policy representations, while operationally retaining consistency with KBCL's own organisational needs – a delicate balancing act skilfully executed by the project management. For policy to succeed it is necessary it seems that it is *not* implemented, but that enough people firmly believe that it is.

Coda

My close involvement with the IBRFP came to an end early in 1998 when the project was riding a high wave of success. Three years later in April 2001, and I was back investigating the *failure* of the same project, now threatened with closure. As I worked with my colleague Supriya Akerkar, meeting village groups, holding staff workshops and talking through long journeys and late nights, I was as puzzled by the project's 'failure' as I had been by its earlier 'success'. Project practice seemed to me unchanged – meaningful engagements between staff and villagers still produced important local benefits even under conditions of severe drought. But a fundamental change *had* occurred, not in the project, but in the donor policy which the project was required to affirm in order to exist. DFID's India programme had become reorganised around the funding of state-wide government programmes, sectoral reform and donor-government partnerships. Unable to articulate this policy, the IBRFP project began to lose its support and consequently its reality. It bore new policy labels of exclusion: 'enclave project', 'niche project', 'replicable model', 'parallel [to the state] structure', 'sectoral, downstream, micro-managed project'. IBRFP had suddenly become the flared trousers of the DFID wardrobe. Unless it could find ways to instantiate, sustain or protect the new incarnations of international policy, this project – which had brought a version of 'development' more meaningful than any previous to Bhil tribal communities excluded from even the most basic state services – would be erased as surely as it was raised by the ambitions of policy.

Notes

1 This chapter is informed by over eight years' work as a consultant (1990–1998) supported by the UK Department for International Development (DFID) with the Indo-British Rainfed Farming Project (IBRFP). The views expressed here are my own and do not reflect those of DFID, 'KBCL' or the IBRFP project. Nonetheless I am grateful to all in the project who have given me ideas and critical feedback over the years, and, in relation to this chapter in particular, Steve Jones, Arun Joshi, P.S. Sodhi and John Witcombe.

2 Edwards (1999: 117).

3 I am sure that project managers the world over are aware of the power of representations. They are also aware that managing representations is a good deal easier than managing social order. (It is also striking how much published material of a donor such as DFID deals with recent policy, new designs manifesting the latest trends in development theory rather than the events and evaluations of existing projects.) But the very suggestion that projects are not about direct implementation with real effects is scandalous, far more so than criticisms of the imperfections of the model or even its unanticipated impacts. Similarly, the self-representation of policy as (rational) *decision making* is scandalised by the idea of 'policy as proposition, statement and style' (Gasper and Apthorpe 1996: 6), or in contemporary British parlance politics as 'spin'.

4 Simple linear models of implementation are today challenged by more sophisticated models dealing with the interactive processes which link policy goals and outcomes (e.g., Brinkerhoff 1996). But even these derive from an instrumental perspective.

5 As Gasper and Apthorpe (1996: 4) point out, notions of development's 'discursive practices' or development as 'a modernist regime' or 'discursive field' involve a dangerous loss of distinction between discourses and practices; and it is precisely the relationship between the two that has to be explored in an ethnography of development. The analysis does not cease to be concerned with ideas of development and their textual expression, but has to explore both their social context *and* consequences.

6 The distinction between normative and pragmatic rules, deriving from F. Bailey, has been applied to development planning practices by Wood (1998).

7 The notion of producing *knowledge* is itself overrestrictive when reflecting on my role as anthropologist consultant. My work is as much about the generation of habits (Uchiyamada, personal communication) or aesthetics (Stirrat 2000).

8 A transitory knowledge building community around which would crystallise a more stable 'interpretive community' as the project model was put in place.

9 See Porter (1995) for elaboration of the ideas of master metaphors in development.

10 In 'writing the project' the donor idea of 'a participatory agriculture project' could become the basis of wide-reaching development ambitions, not only in the area of technology innovation, but also public sector reform, empowerment, environmental protection, and so forth.

11 As a 'master metaphor', participation was able 'to promote the impression of radical change without threatening the basic project of controlled and orderly manipulation of change' (Porter 1995: 64). The pseudo-radicalism of the 'participatory approach' was ensured by a series of polarities which contrasted the approach to old, non-participatory, and top-down alternatives.

12 To locate power does not, as Cooper and Packard note, 'show that it is determinant, or that a particular discourse is not appropriable for other purposes ... what at one level appears like a discourse of control is at another a discourse of entitlement' (1997: 3–4).

13 In a more regular and routine way the interpretive frame of the project had to respond to the ideas and reports of each of a succession of consultants and their recommendations.

14 The LogFrame – especially its joint planning TeamUp version – proved an especially powerful instrument of such dominance in the ODA/DFID programme in India in the mid-1990s.

15 Thus the innovatory participatory approach of IBRFP was portrayed as an extension of the project agency's (KBCL's) flexibility, client-orientation, freedom from bureaucracy and innovative organisational culture (see below).

16 A parallel suggested by reading Sutton (1999: 15ff).

17 To pre-empt confusion later let me here set out the project's different institutional actors. First there is a donor, in this case DFID, second a partner or 'host' agency, the Indian cooperative KBCL, and third the special project management unit created to implement the project. There is also a team of consultants, in this case from the University of Wales, contracted by DFID to support the project unit in planning, implementation and monitoring the reports to both DFID and the project manager. The project is governed by a Steering Committee on which DFID, KBCL and the Government of India are represented and to which consultants are invited. Line management runs through the KBCL hierarchy.

18 With the election of a Labour government in May 1997, ODA was re-named the Department for International Development or DFID.

19 All too aware that practices did not conform to the models and worried by the lack of farmer control, I found myself urging project staff to recommit themselves to the model of participation in ways which only served to underline its assumptions and confirm its unassailable position.

20 A focussed study on seasonal labour migration from project villages made an important contribution here (Mosse et al. 2002).

21 The distribution of benefits and the socially differentiated nature of project effects is a complex subject requiring a separate account. Certain individuals gained disproportionately as key brokers, *jankars* or leaders. More generally, the principal economic gains from project activities such as soil and water conservation, minor irrigation, improved seeds, agro-forestry, or vegetable cultivation accrued to households in proportion to the land they possessed (quality – i.e., lower valley rather than upper slope – as well as quantity). The poorest (including the land poor) received less of the project's subsidies, while contributing more (to common assets) through their own subsidised labour on project works. But at the same time, what the project offered – especially wages and low-cost credit – was also of greatest importance to the livelihoods of the poorest, most heavily indebted households.

22 Credit groups (at least in the form they eventually took) were not part of the original project model, and they produced an effect on production through increased fertiliser purchase (on credit) which had specifically been underemphasised, at least in the donor/consultant interpretation of the project design, in relation to new crop varieties and soil and water conservation. Also, the project model anticipated a reduction in seasonal migration following agricultural development, while at least some village studies showed that the number of people migrating had actually increased over the period of the project, even though shifts in the pattern of migration (i.e., independence from money-lending brokers) meant that migration had become more profitable.
23 Later formulated as the 'sustainable rural livelihoods framework'.
24 In 1999, finally realising the difficulty of participatory development under the prevailing institutional arrangement, the donor negotiated the creation of an independent project agency, a Trust, as a condition of funding for the next project Phase. Whether or not this new institutional arrangement was better at implementing participation and creating autonomous community institutions is the subject of another narrative.
25 ... of which I was undoubtedly more guilty than my technical consultant colleagues.

References

Agrawal, Arun (1996) 'Poststructuralist approaches to development: some critical reflections', *Peace & Change* 21 (4): 464–477.

Alvesson, Mats (1993) *Cultural Perspectives on Organisations*, Cambridge: Cambridge University Press.

Apthorpe, Raymond (1997) 'Writing development policy and policy analysis plain or clear: on language, genre and power', in S. Shore and S. Wright (eds) *Anthropology of Policy: Critical Perspectives on Governance and Power*, London and New York: Routledge, pp. 43–58.

Arce, Alberto and Norman Long (2000) 'Consuming modernity: mutational processes of change', in Alberto Arce and Norman Long (eds) *Anthropology, Development and Modernities: Exploring Discourses, Counter-tendencies and Violence*, London and New York: Routledge, pp. 100–111.

Bourdieu, P. (1977) *Outline of a Theory of Practice* (trans. R. Nice), Cambridge: Cambridge University Press.

Brinkerhoff, D.W. (1996) 'Process perspectives on policy change: highlighting implementation', *World Development* 24 (9): 1395–1401.

Cooper, F. and R. Packard (1997) *International Development and the Social Sciences: Essays in the History and Politics of Knowledge*, Berkeley: University of California Press.

Craig, D. and D. Porter (1997) 'Framing participation: development projects, professionals, and organisations', in D. Eade (ed.) *Development and Patronage: a Development in Practice Reader*, introduced by Melakou Tegegn, Oxford: Oxfam.

Edwards, Michael (1999) *Future Positive: International Co-operation in the 21st Century*, London: Earthscan Publications.

Escobar, Arturo (1995) *Encountering Development: the Making and Unmaking of the Third World*, Princeton: Princeton University Press.

Fairhead, James (2000) 'Development discourse and its subversion: decivilisation, depoliticisation and dispossession in West Africa', in Alberto Arce and Norman

Long (eds) *Anthropology, Development and Modernities: Exploring Discourses, Counter-tendencies and Violence*, London and New York: Routledge, pp. 100–111.

Ferguson, J. (1990) *The Anti-politics Machine: Development, Depoliticisation and Bureaucratic Power in Lesotho*, Cambridge: Cambridge University Press.

Gasper, Des and Raymond Apthorpe (1996) 'Introduction: discourse analysis and policy discourse', in R. Apthorpe and D. Gasper (eds) *Arguing Development Policy: Frames and Discourses*, London: Frank Cass.

Gupta, Akhil and James Ferguson (1997) 'Culture, power, place: ethnography at the end of an era', in A. Gupta and J. Ferguson (eds) *Culture, Power, Place: Explorations in Critical Anthropology*, Durham and London: Duke University Press, pp. 1–29.

Hobart, Mark (1995) 'Black umbrellas: the implication of mass media in development', unpublished paper, EIDOS Workshop on Globalisation and Decivilisation, Agricultural University of Wageningen.

Marcus, G. (1995) 'Ethnography in/of the world system: the emergence of multi-sited ethnography', *Annual Review of Anthropology* 24: 95–117.

—— (1998) *Ethnography through Thick and Thin*, Princeton: Princeton University Press.

Mosse, David (1996) 'The social construction of "people's knowledge" in participatory rural development', in S. Bastian and N. Bastian (eds) *Assessing Participation: A Debate from South Asia*, New Delhi: Konark Publishers, pp. 135–180.

—— (2001) '"People's knowledge", participation and patronage: operations and representations in rural development', in Bill Cook (ed.) *Participation – the New Tyranny?*, London: Zed Books.

Mosse, David (with the IBRFP Project Team) (1996) 'Local institutions and farming systems development: thoughts from a project in tribal western India', *ODI Agren Network Paper* no. 64.

Mosse, David, Sanjeev Gupta, Mona Mehta, Vidya Shah, Julia Rees and the IBRFP Project Team (2002) 'Brokered livelihoods: debt, labour migration and development in tribal western India', in Arjan de Haan and Ben Rogaly (eds) *Migration and Sustainable Livelihoods*.

Osella, F. and Osella, C. (1996) 'Articulation of physical and social bodies in Kerala', *Contributions to Indian Sociology* (ns) 30 (1): 37–68.

Porter, Doug J. (1995) 'Scenes from childhood: the homesickness of development discourse', in Jonathan Crush (ed.) *Power of Development*, London and New York: Routledge, pp. 63–86.

Quarles van Ufford, Philip (1993) 'Knowledge and ignorance in the practices of development policy', in M. Hobart (ed.) *An Anthropological Critique of Development: the Growth of Ignorance*, London and New York: Routledge.

Shore, S. and S. Wright (eds) (1997) *Anthropology of Policy: Critical Perspectives on Governance and Power*, London and New York: Routledge.

Sivaramakrishnan, K. and Arun Agrawal (forthcoming) 'Introduction: regional modernities in stories and practices of development', in K. Sivaramakrishnan and A. Agrawal (eds) *Regional Modernities: the Cultural Politics of Development in India*, Stanford: Stanford University Press.

Stirrat, R.L. (2000) 'Cultures of consultancy', *Critique of Anthropology* 20 (1): 31–46.

Sutton, Rebecca (1999) 'The policy process: an overview', *ODI Discussion Paper* no. 118.

Witcombe, John R., Daljit S.Virk and John Farrington (eds) (1998) *Seeds of Choice: Making the Most of New Varieties for Small Farmers*, London: Intermediate Technology Publications.

Wood, G.D. (1998) 'Consultant behaviour: projects as communities: consultants' knowledge and power', *Project Appraisal* 16 (1): 54–64.

Chapter 3

The Icarus effect

The rise and fall of development optimisms in a regional development project in Luwu District, South Sulawesi, Indonesia

Philip Quarles van Ufford and Dik Roth

> Next he prepared his son. 'Take care', he said,
> 'To fly a middle course', lest if you sink
> Too low the waves may weight your feathers; if
> Too high, the heat may burn them. Fly half-way
> Between the two ...
>
> (Ovid 1986: Book VIII, *Daedalus and Icarus*)

Introduction

This is a case study about the moral dimensions of institutionalised development optimism. A major characteristic of development interventions is the gradual loss, in the process of going through what is veilingly called 'the project cycle', of a sense of proportion, of an acknowledgement of limits to planned intervention in local processes. Excessive notions of and belief in governability and control have become the wax with which policy objectives are glued together like the feathers of Icarus's wings. In this chapter we intend to problematise the development process as a process which is only partly constituted by local circumstances that more or less determine the options and choices available for intervention. In our view, its dynamic is very strongly influenced by factors of quite a different order, unrelated to the local context of intervention. First, there are the policy objectives that form the normative basis of donor development practice. Second, there is the rather compulsive policy cycle, setting the stage for the various actors, each with their own background to act in an orderly way.

In circles of policy makers and other actors involved in development policy, the policy process is usually taken for granted as a logical sequence of rational steps, each 'stage' of which naturally and rationally follows from the previous one under the basic assumption of control and manageability. Contrary to such analysis in terms of basically rational 'project cycles', the processes involved can also, and perhaps more realistically, be analysed as involving a different kind of cycles: 'cycles of optimism' characterised by a sequence of initial excessive optimism, high expectations, and claims of governability, followed by increasing complexity, growing pressures and internal contradictions, and finally erosion and loss of control. The downfall of old optimisms involves the gradual downplaying of old claims and replacing them by new ones, into a new cycle of optimism.

The various 'stages' of what in developers' discourse is called the project cycle, such as identification, formulation, and evaluation, play a crucial role in initiating, interconnecting, and closing those other cycles – cycles of optimism – on which we concentrate our attention in this chapter. We analyse those short periods, during which development activities are identified, formulated or evaluated, as rather dramatic episodes of high stress, in which the complex articulations between the various actors are condensed into one single, apparently coherent narrative about past, present and future. Evaluations, for example, with their direct interactions, observations and field visits, pose a special challenge to all project actors involved. They bring an unknown mixture of opportunities and threats for the various actors, who will try to impress upon evaluators their views about project past, present and future. However big the differences of interests, motivations, strategies and moral frameworks between actors may be, in the outcome of such periods of condensation the field of actors is represented as basically coherent, agreeing about what should be done, and driven by common objectives. This image of basic unity among actors finds expression in unproblematic jargon such as 'integrated development', 'participation', and 'sustainable development'. After such periods of dramatic 'condensation', when life has returned to 'normal', the articulations, contradictions and conflicts that exist in the complex field of actors will strike with renewed force.

Excessive optimism about governability and the possibilities of (social) engineering have become the symbolic capital of the development policy process. And for good reason: development policy puts a reward on such optimism and the continuing generation of new cycles of optimism, or at least the preservation of old optimisms through various techniques of representation or 'image management'. In the short time spans prevailing in the volatile development world, then, a considerable amount of *hybris* in planning and secrecy in reporting is synonymous with wise policy.

But on the way we seem to lose our sense of proportion, our ability to stand back and critically reflect on what 'development' actually is all about. Does our understanding of local processes grow in proportion to the emergence of new buzzwords in development? We believe not (see also Hobart 1993). On the contrary: the use of such veiling language has increasingly screened us off from the major complexities, dilemmas and conflicts inherent in development policy processes and practices. An alarmingly wide gap has grown between words and practices, between bureaucratic-administrative routines and understanding. We may even ask, how far are 'actors' still able to determine the contents of the part they play? Are they not just playing their role in a script largely predetermined for them by more structural forces? And might that be the cause of the fact that in the development world there is surprisingly so little 'learning'? (see Hulme 1989; Quarles van Ufford 1993).

To illustrate these processes we describe and analyse a case of development intervention in the framework of Dutch–Indonesian bilateral development cooperation. This case analyses some aspects of the Pompengan Integrated Area Development Project (PIADP), situated in Luwu District in the province of South Sulawesi (see Map 1). This was a project for 'integrated rural development' with a complex combination of activities: construction of an irrigation system and other infrastructure, a redistributive land reform and settlement programme, involving the construction of housing and sanitary facilities, agricultural extension, and formation of water users' associations for irrigation. Started in 1980 as a mainly technical/infrastructural project for irrigation development under the name of Pompengan Implementation Project (PIP), in 1986 the project was continued as PIADP. We take as the point of departure for our analysis the 'final' evaluation of the project in 1990. Both authors were directly and crucially involved in the evaluation process as leader of the visiting evaluation team (Quarles van Ufford) and as permanent consultant for the land reform and settlement programmes (Roth) respectively. We intend to critically reflect on the processes we were part of and tried to influence.

In analysing this case we neither want to be trapped into concluding astonishedly that the project outcome differed from the initial intentions, as we take that as a given; nor is our objective deconstruction *per se* (see Long and Van der Ploeg 1989), nor do we associate ourselves with a post-structuralist stance that would force us into a position of non-involvement and denial of responsibility (Ferguson 1990; Escobar 1995). Rather, we take a critical stance towards the development policy process, with the objective of illuminating the processes involved, gaining a deeper understanding of the roles of various actors, and the choices made at crucial points in the development policy process. Can we identify the point where in the project history of increasing ambitions and growing pretensions the *hybris* of planning and social engineering took over from a realistic weighing of what was feasible and what impossible, where sense dissolved into nonsense, gradually leading PIADP into a cycle of erosion and final downfall? How high should we aspire to fly? This is not only a question of strategy, but also, and perhaps primarily, a question with an important moral dimension to it. Should we impress our morally informed policy objectives upon unknown and hardly understood local situations? How far should we go in turning the development policy process into an arena for the articulation of conflicting perspectives and competing moral frameworks and justifications of actors, largely for the sake of motivations generated, and justifications needed in the donor world?

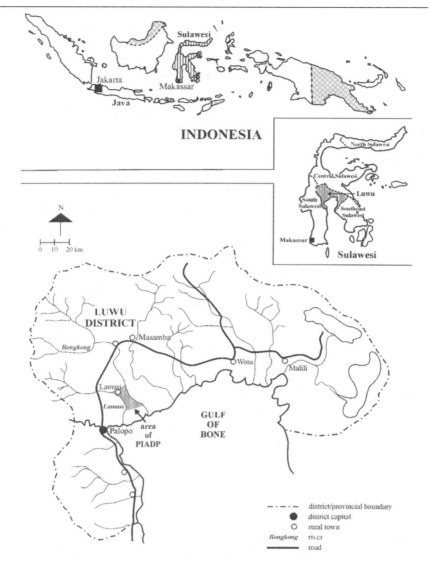

Map 1

After this introduction, in the second section of this chapter we describe and analyse the process of 'final' evaluation of PIADP as we experienced it 'from above' and 'from below'. Particularly, we analyse evaluation as a process in which, basically, the notion of contingency is relegated to the past, thus allowing for a high degree of optimism for the future. In the third section we plunge into the project history of PIADP: how did it all come about? In what way do 'cycles of optimism' in the project relate not only to the local project context, but also to the interaction between institutional actors and changing development policy priorities? In the final section we present a short comment on and analysis of the case.

Rational machines or pressure cookers? Evaluating an 'integrated' rural development project

A project staff preparing for evaluation

One morning in October 1990, a report written by the leader of the Dutch consultants' team in preparation for the arrival of the evaluation mission for PIADP was distributed to the team members (DHV/ISSAS 1990). As could be expected for such a momentous occasion, it was a perfect piece of image management. Formally the report meant to give the mission members a quick, 'objective' insight into the state of affairs. It also fulfilled another, more elusive, objective: more or less to set the margins within which discussions with the evaluation team about past project performance were expected to take place, as well as to convey a message about which direction, according to the teamleader, recommendations of the evaluation mission should ideally take. The report, written by the team leader, was presented as a joint product of all team members involved.

The chapter on land reform and settlement gave quite a distorted, unwarrantedly optimistic, image of the field situation in PIADP. While something of the problems experienced in project implementation was allowed to shine through, it was above all meant to preserve a comfortable degree of secrecy. The outside image of PIADP as a relatively successful programme that could be presented as a 'model' for integrated rural development throughout Indonesia should not be allowed to be shattered by too full a view of its problems. In view of actual field conditions, this time the consultancy firm was remarkably modest in its recommendations. Rather than taking the risk of (again) being found too 'demanding' by the principal, the consultant seemed now to let its long-term interests prevail by being satisfied with a 'limited extension' of the project and getting away undamaged from the hornets' nest that PIADP had long since become.[1] While it was stated in the report that a short extension should suffice to guarantee an acceptable result for PIADP, the report about the 'present status' was used to look ahead to new project activities in the region 'to use the knowledge and experience gained' (DHV/ISSAS 1990).

'What about the report?' asked the consultant responsible for the land reform and settlement programmes. Could it still be adapted so as to be more open and informative about the major problems in these programmes? About the growing discrepancy between actual conditions of the land reform programme and its administrative representation on maps and in land title documents? About the possibility of social conflict and loss of capital in the settlement programme? 'No' was the answer; that was out of the question. The mission was already on its way, and the report had already been distributed among the parties involved, so no further discussion was possible about its contents. Some days later another report, providing an alternative view of land reform and settlement, was born.

Long before the arrival of the mission, other project actors also gave signs that they were, to say the least, not in favour of continuation. Towards the arrival of the mission, tensions mounted perceptibly. During project meetings attempts were made to speed up 'delivery' of project facilities, to conceal the enormous problems experienced in land reform and settlement behind a formal administration in which targets were met, and act as if everything were under control and PIADP could be terminated successfully after the running period. For one reason or another, most of them were fed up with it: because the erosion of PIADP had become a threat to their careers; because implementation had become too heavy a workload for their agency; because they had personal speculative interests in land to hide and feared that project extension would provide a newly-formed team with time and support to critically investigate earlier decisions in land reform; because another extension would be incompatible with the stream of optimistic reports they had been sending to their superiors for many years; or because new private enterprise and development projects were financially more promising and brought new opportunities for private gain. Most actors at project level regarded the mission as a real *final* mission: a good opportunity to terminate a project in dire straits, while presenting it once more as relatively successful, and propagating it as a 'model' for integrated development.

Evaluation as administrative ritual: the unfolding of optimism

The evaluation team sent to PIADP by the Indonesian and Dutch authorities consisted of five people: two Indonesians and three Dutchmen.[2] The activities of the team were sharply bounded in terms of time and substance. The research was started and the final report completed within two months. The three Dutch team members actually writing the report started the mission with an almost total ignorance of the programme. After two months they produced a report of the project's history and of the various subprogrammes, as well as a series of recommendations. In two months' time, ignorance was transformed into decision making: insight into past contingencies gave rise to detailed proposals for solving some of these problems. In the evaluation process, the notion of contingency was relegated to the past, allowing for a high degree of optimism for the future.

Indeed, this kind of evaluation is the normal routine in development cooperation. Two months, seventeen days of which were real 'field days'. Ignorance about a ten-year project history in the beginning; clear, unambiguous recommendations in the end. During these seventeen days, the team allowed itself four days to gain an understanding of what had been going on in the last years. On the fifth day, in internal team discussions the question was raised whether some views concerning the project's future were already emerging. Was it possible to define some shared views? The priority in the activities of the team now shifted from an effort to understand what had been going on in five years of PIADP to the task of defining a view of the future – if any. This was quite a shocking shift, as the tasks of understanding project history and making recommendations, inherent to any kind of evaluation, are in fact quite contradictory and do not run parallel at all. After four days, further research into project history had become subordinate to the execution of the team's major task: defining priorities and recommendations. In a short time span, the preceding project cycles of PIP and PIADP were compressed and rewritten, and the expectations of a new cycle formulated. The past was given a renewed understanding, while commitments for the future were formulated. Notwithstanding its quasi-neutral and 'professional' language, the evaluation exercise is not a description of the project, it transcends and rewrites project reality. The evaluation exercise so acquires the dimensions of a quasi-religious ritual.

'Arbitrary' recommendations

As the recommendations were presented by the mission to the various administrators at different levels of supervision of the programme, most of them seemed inclined to accept most of the recommendations, even though these were sometimes contrary to their own views and preferences. The report claimed to have found a way to overcome problems that had emerged in the past, a way out of the dilemmas confronting the project staff. Indeed, the proposals claimed to contain the seeds for transforming the imminent disasters lying in wait for PIADP as described and analysed in the descriptive part of the report, into a series of (relative) successes which would be more or less lasting. The notion of 'sustainability' had become the key word in the new script relegating failure to the past and an acceptable modicum of success to the future.

What had actually been going on when the team members were 'doing their evaluation'? What actually happened? How is it possible to understand our jump into optimism concerning the future of the project, contrasting so much with the analysis of the past? In order to answer these questions we must say more about the nature of the evaluation exercise. The team's activities can of course be described as impassioned and professional research, a scientific endeavour aimed at presenting a reliable description and analysis. Indeed this is the view cherished by most consultants. But if we are to understand the role of evaluators and the kind of knowledge they produce this does not help much. It does not explain, for instance, how it was possible to gather and analyse such a wealth of complex data in a short time. Experiences of anthropological fieldwork, resulting after a long time in 'only' a scientific publication, are totally different from these. As scientific researchers we have become used to being absolutely marginal whenever we study problems with some relevance for policy making. But now information was there at hand whenever we asked for it. Reports were produced, explanations given whenever needed, and 'relevant' or 'strategic' field visits were possible whenever we insisted on having a 'local touch'.

Apart from the intensity and bounded nature of the mission, another element must be mentioned. The activities of the mission were 'arbitrary' in the most literal sense. As evaluators we were the arbitrators of the various 'stories' about the project that different (figurations of) actors brought forward. An evaluation is not primarily a research endeavour, an effort to gather the relevant data. Rather, it allows other actors to deposit their 'stories' of the past and expectations of the future in an empty space. Therefore, rather than entailing the relationship between a researcher and his informants, evaluation is a temporary event, a series of activities aimed at collecting the various stories of (groups of) actors, each with their own interests, points of view, expertise and experiences. Evaluators collect, judge and rewrite 'stories', differing and often conflicting actor views about past experiences and future courses of action. Evaluation allows a number of 'knowledgeable' parties in the programme to tell their stories. For a limited period, the social hierarchies controlling the daily mechanisms of access of the different stories are broken down. Thus, evaluation is not 'research', an effort to gain knowledge. It is, rather, a ritual, that is: an exercise in countering the daily balances of power, at least for some time.

The ritual of evaluation is rather a contradictory affair. The team members are in a curious way *helpless* in their relations with the other parties concerned as well as *powerful* at the same time. The weakness of the evaluators is their ignorance. That means that they are dependent on other actors, who must tell their stories. This initial ignorance at the beginning of the exercise is important indeed because it somehow guarantees that no story has reached the status of 'orthodoxy' over other stories. Yet, at the same time evaluation missions are in principle also formidably powerful. Their source of power is their *exclusive access to the programme's future*. This power base is as strong as it is temporary. It does not transcend the time limitations of the ritual of evaluation itself. Its power lies precisely in the fact that evaluation entails a divorce from the daily routines of the programme.

This power base lies in writing the structures of legitimacy for future administrative action and routines. Once the report becomes accepted by the main representatives of the two governments, a new structure of substantive legitimacy has been created for the project. The various decisions which follow have to be defendable in terms of the priorities and analyses put forward by the evaluation report. But the evaluators have no control over the ultimate decisions. Once their mission is over and the report written, they slide back into blissful ignorance. They have created a new structure of legitimacy, but are helpless as regards the degree to which their views are going to be used. Others have that power. But those others are bound to defend and justify their decisions in terms of that new structure of legitimacy.

Four stories

The ultimate 'conclusions' of the evaluation mission were based on a '*Fingerspitzengefühl*' concerning the relevance of each of the stories we were confronted with. It may well be that nobody in the team actually realised what was going on during the first decisive week; that we were pressure-cooked into an agreement because disagreement within the team would mean chaos and disaster for everybody. We were actually writing on the basis of a series of half-known, shared 'gut feelings' and extremely hard work. During our stay in the field four different 'stories' had come forward, each competing for prominence with the others, each with a particular rationale for judging the past and formulating recommendations. All of us realised that our capacity for admitting and absorbing such stories was very limited. In the ritual of evaluation any effort to incorporate the local population directly in our arbitrary opinion making could easily work counter-productively. If 'local stories', that is those of the 'beneficiaries', could reach us at all, it was in a mediated form, through the stories of other actors. What follows here is a short account of four major stories with which the mission had to cope in order to construct its view of project past and present, and give recommendations for either project termination or a new future.

First, it quickly became clear that on the side of the Dutch principal it was felt that the project, which had been going on for ten years, had to be terminated. Upon arrival in Indonesia the Dutch team members were received at the Dutch embassy by three development specialists and diplomats. These gave them an overview of the state of affairs. Finally, the team members were routinely informed that it would be best to conclude that the programme be definitively terminated after the running period. It became clear that, in the government view, the consultant carrying out the programme had failed miserably to meet agreed targets in various programmes. Even an intensive supervision by the embassy had not led to a substantial improvement. Yet the major considerations did not have anything to do with the project at all. These emerged from a much higher level of administration. The embassy had been instructed by the newly appointed minister for Development Cooperation to free some of the bilateral funds for new initiatives, in accordance with the new policy profile of the minister. By concluding that the project had to be terminated, the embassy chose faithfully to serve the views of its new minister. In order to press this point upon the Dutch actors, an embassy official accompanied the mission to Sulawesi for two days. When he introduced the mission to the Dutch expatriate experts, he explained what the 'agreed outcomes' of the mission would be.

Second, there was the Dutch consultant responsible for implementing the programme, one of the large firms of consulting engineers in the Netherlands generating considerable income from bilateral and multilateral development cooperation. At the time, the consultant was quite aware of the views held at the Dutch embassy in Jakarta. In view of the fact that the decision to terminate the project had already been taken by 'the customer', what counted for the consultant was as smooth a termination of the programme as possible. An overall good relationship with funding agencies and the governments of Indonesia and the Netherlands was its overriding concern, rather than any substantive view it might have concerning the problems and tasks in the field. Any suggestions concerning new priorities for the programme on the part of the consultant's branch office in the capital or its field representative were strongly discouraged by head office. As it became clear that the principal was in favour of termination, the engineering firm complied. Whatever views its local staff members might have, the team leader was assigned to start writing an overall report concerning the various activities carried out in the past. What counted now was keeping good relations with the two governments. The story of the project was one of moderate success, that is 'moderated' by various 'lessons learned'.

Third, the story on the part of the Indonesian project administrators was different again. During the first week a delegation of some Indonesian officials responsible for the programme through various offices in the district came to visit the evaluation team. The Indonesian team members had made sure that their colleagues' story could be told. It was one of conflicts between Dutch and Indonesian staff members, of different priorities and working styles of the Dutch and Indonesians. A series of events had antagonised the Indonesian administration towards the programme as it was defined by the Dutch. The Indonesians were afraid that they would be blamed for the shortcomings of the project. Two issues were at stake. First, the zeal of the Dutch team to carry out the tasks as defined in the project documents had put extreme pressure on the Indonesian administration. There was considerable pressure on them to help meet the targets. While they were loyal to the project and indeed derived quite substantial financial benefits from it, this loyalty had, according to them, been stretched too far by the Dutch staff. Project goals conflicted with their daily routines. Compliance with Dutch demands would result in a systematic negligence of other district tasks. A way out of this dilemma had to be found. Second, a rather sensitive conflict had arisen between Dutch and Indonesian staff members. As it was put forward by the Indonesians, this was a conflict between, on the one hand, the Dutch expatriates parading themselves as defenders of 'quality' in the construction of facilities like irrigation canals, houses and wells, and, on the other, the Indonesian administrators who were held accountable for meeting their quantitative targets much more strictly than the Dutch. As much was at stake, these conflicts had taken on rather heated dimensions. Not meeting the targets defined by the Indonesian government could, for instance, negatively affect the careers of the administrators. This could not be tolerated any more, the mission was told.

Fourth, some of the Indonesian and Dutch staff members took a view diametrically opposed to the other accounts. Their story, based on their experiences with implementation of land reform and settlement, derived its impetus from their view that the land reform programme had created problems rather than solving them, and was continuing to do so. The land reform area was afflicted by conflicts over land; complexity of land tenure in the area had only increased as a result of project intervention, and consequently security of tenure of farmers had decreased; land ownership titles for 'beneficiaries' of the programme threatened to become the paper symbols of bureaucratic targets that had only been met in an administrative sense but not in the field; more conflict and loss of project capital was at hand in the settlement areas. The programme, then, was a time bomb. The provision of land titles and the settlement of conflicts over land had only just started. Much more time and attention than had been allowed for so far was needed to reach a minimally acceptable degree of stability in (security of) land tenure, and to avoid an 'administrative solution' through massive routine distribution of land titles without taking into account its consequences: a multiplicity of conflicting claims on the same land. The threat of this 'solution' was ever present; every monthly meeting of the project Steering Committee it was propagated by the project officers of almost all agencies engaged in project activities, especially the sub-programmes of the settlement programme, the success of which were measured in purely quantitative targets.

The evaluation team chose to base its analysis and recommendations largely on the last two stories. The land reform and settlement programmes, as well as the strengthening of regional and local administrative structures became the focus of attention. New goals were defined. The governments of Indonesia and the Netherlands, the firm of consulting engineers, and the district administration endorsed the new priorities and justificatory structure of a new phase for PIADP. Failures and contingencies were acknowledged, but again, *in the past only*. The insight into and ultimate control over these contingencies was – again – translated into new optimism for a new period.

The sociogenesis of institutionalised development optimism

As remarked above, evaluations are, in a number of ways, crucial and dramatic moments. First, various often contradictory and conflicting actor views on past performance and actor interests in how this performance is represented and turned into official discourse have to be integrated into one consistent account. Second, while evaluations may be critical towards the project past, they are not expected to deconstruct the basic optimism on which intervention is based. On the other hand, they often have the additional function of convincing the donor that, with success within reach, there is more to be done. With reference to the future, evaluations should form the basis for unrestrained optimism about additional activities. In the case of the PIP/PIADP, two crucial moments of change can be discerned: first, in 1986 the Pompengan Implementation Project (PIP) was transformed into the Pompengan Integrated Area Development Project (PIADP). This transformation led to an exponential growth of pretensions and ambitions in the field of social engineering. Second, the 'final' evaluation, of which we gave an impression above. The latter, while giving room for further extension to redress the negative effects of towering ambitions during the foregoing period, would only lead to further erosion and chaos.

Far before the 1990 evaluation, PIADP was already in dire straits. How had this crisis situation grown historically? How could the project become entangled in an increasingly complex, largely self-created web of internal contradictions, conflicting interests, and painful dilemmas? Here we intend to show how project history can be understood as a series of cycles of optimism, gradual erosion and final downfall, followed by a new cycle with its own assumptions, goals and objectives, and optimistic ambitions. We show that the PIADP period evaluated in 1990 had been preceded by another such cycle, and, in fact, was followed again by a new one. In describing and analysing this case, we focus mainly on the programmes for land reform and settlement, the main components of PIADP.

Technology-based optimism: the Pompengan Implementation Project

After the 1965 coup, which brought to power President Suharto and marked the beginning of his 'New Order' government, large amounts of international development donor funding became available for Indonesia.[3] Priorities were mainly infrastructural: the construction of roads and other infrastructure, and of irrigation systems for intensive rice cultivation.[4] One of the regions in which these national priorities met in a large regional development programme was Luwu District in South Sulawesi, and especially the North Luwu plain. Here a multi-sectoral programme for rural development sponsored by USAID was implemented, focusing on the construction of irrigation systems and other infrastructure, in combination with transmigration, agricultural development, and marketing and cooperatives. Indonesia still being a major rice importing country at the time, regions such as Luwu were crucial in reaching the national objective of (staple) food self-sufficiency. From 1975 Dutch development aid was involved in making feasibility studies on irrigation development for proposed sites in the North Luwu plain.

In 1980, implementation of one of the sub-projects identified in the masterplan for irrigation development took place in the framework of Indonesian–Dutch bilateral development cooperation: the Pompengan Implementation Project (PIP). Its main objectives were the upgrading and expansion of infrastructure for irrigation, drainage and transport, and flood protection in a 9,000 ha. area with an estimated irrigable potential of 4,450 ha. Like the Luwu Area Development project as a whole, PIP was severely biased towards construction of physical infrastructure. Minimal attention was paid to social and institutional aspects of intervention.

This technocratic bias of PIP soon ran against its limits in the lack of fit between the basic social-demographic complexity of the project area and the blueprinted uniformity of engineering approaches to development. Soon the initial engineering optimism, defining development in terms of volumes of sand, metres of irrigation canals, and other quantifiable physical characteristics, came to be put into perspective. What had initially been routinely defined as one 'project area' on the sole criteria of river hydrology and potential for irrigated agriculture, was in reality an area of considerable physical, social, demographic and ethnic diversity. Most importantly, there were crucial differences between the upper and lower parts of the project area. The former, gently sloping and ideally suited for irrigated agriculture, had a relatively long settlement history. It was densely populated, irrigated through village-based systems, and intensively cultivated when the project started. The latter had long been sparsely populated and extensively cultivated. Settlement on a larger scale was a recent development. From the 1960s, land in this part was allocated to settlers by the local administration, while spontaneous migration also increased from this period. However, as the rivers enclosing the area regularly flooded and changed their course, land was often worked for a short period and left again when flooding made agricultural activities impossible. In the 1980s, when river protection dykes were constructed under PIP, the agricultural potential of the area increased. Old claimants returned, while new ones were attracted by the expected benefits of project implementation.

In the intensively worked upper project area some attention had been paid to the establishment and guidance of water users' associations, responsible for the operation and maintenance of the rehabilitated irrigation system.[5] But what about the lower part of the project area with its low population density? Agriculture was rainfed, and the tenure status of land was unclear. As a consequence of the recent history of migration to and settlement in this downstream part, many farmers had cleared, worked, and held claims on what formally had the status of state land (in Indonesian, *tanah negara*). Farmers had mostly settled spontaneously, with or without a permit from the local administration to settle, clear and work land. Formal land titles and cadastral registration were almost absent. Land had once been partly and coarsely surveyed for the purpose of land tax collection, and a very small part had been routinely titled, but usually not adequately surveyed or mapped.[6] Data available, then, were incomplete, outdated and, moreover, could not reflect the dynamics of real-life processes such as inheritance and other land transactions, periodic floodings and rivers changing their course, and the pull factor of rising expectations generated by plans for project intervention.

In a formal sense, there was no problem: all land, except the small part that had been titled, was state land. Thus, land already in use had the status of 'claims' on state land, the validity of which was finally to be decided upon by the state. In practice, however, the situation was more complex. The core of the problem was the existence of a huge gap between the formal state right to regulate existing land tenure, and the historically grown patterns of tenure and self-defined rights to land, the inflow of claimants and speculators attracted by the project, as well as the lack of state capability to intervene in these processes. From the first surveys, even before the actual start of PIP, the lower parts of the project area had often been regarded as 'underpopulated' (or 'empty'), leaving room for the resettlement of between 1,000 and 2,000 additional farmer families. Even before the implementation of PIP, farmer settlement in the lower part of the project area had been under consideration.[7] Shifting cultivators living in the upper catchment area of the river Lamasi, whose agricultural practices were regarded as a threat to the sustainability of water resources and irrigation infrastructure, were then seen as the potential target group for resettlement in the project area. However, in the initial years of PIP such resettlement plans were not a priority. In the lower part of the area, activities concentrated on land clearing and construction.

How problems became promises

In the course of the implementation of PIP, when irrigation development reached the downstream part of the area, the situation changed. The lack of knowledge of and control over land tenure now came to be seen as a threat to the long-term sustainability of the benefits of irrigation development. In the lower part of the project area a completely new irrigation system was being built for people unknown. Continuation of the already heavily delayed construction programme for irrigation infrastructure without paying attention to land tenure was regarded as a major threat to sustainable use of the irrigation system. Hence, the settlement option came increasingly to be regarded as a way to solve the problems of 'underpopulation' and lack of labour power for (future) intensive rice cultivation and system operation and maintenance. In order to avoid additional problems caused by encroachment on fallow land by spontaneous settlers from outside, and to counter large-scale speculation and absentee ownership, such additional settlement should be carried out in a planned and controlled manner, by bringing in new farmer families through a project-organised resettlement scheme.

Without attention to land tenure, PIP would be at risk of becoming a project without a clear 'target group', without 'beneficiaries'. But projects without beneficiaries had no future any longer in a donor world that was changing its focus from 'hardware' to 'software'. The settlement programme that was now coming within view should give 'the beneficiary' a face. The face of a by definition needy, participative, full-time, initially male, later also female, farmer, loyal to his/her benefactor: the state and its agencies, laws, regulations, and allocational decisions. A gregarious animal, finding his/her 'sense of belonging' in groups established on the initiative of state agencies or foreign consultants: groups for the construction of housing, for construction and maintenance of sanitary units, for women, for tertiary irrigation management, for farming.

The social-demographic context of PIP was, of course, important in shaping the general direction into which new approaches to the problems faced in implementation gradually developed, that is, a shift from physical (irrigation) engineering only to combined efforts addressing the technical and social aspects of irrigation development. But it is important to stress that other forces were at work that influenced views of what was to be done. First, already alluded to above, there were the changing donor policy priorities in which 'traditional' approaches to development like the exclusively physical/infrastructural PIP became outdated, and were gradually replaced by new priorities and approaches. Reaching the target group of 'the poorest', participative 'bottom-up' development and 'integrated development' gained ground as the new 'capital' of consultants and development planners. Second, there was the actual presence of both orientations as dynamic forces in the project environment of PIP: engineers and social scientists, both belonging to a different Dutch consultancy firm and representing different interests, competed for scarce project resources by claiming a monopoly on 'real' development. Organisationally, in PIP the social scientists played second fiddle to the engineers. However, as problems in the lower project area became visible, the tide was gradually turning in favour of a social engineering contribution to the project. The path had been cleared for the social engineers to claim a distinct professional input which, moreover, was now increasingly held to represent a surplus value over civil engineering.

Irrigation engineers and social engineers, then, were condemned to each other. The engineers, confronted with the threat of a negative project outcome, somehow had to face the problems in the downstream part of the project. Furthermore, in a changing development policy world, the physically biased approach of the former was out of vogue, and had to be complemented by inputs catering to new policy priorities of the donor country such as 'reaching the poorest', 'participation' and 'integrated development'. These were the capital of the social scientists. The social scientists, in their turn, could not do without the engineers; in the end, irrigation development and the outcome of the final cost–benefit analysis of the project was what it was all about. In practice, except perhaps at the level of rhetoric, there turned out not to be that much difference between civil engineers and social engineers. Where social engineers had been extremely critical of civil engineering inputs and their social consequences (and rightly so), it seems that, once they could claim their own niche of professional input in the project, they had lost their capacity to critically reflect on the sense and nonsense of their own development planning. For the social engineers, the sky now became the limit.

The breakthrough of new optimism: towards 'integrated area development'

Settlement gradually came to be seen as a precondition for the successful continuation of construction and the finalisation of irrigation development in the lower project area. However, large-scale project-organised settlement required a pervasive intervention in land tenure as well. As remarked above, it was this land tenure status which was still completely unclear. Field data on this issue showed that there were good reasons for being very cautious with any planning in the downstream area, and that there might even be a land shortage rather than 'empty' land. Warnings to this effect were given in several project reports. In vain, for in 1985 a draft settlement plan for the lower project parts was issued, stating that 'at the core of the approach is the redistribution of large areas of potential sawah land. Apart from the present population, also a large number of newcomers will be among the beneficiaries of the land redistribution' (DVV/ISSAS 1985). Resettlement and land reform were now envisaged as one 'package' for the development of the lower project area. The redistributive land policy, based on the Indonesian 1960 Basic Agrarian Law, was supposed to be an effective instrument for adapting existing land claims and settlements to the new irrigation infrastructure and planned new settlements, as well as for preventing illegal land clearing and settlement, land speculation and transactions, absentee ownership, and land fragmentation. Moreover, 'empty' land could in this way be distributed to farmer households belonging to the priority beneficiary categories as developed in the framework of land policy. Increased state influence in land tenure through land redistribution and titling was not only seen as basically unproblematic, but even regarded as a major stimulus to efficient land use. Redistributive land reform, it should be added, was mainly a Dutch development priority. It fitted in perfectly with the growing donor policy concern with 'reaching the poorest', but found little support, apart from lip service, on the Indonesian side.

Selection of 'beneficiaries' was based on the results of an inventory of claims and claimants in the land reform area. Farmers with 'strong' claims (i.e., those who could prove the existence of their claim through tax payment registration, land titles and other written proof) would have priority in the selection procedures.[8] They would in principle be entitled to one hectare of irrigated land, a 0.25 ha. house plot in the settlement area, housing and sanitation facilities, agricultural extension, seedlings, and a one-year living allowance to bridge the first period of land development, house construction, and other activities. Project regulations about land redistribution stated that claims smaller than one hectare would be enlarged to one hectare, while claims exceeding this size would be reduced to this standard plot size. However, it was decided that the redistribution of land claims was to take place in a tolerant way, making possible registration of land claims in more than one name.

Land policy for the lower project area was laid down in a special land policy document, stating procedures for implementation, farmer selection, and allocation of land and additional facilities. Thus, from 1986, Dutch involvement in the Pompengan area continued in a new shape that reflected the new development policy priorities as well as new objectives for the Pompengan project. While construction of roads, dykes and the irrigation system continued as before, pride of place was now given to the, in development jargon, 'integrated' approach to development of the downstream part of the project: land reform and settlement, agricultural development and extension, institutional development in the tertiary units of the irrigation system, and, from 1988, a 'women in development' programme. To stress this transition to an 'integrated' approach, PIP was renamed PIADP (Pompengan Integrated Area Development Project; see Roth 1994).

Thus, the initial optimism about the beneficial effects of technically biased irrigation development, demasked in a complex reality, had now made way again for a new cycle of optimism featuring social engineering through 'integrated development'. Typically, greater awareness of the complexity of the project and its environment during the PIP period ultimately resulted in even more ambitious, diverse, complex, mutually dependent and sometimes even contradictory project goals and objectives. Goals and objectives of PIADP were routinely translated into simple, quantitative targets for the sake of planning and implementation. Initial recognition of complexity and limits to technical planning degraded into a system which paired the new, sky-high ambitions and pretensions to a project organisation which was as mechanistic and blueprinted as PIP, its concrete-biased predecessor had been. After the project context had been defined as a 'problem' and a hindrance to development, through that mysterious magic of development policy the problem had now been transformed into a set of optimistically formulated promises. Icarus was now heading for the sun, paying due attention to participation, gender and the poor.

From the beginning, implementation of these 'integrated' plans for land reform and settlement was full of conflict. It is not our intention to go into the many details about the process of implementation or the outcome of land reform. Suffice it to say that even in the so-called 'pilot project'[9] a diversity of problems had become manifest: the large number of existing land claims (a land inventory held in 1986 showed that all project land had already been claimed); the strategies of administrators involved in project implementation, their friends and relatives, to obtain land and additional facilities (the same land inventory had been used by various interest groups, mainly district government officials, as an instrument to have themselves registered as claimants and thus sneak into the selection procedure); the unwillingness of farmers to accept decisions of the selection and land allocation team; and the increasingly difficult and awkward position of the Dutch consultants within this arena. For the latter, keeping up the initial objectives of implementation meant a greater depth and intensity of intervention in local affairs, to the point of paternalistically 'taking over' local tasks and responsibilities.

From optimistic project objectives to survival and chaos

As PIADP showed, 'integrated area development' is a high-sounding concept but problematic in daily reality. What the concept conveys is systemic order, a sense of purpose and direction, a well-coordinated machine-like whole. However, in practice, PIADP was from the beginning plagued by conflicts of interest, fragmentation, and competition. The agencies responsible for the various sub-programmes making up the 'integrated' structure carried out their project activities in relative isolation from each other, and in complete isolation from the 'beneficiaries'. Each agency had its own time schedules, quantitative targets, budgetary procedures, administrative requirements and clients.[10] The same goes for the other actors: the government of Indonesia, donor representatives, and consultants. All were extremely target-minded; especially in periods of increased stress and pressure like before project evaluations, the closing of the financial year etc. 'Integrated development' in PIADP was a normative, ideological notion, an ideal to be achieved in the midst of various mechanisms leading to the contrary.

As implementation continued after the pilot project, it became clear that the situation in the other areas would become at least as uncontrollable. But one lesson had been learned from the pilot project: as land reform and settlement in this area dragged on without hope of solutions or even progress, the agencies responsible for implementation of the various programmes started to lose whatever interest they initially had in the project. The agency for Village Development (Bangdes), providing material facilities such as housing and sanitation as well as living allowances to the settlers, began propagating the routine distribution of these facilities without bothering too much about whether the recipient fulfilled the conditions specified in the land reform programme. The Agricultural Service (Pertanian), the field team of which had always assisted the Land Registry Agency by making field reports of land tenure in the land reform areas, suddenly started to play it safe and routinely issue quantitative reports which stressed their own progress and fulfilment of targets, but no longer provided any field information on land reform. In the Land Registry Agency (BPN), responsible for land titling, a small group of quality-oriented personnel was put under increasing pressure to routinely distribute land titles, regardless of the actual field situation. In short: soon after the start of PIADP, the survival of agencies and project officials gained priority over ambitious project objectives.

PIADP fell victim to basic tensions and contradictions generated by its complex and unattainable objectives, and to its ambitious and blueprinted planning. First, there was the tension between, on one hand, the objective of land redistribution and controlled settlement to avoid large-scale speculation and spontaneous settlement, and, on the other, the donative orientation of PIADP. Project regulations had put an enormous donative price on becoming a 'beneficiary' of the programme. In sharp contrast to its rhetoric of participation and bottom-up development, basically PIADP was a dole-out project. As claiming land was the major way to get access to facilities provided in the settlement programme (housing, sanitation, living allowance, etc.), in the end the donative orientation of PIADP stimulated speculative behaviour with land. It was the relation between land claimed and access to material spoils that made farmers stick to their land claims and reject redistribution of their claims, and groups from outside with speculative intentions became even more interested in gaining access to land in the project area. Thus, a project policy designed to fight speculation on land and conflicts about redistribution of claims, in practice led to quite the contrary.

There was another contradiction inherent in the land reform in PIADP. The volatility, due to continuing land transactions (e.g., buying, selling, inheritance), of the 'data' on which decision making was based necessitated rapid implementation.[11] The longer the time lag between surveys and implementation, the wider the gap between survey 'data' and actual field conditions. On the other hand, the sheer complexity of the process and the context in which it was implemented required a cautious approach, contrary to the kind of blueprinted planning that characterised PIADP. Thus, there was an unsolvable dilemma within the land reform programme: while a speedy implementation with less concern for complexity was bound to fail because farmers would never accept its outcome, a more cautious implementation was almost certain to lead to more or less the same result because the longer implementation would take, the wider the gap between data on land tenure and the actual field situation.

Then, there was the increasingly awkward position of the Dutch consultants. The introduction of redistributive land reform was clearly based on Dutch policy priorities such as a target-group orientation of 'reaching the poorest', giving land to the landless, etc. Formal responsibility for the process was, of course, in the hands of the Indonesian administration. However, in view of the massive speculative behaviour of some individuals from the implementing government agencies and the administrative apparatus, the Dutch expatriate staffs felt that a policy of leaving responsibility to the Indonesians would backfire on the project as a whole. This would be a major threat to the land reform and settlement programmes. In an effort to restrict possible misuse of project regulations by project officials and local elites, consultants appropriated many tasks and responsibilities from the Indonesian government agencies. As a consequence, implementation leaned increasingly heavy on Dutch initiative, logistics and financial inputs. Such a deep involvement was not only paternalistic, taking responsibilities for decision making away from the responsible agencies, it was also counter-productive. Massive land speculation had already occurred earlier (especially during the land inventories), and could hardly be redressed at the stages of farmer selection and land allocation. The Dutch had bought a very limited degree of influence on the selection process by financing a settlement programme that stimulated speculation, and by accepting a process characterised by arbitrariness and manipulation. Thus, consultants had lost the capacity to take a critical stance towards modalities of planning, implementation, and decision making concerning land reform and settlement. Willy-nilly they had become accomplices to, rather than critical advisors of, a programme that, though presented as 'participative', 'bottom-up', providing farmers with 'security of tenure' and 'sense of belonging', was actually enforced upon a local population sensible enough to pick out the material spoils of the settlement programme and reject the land reform part.

Last, there was the growing conflict between 'quality' and 'quantity'. Under pressure from the local administration and other agencies, in 1989 the Land Registry Agency had implemented massive routine titling in the pilot project. It became a complete failure; land titles that had already been distributed had to be returned again to BPN, due to ongoing conflicts. As a consequence, after this failed titling, some project officials of the Land Registry Agency, responsible for the possibly negative impact of such routine titling, were in favour of implementation of land reform with an eye to quality. However, by 1990, shortly before the arrival of the evaluation mission, they were under increasing pressure from other agencies in the 'integrated' structure to dole out land titles that did not correspond with actual field conditions. Attention to quality in the land reform programme meant delay for the other agencies responsible for housing, sanitation, establishment of water users' associations, women's groups, etc. These agencies had other priorities and commitments than quality alone: they were designed for matching material outputs with bureaucratic inputs (targets) in the shortest time possible. Preferably in accordance with project objectives but, if necessary, by dumping facilities or producing paper only. Rather than accepting delays in land reform as 'part of the game' or as a possible sign of quality of implementation, representatives of the agencies responsible for the distribution of project facilities became nervous. And not without reason; their performance was evaluated in terms of budgets spent, volumes distributed, units built, number of farmers' groups or neighbourhood groups established. For how long could they continue to present PIADP to their far-away superiors as a story of success and progress rather than failure and decay? Thus, the opposed interests of the various agencies involved in the implementation of PIADP, surfacing most clearly in the conflict between, on one hand, an orientation towards quality and long-term sustainabilty of project results, and, on the other, towards quantity and the routine fulfilment of targets, were the daily reality behind the superficial notion of 'integrated development'.

The internal tensions and contradictions generated by the transition from PIP to PIADP and subsequent developments caused the wax on Icarus's wings to melt. However, the final crash was to take place after the 1990 evaluation mission had succeeded in securing a considerable extension for PIADP. As PIADP had replaced PIP in the hope of redressing some of the shortcomings of the latter, caused by the *hybris* of civil engineering, the rationale behind the extension of PIADP recommended by the 1990 mission was the hope, that in this way the serious shortcomings of PIADP, this time caused by over-ambitious social engineering, could be reduced to an acceptable level. Another extension of PIADP was the last hope of saving Icarus from his final crash.

Within half a year after the visit of the 1990 mission, chaos ruled in PIADP. Members of the field team of the Land Registry Agency who were in favour of preventing the land reform programme from becoming a meaningless administrative routine were replaced by new staff members, who were given the task of getting rid of the PIADP problem as soon as possible. The agenda had definitively shifted towards rapid routine land titling. The programme had now completely lost its initial meaning. It had degraded into a senseless bureaucratic routine. A final separation had now become established between the complex field reality on one hand, and the paper reality represented by land titles, progress reports, and targets met on the other. PIADP was now reduced to the massive dumping of the last infrastructure and remaining material facilities of the settlement programme, with an open disregard of quality, rights and interests of 'the beneficiaries', or sustainability of project results. By the end of 1991, the consultants were told by DGIS and the Dutch embassy to sit it out, to avoid any disturbance of the good bilateral relations between the two countries. Soon another issue was to damage those relations: in April 1992 PIADP was suddenly terminated as a consequence of a political conflict between the governments of Indonesia and the Netherlands about the human rights issue in Eastern Timor, leading to the immediate termination of Indonesian–Dutch development cooperation. But Icarus had already crashed a long time before. 'For the Pompengan project, this political crisis is a blessing in disguise' were the last words heard from one of the planners who had made PIADP fly so high. And indeed, why should we learn from such experiences if there is no chance of new assignments?

Concluding remarks

We have analysed some of the mechanisms which have shaped an excessive and quite unwarranted optimism in development programmes, and conclude by making some final comments here. What can we learn from cases like this? We feel that we have touched upon a process of cyclical repetition which, for some fundamental reasons, took the course it did in the case discussed above. It is as if a play of development processes is performed which, though the different actors may change and vary, remains the same. Why this repetition of 'cycles of optimism', this unwarranted belief that the sky is the limit, that we can reach for the sun? Have we learned to mask the downfall? Have we relegated the 'falling part' of the story to another – past – 'project stage', keeping the optimistic part for the future?

In our respective functions as evaluator of and expatriate advisor to PIADP we ourselves have fallen victim to the same optimism about future courses of action. When the evaluation team was at work in PIADP, there was agreement between us about the existing situation, about the problems and what caused them, and about what should happen to overcome these problems. We agreed that it was not justified to back out from the enormous problems caused by implementation of the land reform and settlement programmes, while at the same time presenting the project as a successful 'model' for integrated rural development. If some degree of stability and sustainability was to be reached at all, more attention should be given to the tensions in the land reform and settlement programmes. This required another extension of PIADP. However, soon our initial optimism and winning mood turned sour, having been seriously put into perspective by local reality. Now, taking a critical distance and looking back to our earlier points of view, opinions, moral judgements and recommendations, we can only conclude that together – as an evaluator receiving and weighing 'stories' and as a consultant providing the evaluation team with one specific story – we started just another cycle of excessive optimism. Why?

One of the main factors underlying these repetitive patterns of rising and falling expectations is that the project cycles that we have analysed are systematic distortions of real-life historical processes. What can we say about the administrative discourse of the 'project cycle'? To what extent is it a virtual reality which is almost unrelated to the actual political, economic and other histories of local people? Do our planning, implementation and 'learning' bear any relationship to the real-life processes and transformations that take place? A conclusion from our analysis may be that there is a basic danger in conceptualising real-life processes in terms of cycles for development administrative purposes. Distinguishing a series of separate time cycles gives unwarranted support to the idea that such administrative cycles are identical to 'stages' that can be distinguished in real-life situations. Rather, these cycles and administrative routines lead their own lives, related in an unknown way to the real-life situations that they claim to represent. If each new cycle indeed represents a new 'project', we have found a sound basis to relegate the contingencies of real life and the 'failure' resulting from it to a past cycle, while reserving optimism for a new cycle characterised by new ambitions and promises, new manifestations of the assumption of manageability and control, and also by a new preoccupation with 'success' and 'failure' in terms of the objectives set in the next cycle. As the administrative cycle has been 'liberated' from historical processes and other contextual factors, there are no inherent limitations to improvement any more. Optimism concerning professional administrative capacities has been set free like birds flying away from their cages of historic contingency; like Icarus putting on his wings and taking off, defying gravity and the heat of the sun. We can do away with the inevitable inherent conflicts of goals, conflicting views or interests. Becoming worshippers of the project cycle we turn the setting of development interventions into an a-historical object. We do away, in fact, with history itself.

The images of development intervention as time cycles, clear cyclical demarcations in time from start to finish, as well as the images of projects as integrating machines, are not just false or inadequate. The point here is that these very official images themselves must be seen as key factors engendering chaos, conflicts and failure. Conceptualising the development process in terms of repetitive cycles, then, means investing in virtuality rather than in development. We cannot know the real significance of endeavours for development. The administration of excessive optimism has replaced critical and historical understanding. We make plans and implement them, but we lack the means to interpret what is going on in a reliable manner and by fixed, uncontested and unproblematic 'rational' standards. In this respect, notions like 'success' and 'failure' are totally unrealistic and lacking meaning. In our analysis we have tried to argue that it is almost impossible to know what is going on. The kinds of 'knowledges' which are produced in the course of the project cycle can only be understood as expressive of the actors in that encapsulated world, the play which was written before the actors actually played their role, isolated from ongoing historical processes and the people taking part in them.

It can be concluded that, to a large extent, the story of development goes its own way, irrespective of historical settings or audiences. This explains why belief in the manageability of development remains so strong, regardless of what we might have learned from the past. 'Integrated area development', 'participation', and 'empowerment' are part of a repetitive pattern of hopes and intentions that lead their own cyclic lives, irrespective of their relationships with the people whose lives are staged in the play. Such concepts are like magical tools. Magical, because they seem to transform reality without having any relationship with it. Scene one goes to scene two and scene three; after the booing or the applause the play is reiterated again. The main task ahead, then, is to try and enlarge our understanding of the linkages between development interventions and historical processes, and at the same time convince the development planners to show more restraint and modesty in enforcing their policy priorities upon unknown people in contexts hardly understood. There may be a major role here for researchers outside the confines of the development policy world. The actors directly engaged in the play are too caught up in their routines to be able to answer the question: what difference does all their hard work make for development?

Notes

1 The principal here is the Dutch development agency DGIS (Directorate-General for International Cooperation).
2 On the Dutch side, the mission consisted of an economist, an agronomist and a development sociologist. The Indonesian members of the team represented two of the leading national agencies: the National Planning Agency (Bappenas) and the Land Registry Agency (BPN).
3 Since 1997 Indonesia has been deeply immersed in a political and economic crisis. Recently, Megawati Sukarnoputri was installed as the third post-Suharto president, after the Habibie and Wahid administrations.
4 Another spearhead was 'transmigration', the resettlement of farmers from densely populated islands such as Java and Bali to islands with a lower population density such as Sulawesi.
5 This was, revealingly, called the 'non-physical component' of PIP.
6 Titling was implemented on a small scale by the Land Registry Agency (Agraria; after 1988, BPN).
7 It had first been mentioned in the 'Administrative arrangements' for the implementation of PIP, in which, for the downstream part, land clearing and 'the provision of adequate facilities and support, allowing a resettlement programme which involves around a thousand families', are mentioned.
8 In the meantime, plans for the resettlement of farmers from 'outside' had been silently taken off the agenda. Attention shifted now to other priority groups

within the project area: claimants in the downstream area, farmers harmed by construction, and landless inhabitants (DHV/ISSAS 1986).

9 PIADP had been subdivided into four 'stages' of implementation, the first known as 'the pilot project'. However, pilot experiences were never evaluated. Notwithstanding enormous problems in the pilot area, neither Indonesians nor the Dutch have ever considered a fundamental reorientation of the project, its objectives and methods. Apart from minor adaptations of the programme, activities continued in the same blueprinted way. In both bureaucratic environments, a serious questioning or reorientation of the programme in the light of field experiences would almost certainly be interpreted as 'failure' of implementing agencies and consultants. For both groups this was a potential threat to interests, positions, and careers. So, rather than initiating a 'learning process', implementation could not be stopped or changed.

10 As to such targets: for instance, land reform was reduced to 'number of hectares allocated' and 'number of titles issued', settlement to 'number of houses and sanitation units built', and institutional development to 'number of farmers' groups established', etc.

11 Project regulations forbidding such land transactions did not have any restrictive impact on actual behaviour.

References

DHV/ISSAS (1985) 'Settlement plan for the Pompengan area', project document.
—— (1986) 'Pompengan Integrated Area Development Project. Settlement plan area B', project document.
—— (1990) 'Pompengan Integrated Area Development Project. Short explanation of present status for evaluation mission', project document.
Escobar, A. (1995) *Encountering Development: the Making and Unmaking of the Third World*, Princeton: Princeton University Press.
Ferguson, J. (1990) *The Anti-politics Machine: 'Development', Depoliticization and Bureaucratic Power in Lesotho*, Cambridge: Cambridge University Press.
Hobart, M. (ed.) (1993) *An Anthropological Critique of Development: the Growth of Ignorance*, London/New York: Routledge.
Hulme, D. (1989) 'Learning and not learning from experience in rural project planning', *Public Administration and Development* 9: 1–16.
Long, N. and J.D. van der Ploeg (1989) 'Demythologizing planned intervention: an actor perspective', *Sociologia Ruralis* XXIX (3/4): 226–249.
Ovid (1986) *Metamorphoses*, Oxford/New York: Oxford University Press.
Quarles van Ufford, Ph. (1993) 'Knowledge and ignorance in the practices of development policy', in M. Hobart (ed.) *An Anthropological Critique of Development: the Growth of Ignorance*, London/New York: Routledge.
Roth, D. (1994) 'How "integrated" is integrated rural development? The case of the Pompengan Integrated Area Development Project (PIADP), Luwu District, South Sulawesi, Indonesia', *Public Administration and Development* 14: 377–393.

Chapter 4

The monolithic development machine?

Elizabeth Harrison[1]

Introduction

Recent discussion of 'resistance', especially resistance to development intervention, has stressed that it is all too easy to overemphasise the opposition of the supposed resisters. To construe the actions of apparently less powerful groups as resistance leaves the developers at the centre of the analysis and defines agency in very limited terms. Put simply, what people do may be neither acquiescence nor resistance to development, but formed and influenced by all sorts of factors which are unconnected to development activity. Relatedly, a sharp division between those who resist and those who are resisted is not always tenable; relations of domination and subordination are not so fixed. As Ortner (1995) has pointed out, a weakness of many resistance studies is their 'ethnographic thinness'; their partial and limited view of the constitution of complex societies.

Nonetheless, for a number of writers now identified with the 'deconstruction of development', notions of resistance have a particular appeal; they provide a plausible answer to the question 'what is to be done?' which creeps, apparently unavoidably, into the conclusions of their critiques of development. For example Arturo Escobar's solution to the problem of 'imagining a post-development era' is a focus on 'new social movements' (1995a, 1995b), and James Ferguson (1990) in a similar vein suggests that anthropologists should support 'counter-hegemonic social forces'. In both cases their critical dissection of the discourses and practices of development ends as a rather idealised picture of social relations among the 'other' – those who have been subject to development.

This problem is part of a wider failure to escape simplifying dichotomies, even (or particularly) among post-modern theorists avowedly stressing complexity, nuance and hybridity. One of the most pervasive of these dichotomies is that between us (developers) and them (recipients). Escobar argues on several occasions that the 'development encounter' should not be seen as a clash between two cultural systems. There is however a tension between this position and a wish to make certain, essentially political, points – to make judgements and identify the goodies and the baddies in the development encounter. Nonetheless, for many authors the wish to specify a singular 'development discourse' with a monolithic power rather than multiple discourses is apparently irresistible.

Some writers have presented the difference between us and them as acute and, ultimately, irreconcilable. For example, Hobart (1993) writes in the introduction to a collection of papers on the anthropology of development: 'just how separate and indeed incommensurable are the respective discourses of developers, developed and governments is a striking feature of many of the essays in this volume' (1993: 12). As Grillo has pointed out, such thinking borders on cultural solipsism with its implication that communication between 'local' and 'Western' knowledge is impossible; 'rationalities are not shared or share-able' (1997: 14). While it is arguably true that there may be important differences in meanings and understandings which may be overlooked in the practices of development intervention, a position of incommensurability is equally untenable. The problem is not that there are not shared meanings; it is one of identifying how these are created and sustained by material circumstances.

Anthropological studies have long focused on discrete, identifiable 'communities', frequently paying attention to the effects of their interaction with the outside world. They have been joined (or even influenced in some cases) by what Richards (1993) calls the 'priests of humanistic plurality'. These priests espouse bottom-up, participatory approaches to development, but with a romantic, even naive, view of the formulation and articulation of interests. Simple dichotomies (insider/outsider, top-down/bottom-up, us/them) possibly play a role in the popularity of such approaches. But who are the 'local' people exactly? And what makes local people local? There is a need for caution in the use of simple statements about what is local because labelling particular groups of people as insiders or outsiders may overlook the ways that 'people may be outsiders and/or insiders according to their activity or purpose' (Cornwall *et al.* 1994: 101).

If identification of 'them' is problematic, is the category of 'us' any easier to either identify or characterise? At an obvious level, of course, it is. Institutions of development such as the UN agencies, the World Bank, bilateral donors, and international NGOs are all part of the development establishment – as are their employees, academics concerned with development, international consultants, and civil servants in the donor countries. But what about recipient governments, who are simultaneously the agents of development for their countries, and subject to the strictures and controls of international development? Are they part of the establishment, servants or opponents? And indigenous NGOs who may both promote particular ideologies of development and see an opposition between themselves and the ultimate beneficiaries; are they recipients of development?

Equally, however, there are differences even within apparently homogeneous organisations. In *The Anti-politics Machine*, James Ferguson (1990) draws an analogy between the 'development apparatus' and Foucault's writings on the prison. Foucault argued that while the prison had failed to reduce crime, it had succeeded in producing delinquency which was politically and economically less dangerous; 'so successful has the prison been that, after a century and a half of "failures", the prison still exists, producing the same results, and there is the greatest reluctance to dispense with it' (cited in Ferguson 1990: 20). In Ferguson's case, the 'development apparatus' in Lesotho is a machine for reinforcing and expanding the exercise of bureaucratic state power. But is the machine really such a monolith? In an obvious way, the development apparatus is fragmented; not only is there a great diversity in types of organisation, but the ways they work, the motivations of individuals within them, and their political context vary greatly. The apparent power of one set of actors, for example the promoters of a technology, is not simple or unitary. Different actors act under variable constraints, making power more fluid than it might appear.

This chapter explores how the boundaries between one apparent category of social actors and another are bridged, transformed, and shifted. Using the case of a development project in sub-Saharan Africa, it traces competing interpretations, incentives and actions of diverse actors in the development process. Rather than focus on the most obviously 'local' (farmers), the case study evidence is of actors who are arguably all 'us'; project personnel and government employees. The chapter reveals how the interface between different actors combines with the structural and historical specifics of their institutional location to create very different manoeuvring spaces. This creates a messier view of reality than many of the 'deconstructors of development' imply, but arguably a more accurate one.

However, an argument for messiness presents an ethical problem. Specifically, there are dangers of political paralysis in continual contextualisation, or a suggestion that no patterns exist. There is no coordinated conspiracy in the development industry, and not all projects obviously 'fail'. Still, a yawning chasm remains between the stated goals of development and many of its practices and outcomes. This is a problem with which I engage in the concluding section of this chapter.

A failure?

Small-scale aquaculture (fish farming) has been promoted in sub-Saharan Africa since at least the 1940s. Colonial, and later donor, aspirations for the technology centred on its potential to improve nutrition, generate income and diversify livelihoods. In a continent with little or no history of fish farming, the results of all this promotion have been mixed at best. Fish ponds might be dug but often produce few fish and are later abandoned;

government contributions are construed by donors as inadequate. As with many similar introductions, blame has been attributed to an overly technical focus and a failure to understand the needs and motivations of the intended beneficiaries.

In 1986, a fish farming programme was introduced to the region which aimed to learn from the lessons of the past. Supported by a number of bilateral donors and implemented by the FAO, the programme also reflected the interest among some donors in taking a more participatory and 'bottom-up' approach to development. The programme's experimental nature meant that rather than introducing infrastructure and extension packages, or trying to persuade people to farm fish, its focus, especially at the beginning, was on studies and 'methodology development'. The idea was that the results of these studies would then be field-tested in a series of 'pilot projects' throughout the region.

My contact with the programme dates from 1990 when it agreed to host the fieldwork for an ODA-funded research project into the socio-economic aspects of aquaculture development. The bulk of this fieldwork was located with a pilot project in Luapula province, Zambia. The pilot project aimed to achieve essentially two things: the consolidation and improvement of existing fish farming and strengthening of the local department of fisheries (DoF). Over four years a range of activities took place including on-farm trials, studies, extension, and farmer training. Three expatriate workers were employed, initially an aquaculturist and a sociologist, then an aquaculturist on his own from 1991. The project supplied a four-wheel-drive vehicle and operating costs. It was thus relatively small by the standards of many development projects.

When it was wound up in 1993, a review suggested that neither of the major objectives of the pilot project had been achieved; impact on farming practices had been minimal and pre-existing weaknesses in the department had not been improved. The programme more generally has also been criticised. An evaluation suggested that although much work had been done, especially with regard to the collection of information, substantive evidence of either improved fish farming practices or strengthened institutional capacity was thin on the ground. The evaluation suggested that the programme was over-centralised and had poorly defined objectives.

This brief description appears relatively straightforward. The project was not one of the pariahs of development that many of its deconstructors love to hate (it is unlikely that any poor farmer was seriously harmed by the programme). It nevertheless illustrates factors apparently common to development 'failure', such as the expenditure of money with little evidence that the supposed beneficiaries were indeed benefiting and a tendency to make misjudged assumptions about local capacities and inclinations to cooperate. In the remainder of this chapter, I want to take a closer look at this development 'failure' in order to show that 'us' – the development machine – is not as simple as it appears. Rather than attribute failure, we need to look at the complicated interactions of organisational and individual priorities, to see how different people and groups are constrained yet able to subvert, and to question the cohesion of the machine. For the purposes of this chapter I focus on the Zambian pilot project, although disjunctures and differences in understanding took place all the way from Rome to Zambia and back again. On the face of it, I am considering an FAO project with FAO employees, and their interaction with their 'hosts', Zambian and other African government employees. But what is the 'us' in all this? It is not so simple or easy to define. Clearly in some ways the 'hosts' could be said to be part of the development bureaucracy. In others, they are not; the project was conceived in Rome, not Harare or Lusaka. Equally, at what point does it make sense to stress separation rather than overlap between project workers, extensionists, and even farmers? These questions are explored below.

The Zambian project – big fish and small ponds

Villareal (1992) has argued that the front-line workers in development projects have to work out appropriate strategies in the face of numerous constraints. They are faced with the task of presenting a package and making it work. Although strategies and standards for action are created outside,

> the implementor's practical analysis cuts through these categories, as he or she now has to face people and their interests, their different understandings, their constraints, their abilities etc. Here is the crucial moment of decision making, of actual accomplishment of projects, which mostly turn out to be drastically different from written plans.
>
> (Villareal 1992: 251)

In Luapula, the 'implementors' were both the expatriate workers posted by the programme and the local Department of Fisheries (DoF). Within the DoF, different roles were played by extensionists (known as fish scouts) and their boss, the Provincial Fisheries Development Officer (PFDO). The conditions and constraints they faced were very different. Arguably though, all of these people were, in their different ways, part of the development machine. As becomes clear below, however, this identity was only sporadically meaningful. Membership of categories such as developer, developed, local and outsider is not mutually exclusive or static.

The Big Fish

A key element was crucial for the success of the pilot project: the cooperation of the DoF. However, from the inception of the project, that cooperation was assumed rather than the basis for it explored. The pilot project was conceived and developed in Harare. Discussion between the various collaborators took place in the provincial capital, Mansa, but from unequal positions; although the language of cooperation permeates all planning documentation, this disguises both real and incipient conflict.

Firstly, there was conflict over objectives. The main DoF objective was the maximisation of fish production through rational exploitation of fish stocking. This has nothing obviously to do with smallholder food security or rural income increase – which were the project's main objectives. Luapula is Zambia's principal fish producer but suffers from declining yields and over-exploitation, creating a need for policing and monitoring. The provincial fisheries development officer (PFDO) held this role to be very important. Arguments used to support aquaculture development stressed that, despite the overall provincial importance of fisheries, away from the lake shores and valleys, people had only restricted access to fish. However, so far as the DoF was concerned, it could make as much sense to concentrate on improving marketing facilities and management of existing fish stocks as to promote fish farming. Moreover, as elsewhere in Zambia, the department was constrained by shortages of cash, by non-availability of fuel, and by low morale among staff who were seldom paid their allowances on time.

There were also differences in perceptions about how objectives should be reached. Two major points of conflict emerged: whether or not the government should be trying to supply fingerlings (fish seed), and the question of which farmers should receive assistance. The PFDO maintained that the supply and distribution of fingerlings to farmers were essential. Two government fish farms were constructed partly for this purpose during colonial days. So far as the PFDO were concerned, the rehabilitation of the run-down fish farms should have been a priority. The project on the other hand strongly believed that farmer–farmer supply was a much more sensible approach.

Furthermore, ideas about suitable target groups for development did not converge. The project's official focus was on the fish farming activities of small scale, mainly self provisioning farmers. Richer, semi-commercial or more intensive fish farmers, particularly those with an urban base, were not such appropriate subjects for development assistance. The PFDO believed that assistance and extension advice should be given to 'knowledgeable and progressive people' – who, he argued, could then create a firm economic foundation for fish farming. The PFDO expressed frustration that the project was not interested in giving loans to the few richer, semi-urban fish farmers in the province. Crehan and Von Oppong (1988) describe a development project in north-western Zambia. They quote an angry politician: 'You promote small-scale farmers, small-scale equipment, small-scale industries ... small! small! small! You have grown big and you want to keep us small! Worse than the colonialists!' (Crehan and Von Oppong 1988: 126). Parallels can be drawn with the feelings expressed by the PFDO.

From his point of view, the project entered with potential clout (which was not translated into tangible gifts), but with too many pre-conceived ideas. Donor assistance was a potentially useful way of enabling the smoother running of the department. It also carried with it the danger that staff time would be used, and policy directions changed away from predetermined lines. The FAO project was in an unclear role as a donor. It entered as a donor-financed operation, with stated objectives concerned with fish production. At the same time, the project provided only a vehicle for its own use and staff time over which the DoF had no control. Simultaneously, the DoF was expected to allocate its staff to activities which the PFDO thought were of dubious benefit. There were personal considerations too, compounding professional resentment. These centred on the repeated reminders of his own disempowered status in relation to the project and its representatives. The PFDO had held his post for many years. Among the nine PFDOs in the country, he felt his position to be relatively important, because of the significance of capture fisheries. He was a native of the province and believed he had good understanding of its problems. In Mansa, he was widely known as 'The Big Fish'. He had also, during his time as PFDO, seen both his personal standard of living and the resources of the department severely eroded. In the early 1970s, he had his own car and the DoF had a new vehicle and a functioning fish farm. By 1992, the car had gone, his salary, like other government salaries, was worth little, the departmental offices were crumbling, and the DoF vehicle was scarcely roadworthy.

While he had had years of experience, creating an understandable belief that he should be accorded respect and status, he was forced to live in poor housing, with no transport or visible evidence of his position. The FAO workers were half his age, white, and newly arrived in Zambia. However, they were paid international salaries which enabled them to live in comfortable housing and have 'personal' vehicles in addition to the project vehicle. The response of one to the rather shabby office he was given (next to that of the PFDO) was to repaint it, complete with royal blue woodwork and FAO logos.

These symbols of difference – in power, in resources and in choices – were obviously present among the many other expatriates in the town. What made them more galling to the PFDO was that they were not something to be put up with for obvious benefit. He often complained there was no reason for the FAO project. However, straightforward obstruction was not an option for him. His room for manoeuvre was curtailed by the hierarchy within which he was situated and, to an extent, he had to play the game – maintaining an illusion of collaboration. Thus, he was formally grateful to the project in his written reports. But he also did not go out of his way to assist the project activities: the majority of his time was spent in work connected with capture fisheries. At programme headquarters in Harare, people complained about the local bureaucracy: 'That [X] – he's a disaster. The whole department does nothing. How can we be expected to get anything done ourselves.' However, these complaints, like the complaints of the PFDO himself, did not enter the public presentation of the project, in which shared objectives were paramount.

Small fry

The one aspect of the pilot project which involved sustained direct contact with farmers was a sub-project in Chibote, an area of the province about 300 km from Mansa. A fish scout was posted there to improve the fish farming activities which had begun some years previously with the support of the White Fathers. The White Fathers had left, but there was a base of fish farming which, it was believed, could be fostered, supported and improved. Posted against his will while nearing retirement, the fish scout was expected to cover an area of 930 km^2 on a moped with insufficient petrol or spare parts, and had to live in a poor quality thatched hut with his wife and seven children. In some ways part of the village, but in other ways not, his position as local partner is worthy of examination; it illuminates further the fluidity of apparently simple categories.

The fish scout had to contend with both his relative powerlessness at the bottom of the departmental hierarchy and in relation to the FAO project, and his slightly ambiguous position in relation to farmers. He claimed that his seniors never visited him or read his reports. He was a potential distributor of largesse, but faced with a limited practical ability to do this. In material terms he was no better-off than many of the farmers with whom he worked. At the same time, his position as representative of the government distanced him. In this respect he is similar to a Zambian agricultural extension worker whose experiences are described by Hedlund (1984). Hedlund argues that interaction between the extensionist and the villagers was sporadic because his ideology and ambitions were so totally in contrast to the villagers' point of view. At the same time as being at the bottom of the extension hierarchy, he saw himself as the representative of the government and the nation in the village. To the agricultural extension officer, 'villagers represented disorder, irrational values, conservatism and not least an indifference to his own development ideology' (Hedlund 1984: 242).

However, for the fish scout, opposition between himself and the village was not straightforward. He had to manage a number of competing priorities: doing what the FAO project and the DoF had designated in his work plan (visiting and training farmers, rehabilitating Mission-built breeding ponds and carrying out a census of fish farmers); supervising the construction of a new house for himself; and getting on with the people among whom he lived. Coming originally from the neighbouring district, he was not a stranger. His wife had many relatives nearby and was enmeshed in social relations in Chibote. Thus the need to assert difference was tempered by the need to belong.

Given these circumstances there were a number of outcomes which were, if not inevitable, at least not surprising. On a day-to-day basis, the construction of his house came first. After this, he concentrated on what he perceived to be both the project's priorities and a way of making allies; a limited number of 'model farmers' and the Mission ponds. The project expatriate worker was conducting on-farm 'trials' with two contact farmers. It was these farmers who were visited: 'they understand easily, and we want to work with those who understand, then others will copy'. Extension work with others was sporadic at best, but predominantly non-existent. The rehabilitation of the Mission ponds enabled him to make friends through his control over resources; the ponds were to be repaired using pieceworkers. Given a lack of employment opportunities in the area, working for the fish scout was a potentially valuable source of income for those farmers who befriended him.

In 1988 Chibote had been identified as a flourishing site of fish farming. By 1992, the project was deemed to have been a fiasco. The house had not been built, very little extension had taken place, there was no visible evidence of improved pond management, and the village hatcheries did not look promising. Unofficially, most of the blame was pinned on the personal failings of the fish scout. However, these personal failings could also be seen as a fairly reasonable response to the situation he found himself in. With personal motivation and commitment lacking, there was little that was likely to engender them. As Arce and Long (1993) argue, although it might seem that the particular strategies of an individual are highly idiosyncratic, 'in fact they are shaped by the possibilities for manoeuvre and discourse that already exist' (Arce and Long 1993: 181).

In many ways, the fish scout should be seen as a local. He lived as a local, he was part of village relations of exchange and negotiation, he took part in, as well as being the subject of, local gossip. But his position was more complicated than this. He was simultaneously an insider and an outsider whose primary affiliation adapted with circumstances. Similarly his friends the model farmers did not unambiguously see themselves as 'villagers'. Their association with the project and with the fish scout meant that other identities were also important. However, once we begin to accept the fluidity of such identities, clearly the whole idea of the village and the local becomes contestable.

One of us?

The three associate professional officers (APOs) who were the 'face' of the pilot project were in complex positions. They were involved in a number of contrasting, but overlapping worlds: the demands of Rome and Harare, the needs of the local department, and the farmers with whom they were supposed to be working. All of these were of course cross-cut with the personal histories, aspirations and characters of the individuals concerned.

APOs are the most junior among FAO's 'expert' staff. They are in part trainees. The idea behind the scheme is that the country of origin of the APO pays their salary and they receive on-the-job training with an international organisation from an expert in their field. Obviously the notion of training and supervision was hard to put into practice in the context of the pilot project; the APOs were at least two days' journey from their supervisor in Harare. This also meant that they had to interpret their work plan as best they could. The first two APOs left before the end of their contract. The reasons for this remain speculative. However, there is little doubt that relations with DoF were not good, perhaps because of the department's disappointed expectations.

The APO who arrived in 1991 therefore had to pick up the threads of the project and the legacy of ill-feeling which had developed between it and DoF. He was in his first posting in Africa, having been briefed in his home country (Denmark), in Rome and in Harare. He was trained principally in marine biology, but had also studied aquaculture. From Rome and Harare, two messages were clear: the importance of the correct adoption of procedures, and the need to show evidence of work, particularly the production of fish. Although the objectives of the project focused on methodology development, among the official outputs were improved production of fish and improved nutritional status among farmers. Equally though, he needed to respond to donor agendas influencing the direction of the project, the most significant of which was the need for participation and interaction with farmers. At the same time, the resources with which he had to work were limited.

The APO was thus faced with a complicated set of problems. On the one hand, the notion of technical support to a non-functioning extension service was meaningless. On the other, he was aware of the main criticism of the first phase of the pilot project – essentially that 'nothing happened', and that he had a limited period of time in which to make his mark. However, making things happen fast and effectively was, he knew, not necessarily in the spirit of participation. He needed to find a way of resolving top-down and bottom-up. His response was to try to steer the project away from its previous emphasis on studies and station-based trials, towards training, monitoring, and trying to improve relations with extensionists. The result was a considerable increase in the profile of the project: a series of 'mobile training courses' in villages throughout the province (funded by another donor), concentrated trials with a small number of 'model farmers', and a concerted attempt to get the extensionists to travel with him as much as possible (they generally had no other form of transport). For the young APO, what he perceived as the apathy and lack of commitment in the fish scouts was a serious challenge. He believed that an important part of his job was to motivate them. Lastly, he paid scrupulous attention to the reporting demands of his employers, realising that, ultimately, Rome and Harare would judge him by the quality of his reports.

The wish to bring the extensionists on board met with problems arising from their own detachment from the project. In March 1992, all of the fish scouts were invited to a seminar in Mansa, organised and funded by the project. On the first evening, many of the scouts threatened to leave when they discovered that they were not to be paid allowances as food and lodgings were already provided. They felt they had been misled and complained that they would not have come if the situation had been clearer. For fish scouts, allowances were a critical source of income. At the time, the disparity between allowances for field trips and attendances at conferences and their salaries was vast.

The APO's surprised and disappointed response was to stress that the seminar was for 'learning together'. Fish scouts were asked to present papers on their views concerning constraints to fish farming and encouraged to use a 'problem-solving' approach to addressing those constraints. He intended that through sharing ideas, mutually advantageous solutions could be reached. For the fish scouts this approach was incomprehensible. Notions of group decision making and problem solving were alien in the hierarchical context with which they were familiar and with which the project was closely associated. For them the paradox was that the request for their opinions took place at the same time as reminders of very clearly defined boundaries of expression as 'inferiors' in relation to their 'superiors'. It was repeatedly stressed (by their departmental superiors) that fish scouts are not involved in planning, that their job was simply the collection of data and teaching farmers. The scouts themselves were therefore understandably unwilling to venture opinions on possibilities for improved aquaculture development other than those relating to the provision of items of equipment.

Clearly, aspirations towards participation, however genuine, take place in preformed relations of power and hierarchy. Thus, participation of both fish scouts and farmers was superficial at best. In the evaluation of the pilot project, the energy of the APO was applauded. The list of his activities was impressive. However, it was also suggested that the pilot project had moved away from what it should have been, 'methodology development', and thus might have created demands which could not be met. The APO had acted reasonably given the situation he had to live with. This did not, however, tie in with objectives elsewhere in the project (his seniors in Harare). They, in turn, were not in a position to dispute the Rome-derived pressure for 'results'.

Beyond 'us and them'

In Rome, the Luapula project was viewed in terms of figures, outputs and reports. Budgets were spent as planned, there were some tangible outputs in the form of training manuals. It was conceded that nothing dramatic had happened with fish farming practices.

However, in Luapula, there was much more to the project than this: complicated and negotiated personal relationships between people in different, but not fixed, positions of power. Although all of the individuals described had seen themselves as being part of the project of development, there were many other aspects of their identity which were, at different times, also of greater importance: Zambian, Danish, black, white, older, younger, rich, poor, knowledgeable, ignorant, male, female. The fish scouts' relationship with the APO combined grudging respect for his hard work, occasionally a sense of alliance against both his bosses in Harare and 'the irrationality of farmers', and resentment when they thought he was bullying them. In turn he was frustrated by what he saw as subservience and delighted whenever, once in a while, he felt they were working as a 'team'. The Big Fish and his subordinates were joined in their antagonism towards certain aspects of the FAO project, but separated by their relative status and local respectability. Both the Big Fish and the APO were proud of their position as Rotarians in Mansa.

As I noted in the introduction, there is a growing literature which takes exception to writings that portray 'local people' as passive, powerless, subjugated, and repressed. They argue that in different ways, people resist their dominators and that the 'powerful' are not always in complete control. However, a focus on 'local' (meaning villagers/farmers) diverts attention from dynamic agency at other levels and in other spheres. Benhabib (1995) discusses this in relation to the work of Richard Rorty, who also makes continual references to 'us' and 'them' as if such terms were simple and uncontested. She points out that the lines between us and them do not necessarily correspond to the lines between one culture and another; 'I think where "we" are today globally is a situation in which every "we" discovers it is in part a "they", that the lines between "us" and "them" are continuously redefined through the global realities of immigration, travel, communication, the world economy, and ecological disasters' (Benhabib 1995: 244).

Benhabib suggests that rather than looking at such relationships in terms of discrete cultures, we might call them 'communities of conversation'. These communities have shifting identities and no discrete boundaries. They do not necessarily coincide with ethnic boundaries; 'we are all participants in different communities of conversation as constituted by the intersecting axes of our different interests, projects, and life situations' (1995: 247). This concept may be a useful way of addressing the permeable relationship between us and them. It reinforces the notion that people in very diverse settings do in fact speak the same language. It also leaves space to acknowledge that another necessary part of this is the exclusion of certain groups.

Thus in Zambia, the expatriate project workers, the Big Fish, the fish scouts, the farmers with whom they all worked, and those they never met, acted within the limits of their particular manoeuvring spaces. Nonetheless, there were also differences in material status which directly influenced their room for manoeuvre. The absent farmers – the ones the project never met – might have been silent for many reasons. Those who made themselves visible had at least some advantages: physical strength, or education, or money. The fish scout had symbolic status above some farmers, but lacked the material resources to back it up. The Big Fish might have done his best in the circumstances, but he could not make a phone call and get the next plane out. The expatriate worker might have been able to do that, but he couldn't be sure of another job in the organisation.

In much analysis of development, the greatest anti-heroes are the developers themselves, as if they were part of a conspiracy. But this assessment is too simple; a more measured critique is warranted. The development 'machine' is comprised of a number of parts which are clearly capable of independent action – and whose identities are themselves not fixed, but to some extent adaptable to circumstance. This is a recurring theme in some studies of development. Porter *et al.* (1991) argue against the idea that development is something that is done by us to them because of competing and sometimes conflicting objectives among us. In their case of a resettlement project in Kenya, there were different objectives ascendant at different times within the donor agency itself. The gulf between these objectives and those of the host government was even greater. Tim Morris tells a similar story for a primary health-care project in Yemen, where 'none of the other players in our aid game … shared our vision' (1993: 208).

Complexity or 'post-modern hesitation'?

In the project described above, although there was a misunderstanding about the institutional 'partners', the effects of the intervention were not too serious for anybody. However, in more critical situations of subordination or injustice, decisions about how and whether to intervene become more difficult. This gives rise to the ethical problem alluded to in the introduction: how and whether to avoid essentialism.

Charges of essentialism have been levelled against various attempts to give content to the meaning and aims of the project of development, particularly when these imply policy and intervention. A wide range of post-modernist thinkers have taken exception to universalising generalisations which apparently put the value and meaning systems of the West to the fore – to the detriment of those who are silenced or unheard. For example, much early work in the field of gender and development has been substantially criticised for its tendency to generalise about the needs and interests of all women from the perspective of a privileged few (Mohanty 1988; Marchand and Parpart 1995; Spivak 1985). This is what Putnam (1995) has called 'substitutionalism' – subsuming all women under the category to which the writers themselves belong. Feminists and non-feminists from diverse parts of the globe point to the essentialism of referring to 'women' as if this were an unproblematic category, not cross-cut with differences of race, class, age, and sexuality.

Similarly, Eva Sylvester (1995) stresses the unsettled, unfixed, and negotiated nature of gender identity in Zimbabwe. She argues that it is sensible to view Zimbabwean women as 'women', 'that is, as bearers of an unsettled, unfixed, and indeterminate subject status that the people thus labelled may or may not embrace' (Sylvester 1995: 185). She argues that we should problematise this category of meaning, not taking it as given, especially in the context of competing and conflicting messages. While the device of sitting back critically, even from such an apparently straightforward category such as woman, succeeds in drawing attention to the fact that meanings vary, the refusal to accept any one meaning has worrying implications. In a sense, what it does is to deny the concrete conditions under which women clearly *are* women, and have shared experiences of both material and symbolic subordination, in access to resources, to land, to control over their own bodies, and so on. Interestingly, Sylvester is drawn back to this herself towards the end of the piece, when she asks 'where's the truth?', and answers 'no one questions gender as a meaningful identity: there are men and there are women and everyone knows who is who' (1995: 201).

There is a tension within Sylvester's argument which is reflected more widely in current thinking about development. Raiser (1997) characterises this as, on the one hand, the worrying implications of post-modernism for a global analysis of the causes of poverty versus the danger of reducing diverging contextual experiences to one set of causal explanations. Over-generalised dichotomies such as that between 'us', the developers, and 'them' on the receiving end, are inaccurate and misleading. On the other hand, does a concern to avoid essentialism lead us into a post-modern maze in which we are unable to say – or do – anything? A stress on difference, especially when focused on meanings and representations rather than materialism, can be the beginning of a slide into relativism which many find morally repugnant. For example, Benhabib has argued that the methodological sophistication of many recent writers, 'their contextualist scruples and post-modern hesitations' (1995: 236), run into a variety of cultural relativism which can be both callous and indifferent to human suffering and injustice. This is a point echoed by Jackson (1997), who is also concerned by an apparent trend away from the acceptability of saying anything substantive about inequality or injustice. Martha Nussbaum puts the point strongly when she argues that 'Under the banner of the fashionable opposition to essentialism march ancient religious taboos, the luxury of the pampered husband, educational deprivation, unequal health care and premature death' (1995: 66).

Within anthropology a distinction between development anthropologists and anthropologists of development has gained currency (Grillo and Rew 1985; Escobar 1991). Development anthropologists are supposedly on the inside; they work for and with development organisations, often critically, but not necessarily questioning the project of development itself. For development organisations they perform a role as cultural translators. Anthropologists of development distinguish themselves from this potentially complicit involvement, making development itself the subject of examination and the focus of criticism. This neat distinction between development anthropology and the anthropology of development is, like most other simple dichotomies, both problematic and illustrative of a wish among those who use it to take a moral high ground. In particular, self-conscious identification with the anthropology of development implies a detachment from the morally compromised object of enquiry. Such detachment is both theoretically and empirically implausible. However, it is lent credibility by a stress on discourse as texts and representations rather than analysis of crude materialism.

However, as Jackson points out, the post-modernist stress on discourse, particularly on words, narratives, and texts, is often worryingly silent on material conditions, particularly with regard to poverty: 'the shift from materialism is a feature of postist understandings of poverty, where culture, ideas, and symbols are discursively interesting and constitutive of power, whilst materiality is of questionable status and at least suspect' (1997: 147). Even Escobar, who pays great attention to the monolithic power of the 'West', does not give a substantive account of how this relates to material conditions and outcomes.

To say anything substantive about injustice, one must (rather obviously) be working with a concept of justice. This entails a measure of universalism, and a willingness to step off the fence and say that a practice or state of affairs is morally right or wrong – not just in a particular context. Ethical considerations which have been taxing philosophers since at least Aristotle are only beginning to receive specific explicit theoretical attention in development studies. This in turn is partially in response to the challenges posed by the relativism of post-modernism. The work of Nussbaum and Sen (1993) and Nussbaum and Glover (1995) has been particularly important in presenting a sustained defence of some forms of universalism, mainly developed from Sen's work on capabilities.

Glover argues that 'It is not readers of books on anthropology who pay the price for this cultural variety. It is paid in the Third World by women and children who have too little too eat. The anthropological case pulls one way but concern with misery and oppression pulls the other' (Glover 1995: 126). The relativist response would be that it is impossible to have a universal account of justice independent of the shared understandings of a particular society or community, therefore external criticism or intervention is not justified. There is an inconsistency in arguing that all morality is relative at the same time as making an absolute moral prohibition on intervention in other societies. Nevertheless, despite this inconsistency, there are also significant problems in effectively deciding that particular people are victims of false consciousness – that they do not recognise what their real interests are. As Steven Lukes (1974) and others have argued, one aspect of the exercise of power can be, through institutionalised practices, to obscure people's interests. Few anthropologists are relativists in the extreme sense implied by Glover. Therefore, alertness to the way that institutions underlie power relations, combined with a flexible approach to the formation of interests, might enable the case for a degree of universalism and the need for contextualisation to pull in the same direction.

Note

1   This article is based on a book co-authored with Emma Crewe entitled *Whose Development? An Ethnography of Aid* (Zed Books, 1998). A number of aspects of the introductory discussion should therefore be jointly attributed to Emma and myself.

References

Arce, A. and N. Long (1993) 'Bridging two worlds: an ethnography of bureaucratic-peasant relations in Western Mexico', in M. Hobart (ed.) *An Anthropological Critique of Development: the Growth of Ignorance*, London: Routledge.

Benhabib, S. (1995) 'Cultural complexity, moral independence, and the global dialogical community', in M. Nussbaum and J. Glover (eds) *Women, Culture and Development: a Study of Human Capabilities*, Oxford: Oxford University Press.

Cornwall, A., I. Guijt and A. Welbourn (1994) 'Acknowledging process: challenges for agricultural research and extension methodology', in I. Scoones and M. Thomson (eds) *Beyond Farmer First*, London: IT Publications.

Crehan, K. and A. Von Oppong (1988) 'Understandings of development: an arena of struggle', *Sociologia Ruralis* XXVIII.

Escobar, A. (1991) 'Anthropology and the development encounter: the making and marketing of development anthropology', *American Ethnologist* 18: 658–682.

—— (1995a) *Encountering Development: the Making and Unmaking of the Third World*, Princeton: Princeton University Press.

—— (1995b) 'Imagining a post development era', in J. Crush (ed.) *Power of Development*, London: Routledge.

Ferguson, J. (1990) *The Anti-politics Machine: Development, Depoliticization and Bureaucratic Power in Lesotho*, Cambridge: Cambridge University Press.

Glover, J. (1995) 'The research programme of development ethics', in M. Nussbaum and J. Glover (eds) *Women, Culture and Development: a Study of Human Capabilities*, Oxford: Oxford University Press.

Grillo, R. (1997) 'Discourses of development: the view from anthropology', in R. Grillo and R. Stirrat (eds) *Discourses of Development*, Oxford: Berg.

Grillo, R. and A. Rew (eds) (1985) *Social Anthropology and Development Policy*, ASA Monographs No. 23, London: Tavistock Publications.

Hedlund, H. (1984) 'Development in action: the experience of the Zambian extension worker', *Ethnos* 49.

Hobart, M. (ed.) (1993) *An Anthropological Critique of Development: the Growth of Ignorance*, London: Routledge.

Jackson, C. (1997) 'Post poverty, gender and development', *IDS Bulletin* 28 (3).

Lukes, S. (1974) *Power: a Radical View*, London: Macmillan.

Marchand, M. and J. Parpart (1995) *Feminism/Postmodernism/Development*, London: Routledge.

Mohanty, C. (1988) 'Under western eyes: feminist scholarship and colonial discourses', *Feminist Review* 30: 61–68.

Morris, T. (1993) 'Eze-Vu – success through evaluation: lessons from a primary health care project in North Yemen', in J. Pottier (ed.) *Practising Development: Social Science Perspectives*, London: Routledge.

Nussbaum, M. (1995) 'Human capabilities, female human beings', in M. Nussbaum and J. Glover (eds) *Women, Culture and Development: a Study of Human Capabilities*, Oxford: Oxford University Press.

Nussbaum, M. and J. Glover (eds) (1995) *Women, Culture and Development: a Study of Human Capabilities*, Oxford: Oxford University Press.

Nussbaum, M. and A. Sen (1993) *The Quality of Life*, Oxford: Oxford University Press.

Ortner, S. (1995) 'Resistance and the problem of ethnographic refusal', *Comparative Studies in Society and History* 37.

Porter, D., B. Allen and G. Thompson (1991) *Development in Practice: Paved With Good Intentions*, London: Routledge.

Putnam, R. (1995) 'Why not a feminist theory of justice?', in M. Nussbaum and J. Glover (eds) *Women, Culture and Development: a Study of Human Capabilities*, Oxford: Oxford University Press.

Raiser, M. (1997) 'Destruction, diversity, dialogue: notes on the ethics of development', *Journal of International Development* 9 (1).

Richards, P. (1993) 'Cultivation: knowledge or performance?', in M. Hobart (ed.) *An Anthropological Critique of Development: the Growth of Ignorance*, London: Routledge.

Spivak, G. (1985) 'Can the subaltern speak? Speculation on widow sacrifice', *Wedge* 7/8.

Sylvester, E. (1995) 'Women in rural producer groups and the diverse politics of truth in Zimbabwe', in M. Marchand and J. Parpart (eds) *Feminism/Postmodernism/Development*, London: Routledge.

Villareal, M. (1992) 'The poverty of practice: power, gender and intervention from an actor oriented perspective', in N. Long and A. Long (eds) *Battlefields of Knowledge: the Interlocking of Theory and Practice in Social Research and Development*, London: Routledge.

Chapter 5

Tapping the bell at governance temple

Project implementation in Sarawak as moral narrative

Alan Rew

> Concepts are not jargon and the conceptual roots of development are not the jargon of development. Jargon, as Theodor Adorno makes clear, arises when the conceptual basis of phenomena is eclipsed by treating phenomena as the administrative matter and means of policy. The jargon of development, therefore, makes 'development' serve as the administrative means of policy.
>
> (Cowen and Shenton 1996: x)

Introduction

In February 2001, I stayed in Bombay for some days in a small guesthouse beside a Jain temple. Unlike Hindu temples, with their prominent shikhar spires, the Jain temple looked from the outside more or less like an ordinary house (see Laidlaw 1995: 96). Throughout the day visitors came to it. I was struck by the fact that, as they ascended the temple steps, they all paused to tap a bell hanging at the entrance. The visitors appeared both various and independent. But they also seemed to reflect some single purpose as they moved in similar ways to mount the steps, tap the bell and enter.

The sound of the bell was gentle and not discordant; but it was insistent. So I asked friends living nearby why the bell was sounded so regularly; I found I had hit on a topic of considerable curiosity and some amusement. One simple explanation was the bell announced to God that you had reached the temple, like any visitor wishing entrance to a house. Another more detailed explanation was that it woke up Vishnu who was asleep on the Sheshag (snake). A third was that the bell vibrations stimulated the *yoga* (meditative breathing) or *dhyana* (concentration) of worshippers in the temple. There had been childhood jokes about 'god sleeping on the job'. There was a central tendency in the explanations but the answers were essentially open to the views of each respondent.[1]

There is certainly the pervading presence of the power or numen within the temple and the specific public behaviours of the worshippers as they come to its threshold. Seen from the outside, the temple is a black box.

The worshippers come to the threshold and provide a sign of their arrival; but the only way of understanding the operations of the box is to follow the worshippers as they cross the threshold and then to listen, watch and ask questions (when these are permissible/appropriate). The bell tapping announces arrivals at the box's boundary and so helps define its importance and shape – but without indicating much of the mission or vision within. Nor can one guess at what is going on from the departures. The periods of arrival and sojourn do not lead to any single discernible outcome. Knowledge about the outcomes of the visits can only be obtained through access to the stated satisfaction of the participants; there is no other independent means of establishing what has happened.

Empirically we see the low foundations of adherence to a distinctive system. Making the sign of the cross on the forehead with holy water by visitors to a Catholic church is comparable. Vaclav Havel's exemplar of the low foundations of power in the post-totalitarian regimes of Eastern Europe is the 'Workers of the World Unite' sign in a greengrocer's shop window (Havel 1992).

This image of an ordinary house on an ordinary street in Bombay with well-announced arrivals at the entrance and, according to a variety of narratives, a powerful presence within, sets the scene for a different set of arrivals at a different 'black box' – that of international development projects. A project is in many ways a house of government set aside for concentrated powers, and a set of arrivals by officials and clients at the threshold of the government machinery. There may be a need for some additional inputs in the form of international consultancy and donor funds. There may be special conditions and costing and budgeting procedures; there may be a need for the recruitment of dedicated project staff. But in most other ways 'the project' only assembles and concentrates departments and units of government that usually have similar remits in government's more quotidian presence. Through concentration in projects, government servants announce their willingness to tackle the challenges of integration of services and interventions and to achieve more streamlined or 'joined-up' efforts. The bell, so to speak, is being tapped; but what are the outcomes and what goes on inside?

To deliver development interventions efficient implementation is essential. This means chains of resources, procurement, supply and construction, and purposive and clearly structured management systems. Yet there are frequent problems – communication and implementation breakdowns, a general untidiness, corruption and maladministration (cf. Guhan and Paul 1997; Crawford et al. 2000). When these failures become endemic they are often identified as 'poor political will'. There must be some set of superior decision makers, a policy and governmental elite, it is argued, who could order implementation if they really wanted it to succeed. Grindle (1980: 15) argues that this is mainly a developing country problem as the representation of interests and the resolution of conflict occurs at the output (project) stage rather than the input (policy) stage.

The problem is more generic than Grindle proposes. Implementation arrangements are, everywhere, full of power, moral frames, disorder and ambiguity. Administrators make operational decisions about services and allocations to people that have major consequences for social equity and for people's moral and physical well-being. The detailed outcomes of the policy implementation chain can be uncertain, ambiguous or flawed in both northern and southern countries (see, for example, Rew and Batley 1977).

'Messiness' in implementation is greatly aided by the almost universal split between 'policy' and 'operational' spheres. In the policy sphere, the focus is on abstract 'knowledge about' issues and the distribution of power among governmental units. The unresponsiveness in practice of public bureaucracies to new policy initiatives is often because of a failure to connect the large canvas of policy aims to the small brush-strokes made by the coping mechanisms of junior implementing staff. These junior staff may have concrete 'knowledge of' the ground realities but often lack the support of any pre-planned match between their tasks and their skills or numbers. When, as it must, responsibility shifts to the operational sphere, there is usually little in the way of useful guidance for the operations staff in how to manage the policy initiatives. Major status and rank divisions underlying recruitment to civil service grades in southern countries compounds and confirms this division.

Case study

Introduction

For some years now I have been using a case study of aid-assisted hydro-power and area development in Sarawak in postgraduate teaching.[2] I have done so because the project illustrates very neatly the difficulty of ensuring adequate co-ordination between institutional stakeholders and the incommensurate and moral basis of the planning of displacement projects. The welfare of indigenous people was seriously compromised despite the exercise of much 'political will' to try to ensure that the project would be successful; and without any set of senior, middle or junior ranking institutional stakeholders really understanding why. It ended up 'messy' and beyond simple rational explanation despite integrated planning.

Project shape and justification

The case study concerns a hydro-power project of the early 1980s on the Batang Ai River in the state of Sarawak. In the context of Malaysia's push towards industrialisation and away from over-reliance on primary commodity exports, a major constraint was power. In Sarawak, power was provided from oil-fired stations. This was environmentally polluting and expensive as all oil had to be imported. The final impetus for the project was the sharp rise in the price of oil in the 1970s. Kuching, the capital city of Sarawak, was constrained in its industrial potential because of high power costs. Possible hydro-power sites were sought. From an engineering and project economics point of view, a site on the Batang Ai River was selected as a high priority for hydro-power development.

The site also had other features that recommended it for development planners' attention. The site was in the Iban population heartlands and, over time, population increases had led to environmental pressures. Hill-rice swidden cultivation was practised on plots established on the forest margins. Productivity and environmental stability depended on a longish fallow period (perhaps thirty to forty years). Population concentration in the lower reaches of the watershed towards the dam site had led to fallow lengths, however, of only ten years or less.

The site was also relatively close to Kuching and expectations of employment and social services were high. The government of Sarawak felt that it should try to provide health and school services at a new town near the dam site, and families dispersed around the watershed should be persuaded to move into it in order to take advantage of key services. The production of cheap electricity might also allow the development of light rural industries there. A reservoir would also allow the development of commercial fisheries.

The reservoir bed and a surrounding safety zone needed to be free of all human settlement and this would mean displacement of some Iban long-houses. The number of displaced persons (DPs) was low – less than 1,000 – by the usual standards of development-induced displacement in Asia. On the other hand, resettlement offered the chance to develop new high-value settled tree-crop agriculture to provide income for the displaced communities. The purchase of a major area of cultivated land from landholders in the host area below the dam wall was needed to allow the planned development of both the new town and high-yielding hybrid tree-crop plantations of cacao and rubber.

Government consulted widely among the state politicians and local leaders. It appointed a High Level Committee chaired by the Chief Minister. The dam was built. It was well within cost – 20 per cent below appraisal estimates – and six months ahead of schedule. The dam structure and the power sets were well designed and well constructed. Land for the new town and for the tree-crop plantations was acquired. Construction of the new town was well advanced with new schools and shops, a clinic, and a residential settlement of 120 houses newly built to high architectural standards and seeking to blend modern materials and traditional Iban features. The project was designed to meet high international and national standards.

Problems and dissatisfaction with the results

A number of worrying allegations began to surface in the two years following the completion of construction. The immediate reason for the evaluation mission I joined was a campaign of protest made by regional NGOs. Letters from NGOs received by the donor and the governments alleged many negative environmental and social impacts, including reports of the extreme dissatisfaction of the Iban people displaced by the reservoir and other works. The tone of many of those reports was shrill and about 'environmental and tribal society rape'. A post-completion mission of myself, an environmentalist, an accountant and an engineer was sent to investigate the complaints.

Indicators of dissatisfaction about the project were not hard to find when we arrived on site. The reservoir and the hydro-power works both looked impressive and were likely to realise the engineers' and national planners' fondest hopes. Discontent among the resettled Iban was, however, pervasive.

One indication of this discontent was that in 60 per cent of cases, people were refusing to sign the mortgage papers for the new houses. The reasons given were mixed. Significant amounts of compensation money had been spent on previous debts and various transport and other projects, and the mortgage and utility bills for the houses coming slightly later were a major shock. It was argued, in some cases, that the houses were sub-standard for the amount of money the authorities expected the displaced Iban to pay. There was deep unease about the need to pay for any services that had previously been costless, together with a strong sense from some households interviewed of being cheated.

Hybrid tree-crop plantings in the new agricultural areas were well behind schedule. In fact only 50 per cent of the horticultural planting targets had been reached by the time the displaced long-house communities took up their new residences. The people displaced were also extremely uneasy about the lack of land available on which to plant rice, both immediately and in the future. The small business and fishing projects promised at the time of the original consultations had also not been started. There were increasing worries about immediate and long-term food security as it became clear that compensation money would not last for ever and that alternative business and income-generating projects were not materialising at the necessary speed. One indicator of the need for new, more intensive, economic activities to be initiated was that average total landholding sizes had, for the project-affected persons (PAP), shrunk from nearly 5 hectares per household before inundation to just less than 1 ha. per household after inundation.

Another problem lay in the visible restriction of opportunities for newly established and shortly-to-be established households. One hundred and twenty new houses had been built for those physically displaced by the creation of the reservoir. This was only two more houses than the number of households established as in need of re-housing when the project area was surveyed at an advanced stage of planning. As often happens, however, awareness that land is being lost and a new town developed had led younger people to bring forward their marriages and to establish new households. This led to some limited demand for extra houses in the town which could not be met. Far more difficult to manage was that it led to an unexpectedly heavy extra demand, of around 40 per cent, for agricultural plots because of Iban expectations that every adult male required a cultivable plot. Some of this demand was met through emergency subdivisions in the newly laid out agricultural area below the dam wall; but a sizeable element of the demand remained unmet and this was a cause of concern in the community.

Many complaints about compensation surfaced in the discussions. Compensation payment in total and per person was in fact high by international standards. The donor had played an active role in trying to ensure that levels were relatively generous and had achieved this aim. The rates agreed were being paid, to the great majority of DPs, in full and promptly, as far as we could discover. Nonetheless, a number of compensation claims were still unresolved, and all agreed they were likely to remain so for an indefinite time, and these unresolved claims aroused considerable passion.

General explanations of the difficulties

The level of discontent and demoralisation in the resettlement component was very high, had fuelled international protests, and was fully apparent to all visitors and consultants. Inevitably, many participants sought a single cause for this demoralisation. One possible explanation (not actually made much of by any of the institutional participants and subsequent academic commentators, although mentioned from time to time) was that demoralisation must be the inevitable outcome of the trauma of loss of home and familiar settings and would diminish over the years (Scudder 1993). A related but more frequently stated slant on the inevitability issue was the notion that some demoralisation is unavoidable with development-induced displacement and resettlement. Displacement of human communities is regrettable but is essentially a utilitarian question for the nation and the state of Sarawak. Some hundreds of people would be displaced from increasingly less sustainable and hard-to-service riverine environments while infrastructure improvements, employment and social services would be created for tens of thousands in both the rural and urban areas. The new development included the DPs but they should not be thought of as especially privileged. Radically opposed to this view is that riverine development through large dams is a form of desecration (McCully 1996).

Other *portmanteau* explanations included the unequal political/economic power of the Iban compared to non-Iban ethnic interests in the state; and the determination of the non-Iban elements to create a modern urban economy and society. The implication is that the operational and implementation details of any specific hydro-power project are largely irrelevant to this macro context (King and Jawan 1996).

Professional explanations

The way to understand the dynamics and ultimately un-coordinated character of the project is through the perspectives of the different institutional actors and interests. First, there were those institutional actors who saw their operational work as essentially unproblematic. The complete project was something of a black box into which they were asked to contribute specialist professional services. On the whole they did not need to ask very much more than that they had carried out their orders adequately and, hopefully, even with distinction.

The hydro-power engineers, for example, were very proud of the design and construction achievements and of the quality of the civil and mechanical engineering. They were disappointed that this otherwise excellent project had become contaminated by NGO complaints about 'environmental and social rape'. The accountants and project finance specialists were surprised at the high amounts of compensation paid and the efficiency with which these had been paid. There were a few outstanding compensation cases but these had been created by delays in getting land survey calculations agreed not because of delays in financial work. They were not responsible for land problems. Indeed, the accountants found it extremely difficult to understand why people were complaining given the high payments already made.

Environmental assessments by the evaluation mission agreed with the appraisal report. Hydro-power had effectively replaced polluting hydrocarbon burning. The area now forming the reservoir bed had been degrading in terms of its swidden agriculture purposes. Accusations about the 'rape of the tribals' was hyperbole; these Iban were not wild isolated people but residents of a long-settled heartland district and with a tradition of long-distance overseas labour migration.

The PWD engineers could not see any problems with the project, either. There was a new town with 'vernacular' style housing and excellent social services. The dam would bring commercial fishing employment and the power would bring start-up businesses.

The initial social appraisal was not shockingly inadequate by the standards of the period (see Rew 1997) but it was, perhaps deliberately, amateur and understated. An ex-colonial administrator, who had lived in the area for many years, had carried it out. He was acknowledged as an authority on local customs, and well liked by all local residents. The report adds little to our knowledge of the difficulties the people would face but does report the presence of a groundswell of support for the project. Subsequently, with encouragement from the donor, sociologists from the state's university were appointed to a sociological unit within the electricity authority. They had sufficient resources to deal with the displaced and host communities. They agreed that the compensation money paid was high and was seen to be so. One major cause for discontent, they suggested, could be the large differences in compensation paid to individuals reflecting wide variations in the wealth of tree plantings on native land. The compensation had served to publicise wide differences in wealth in what was a fiercely egalitarian society (cf. Freeman 1970).

In parallel to the initial social appraisal, district politicians and local community leaders consulted widely with the long-house communities in what was reported as a relaxed informal style. They had reported, emphatically, that the project had local support. The state government felt it had learned the lessons of other poorly implemented schemes elsewhere and so insisted that the quality of initial project planning was high and that all aspects should be covered in a comprehensive manner. It also instituted an active, high-level committee chaired by the Chief Minister to supervise implementation.

All of the above categories of institutional stakeholder did exactly what was expected of them, and so they were surprised, disappointed, and not a little aggrieved, that this supposedly prestige project was now attracting adverse publicity.

There were those for whom it was a little more problematic, but not radically so. They were doing their job well enough but did recognise that they had encountered some constraints that, in an ideal world, would have been better not there. The extent to which they did their jobs with pride and confidence in part depended on their empathy for the long-house residents of that area and their closeness to them in cultural terms.

The planners/economists within the electricity supply authority, for example, were convinced that the income of displaced persons (DPs) would improve as a result of the project. There were the considerable short-term wages from project construction and then there would be hybrid tree-cropping and employment or commercial opportunities in the fishery and the new industrial and other start-up units. The town would grow in time and create more jobs. Moreover the Iban's existing hill-rice cropping gave very poor returns. Although recognising that rice was their main food, they pointed out that upland rice in Sarawak yielded scant harvests. The Iban would be better off gaining income from tree crops and other activities and, with the proceeds, buying imported rice from the local stores.

The development of the tree-crop plantations depended on the work of the agricultural unit. A supply of appropriate nursery stock was obtained but the unit ran into an unexpected snag concerning labour for planting. As a unit of state government the agricultural unit was obliged to pay prevailing wage rates. It found itself competing, and not very favourably, with the civil engineering works at the dam site and in the town for the little labour that was available. Targets for planting were therefore not met. Moreover, in the semi-cleared ground left as a result of plantation clearance, the existing and soon to be displaced communities were firing the under-growth and planting rice – and as a consequence burning some of the newly planted cacao and rubber stock. This led to conflicts that further delayed planting and further antagonised the resettled communities.

The government officials with the best sense of the problems besetting project implementation were the land surveyors. The surveyors had recog-nised, very early in the planning stage, that discussions with anxious rural residents would take time, even if local people had been convinced by their leaders and by politicians, and so asked for more staff and a longer time-scale for implementation. The state government dismissed this request. The lands department was criticised for being insufficiently energetic and posi-tive about the project. Events proved the surveyors right. The long-house residents wanted every detail of their existing houses, land and trees recorded in order to gain the highest available compensation. Often surveyors had to re-visit and then re-re-visit a community or individual to achieve an agreed assessment. Finally, completion of dam construction six months earlier than expected meant that the reservoir began to fill when land surveying work was still under way, burying the evidence for some unresolved compensation claims under water.

Results of weak institutional and social appraisal

The survey of institutional stakeholders suggests that there were no obvious grossly offending departments or categories in the project process unless, that is, the unravelling process at community level could be found to lie in one or other of a number of apparently minor administrative problems. These might include the denial by government of the survey department's request for more staff, the inexperience of the agricultural planting unit, or the relatively minor but cumulatively significant demographic mistakes of the planners.

My own evaluation at the time was that three more pervasive, but still preventable, factors had created the severe discontent among the Iban. First, there was a major imbalance between the hydro-power and area develop-ment components. The international, largely Australian, consulting engineers in charge of dam design and supervising construction had worked in isolation from those government officials, often Iban and sometimes Malaysian Chinese, charged with implementing the area development component. The foreign engineers should not have been allowed to work with such enthusiasm and energy that the dam was finished six months ahead of schedule, thus jeopardising the work of the land surveyors and rushing the relocation process. The engineers should also have liaised with the agricultural department because it also needed the labour being drained away by dam construction. The project needed success in both the hydro-power and area development components to be judged fully successful. It achieved an 'outstanding' grade in the hydro component; but this achievement prevented the area development teams from achieving even an adequate performance.

The second major factor creating the subsequent problems was the amateur nature of the social appraisal. Although most likely well intentioned in the interests of 'obtaining' the project, the failure to show how existing social and economic activities and relationships would match or fail to match the design of the project led to difficulties for the Iban. More cultivable plots and houses for DPs could have been made available if demographic and social response issues had been properly appraised. The failure to spot the gap between the assumptions of planning economists about rice cultivation and actual Iban agricultural practices was serious. The DPs were not interested in continuing to cultivate upland rice for food security purposes alone. Iban religion stresses the link between the maintenance of each rice seed's breeding lineage through planting and the continuity of human social forms through each Iban lineage. At a time of displacement and threat to Iban society, planting rice in the areas planned for tree crops was a sign of salience for what was essential to Iban living. This aspect was completely ignored by the power economists, all of them Chinese and with urban backgrounds.

The third factor was the lack of detailed administrative planning to support implementation. The project planners thought it sufficient that there was high-level co-ordination within government and that the work was given high priority. In fact, the high-level decision makers were largely indifferent, and even became impatient, at the administrative detail at the heart of the operational sphere. This is less a specific deficiency in this one project case than a general tendency in implementation. There is complicity in a mutually reinforcing process of policy 'evaporation' and policy 'subversion'. There can be, that is, both an implementation deficit seen from the perspective of the top policy makers, and a policy deficit seen from junior staff's need for clear guidelines. As policy gets implemented, those in middle and junior levels successively subvert the broad policy goals through a combination of discretionary decision making and inertia. There is often a parallel failure of policy makers to set absolutely clear policy goals that can be implemented in the face of resource constraints, the well-known compartmentalism of government units, and the legacy of existing, often contradictory, policies and civil society commitments.

Some deeper conclusions

In his deep ecology critique, McCully (1996) refers to large dams, without further explanation, as 'temples of doom'. The view taken in this chapter is that it is the moral and practical consequences of governance around major projects that constitute the temple, not the construction works. Projects are special houses of governance, set aside as 'sacred' and requiring an understanding of the signs of adherence on the part of the visitors and of the power and numen within revealed by development narratives and visions. The many detailed activities of routine government and special project operations all 'tap the bell' to announce their presence at the entrance to government power and to arouse the vision – which is always there but may have been sleeping at that point, always in this spot, or for these people.

In part, changes to hydro-power and area development governance can be handled through specific reformist improvements. Engineers should adjust their construction timetables to fit in with agricultural planting and resettlement schedules; top government officials and ministers should commit themselves to detailed administrative planning before implementation starts; and donors should insist on top quality professional social appraisal and see it supplied. This was my original view of the research need: a series of applied recommendations about administrative duties and enhanced awareness of social dynamics based on detailed field evidence. Increasingly, however, as I have analysed the case study with groups of postgraduate students, I have felt that something is missing in this account of management and planning.

Societal context

That missing element includes the macro-social and moral context. Langton (1992: 293) has reminded us, in his review of an exchange of correspondence between Immanuel Kant and Maria von Herbert, that supposedly absolute moral duties can look much more open-ended and contingent when seen in the context of the gender relations of the late eighteenth century. One macro-social context of particular importance in this case is the character of the interaction between officials and communities. The consultations held by politicians and local leaders with the long-house communities to be displaced were relatively informal. The aim was to convince people to move, not to conduct a survey or keep written records. One cause of discontent subsequent to resettlement was that, because of this informality, the resettled people thought they had been promised free modern services in the new town while the leaders conducting the meetings denied this. No records had been kept and so the disputes could not be resolved.

The high political priority in the state was to implement the 20/20 vision of an industrialised Malaysia with an efficient, hierarchically controlled, and responsive, civil service. Ong has described the priority as 'stability through bureaucratic benevolence'. The art of government is to translate 'citizenship capacity into the ability to hold the state accountable in terms of the delivery of material and social goods' (Ong 1999: 54). She criticises Scott's analysis of Muslim Malay peasants in *Weapons of the Weak* (1985) as the projection of the ideal Western citizen-subject seeking rights, and as lacking an understanding of the complex ways that religion and the state shape the political subject in Malaysia.

When translated to Sarawak, the state faces Iban, not Malay, 'sons of the soil'. Its civil servants are a mixture of people of largely Iban and Chinese ethnic origin, although still shaped by the pressures of bureaucratic hierarchy and by the need to maintain 'guardianist government'. The norms of Iban social structure are, by contrast, egalitarian and focused not on hierarchy and state Islamic political traditions but on interpersonal support and exchange flowing through wide-ranging kindreds.

The dynamics of the encounter between an acephalous rural society and the complexities of state-engineered social liberalism that is simultaneously corporate, urban, overseas Chinese and Malay, are beyond the limits of this chapter and my knowledge. But these dimensions do help structure the power hierarchy and provide a difficult set of challenges for local leadership. The pressures of hierarchy require compliance and willingness to communicate orders from on high, though detailed instructions are sometimes lacking. The local leaders and politicians could not have been immune to these calls for cooperation in Malaysia's and Sarawak's futures, and tried to mediate and lead opinion in the long-house communities and also to adjust the pressures from above. The consequence was that local leaders easily became discredited as their offers to mediate failed to satisfy local hopes or to reduce disappointments as the project went ahead. One major cause of discontent among the DPs in this project was that some influential people seemed to have benefited unduly from compensation payments. This led to accusations about the quality and possible corruption of the very leadership that was needed to find a way forward after displacement. Demoralisation was the result, not any easy deployment of social provision and cultural idioms through 'pastoral power' (see Ong 1999: 57). The administrative style was not 'guardianist' or 'pastoral' but 'disjointed responsiveness-intolerant'.

It would be wrong to blame only the representative capacity of leaders, the poor social engineering techniques of officials, or even 'the vision' of an industrial modern Islamic Malaysia. The combination of hierarchical control and urban consumer pressures creates what Havel (1992: 344) has insightfully termed 'social auto-totality'. His key illustration of the system of auto-totality, and the 'low foundations' for power in post-totalitarian Eastern Europe, is a sign in a greengrocer's shop window urging 'Workers of the World Unite'. The sign is delivered to the shopkeeper, together with the onions and carrots, by the headquarters of the state enterprise. It is again re-presented by other shopkeepers in their windows, without comment, as an auto-totality that 'has to be'. If our greengrocer refused there could be trouble. Displaying the sign is 'one of the thousands of details that guarantee him a relative tranquil life, in "harmony with society" as they say'.

By pulling everyone into its power structure, the post-totalitarian system makes everyone instruments of a mutual totality, the auto-totality of society. ... Everyone is in fact involved, not only the greengrocers but also the prime ministers. Both are unfree, each merely in a somewhat different way. The real accomplice in this involvement, therefore, is not another person, but the system itself. Position in the power hierarchy determines the degree of responsibility and guilt, but it gives no one unlimited responsibility and guilt, nor does it completely absolve anyone. Thus the conflict between the aims of life and the aims of the system is not a conflict between two socially defined and separate communities ... everyone in his or her own way is both a victim and a supporter of the system. ... In highly simplified terms, it could be said that the post-totalitarian system has been built on foundations laid by the historical encounter between dictatorship and the consumer society.

(Havel 1992: 334)

Moral narratives

The result of the process was demoralisation as much as, or more than, specific policy and project management failures. The familiar riverine environment had been lost for everyday living. The absolute loss of upland rice cultivation, and therefore of key elements of Iban vitality and religion, was now fully apparent. Some families, especially younger ones, were torn between the pleasures of new entertainment systems and transport purchases and the difficulty of finding cultivable land. There was the anxiety that leadership may have been, perhaps was, compromised.

Losses of individual and group integrity were being experienced and hence the sense of anger. The inability of almost all institutional stakeholders to understand these angry reactions came from a combination of administrative compartmentalism – 'I was doing my job correctly' – and the complex utilitarian/guardianist moral narratives they told – 'their children will have better things in the town'. The impasse in the discussions and understanding was reminiscent of the debate, in *Brave New World*, between Mustapha Mond, World Regional Controller and happiness guardian, and the Savage, who wanted unhappiness as part of life (Huxley 1971).

A background to these contrasted moral narratives is formed by a combination of policy and project factors. First, there are continuing uncertainties about cultural rights in political theory (Kymlicka 1993; Green 1993; Kukathas 1993) and in the ideas about administration and governance that shape the assumptions of (Western) project planning (Mohan 1997). Second, there is the attempt in Malaysia to create distinctive state-to-citizen relations based on ethnic politics, Islamic religion and the expansion of consumer and public goods. Third, the international-aid-assisted project creates a concentrated area of governance where integration and coordination are at a premium. Why else have a project unless it is to achieve a greater focus and to channel energies into a smooth well-planned path? The project creates almost a sacred area of government in which officials can say that they are redoubling their efforts, have a special mission and special funds. In this context, the contingencies and possibilities emerging are multiple and are the project reality, not the original planning assumptions or policy imperatives (cf. Toulmin 2001).

The problems were ameliorated somewhat by the shared Iban experiences of communities with some of the officials – especially with those from the departments connected with land. The DPs were, for these Iban officials, actual people at risk rather than people 'elsewhere' as they appeared to the largely Chinese urban-based planners, or 'consumers in the future' as they appeared to the engineers, or even 'hypothetical', as they were to the donor representatives at the appraisal stage. But even those Iban operating staff on the ground dealing with real people at risk could not counter the project's lack of detailed administrative planning and compartmentalism or government's uncompromisingly utilitarian approach in policy formulation. It was expected that every officer would come to his workplace and 'tap the operational bell' while the 20/20 vision chose to wake up for some people and not others.

The answer for Havel to any systemic undermining of integrity is to understand the lie against humanity and to challenge it through personal dissent.

> In everyone there is some longing for humanity's rightful dignity, for moral integrity, for free expression of being and a sense of transcendence over the world of existences. Yet, at the same time, each person is capable, to a greater or lesser degree, of coming to terms with living within the lie. Each person somehow succumbs to a profane trivialisation of his or her inherent humanity, and to utilitarianism. In everyone there is some willingness to merge with the anonymous crowd and to flow comfortably along with it down the river of pseudo-life. ... Human beings are compelled to live within a lie, but they can be compelled to do so only because they are in fact capable of living in this way.
>
> (Havel 1992: 345)

Havel's advice to the Czechs and other subjects of authoritarian regimes was to 'live within the truth'. Gandhi gave similar answers about the independence of India:

> Real swaraj will come not by the acquisition of authority by a few, but by the acquisition of the capacity of all to resist authority when it is abused. In other words, swaraj is to be attained by educating the masses to a sense of their capacity to regulate and control authority.
>
> (*Young India*, 29 January 1925: 52, quoted in Jesudasan 1987: 106)

Development narratives and learning processes

Given the need to dissent from disjointed utilitarian solutions offered for the loss of cultural integrity, what then are the implications for development practice and anthropological research? The efforts of anthropologists of development to articulate macroscopic with microscopic analysis, economics and anthropology, are firmly noted as part of the mainstream discipline (Carrier and Miller 1999: 27). Ethical guidelines for good research practice including that by non-academic sponsors have been adopted (ASA 1999). Yet anthropologists continue perhaps to feel uneasy with concentrated power at such close quarters (cf. Redclift 1985). Compromises by the development researcher are suspected, if only through association. As activists of the Czech Velvet revolution and of the Indian independence struggle found when they gained ministerial office, despite their ideals of swaraj and 'living within the truth', governing provokes compromise (Shepherd 2000; Kothari 1997). It may be feared that some of this pitch will rub off on the applied researcher. Yet it is in the middle of implementation processes that the anthropological description of context and of learning and non-learning processes can provide reform and management analyses, and not just serve as aesthetic elaboration or a statement of pathos.

In his attempt to reclaim 'blueprint development' for serious attention in the face of the 'learning process' thinking of the time, Roe (1991) argues we should improve 'just-so' development narratives rather than reiterate process research without evident lessons in it. Unfortunately, he himself shows that most of the narratives he would use and adjust – for example, 'the tragedy of the commons' – are either false or seriously partial. Nonetheless, they require further attention because they have enabled decision makers to take action(!), are the best guides we have in sectoral planning, and so must be improved rather than discarded.

It should be remembered, however, that the narratives are not equally benign. The favourite just-so statement once used to justify population displacement in infrastructure projects was 'you can't have omelettes without breaking eggs'. Armed with this 'development narrative', many engineers and project economists helped create tragedy through indifference to cultural form and detail.

So the accuracy of any blueprint or narrative is critical or it can be used to justify even more extreme forms of the kind of unbalanced utilitarianism and disjointed planning emerging from this project. Of particular interest here is that, as Bernard Williams (1973: 342) notes, utilitarianism has a tendency to 'leave a vast hole in the range of human desires between egoistic inclinations and necessities at one end, and impersonally benevolent happiness-management at the other'. The slide to acceptance of a bi-polar split between mundane, almost always contingent, first-order human projects and the second-order project of maximally satisfying the first-order projects is typical of the 'trade-offs in utility' method. To put it another way, there is the nobility and calm of the temple-like plan; and the everyday disorder of the comings and goings needed to make it work.

Untidiness or tragedy (depending on whose view was taken) emerged despite precautions taken at the appraisal stage. The area development plan adopted was shaped following good advice on resettlement planning available from the donor community. The basic advice circulating then is now, with a few significant amendments, encapsulated in unified policy guidelines adopted by all member countries of the Organization for Economic Cooperation and Development (OECD) (Cernea 2000: 44).

There was certainly scope for improvements to the area development blueprint in this case. As a visiting 'fireman' I had spotted three weaknesses in the planning – in the social and institutional appraisals and in the imbalance between the engineering and resettlement components. It follows that one important approach to recurrent shortfalls in resettlement policy and operations has been to urge better initial planning. Michael Cernea, in a large body of publications over more than twenty years, has been pre-eminent in this strategy, seeking, often successfully, to influence the planning standards in use by governments and donors and to expand our understanding of the circumstances of displacement and resettlement. He has developed a very comprehensive 'impoverishment risks and reconstruction' (IRR) planning framework for resettling displaced populations with eight types of risk defined. The main targets in implementation are to secure the participation of DPs, make changes to existing economic methodologies, understand and reverse risks and set new international planning standards (Cernea 2000: 34).

There is a further view of priority, and it surfaces when Cernea's IRR model is applied, by Voutira and Harrell-Bond (2000: 56–72), to the rehabilitation of refugee populations. They conclude that the major obstacles to rehabilitation are 'institutional, originating in the practices of major agencies' (2000: 57) and not conceptual.

This chapter takes the view that, ultimately, both planning and institutional approaches are needed. I give priority to the institutional and moral context partly because it has received far less attention in the literature to date. Moreover, it is through their understanding of context that official participants in the operational sphere experience career risks and policy-to-operations resettlement processes. For example, donors and governments now provide training in up-to-date resettlement planning methodologies. But the 'trainees' often see their time in resettlement as a punishment posting (Rew *et al.* 2000) and may have little commitment to implementation. So a first priority for reform is not so much the planning content of training as the quality and recruitment of the trainees. They should, moreover, be selected on the basis of their high personal tolerance for ambiguity; and their general ability to deal with parts of complex processes in teams, and with any results as provisional.

Similarly, the practical recommendations of the case study are less the potentially universal generalisations concerning displacement risk, cost–benefit balance or inter-departmental collaboration, etc., but the practical importance of organisational development and learning process approaches to policy implementation (Mosse *et al.* 1998). Integration should have been actively sought, not assumed through planning. Operational administration was essentially political and what was needed was explicit recognition of this in learning process management, process monitoring, and controlled amendment as the project proceeded. Both development jargon and the national vision sabotaged recognition of the need to integrate the project in terms of Iban rural and official contexts, not only in abstract or generalised terms. 'Thick descriptions' of moral content and official, institutional processes are also two key areas for anthropological research.

Hierarchical control and consensus are the dominant norms in public bureaucracies. Officials will never admit publicly that the policy norms are wrong – they have come from on top – but will try to find other means to ensure people accede, or at least conform, so that they can report 'policy success'. On the village street, however and so to speak, the reality is not hierarchical control of policy instructions but open-ended bargaining and conflict between officials and communities that lacks any objective definition of success or failure. It follows that my last practical recommendation is to advise that policy does not exist in any concrete sense until implementing staff and communities have shaped it and claimed it as their own. Team building, moral commitment, and ownership of implementation tasks and bottom-up monitoring systems in context are needed rather than the formulation of new planning guidelines or abstract policy trade-offs.

Notes

1   I am grateful to S.A. Khan and Dr G. Gangoli for extended discussions about the temple bell.
2   It has been convenient that the project is clearly 'history' and so can be used for teaching without controversy. The project was evaluated in the early 1980s and so contemporary discussion does not reflect on the current priorities or operational procedures of the aid donor or the implementing governments.

References

ASA (1999) *Ethical Guidelines for Good Research Practice*, Association of Social Anthropologists Annual Business Meeting, Durham.

Carrier, James G. and Miller, D. (1999) 'From private virtue to public vice', in Henrietta Moore (ed.) *Anthropological Theory Today*, Cambridge: Polity Press, pp. 24–47.

Cernea, Michael (2000) 'Risks, safeguards and reconstruction: a model for population displacement and resettlement', in Michael Cernea and Christopher

McDowell (eds) *Risk and Reconstruction: Experiences of Resettlers and Refugees*, Washington, DC: The World Bank, pp. 11–55.

Cowen, M.P. and R.W. Shenton (1996) *Doctrines of Development*, London: Routledge.

Crawford, David, Michael Mambo and Zainab Mdimi (2000) 'A day in the life of a development manager', in Tina Wallace (ed.) *Development and Management*, Oxfam and Open University: Oxfam Publishing, pp. 280–287.

Freeman, Derek (1970) *Report on the Iban*, London: Athlone Press.

Green, Leslie (1993) 'Internal minorities and their rights', in Will Kymlicka (ed.) *The Rights of Minority Cultures*, Oxford: Oxford University Press, pp. 256–274.

Grindle, Merilee (1980) 'Policy content and context in implementation', in M.S. Grindle (ed.) *Politics and Policy Implementation in the Third World*, Princeton: Princeton University Press, pp. 3–39.

Guhan, S. and Samuel Paul (eds) (1997) *Corruption in India: Agenda for Action*, New Delhi: Vision Books.

Havel, Vaclav (1992) 'The power of the powerless: citizens against the state in central Eastern Europe', in *Open Letters: Selected Writings 1965–1990*, New York: Vintage.

Huxley, Aldous (1971) (first published 1932) *Brave New World*, Harmondsworth: Penguin.

Jesudasan, Ignatius (1987) *A Gandhian Theology of Liberation*, Anand, India: Gujarat Sahitya Prakash.

King, Victor T. and Jayum A. Jawan (1996) 'The Ibans of Sarawak, Malaysia: ethnicity, marginalization and development', in Denis Dwyer and David Drakakis-Smith (eds) *Ethnicity and Development*, Chichester: Wiley, pp. 123–456.

Kothari, Rajni (1997) 'The agony of the modern state', in Majid Rahnema and Victoria Bawtree (eds) *The Post-Development Reader*, London: Zed Books, pp. 143–151.

Kukathas, Chandran (1993) 'Are there any cultural rights?', in Will Kymlicka (ed.) *The Rights of Minority Cultures*, Oxford: Oxford University Press, pp. 228–255.

Kymlicka, Will (1993) 'Introduction', in Will Kymlicka (ed.) *The Rights of Minority Cultures*, Oxford: Oxford University Press, pp. 1–30.

Laidlaw, James (1995) *Riches and Renunciation: Religion, Economy and Society among the Jains*, Oxford: Oxford University Press.

Langton, Rae (1992) 'Maria von Herbert's challenge to Kant', in Peter Singer (ed.) *Ethics*, Oxford: Oxford University Press, pp. 281–294.

McCully, Patrick (1996) *Silenced Rivers: the Ecology and Politics of Large Dams*, London and New Delhi: Longman.

Mohan, Giles (1997) 'Globalisation, liberal theory and the spatiality of governance in sub-Saharan Africa', *Space and Polity* 1 (1): 83–101.

Mosse, David, John Farrington and Alan Rew (eds) (1998) *Development as Process: Concepts and Methods for Working with Complexity*, London: Routledge.

Ong, Aihwa (1999) 'Clash of civilisations or Asian liberalism: an anthropology of the state and citizenship', in Henrietta Moore (ed.) *Anthropological Theory Today*, Cambridge: Polity Press, pp. 48–72.

Redclift, M.R. (1985) 'Policy research and anthropological compromise', in Ralph Grillo and Alan Rew (eds) *Social Anthropology and Development Policy*, London: Tavistock, pp. 198–202.

Rew, Alan (1997) 'The donors' discourse: official social development knowledge in the 1980s', in R.D. Grillo and R.L. Stirrat (eds) *Discourses of Development: Anthropological Perspectives*, Oxford: Berg, pp. 81–106.

Rew, Alan and Richard Batley (1977) 'Urban development: the redistribution of persistent deprivation', *IDS Bulletin* 9 (2): 49–53.

Rew, Alan, Eleanor Fisher and Balaji Pandey (2000) 'Policy practices in development-induced displacement and resettlement', proceedings of the 10th World Congress of Rural Sociology, Rio de Janeiro, August 2000, pp. 1–19.

Roe, Emery (1991) 'Development narratives, or making the best of blueprint development', *World Development* 19 (4): 287–300.

Scott, J. (1985) *Weapons of the Weak: Everyday Forms of Peasant Resistance*, New Haven, CT: Yale University Press.

Scudder, Thayer (1993) 'Development-induced relocation and refugee studies: 37 years of change and continuity among Zambia's Gwembe Tonga', *Journal of Refugee Studies* 6 (2): 140–144.

Shepherd, Robin (2000) *Czechoslovakia: the Velvet Revolution and Beyond*, London: Palgrave.

Toulmin, Stephen (2001) *Return to Reason*, Cambridge, MA: Harvard University Press.

Voutira, Eftihia and Barbara Harrell-Bond (2000) ' "Successful" refugee settlement: are past experiences relevant?', in Michael Cernea and Christopher McDowell (eds) *Risks and Reconstruction: Experiences of Resettlers and Refugees*, Washington, DC: The World Bank.

Williams, Bernard (1973) 'A critique of utilitarianism', in J.J.C. Smart and B. Williams (eds) *Utilitarianism For and Against*, Cambridge: Cambridge University Press, pp. 110–117.

Part III

Coping with different kinds of knowledge

Chapter 6

Development, displacement and international ethics[1]

Peter Penz

Displacement and international ethics

People displaced by the actions of other people can be deemed, *prima facie* at least, to have been wronged. Development refugees, i.e. those displaced by development projects, policies and processes, have been harmed or coerced by the actions of others. This applies also to those environmental refugees who have been displaced by anthropogenic environmental processes. What is morally owed to the potential and actual victims of such displacement? This question will be addressed first, in order to then move on to focus on a further question: What are the moral obligations of foreign participants in the development process when the displacement of people is a possible or actual result of such development?

This latter question will be addressed within the field of tension between an ethic of state sovereignty and cosmopolitan ethics. The former treats states as morally fundamental and sees international ethics as moral relations between states. Beitz (1979: 63–66) has referred to this perspective as 'the morality of states' and Janna Thompson (1992: 78) as 'just interaction theory'. Cosmopolitan ethics, on the other hand, is based on seeing humanity as part of one global society, and states as institutions that may or may not be conducive to the good governance of this global society. In other words, the ethics of sovereignty treats the state system as the framework for articulating an appropriate international ethic, while cosmopolitanism views international ethics as conceptually prior to the state system and as a basis for evaluating the state system and its propensities. In this chapter, I will argue for the cosmopolitan approach to determining the moral obligations of foreign participants in the development process.

Development refugees, environmental refugees and the Chittagong Hill Tracts case

Before turning to the question of international obligations, it is useful to first briefly clarify ethical obligations within states regarding displacement induced by development and environmental degradation. This task will be contained by limiting it to the obligations of states to their citizens in this policy domain. This will be sufficient for the ensuing discussion about international ethics.

Displacement here refers to forced migration. It occurs in at least two distinguishable forms. Direct displacement consists of evictions. Thus, direct development refugees are people removed for the construction of dams and their reservoirs and other infrastructure projects, such as ports, roads and irrigation canals, by slum clearance and urban redevelopment, and, in forests, for conservation or logging purposes. Indirect displacement by development, on the other hand, is displacement that is mediated by processes not directly under the control of decision makers, such as market processes and environmental degradation resulting from different, interacting development activities. If people move because they have been impoverished by the market-mediated or environmental consequences of development decisions, we can refer to them as indirect development refugees.

Environmental refugees are those displaced by environmental degradation. To the extent that such degradation is the result of one particular economic activity, such as the displacement of river fishers by the pollution of an upstream tannery, it can be taken to be direct displacement. On the other hand, if the displacement occurs as a result of a more interactive pattern of development, the resulting environmental refugees represent indirect displacement. Environmental displacement is thus a form of development-induced displacement that cuts across the distinction between direct and indirect displacement.

An example that illustrates development-induced displacement, including its environmental form, is the region of the Chittagong Hill Tracts in Bangladesh. It is a hilly area in the south-east of the country with thin tropical soil and generally low fertility. It has been inhabited by ethnically distinct hill peoples who have since the introduction of development experienced displacement by a number of different, but interacting, processes. One has been a big hydro-electric dam that displaced about 100,000 hill people. In response to guerrilla activity that this displacement induced, the area was militarised and Bengali settlers, deemed more loyal to the government and in need of land, were moved by the military onto land left fallow in the shifting agriculture that has been practised on this region's hillsides. Apart from the civil war that this set off, it involved a loss of land and livelihood for the hill people. At the same time, intensification of cultivation, including by the hill people, who have experienced substantial natural population growth and have also been left with less land, has led to soil depletion and erosion and some displacement for that reason. The Chakma, Mrong, Marma and other hill peoples have thus experienced a multi-dimensional syndrome of displacement due to a variety of interacting causes (Penz 1993).

Displacement is morally objectionable in the first instance because it involves coercion. This is evident in the case of direct displacement. In the case of indirect displacement, the element of coercion is not always straight-forward. If one views forced and voluntary migration as mutually exclusive categories, then it is easy to view much of the migration that is induced by development or environmental degradation as voluntary, since much of the time there is a considerable element of choice as to whether to move or to put up with deteriorating conditions. What is misleading here is to view coercion and choice as mutually exclusive. Even when threatened by death, individuals still have the choice to defy that threat. Thus, members of the Narmada Bachao Andolan, a movement that opposes the construction of the big Narmada dams in India, have announced that they will refuse to move and will accept being drowned when the waters rise. Nevertheless, we would accept that coercion is involved here on the part of those undertaking the dam projects. This can be understood, not as a complete removal of choice, but as a contraction of choice. Thus a person can be deemed to have been coerced when the range of options that are significant to the person are restricted. Choice is not eliminated, but merely restricted.

Displacement is also objectionable to the extent that such forced migra-tion typically makes people worse-off. They are often inadequately compensated for what they lose; they often have to move to areas more poorly endowed; and they often are unfamiliar with the new environment and the skills it requires, and therefore lose in terms of making a living (see McDowell 1996).

Some might respond with the claim that displacement has been ubiqui-tous in the process of industrialisation and economic growth, that it is unavoidable, that it is better than immobility or that it serves the public interest. Others, on the other hand, treat all displacement as morally un-acceptable. The question is whether displacement can, under certain conditions, be justified.

Applied ethics and its methodology

The process of justification, applied as it is to the concrete issue of develop-ment and displacement, raises the question of the methodology of applied ethics. Essentially three methodological approaches can be found in applied ethics.

1   The first is the theoretically committed approach of deriving practical judgements and prescriptions from a particular normative theory, to which a foundational commitment has been made. Thus, the theoretical starting point of a utilitarian will be different from that of a Rawlsian social-contract theorist. One difficulty here is that disagreements about normative theories are typically much greater than about practical

judgements and prescriptions emanating from competing theories. Much contestation is thus liable to be devoted to the theoretical foundations, even though the underlying differences may not create much difference at the level of policy evaluation. A second difficulty, at least for applied ethics that is to be useful to non-philosophers and policy makers, is that, outside of philosophical discourse, ethical judgements tend to be made with reference to concrete issues rather than in a theoretical form and non-philosophers therefore tend to be handicapped in assessing theories and tend to be excluded from the discussion.

2   The opposite methodological approach in applied ethics is to respond to practical problems in an entirely *contextual*, or situational, manner without reference to theories, implicitly relying on moral intuitions. These intuitions may be either those of the practical ethicist or they may be those of the culture, sub-culture or community in which the practical problems arise. In the personal version it is not clear how argumentation is to proceed and what are appropriate criteria for resolving disagreements; this approach is always in danger of sliding into arbitrariness or never rising above it. In the communitarian version of this approach, the criterion is conformity with community values. The difficulty here is that there may be no real agreement within communities. This is even more likely when many communities are involved (e.g., not only dam-displaced communities, but potential beneficiaries of rural electrification or irrigation) and when communities are stratified (e.g., by wealth, caste, or gender). Even when there is substantial agreement about community values, there is always the danger that they reflect patterns of domination within the community and the effective silencing of the disadvantaged (or their internalisation of the rationalisation of their underprivileged position, for example, accepting the lesser worth attributed to them). While it is important to bring community values to light, analysis cannot be limited to them. Jamieson (1991: 477–449) has referred to approaches (1) and (2) as, respectively, the 'dominant conception of moral theory' and the approach of the 'anti-theorists'.

3   That brings us to the third methodological approach, a *middle-level analysis*. It focuses on generalisable principles, but does not commit itself to a particular normative theory (Sumner's [1994] 'principlism' – cf. Jamieson 1991: 479–480). Instead of removing value disputes to the level of theory and attempting to resolve them there, as in approach (1), it addresses them within the concrete issues, in this case that of development-induced and environmental displacement. On the other hand, it is important to articulate the general principles at work in the ethical analysis and not to leave them operating at a level which is not explicit and where inconsistencies and controversial implications may remain out of sight, which the strictly contextual approach (2) is prone to do. These features make this middle-level analysis attractive. It can be employed in a dialectical

fashion, by engaging different theoretical perspectives in a 'dialogue' with each other to arrive at a more sophisticated mixed position.

Displacement, the state and moral justification

In accordance with the methodology proposed, the question of the justification of displacement will be explored in terms of three normative perspectives: (1) the public-interest perspective of utilitarianism; (2) the self-determination perspective of libertarianism and the more communal version of it held by some communitarians; and (3) the equal-sharing perspective of egalitarianism. (Finer distinctions within these perspectives will not be pursued here.)

1   The public interest perspective of utilitarianism is readily represented by cost–benefit analysis (see, e.g., Wenz 1988: ch. 10). The question here is simply whether the benefits of development outweigh the costs of its side-effects, including displacement. The distribution of benefits and costs in itself is not a concern in this perspective. Whether those displaced are compensated or not is not part of this particular moral calculus. Nor is whether it is the relatively affluent that benefit and the poor that bear the sacrifices.

2   The self-determination perspective of libertarianism, on the other hand, treats freedom and choice as central. From this perspective displacement is necessarily immoral. This applies also to communal self-determination, since displacement involves the coercive removal or forced migration of whole communities. This certainly seems like a promising antidote to heavy-handed and business-privileging development from the top. However, it completely ignores broader public-interest considerations, such as enhanced productivity resulting from the electricity and irrigation that dams, for example, provide. It is, of course, possible to convert opposition to consent from those required to move by offering them sufficient compensation to move voluntarily, so that they are, ultimately, not displaced (not *forced* to move). However, this creates an incentive for those required to move to try and capture some of the benefits from the project by demanding much higher compensation than is needed merely to not be worse off, and could make the project too costly to finance. This approach also involves a rather restrictive notion of freedom, in that it ignores that choice can be expanded by development. Amartya Sen's (1992: chs 2–4) notion of capacities complicates the issue, but draws attention to both the choice-expanding and choice-restricting aspects of development. Finally, from the next (egalitarian) perspective, this approach does not ensure a just distribution of benefits and can even stand in the way of redistribution, such as land reform, that would serve social justice.

3   The equal-sharing perspective of egalitarianism focuses on the distribution of costs and benefits from development as well as on inequalities prior to particular development projects or policies. From this perspective, development should serve to reduce inequalities. Thus, development-induced displacement could conceivably reduce inequalities if it primarily benefits the poor and puts the burdens on the better-off. Considerations of horizontal equity among the better-off would, however, limit or complicate such a process. Even more crucial is horizontal equity among the poor in that development can benefit some disadvantaged groups (e.g., by electrifying poor villages), while harming others (e.g., by displacing them). Compensation is one way of dealing with this; having those displaced share in the benefits of development, beyond mere compensation, is another. One major concern about the egalitarian approach is the maintenance of economic incentives. This can be accommodated by qualifying the egalitarian approach by a 'maximin' distribution approach, i.e., Rawls's difference principle of maximising the conditions of the worst-off. This represents a move away from the pure version of egalitarianism.

These three perspectives can be brought together by according each of them a role in a more comprehensive approach to the ethics of development-induced displacement, including displacement by development-induced environmental deterioration. Thus, the requirements of self-determination should be recognised as important by providing substantial community control over environmental decision making and by dealing with the required resettlement of populations through negotiations and roughly consensual consent, but not as an unqualified right to veto development projects and policies with displacement consequences. Refusing such veto power may be justified by considerations of public interest and distributive justice. In that case, however, certain conditions would need to be met: compensating those displaced, minimising displacement in the selection of development options, and giving priority to poverty alleviation in determining development strategies.

Sovereigntism and international responsibilities

The discussion so far has been of development in a national context. Development in Third World countries, however, is typically no longer strictly a national project; it involves foreign actors. It usually did so even before the current era of globalisation, when development was indeed seen as essentially a national project. (For this chronological distinction, see McMichael 1996.) This brings us to the central question of this chapter, namely what the moral obligations of foreign participants in the development process are, when their participation is in processes that displace people.

One cluster of positions that provide answers to this question is that of statist ethics. Statist ethics involve two levels or stages of moral consideration. One is that of intra-state ethics, as discussed in the previous section. The other is that of inter-state ethics. Within this perspective, citizens of one country do not stand in a direct moral relationship to citizens of another country. Rather, they have moral rights and obligations in relation to their own state and their state then stands in a moral relationship with the other state, which in turn stands in a moral relationship to its own citizens. The state is the pivotal mediator between foreign actors and the state's citizens. Whatever moral obligations the citizens of one country may have to the citizens of another country arise from the moral relationship between their respective states. For that reason I refer to it as statist ethics.

Within this general orientation to international ethics, the predominant position is that of sovereigntism. By sovereigntism I mean the moral rationale underlying the state system that has prevailed in Europe since the Thirty Years War in the seventeenth century, and that has been globalised through decolonisation in the latter half of the twentieth century. It gives moral primacy in international relations to the principle of state sovereignty. That means respect for the supreme authority of other states within their own territories and thus non-intervention among states. It does not rule out participation by foreign agencies in the economy and development of a particular country. It simply means that such participation has to be under the authority of the host state. In other words, foreign business, governmental aid agencies and non-governmental organisations have to operate within the laws and directives of the host government.

Does this mean that observing the laws and directives of the host state is the only moral obligation of foreign participants? Sovereigntists can answer this question in two quite different ways: (1) One answer is that the home society or polity may impose additional moral requirements regarding dealings with foreigners and that these have to be observed as a result of membership in the home society or polity. For example, if the laws of the host country concerning pollution are lax, there may be legal or moral obligations to observe the home restraints on toxic pollution abroad as much as at home. (2) A second answer may be that to carry domestic restraints from the home country to the host country is an imposition of values from outside the country and thus interferes with state authority or with the politico-cultural autonomy of the host country, whose trade-offs between living standards and environmental standards may be different. I will distinguish between these two positions by treating position (1) as the *national* sovereigntist position, under which actors in a foreign country have obligations to their national home states, beyond their obligation to obey the authority of the host state, while position (2) can be referred to as *territorial* sovereigntism, in that the authority of the home state ends when nationals leave the territory and enter that of another state. National sovereigntism sees sovereignty satisfied when the sovereign state gives its consent to the activities within its territory, while territorial sovereigntism emphasises that consent may be given under conditions of pressure on the host state, such as the withholding of important capital, and treats this as objectionable.

The problem with national sovereigntism is that it does not recognise the weakness of at least some states in the face of the politico-economic power of foreign capital and even of non-governmental organisations, for example in countries such as Bangladesh. The problem with territorial sovereigntism, on the other hand, is that it does not recognise that states do not necessarily act in the interests of their own citizens. In fact, both forms of sovereigntism do not acknowledge adequately the need to apply ethical evaluation to how states treat their own citizens. This suggests the possibility that the kind of ethical perspectives that were employed in the intra-national evaluation of national state policy with regard to development-induced displacement might be applied across borders, which is what the cosmopolitan approach does.

Considerations in favour of cosmopolitanism

The case for the cosmopolitan approach rests not merely on the difficulties of sovereigntism as an ethic, but also on more positive arguments that refer to current and historical developments in the world. These are (1) the increasing economic, social, cultural, and political integration of the world; (2) the nature and history of state boundaries; and (3) the actual behaviour of states.

1   The increasing integration of national societies through various processes is creating what must be considered to be a rapidly emerging world society. Economic globalisation is making families, groups and national and sub-national societies increasingly dependent on economic decisions and developments in other parts of the world. Thus the recent Pacific Asian economic crisis has been greatly affected by the behaviour of foreign capital, including that from the North Atlantic region. The globalisation of communications has made it possible in affluent countries to see what is going on in poor countries and for those in poor countries to see how those in the rich countries live. Extraordinary global mobility brings affluent tourists to poor countries and immigrants and refugees from poor countries to rich countries. Cities such as London, New York and Toronto are becoming extraordinarily cosmopolitan in their ethnic composition. These interdependencies are recognised in the growth of international governance or coordination institutions such as the UN, the World Trade Organization and a multitude of agencies dealing with everything from refugees to postal services and airline regulation. These are all hallmarks of a society, even though

there may be considerable limits to the extent to which people in one part of the world are concerned about what happens to people in other parts. But this also holds, although to a lesser extent, for national societies as well. World society may thus be a thinner society than national societies, but it is a society nevertheless.

2   Even if the identification of people with each other was, in fact, quite weak, the moral significance of state borders is still an issue. State borders have, historically, not been drawn cleanly around ethnic or linguistic groupings, but have emerged from wars that transferred territory, possibly because of the natural resources they contained rather than the people, or because the people provided a work force, a tax base and a source of soldiers, all of which could strengthen the state. Territorial states may have successfully used nationalism to forge national societies, but this often involved the suppression of minority cultures. Territorial states have typically maintained themselves by denying and restricting diversity. This historical element of force in the determination of state borders raises serious questions regarding the moral significance of such borders. The legacy of force is particularly evident in Africa, where colonial borders have been largely maintained into the post-colonial era, and where these borders developed on the basis of contestation and agreement between European powers, with little recognition of ethnic territories. Ethnic wars within territorial states indicate the weakness of national solidarity and of the national scope of moral concern and commitment.

3   The moral rationale for state sovereignty is based, at least in part, on the idea that states protect their respective societies and advance their interests. Yet the actual behaviour of states often reveals a predatory stance towards their citizenry, or one of neglect. Collaboration by foreigners with such states, either through their own states or through non-state agents such as business or non-governmental organisations, may involve complicity in such irresponsible behaviour. This suggests that the consequences of one's actions, which are international in that either the actions take place abroad or the consequences extend across borders, have to be assessed in terms of their impact on individuals and groups, not just countries or states.

These considerations point in the direction of a cosmopolitan approach. While a full case will not be offered here, these points will be taken as sufficient to warrant the application of a cosmopolitan approach to the issue of this chapter, namely that of the international obligations regarding development-induced and environmental displacement. Within a cosmopolitan framework, the obligations of foreign participants in the development process are to the people being affected and to those institutional agents that act on their behalf, but only in that representative capacity.

Cosmopolitanism and international responsibilities

In this framework, the considerations sketched out above under the heading 'Displacement, the state, and moral justification' apply across borders. In other words, moral concern for the citizens of other countries, such as for their well-being, self-determination and equality (among themselves or with citizens elsewhere), is relevant. There is, however, one crucial difference. In the previous situation the relevant state exercises authority; the discussion was thus conducted essentially in terms of the moral responsibility of the state. In the case of foreign individuals or organisations, whether state or non-state, the relevant agents do not exercise such authority. They operate within the authority sphere or sovereignty of another state.

If the host state is a reliable protector and promoter of the interests of its citizens (and other legitimate residents), then the assignment of moral responsibility within a cosmopolitan perspective may not be all that different from the sovereigntist perspective. However, a distinction should at this point be made between two kinds of foreign participants in development, in terms of their functions. One is business organisations whose function is to contribute to economic production, including services, generally on the basis of the pursuit of profits for their investors; the other is non-profit development organisations (NGOs) whose purpose is to protect or advance the interests of people in a development context. (Foreign states can fall on both sides of this distinction: as promoters of their economic interests, such as exports, they fall on the business side; as providers of genuine development assistance, they fall on the non-profit side.)

Given the assumption of moral and competent states, foreign business organisations can reasonably be deemed simply to have the responsibility to obey the laws, regulations and directives of the host state. It is the responsibility of the host state that productive activities and markets operate in a frame where these processes are beneficial and do not harm people in an unjustifiable manner. Thus, when businesses engage in logging, they need not worry about environmental and displacement effects; that is the concern of the state. Business organisations merely observe the constraints imposed on them by the state. There is thus a division of moral labour. It is, of course, possible to adopt a business ethic that goes further in terms of business responsibilities to communities. But this is dependent on the retreat of the state from assuming full responsibility for managing economic processes such that they do not cause unjust harm. It will thus be considered below as part of the limits to the assumption of the fully moral and competent host state.

For non-profit development organisations, on the other hand, the function is to further the interests of people. Since there are limits to what states can do to harness economic processes to promote the general interest and particularly social justice, non-profit organisations have here an important role to pursue action and innovation beyond state policy. This means that, with respect to development-induced and environmental displacement, to some extent they have to make the kind of broad assessment of the causal connections between development processes and their displacement consequences, and of the moral evaluation of the latter that states ought to be making. In other words, their moral responsibilities go considerably beyond observing host-state law.

The assumption of states as fully moral and competent is, however, a particularly artificial one. It is not uncommon for states to fail to ensure that development really does serve the public interest and social justice, that people are appropriately compensated and that policies that minimise displacement are pursued. These failures may be deliberate, as when state policies serve only the interests of an elite, or they may be due to weaknesses of state institutions, such as protection agencies that have insufficient funding, inadequately trained staff, poor management or inadequate authority in relation to state agencies with other mandates (e.g., the development of infrastructure). Much of the time these two causes are intermingled. (This problem applies to some extent to *all* states, but certain developing countries are particularly subject to it.) This phenomenon extends the moral obligations of foreign participants in development, and particularly those of business organisations.

To assess these, it is important to make a distinction between directly and indirectly caused displacement. Where outright evictions are involved, the consequences of the role of foreign business organisations in development are clear. Even though it may be the actions of local business partners that lead to such evictions, the participation of foreign capital definitely makes such foreign participants responsible, because their participation facilitates the displacement. The same applies to displacement due to environmental damage where the cause of such damage can clearly be traced to the activities of the relevant business organisation. On the other hand, where displacement results from more indirect processes, such as market processes or environmental degradation that is due to a variety of sources, then displacement has to be seen as having a range of causal agents. In that case, the causal connection between any particular business and displacement is too diffuse to reasonably assign moral responsibility. Only the local state can effectively assume responsibility for the overall causal process behind the displacement. However, if the whole pattern of development in a country is seriously exploitative and the participation of foreign business simply helps to maintain or extend it, there is a moral obligation to stay out of the development process entirely. Only if there are good grounds to believe that participation by a foreign business would actually undermine such exploitation or the development pattern that makes it possible can it be justified.

Even where that is not the case, there may be a further moral responsibility for foreign business, specifically with respect to environmental displacement. While a particular displacement process may have multiple causal agents, any particular kind of environmental damage may be attributable to a particular business. In that case, that business is responsible for that damage, even though it may not be held responsible for the displacement because that is due to a broader pattern of environmental deterioration. The particular environmental damage rather than the displacement due to multiple causes is the moral reason for abstaining from such business participation in development.

In the case of non-profit development organisations (and the development assistance agencies of states), the broader pattern of moral obligations continues to hold. It is not sufficient to show that no damage is being done; it is necessary to show that good is being done. It is reasonable to expect that such organisations not only avoid directly caused displacement, but also do not further a more complex process that leads to displacement that overall would be unjustifiable. This is not to say that non-profit organisations should never be involved in such processes. Their role may well be to alleviate displacement that is being generated by such processes. As a matter of fact, that consideration may quite properly lead them to participate even in unjust direct displacement, but as agents that alleviate the deleterious consequences of the evictions (e.g., by improving an otherwise deficient resettlement process). But in terms of moral strategy, NGOs also need to be careful here. They could end up being used by state agencies not concerned with justice for those being displaced ('oustees' in India) by performing the function that makes the process sufficiently acceptable to funding organisations (e.g., the World Bank) or the electorate. The basic point here is that, while the function of business organisations is to contribute to economic productivity by engaging in profitable activities so that their moral responsibilities here are confined to the avoidance of harm that can be clearly traced to them, the function of non-profit organisations is to help people benefit from development and they therefore have to assess their contribution to the broader and more complex processes that affect displacement not only directly, but also indirectly.

These considerations, then, also apply to development assistance provided by foreign states. They have the moral responsibility to ensure that such assistance is used beneficially and therefore have to attach conditions to the provision of such assistance. In this case, because inter-state relations are involved, some of the considerations of the sovereigntist perspective remain relevant. This means that, if one state is to respect another as guardian of its own citizens, it cannot establish aid conditions that have very detailed requirements concerning how the public interest and social justice within the country of the host state are to be served. Nevertheless, choices have to be made about which countries to give aid to and for which sectors or projects, and additional broad stipulations can be made concerning the design of projects or programmes. These all provide scope for exercising moral responsibility by the donor state.

Conclusion

The conclusion is that, under a cosmopolitan perspective, the existence of fallible states means that considerable moral responsibility concerning development-induced and environmental displacement, beyond that of observing the laws and decisions of host states, falls on foreign participants in development. This responsibility differs for the different kinds of participants, with business organisations having responsibility only for directly caused displacement, non-profit organisations for a broader pattern of effects, and state development-assistance agencies for some restraint as a part of respect for state sovereignty, even though the latter is not treated as morally fundamental.

Notes

1   This paper was presented at the International Conference on Forced Migration in the South Asian Region: Displacement, Human Rights, and Conflict Resolution, 20–22 April 2000, Centre for Refugee Studies, Jadavpur University, Calcutta, India. A previous version of this chapter (entitled 'Development refugees, environmental refugees, and international obligations: sovereigntist vs. cosmopolitan ethics') was presented at the joint conference of the Society for Applied Philosophy and the International Society for Environmental Ethics on 'Moral and political reasoning in environmental practice', Mansfield College, Oxford University, 27–29 June 1999. The research for the chapter has been supported by two related team-research projects: a project entitled 'International development ethics and population displacement: the nature and limits of Canada's obligations to developing countries', funded by the Social Sciences and Humanities Research Council of Canada; and an Indo-Canadian project entitled 'Economic policy, population displacement, and development ethics', funded by the Shastri Indo-Canadian Institute's Partnership Programme, which was funded in turn by the Canadian International Development Agency. The author of this chapter is principal investigator of both team projects.

References

Beitz, Charles R. (1979) *Political Theory and International Relations*, Princeton: Princeton University Press.

Jamieson, Dale (1991) 'Method and moral theory', in Peter Singer (ed.) *A Companion to Ethics*, Oxford: Blackwell, pp. 476–487.

McDowell, Christopher (ed.) (1996) *Understanding Impoverishment: the Consequences of Development-induced Displacement*, Providence, RI: Berghahn Books.

McMichael, Philip (1996) *Development and Social Change: a Global Perspective*, Thousand Oaks, CA: Pine Forge Press.

Penz, Peter (1993) 'Colonization of tribal lands in Bangladesh and Indonesia: state rationales, rights to land, and environmental justice', in M.C. Howard (ed.) *Asia's Environmental Crisis*, Boulder: Westview Press, pp. 37–72.

Sen, Amartya (1992) *Inequality Reexamined*, Oxford: Clarendon Press.

Sumner, L. Wayne (1994) 'How to do applied ethics', Keynote Address, Annual Conference, Ontario Philosophical Society, York University, 4 November.

Thompson, Janna (1992) *Justice and World Order: a Philosophical Inquiry*, London: Routledge.

Wenz, Peter S. (1988) *Environmental Justice*, Albany, NY: State University of New York Press.

Chapter 7

Charges and counter-charges of ethical imperialism

Towards a situated approach to development ethics

George Ulrich

A focal point of global ethical discussion in recent years has been the glaring inequities in the access of rich and poor, North and South, to treatment for HIV/AIDS. This brings up many thorny questions. Aside from exposing the injustice of the current world order, the neglect of the great majority of HIV/AIDS sufferers also exposes the intense profit motives of the pharmaceutical industry and yet humanity's radical dependence upon this industry for its continued welfare and health improvements. When it comes to organising research, few other areas are as urgent and as contentious. Presumably, the AIDS pandemic will not be effectively curbed until a vaccine or a cure is developed, yet steps in this direction are extremely costly and often involve considerable risks for research participants. Furthermore, there is serious ambiguity about who bears the burdens of research and who will reap the benefits. Is it possible that treatments are being tested on impoverished Third World populations who will subsequently not be able to afford them? Are ethical standards being lowered when research is conducted in developing countries? Conversely, is it possible to articulate meaningful universal standards of medical research ethics? Is it morally defensible *not* to invest in research in developing countries?

These are some of the questions that will be taken up in this article. I shall focus on a particular case, or rather a particular moment of an ongoing case, which has to do with research into the prevention or reduction of mother-to-infant HIV transmission. This issue has long received special priority due to the realisation that while it seems unrealistic at the present time to secure effective treatment for infected mothers, it might be feasible with relatively limited resources to reduce the transmission of the disease to the offspring. The particular moment of controversy in which I take my point of departure occurred in the autumn of 1997. At this time sixteen UNAIDS-sponsored HIV perinatal transmission trials conducted in Africa and Asia were subjected to intense criticism, first in a prestigious medical journal and subsequently in the international press. As we shall see, the criticism elicited an equally bitter response and led to an exchange of charges of 'ethical imperialism'. On closer examination, the case raises a broad range of questions about the current standards of international research ethics and, more generally speaking, about the ethics of donor-sponsored development interventions.

I begin by recapitulating some of the main moments of the case and the controversy surrounding it. I then seek to draw a distinction between different *types* of ethical issues, some of which are subject to (more or less) absolute standards and others that call for a greater degree of flexibility and need to be treated in a contextual manner. The latter range of issues brings into play an important dynamic concerning the recognition of ethical competence and the need for situated accountability – a dynamic which is also found to be central to the case at hand. In order to situate my analysis of the case in a broader philosophical context, I briefly outline some basic tenets of the ethical theory articulated by Jürgen Habermas under the label of *discourse ethics*. I argue that this approach to moral reasoning provides a constructive framework for negotiating issues of professional ethics in a context of normative pluralism. However, the practical implications of discourse ethics for international professional ethics have not generally been explored, and the present case analysis may be viewed as a step in this direction.

A scandal exposed?

On 28 April 1997 Kenya's leading daily *The Nation* carried a back-page feature proclaiming in large script that 'AIDS studies "kill infants" '. The source of this accusation was an American consumer group, Public Citizen, which had earlier the same year raised concerns about the HIV trials in question with the appropriate institutions in the USA, namely the Congress, the National Institute of Health (NIH), and the Centers for Disease Control (CDC). Since these advances did not produce the desired effect, Public Citizen's next move was to contact the press in the USA and in several African countries. In response, numerous letters in support of the trials were sent to the director of the NIH by implicated African, Asian, European and American scientists. In September, the case was taken up by the *New England Journal of Medicine* (*NEJM*), and Public Citizen's criticism was lent full support, in some respects even trumped, by editor Marcia Angell.[1] What particularly shocked the medical community was a direct comparison with Tuskegee – the most infamous case of scientific medical abuse in the post-Second World War era.[2] President Clinton issued a statement denouncing the comparison. At this point, the international press took note. For a few weeks the story was front-page news. Later in the autumn, official statements were issued by the NIH and the WHO in defence of the trials under attack (Varmus and Satcher 1997). In a final dramatic development, two leading HIV experts resigned in protest from *NEJM*'s board of editors, and the British medical journal *The Lancet*, which had earlier featured an editorial echoing the concerns of Public Citizen, in January 1998 featured a new editorial retracting its earlier position.[3]

To understand why the sixteen HIV trials became so controversial, we have to go back to early 1994 when an American/French study known as ACTG 076 demonstrated that a lengthy regimen of antiretroviral (AZT) treatment is able to reduce perinatal HIV transmission by 67 per cent. Within a few months after receiving the test results from the ACTG 076 trials, health authorities in the affluent countries of the world began adopting the treatment as a 'standard of care' for HIV-infected pregnant women. However, there are numerous reasons why the treatment is not applicable in developing countries. First and foremost, it is far too expensive. On this count alone, it may be viewed as irrelevant to the vast majority of HIV-infected pregnant women around the world. But there are also other complicating factors. ACTG 076 presupposes an early detection of pregnancy and a prolonged contact with the health-care system, both of which are in conflict with common health-seeking behaviour in many parts of the world. Moreover, the regimen presupposes intravenous AZT during delivery, but outside of a few urban centres, the physical facilities for administering this are simply not there in developing countries. Finally, the ACTG 076 regimen presupposes that mothers refrain from breastfeeding their babies, and in situations of contaminated water supplies, this might pose an even greater health risk than HIV itself!

There is, therefore, an obvious need to look for ways of adapting the regimen to Third World conditions, or to find other interventions that, while perhaps less effective, could be of use in the context of the AIDS pandemic in Africa and Asia. All sixteen trials under attack by Public Citizen and *NEJM* were designed specifically with such considerations in mind. The sixteen research teams were associated with a working group under UNAIDS called The Joint United Nations Programme on HIV/AIDS. This group was constituted expressly for the purpose of addressing mother-to-child HIV transmission and identifying interventions of relevance to developing countries in light of the ACTG 076 results. Nine of the trials were thus designed to test less costly and lengthy uses of AZT. The remaining studies were designed to test the efficacy of alternative or complementary interventions, such as the use of micronutrients in order to boost the immune defence system. It must be noted that the UNAIDS group addressed the question of ethical standards at its initial meeting in 1994. A set of recommendations were drafted for the purpose and endorsed by the WHO, and it appears that all sixteen studies complied with these (WHO 1994).

Nevertheless, the UNAIDS studies were targeted as one of the worst breaches of medical ethics in recent years. Why? Fundamentally because all trials but one had built-in placebo controls.[4] This would *not* have been allowed in developed countries, i.e., in the very nations sponsoring the research. It is a general rule of biomedical research that research participants are entitled to the best-known treatment. They must at least be able to expect the current 'standard of care', so in a situation where a regimen such as ACTG 076 is already firmly established, any trials involving placebo controls are completely out of the question. Any new treatment must be tested against the existing standard. In light of the fact that women in the control groups in fifteen of the sixteen UNAIDS studies received no care, it is possible to make a hypothetical calculation of the number of infants infected with HIV who could have been spared. The maths is simple. Roughly 10,000 women were involved in the control groups. According to Western statistics, the ACTG 076 regimen could have reduced the infection rate among these women from approximately 24 per cent to 8 per cent, which is to say in absolute numbers that more than 1,500 infants contracted HIV unnecessarily. Hence the accusation that HIV research 'kills infants'. A passive construction like 'allows infants to die' might have been more accurate. But the end result is the same: it was within the capacity of the researchers to protect infants in their care, and they did not.

Aside from the question concerning the possible abuse of control group subjects, the trials have also been attacked for not obtaining proper informed consent. Thus, the charge is that not only were half of the research participants severely neglected, the women were also deceived into thinking that they would receive the best available care. This point was rendered graphically by some American journalists who managed to round up a few trial participants so unfortunate as to have given birth to HIV-positive children. When asked whether they had understood the concept of placebo controls, the answer was clear: they had not understood it and expressed a sense of bitter betrayal. Against this kind of heart-wrenching testimony, the researchers responsible for the UNAIDS trials insisted that informed consent was in fact obtained, or at least that the standard procedures for obtaining informed consent in developing countries had been followed in all cases. Probably both sides of the dispute are right, to a certain extent. Informed consent is an extremely complicated principle to handle in research in developing countries, and the concept of placebo controls is difficult to explain even in highly literate societies, so it is no surprise that once a controversy has broken out, it is possible to find research participants who feel they were not properly informed. No doubt one of the great challenges of contemporary research ethics lies in finding ways to render consent procedures more meaningful or, perhaps better, to protect the values underlying the principle of informed consent without resorting to a rigid formalism that ends up protecting professionals more than lay research participants. However, this is not a problem that is unique to the HIV trials in question.[5]

The controversy

If we concentrate on the dispute concerning the use of placebo controls, it is obvious that the fundamental problem underlying this 'scandal' is that health services and available resources are so unevenly distributed in the world today. In most of the communities where the HIV research in question was (and to a certain extent still is) conducted, infected patients have no other access to medical treatment. But does this exempt scientists from treating them to the best of their ability? Are we otherwise prepared to endorse a notion of differential human worth? In technical terms, the critical question is whether the 'standard of care' to which research participants are entitled should be interpreted in accordance with the most advanced medical practices – as an absolute, universal standard – or whether it should be established relative to existing conditions in the country where the research is conducted. Public Citizen adopts an uncompromising stance on this question. Research participants everywhere in the world are entitled to exactly the same protections, and scientists proposing to conduct studies in underdeveloped communities are responsible for providing the best-known treatment to everyone taking part in their trials.

The counter-argument to this is that it sets an unrealistic standard, making it next to impossible to conduct research that is actually relevant in the context of developing countries. Is a quest for moral purity getting in the way of conscientious social interventions? Can it really be that stopping all current attempts at finding useful treatments is to be seen as more ethical than trying? Public Citizen has argued that it would be possible, with some ingenuity and imagination, to design so-called *equivalency studies*, i.e., studies that test the efficacy of promising new treatments against the current best-proven therapeutic method. However, this argument seems to be fraught with difficulties. There is something highly artificial about comparing all new interventions with a treatment such as ACTG 076 which has no other use in the given context than to remind impoverished Third World populations of what they are being denied. And since the researchers responsible for the UNAIDS trials do not necessarily expect that their proposed interventions could be shown to be *more* effective than ACTG 076, the trials would at any rate be unethical according to Public Citizen's logic. Furthermore, it has been pointed out that one cannot assume that the ACTG 076 regimen would have the same effect in an anaemic Third World population as among women in Europe and America. There is, therefore, not really a 'proven treatment', and if ACTG 076 were to be introduced in developing countries on a mass scale, it still ought to be tested against a local control group. Whereas Public Citizen rightly emphasises that placebo controls are extremely complicated and often overused, it must be kept in mind that they also serve a protective function. *Not* to include placebo controls would in many cases be equally problematic from an ethical point of view.

Thus, the case clearly illustrates the difficulties in articulating universal ethical standards in a world of extreme differences and inequities. Removing attention somewhat from the particulars of the UNAIDS trials, Lurie and Wolfe (1997) of Public Citizen argue in their *NEJM* article that allowing for differential standards of research is a *slippery slope* that opens the door wide for the exploitation of impoverished Third World populations. If 'no care' is accepted as the minimum standard of protection for research subjects in developing countries, then 'anything goes'. It may be noted that this position concurs with an argument presented nine years earlier in the same journal by editor Marcia Angell. In her article 'Ethical imperialism? Ethics in international collaborative clinical research' (1988), Angell argues that ethical standards, like scientific standards, have to be objective and absolute; otherwise what would follow 'would be true imperialism in the sense of exploitation'. In contrast to this, the chair of the Ugandan AIDS Research Committee, Dr Edward Mbidde, presents an equally forceful argument. These are not European and American trials exploiting developing countries, he insists, loosely paraphrased. They are African studies addressing Africa's problems. Due to a lack of resources, foreign economic and technical assistance is required, and is received with gratitude, but this does not prevent local principal investigators from assuming ethical responsibility. In Mbidde's own words, perhaps deliberately recalling Angell's 1988 article:

> There is a mix up of issues here which needs to be clarified. It is not NIH conducting the studies in Uganda but Ugandans conducting the study on their people for the good of their people. If this is not acceptable ... then this is tantamount to ethical imperialism.[6]

For our present purposes, this is where the case stands. Since 1997, there have been many intricate developments culminating in the highly publicised 2001 court case between the Republic of South Africa and the pharmaceutical industry about the patenting of antiretroviral treatment. Economics and geopolitics aside, many twists in the case hinge on advanced scientific assessments which will not be discussed here. What is of primary concern is rather two ethical issues of general relevance, both of which stand out with particular clarity in the dispute at hand. One has to do with how to protect the basic interests of the poor, neglected and highly vulnerable. Public Citizen's and Angell's strong commitment to this group clearly speaks to their credit. The other key issue concerns the recognition of ethical competence and the need to apply established norms in a context-specific manner. In this respect Mbidde has a powerful point. It is nothing short of remarkable that a case concerning women and infants in Africa and Asia should be treated as an internal American (and to a lesser degree European) affair. There is an unmistakable element of paternalism in this. Not only are the sixteen trials in question treated as American and European research initiatives deploying First World expertise to solve Africa's and Asia's problems. It is also taken for granted that the ethical difficulties arising in this connection are properly addressed in places such as Washington, DC, Geneva, London, and Copenhagen. Clearly this is unacceptable and, as I shall argue, detrimental to any meaningful commitment to development.

As both sides in the dispute seem to have some merit, the question naturally arises as to how to resolve it. The obvious approach would be to look to current international standards of medical research ethics. But these are inconclusive. If one looks to the *International Ethical Guidelines for Biomedical Research Involving Human Subjects* adopted by the Conference of International Organizations of Medical Science (CIOMS) in 1993, one finds that both sides receive a certain degree of support. In support of Public Citizen's position, guideline 15 clearly stipulates that donor-sponsored research must meet the ethical standards of both the sponsoring nation and the host nation and must be able to pass ethical review in both places. But, contrary to this, guideline 8 strongly emphasises *local relevance* as a criterion for conducting research in 'underdeveloped communities'. And it is indicated in a background note to the CIOMS document that the principles contained therein will sometimes have to be applied in a flexible manner in so far as '[t]he mere formulation of ethical guidelines for biomedical research will hardly resolve all the moral doubts that can arise in association with such research' (CIOMS 1993: 7). Surely this could be taken as a warning against adopting too purist a stance.

To get beyond this impasse, I propose that we need to take a step back and embark upon a set of broader ethical reflections. I believe that headway can be made by distinguishing between different *types* of ethical issues, in particular between issues which demand equal treatment everywhere in the world and issues which allow for a greater degree of flexibility. A distinction of this nature is familiar from the legal discourse, where different international legal norms are attributed different so-called 'margins of appreciation'. If a similar distinction is adopted in international ethics, then our attention immediately shifts to the question of determining what types of issues are at stake in the case at hand. A further central challenge consists in identifying the relevant *fora* in which the different issues can be handled.

Before examining our case in this light, however, I wish briefly to touch upon some reflections on moral philosophy. More specifically, I wish to introduce the basic tenets of a school of thought that makes a strong case for the context-specific application of ethical principles and attributes of particular significance to the mutual recognition of competence among partners in ethical discourse. This is Habermasian 'discourse ethics'.

Some basic tenets of discourse ethics

In order to support objective, authoritative pronouncements on right and wrong, Occidental philosophy has persistently sought to attain a universal perspective on ethical problems. It has, in other words, stipulated that 'the moral point of view' must transcend individual interests and assess a given situation in an impartial manner. Arguably, this is what defines the ethical judgement as such. This assumption may be shown to be operative in numerous, otherwise divergent schools of thought (notably schools of thought post-dating a heroic tradition of virtue ethics and antedating Nietzsche).[7] The quest for a transcendence of individual perceptions and interests is thus reflected in the Platonic philosopher's ascendence to the realm of pure ideas; in Aristotle's application of *orthos logos* in moral reasoning as well as in his recognition of an immutable, i.e., divine, moral law; in the Stoic notion of and commitment to universal humanity – a principle that demonstrates a deep affinity with moral thinking in all the great world religions; in the Kantian categorical imperative (which requires us to test whether, in addition to willing a certain action or state of affairs, we could also will that the maxim of our act could be raised to a universal law); and in the utilitarian maxim that what is right is that which will facilitate the greatest good for the greatest number of people. In a contemporary context the same motif is preserved in Rawls's theory of justice in the notion of an 'original position' characterised by ignorance about one's own personal and social interests.

Discourse ethics breaks with this tradition of laying claim to an authoritative standpoint from which to resolve moral dilemmas. In Habermas's thinking, the commitment to universality and impartiality is retained, but this is now done through a *decentring of perspectives* based on the stipulation that the outcome of a given moral judgement must be acceptable to *all* parties affected for that judgement to be valid. In pronouncing moral judgements, we are thus enjoined to adopt the concrete perspective of every interlocutor in discourse rather than an abstract, impersonal perspective assumed to provide privileged insight into the nature of the good. '[T]he impartiality of judgement is expressed in a principle that constrains *all* affected to adopt the perspectives of *all others* in the balancing of interests' (Habermas 1990: 65).

There seem, in Habermas's writing on the subject, to be two operative models for how such a decentring of perspectives may be accomplished. The stronger model consists in putting disputed moral questions directly to the test within the circle of parties concerned. What is needed is a 'real' process of argumentation, Habermas stipulates, and proceeds to suggest that the categorical imperative needs to be reformulated as follows: 'Rather than ascribing as valid to all others any maxim that I can will to be a universal law, I must submit my maxim to all others for purposes of discursively testing its claim to validity' (Habermas 1990: 67, citing T. McCarthy 1978).

This marks a rupture with what might be called *monological* ethical reasoning. The idea is that ethical reasoning can no longer rely on thought-experiments taking place exclusively in the mind of the individual but must instead become dialogical. Hence the designation *discourse ethics*. Habermas notes that this 'stands or falls with two assumptions: (a) that normative claims to validity have cognitive meaning and can be treated *like* claims to truth and (b) that the justification of norms and commands requires that a real discourse be carried out and thus cannot occur in a strictly monological form, i.e., in the form of a hypothetical process of argumentation carried out in the individual mind' (1990: 68).

The direct implication of giving priority to a dialogical approach to ethical reasoning is that emphasis is placed first and foremost on *procedural rules* and *formal norms* which must be shared by all participants in discourse precisely in order to allow substantive differences to be articulated in a free and open manner. A central norm has to do with the recognition of moral competence, i.e., not just what we do *to* and *for* others but the quality of our moral interaction, the manner in which we heed different interests and points of view, and the manner in which we express mutual expectations and treat each other as responsible agents. Arguably, this is of paramount importance in a context of normative pluralism, and thus also in connection with international professional ethics, development ethics, etc. Here discourse ethics has the dual advantage of containing in-built protections both against ethnocentrism and against cynicism and moral indifference. It curbs the ethnocentric impulse to impose one's own values on others by making space for the articulation of divergent perceptions of the good and it opposes cynicism and disillusionment by relentlessly insisting upon moral accountability in social interaction. I view this as particularly important in an international, cross-cultural context, since the problem of maintaining high ethical standards generally has less to do with identifying shared norms than with the weakness of existing structures of accountability.

There is, however, an obvious objection to the central tenets of discourse ethics which points to a weaker articulation of the principle of decentring perspectives. This is that it is rarely possible from a purely practical point of view to heed the call for a 'real' normative dialogue involving all parties affected. Moreover, normative deliberations rarely happen in a coercion-free manner, and to operate with such an assumption would seem to be exceedingly naive. In response to the latter concern, it might be argued that a normative standard should not be confused with a description of reality. Thus, irrespective of whether the expectation of reciprocal communicative interaction is honoured in practice, it remains a valid norm, and indeed a norm which is well suited to expose illegitimate uses of power in moral interaction. Nevertheless, in so far as discourse ethics relies on actually putting normative judgements to the test within the circle of parties concerned, the practical constraints upon free and reciprocal communication do seem to pose a problem. Habermas's response to this, as far as I can ascertain, consists in re-importing a certain element of hypothetical reasoning. He reintroduces the dialogical test in a virtual form by stipulating that '[o]nly those norms may be claimed to be valid that *could* meet with the consent of all affected in their role as participants in a practical discourse' (Habermas 1990: 197; emphasis added). It is significant that what is required is no longer that norms must actually meet with the consent of all affected, only that this must be rationally possible. This 'compromise' recurs time and again in Habermas's writings on moral philosophy and even carries over into his legal philosophy: 'a law may claim legitimacy only if all those possibly affected could consent to it after participating in rational discourses' (Habermas 1998: 160).

Thus discourse ethics leaves us with two core principles. One is a demand for recognition of ethical competence and reciprocity in moral interaction. The other is a factoring in of the viewpoints and interests of all parties concerned in an ethical situation. In returning now to our specific case, both principles will be found to be relevant to the dispute concerning the HIV transmission trials. What needs to be clarified next is the essential nature of the issues at stake.

Degrees of 'situatedness'

If, rather than inquiring into what is good and bad, right and wrong to do, one were to ask what ethics is *about*, i.e., what sorts of issues are subject to ethical discourse in accordance with the formal principles outlined above, then I believe that one would find the prospects for reaching a comprehensive cross-cultural understanding to be greatly improved. Elsewhere I have proposed that discussions in international research ethics and development ethics essentially revolve around three or four different types of issues or thematic clusters. These have to do with protection against harm, with respectful communicative interaction, with justice and local relevance, and, as a fourth important level of ethical consideration, although not quite on par with the three others, with the implications of collaboration, the individual and collective spin-off effects of research, negotiating vested interests in professional activity, etc.

An advantage of developing a taxonomy of this nature is that it reveals how different types of ethical issues display certain fundamentally different characteristics. Protection issues thus tend to involve asymmetrical relations and have to do with how we treat others who happen to be exposed to or depend upon decisions taken by us in our capacity as professionals. Communication issues concern the quality of intersubjective relations – not what we do *to* and *for* others but the *manner* in which we interact. They turn on values of respect, reciprocity, recognition of ethical competence, openness in research, etc., all of which are of immediate ethical concern on a par with protection issues, and at the same time form a meta-norm for how ethical deliberations and decisions are generally to be handled. Justice and relevance issues typically involve a shift of focus from interpersonal to impersonal relations and tend to target the systems level, i.e., a level of ethical consideration which exceeds individual agency. Often the primary concern at this level has to do with how to maximise available social resources and how to balance foreseeable burdens and benefits.

In light of these characteristics, it further becomes apparent that different ethical norms allow for different degrees of objectivity and exactitude in their application. The injunction against inflicting harm thus approximates an absolute norm with a very narrow 'margin of appreciation', which is to say that it is a norm that should be applied more or less consistently everywhere in the world. Issues of respectful communicative interaction, on the other hand, involve a much greater degree of interpretation, negotiation, and balancing of different factors. The same is true of ethical issues that have to do with maximising the benefits of scarce resources, ensuring the local relevance of research and other development interventions, and ameliorating systemic injustices. Issues of this nature clearly need to be addressed in a situated manner with due regard to the specifics of the given context and with a sufficient degree of openness to involve a wide range of parties directly and indirectly concerned. Interestingly, what we encounter here is a need to embed ethical deliberations in a communicative framework precisely of the nature stipulated by the theory of discourse ethics.

In distinguishing between different degrees of 'situatedness', I am thus acknowledging that some ethical issues are subject to the type of categorical judgement that Marcia Angell invokes in her 1988 article on ethical imperialism. A viable cross-cultural approach to ethics must be able to recognise certain absolute limits for morally acceptable human treatment. We may encounter difficulties in determining precisely where such limits are to be drawn, but this notwithstanding, there are certain types of harm and degrading treatment, violations of dignity, etc., that are reprehensible and unacceptable irrespective of culture and social context.

What is less clear, however, is whether – and to what extent – issues of this nature are at stake in the case examined in the present article. As originally formulated, Public Citizen's entire case rests on the claim that denying control group subjects a known treatment constitutes a serious infliction of harm. Both *NEJM* and *The Lancet* have at one point lent this charge their full backing but have since retracted their positions somewhat. In my view, the claim is untenable. If harm were to be demonstrated, it would have to be harm by omission, harm in the form of failing to provide treatment that it was within one's power to provide. Doctors everywhere have a primary obligation to provide for patients in their care to the best of their ability and, certainly, this needs to be taken into account in the case at hand; yet given the scandalous lack of treatments relevant to developing countries, the uncertainty about how the ACTG 076 regimen would behave in a typical

Third World setting, the impossibility of administering that regimen in local settings, etc., I find it doubtful that the expectation of antiretroviral treatment can be construed as sufficiently strong to support a charge of inflicting harm by omission. When it comes to those among the sixteen UNAIDS trials that were designed to test the potential of micronutrients to boost immunity and thereby reduce HIV transmission, the charge of inflicting harm becomes blatantly absurd. Vitamin A does not 'kill infants'; it is generally beneficial and moreover inexpensive, so it could have an important role to play in global HIV campaigns.

My general argument, then, is that the case at hand should *not* be construed as primarily concerning the protection of vulnerable subjects against harm. As soon as this is left aside, other ethical issues come into the foreground. These are no less important than the issue of harm, and they retain many aspects of what led Public Citizen and *NEJM* to react, but they have in common that they need to be treated in a more clearly situated manner and probably also a more modest manner, avoiding the shrill exchange of charges and counter-charges that we have witnessed in the current case.

One dimension of the case that immediately comes to the fore has to do with the suspicion of autonomy violations. Since informed consent seems to have been insufficient in some of the UNAIDS trials, it may be inquired whether the case involves a measure of deception. To this I believe we may have to reply in the affirmative, yet, as mentioned above, I see this as indicative of certain fundamental problems with the principle of informed consent itself. At the heart of the predicament lies the pseudo-contractual form in which consent procedures are usually handled. The problems associated with this go beyond the difficulties encountered in attempting to convey the appropriate technical information to uneducated research subjects. If the idea of protecting the right to self-determination is to be taken seriously, careful attention must be paid to a set of broader issues such as: what does it mean to give consent in the given context? what are the operative decision-making procedures? what are the realistic alternatives? and what are the structures of power and authority that might influence decision making? Does informed consent in the given social setting function effectively as a mechanism of self-protection – and if not, how to compensate for this? Questions of this nature are all subject to context-specific examination and interpretation, and hence take us firmly into the domain of a situated approach to research ethics. I view it as a failure of existing ethics guidelines not to make this clear. In effect, we are left with a central principle that is routinely violated (cf. Ulrich 1999: 135ff).

Another salient aspect of the case concerns our inability to effectively address gross systemic injustices. This problem forms a subtext to the case as a whole and surfaces explicitly on various occasions, notably in connection with Public Citizen's apprehension about global double standards and the unequal treatment of human beings. Needless to say, these are serious ethical problems that demand to be addressed, but I view it as misleading to pretend that they can be meaningfully *resolved* within the arbitrary and somewhat artificial context of a clinical trial group. Justice issues are generally of a completely different order than issues of harm and deception in that they exceed the scope of individual agency. Yes, it is a scandal that the majority of the world's population has no access to the types of treatment that a privileged minority take for granted, but these are injustices which are already given and which no single researcher or research team can rectify. Realistically speaking, most justice issues have to be addressed at higher levels of intervention, for example at the levels of public policy and global economics. This is *not* to say that they are irrelevant to the individual scientist. They do indeed affect specific research designs and do entail certain individual responsibilities, but in order to make sense of this and begin to specify meaningful criteria for decision making and accountability at this level, it must be clear that we are dealing with an area in which we can only make modest contributions and in which we will never get things quite right.

Strengthening ethical competence and situated accountability

More than any other challenge faced by professional ethics, that of responding to systemic injustices confronts us with the need for interactive approaches and the modesty that this entails. As a final remark, I would like to suggest that taking up this challenge means envisioning contemporary global ethics not just as a matter of defining defensive strategies and setting limits to professional conduct, but also as a reciprocal discourse about positive values and aims. In my view this entails an enhanced focus on local capacity-building and an increased onus on visiting experts to honour ethical accountability in a local context. At an earlier juncture, we saw how the case at hand brings out a spirit of paternalism both with respect to who is to solve the Third World's problems and who has the competence to make ethical judgements. If our commitment to development is to be meaningful at all, attitudes need to be reversed on both counts. In light of the colonial and post-colonial legacy of extracting raw data from the Third World – data which, like other raw materials, are refined and consumed elsewhere – it is reasonable to stipulate that *all* research initiatives in developing countries should be approached as collaborative efforts that also involve an aspect of fostering local expertise and resources to confront own problems and to assess proposed international interventions. Indeed, the case at hand is a primary illustration of why developing countries cannot simply rely on importing results from the more advanced nations. When it comes to HIV, the treatments developed in the North are either unavailable or at odds with local conditions, or both.

As far as the tendency to monopolise the right to pronounce ethical judgement is concerned, this too is a sinister expression of paternalism. While scientists committed to the cause of development tend to be motivated by genuinely good intentions, it is my experience that they (we) display a deep-seated unwillingness to be held accountable, or even questioned about ethical standards and decisions, while 'in the field'. The same point can be made about other experts working in development. Indeed, there may be a direct link between having good intentions and experiencing a sense of exemption from common public accountability. But the refusal to engage in reciprocal normative discourse is in and of itself a deeply unethical gesture that effectively disqualifies our counterparts in developing countries as competent subjects. In a contemporary setting, command of the language of ethics serves as an important parameter of power and professional legitimacy, and honest collaboration therefore necessarily involves recognising ethical competence in local colleagues, in lay research participants, and within the civil communities where research is conducted.

This is a minimum requirement, as it were. One could go a step further and propose active measures to strengthen the ethical voice and structures of accountability within research environments in developing countries. I support this too. Against the call to recognise and respect the ethical competence of colleagues, collaborators and community leaders in developing countries, it is sometimes objected that it would be naive to assume that members of the elite in developing countries always act in the best interest of the populations they represent. In my own experience, this point is frequently articulated not only by Western sceptics but also by African and Asian colleagues. But I believe that the reservation rests on a misunderstanding. If the concern about mismanagement of office is indeed pertinent, then all the more reason to get involved in frank, reciprocal interaction and to contribute to strengthening local contexts of ethical accountability.

In conclusion, the point I am trying to make is that cross-cultural professional interaction, the globalisation of science, and the exigencies of development all confront us with a need to develop models for what might be called a situated, interactive approach to professional ethics. The key to this, as I see it, lies in shifting focus from a primary preoccupation with objectified *norms* to an emphasis on the *process* of ethical discussion, dispute, decision making, and review. At the level of philosophical theory, important steps in this direction have been taken by the proponents of discourse ethics. But in terms of the practical implications of this approach to ethical theory, we are entering new territory. In academic centres in both developed and developing countries, the current trend is overwhelmingly towards quasi-legalistic, formal approaches to professional ethics. In practice, however, formal ethical guidelines often do not speak to the actual dilemmas confronted in the laboratory and in the field, and scientists adapt and make do, usually without articulating the deliberations and principles underlying their decisions. If one accepts that many ethical issues are of such a nature that they cannot be effectively treated in a decontextualised manner, then it is relevant to raise questions about who has ethical competence in the concrete situation and what the relevant contexts are of ethical justification. What is being emphasised here is a view of ethics as a matter of public accountability, continuously and in shifting fora. Developing interactive approaches to professional ethics is not a question of reverting to some easily dismissible stereotype of normative relativism. Nor is it a matter of reducing ethical judgement to simple consensus-building. It is about verbalising and confronting multiple levels of normative agreement and dispute, sometimes maintaining differences and sometimes bridging them, through reciprocal communicative interaction in fragile, emerging, common moral spaces.

Notes

1   See Lurie and Wolfe (of Public Citizen's Health Research Group) 1997; Angell 1997.
2   From 1932 to 1972, more than 400 African Americans in the State of Alabama unknowingly took part in a study officially titled *The Tuskeegee Study of Untreated Syphilis in the Negro Male*. Even after the discovery of penicillin, the patients were offered no treatment, and were in some cases actively barred access to treatment in order to make it possible for the scientists to study the development of untreated syphilis. In 1997, President Clinton made a heartfelt speech on behalf of the nation apologising for this travesty.
3   *The Lancet* 351 (24 January 1998): 225; compare *The Lancet* 350 (27 September 1997): 897.
4   Meaning that a randomly selected control group was unknowingly given an ineffective treatment, i.e. no treatment at all.
5   For a more detailed discussion of the complications of working with informed consent in developing countries, see Ulrich 1999: 135–175.
6   Letter to the NIH dated 8 May 1997; quoted in part by Varmus and Satcher 1997:1005.
7   In *After Virtue* (1985), Alasdair MacIntyre reclaims a tradition of virtue ethics, notably in an Aristotelian version, which to a certain extent abandons the strict claim to universalisability of ethical norms. Nietzschean and post-Nietzschean schools of thought make an even stronger case for positioned value judgements. However, due to space constraints these approaches to moral philosophy, and their relation to the theory of discourse ethics, will not be further examined here.

References

Angell, M. (1988) 'Ethical imperialism? Ethics in international collaborative clinical research', *New England Journal of Medicine* 319: 1081–1083.
—— (1997) 'The ethics of clinical research in the Third World', *New England Journal of Medicine* 337: 8847–8849.
CIOMS (1993) *International Ethical Guidelines for Biomedical Research Involving Human Subjects*, Geneva.
Habermas, J. (1990) *Moral Consciousness and Communicative Action*, Cambridge: Polity Press.

—— (1998) 'Remarks on legitimation through human rights', *Philosophy and Social Criticism* 24 (2/3): 157–171.

Lurie, P. and S.M. Wolfe (1997) 'Unethical trials of interventions to reduce perinatal transmission of the human immunodeficiency virus in developing countries', *New England Journal of Medicine* 337: 853–856.

MacIntyre, A. (1985) *After Virtue: a Study in Moral Theory*, London: Duckworth.

McCarthy, T. (1978) *The Critical Theory of Jürgen Habermas*, Cambridge, MA: MIT Press.

Ulrich, G. (1999) 'Globally speaking: report on the ethics of research in developing countries', Copenhagen.

Varmus, H. and D. Satcher (1997) 'Ethical complexities of conducting research in developing countries', *New England Journal of Medicine* 337: 1003–1005.

WHO (1994) *Recommendations from the Meeting on Mother-to-infant Transmission of HIV by Use of Antiretrovirals*, Geneva: World Health Organization, 23–25 June.

Chapter 8

Social science intervention

Moral versus political economy and the Vietnam War[1]

*Oscar Salemink**

Introduction

The recent publication of Patrick Tierney's *Darkness in El Dorado: How Scientists and Journalists Devastated the Amazon* (2000) created a major stir in scholarly circles around the world with reverberations in the press. The book critiques the work of famous US anthropologist Napoleon Chagnon and other anthropologists and scientists among the Yanomami in Venezuela and Brazil for the effects of the research on the situation of the Yanomami themselves. The highly polemical book attempts to undermine the credibility of anthropological research primarily in moral terms. The book triggered much heated debate about the ethics of anthropology world-wide (but primarily within the American Anthropological Association – or AAA), with participation by many senior anthropologists such as Clifford Geertz. Much of the response criticised Tierney for his misleading use of sources and tendentious interpretation of data, in particular regarding measles epidemics which he claims were caused by a US genetic research mission under the leadership of the noted geneticist James Neel and in the context of which Chagnon did his PhD research. This provoked rebuttals from the American scientific establishment which stood accused, especially from the Atomic Energy Commission – the predecessor of the US Department of Energy – and the National Academy of Sciences.[2] The AAA decided to launch a formal inquiry into Tierney's allegations.[3]

The debate about the ethics and politics of anthropological research is comparable with other so-called 'scandals' in the anthropological discipline. Such scandals in the 1960s and 1970s were mostly related to open military or political conflict. This is clear from the response to the advertisement by the US Navy for a 'research anthropologist' for Vietnam in the *American Anthropologist* of 1968 (70: 852). The publicity and collapse of the Department of Defense-funded 'Project Camelot' which investigated peasant insurgency in Latin America was closely related to the Cold War

*I would like to thank Philip Quarles van Ufford, the late Peter Kloos, and the participants at the EIDOS Conference at SOAS, London, for their valuable comments on earlier versions of this chapter. The research has been made possible by grant no W52–456 of the Netherlands Organization for the Advancement of Tropical Science (WOTRO).

tensions (Horowitz 1967). The publication in the *New York Review of Books* of the article 'Anthropology on the warpath' by Eric Wolf and Joseph Jorgensen (1970) alleged that anthropologists played an important role in the suppression of the communist insurgency in Thailand's multi-ethnic North, and gave rise to what became known as the 'Thailand controversy' within the AAA (Davenport 1985; Wakin 1992). These became scandals because of the role that anthropology and anthropologists were perceived to play in interventions of a military nature.

However, it is less common to look at social science research, practice and discourse as interventions in their own right, as Patrick Tierney attempted. In the wake of Mark Hobart (1993) and Arturo Escobar (1995), many social scientists have attempted to deconstruct development by applying a Foucauldian analysis on the practice and discourse of development, thus conceptually distancing social science from practical intervention. This chapter, on the other hand, will analyse anthropological research and the resulting theory as interventions in the life of the group under research. This will be done through a case study of the so-called moral and political economy debate which took place in academic social science in the 1970s and 1980s. The protagonists of that debate were James Scott (*The Moral Economy of the Peasant*, 1976) and Samuel Popkin (*The Rational Peasant*, 1979). Both are political scientists but their influence extends to sociology, economics, historiography, and especially anthropology. I present these theories as social science interventions which take place alongside other scientific interventions, and in conjunction with political, military, market, religious, medical, educational and development interventions. The contextualisation of the 1980s theoretical controversy between moral economy (James Scott) and political economy (Samuel Popkin) within the context of the American involvement in the Vietnam War will serve to illustrate the politics and ethics of social science research in relation to other kinds of intervention. My aim is to reconstruct the genesis of both theoretical perspectives, either in support of the military intervention, linked to varying strategic interests, or in opposition to it.[4]

The theoretical controversy

During the last three decades much scholarly attention has been given to the 'peasant question' within anthropological discourse. Theory on peasants focused mainly on their relations with the State, especially as they posed problems to the State. One such country where the peasants did not act the way their overlords and their allies would have liked, was Vietnam. It is not surprising, then, that Vietnamese peasants are at the heart of two major theories dealing with peasant rebellion, in particular the well-known theoretical controversy of moral economy versus political economy. However, this chapter is not an assessment of the respective explanatory value of both theories, since this has been amply done before by others (Brocheux 1983;

Cumings 1981; Keyes 1983; Kleinen 1988; Moise 1982; Peletz 1983). It purports to show why and in what context these theories were generated. Writing in retrospect, James Scott attributes the interest in the 'peasant question' to left-wing academic romanticism:

> A great deal of the recent work on the peasantry – my own as well as that of others – concerns rebellions and revolutions. ... On the left, it is apparent that the inordinate attention devoted to peasant insurrections was stimulated by the Vietnam War and by a now fading left-wing, academic romance with wars of national liberation.
>
> (Scott 1985: xv)

I agree with Scott that scientific debate is not an autonomous process, but is conditioned by its historical and political context. This insight is fully in line with current thinking about the history of ideas and of science. However, his statement downplays the degree to which the American intervention in southern Vietnam formed the positive context for much research funded by the US military, intelligence and development establishments. I shall argue that the moral versus political economy controversy had its roots in the American involvement in the Vietnam War (or American War for the Vietnamese), and that this has ethical implications for contemporary development practice and social science research. In so doing it is not my intention, however, to revive the ethical debates concerning the 'complicity' of social scientists doing research for the US Army or related institutions, which haunted the social science community in the 1960s and 1970s.

Social science discourse, like any social discourse, is conditioned by political and social practice as well as by scientific criteria. In order to be accepted and acceptable, new, innovative theories have to be written in the normative language of the era in order to be accepted (cf. Skinner 1978; Tully 1988). Scott's *Moral Economy* (1976) and Popkin's *Rational Peasant* (1979) did not come out of the blue, but were framed in concepts that were already commonplace in anthropological and sociological language. Even the content of their theoretical controversy is not entirely new. In different shapes the opposition between community (*Gemeinschaft*) and society (*Gesellschaft*) has haunted social science, and is associated with illustrious predecessors such as Ferdinand Tönnies, Robert Redfield and Oscar Lewis, George Foster, Karl Polanyi, etc.

James Scott's moral economy approach deals with the causes of peasant resistance. It postulates that in traditional village communities peasants tried to provide some subsistence insurance through arrangements that minimised risks, according to a 'safety-first' principle. A subsistence ethic, based on economic practices and social exchanges, guaranteed every member of the village community a moral right to subsistence. Peasants evaluated claims to the surplus of their produce by landlords, moneylenders and the state against a moral standard of what was considered a fair minimum subsistence level. Violation of these moral standards of subsistence provoked resentment and resistance among at least a part of the peasant population. The idea of a moral economy then focuses on those cultural arrangements which would be economically beneficial for the participants within the village community. It thus constitutes a deviation from both neo-classical schools of development sociology and Marxist analyses of class struggle.

Based on analyses of the Saya San rebellion in Burma and the Nghe-Tinh Soviets in Annam (the colonial designation of central Vietnam) during the economic crisis of the 1930s, Scott asserts that, during colonial times, the village community had been progressively stripped of its moral arrangements as a consequence of the imposition of capitalism and of the development of the modern (colonial) state. Peasants became dependent on a capricious market. They lost their lands and means of production, and as tenants or landless labourers had to face the claims of landlords, moneylenders and the colonial state. Peasants tried to resist, and sometimes they rebelled when they felt that their right to subsistence was being infringed upon.

Scott states explicitly that his analysis was not intended to deal with the causes of revolution, but with the preconditions of rebellion. Yet, it was widely believed that he tried to explain why the Vietnamese were able to mount a successful guerrilla war against the formidable military power of the United States and its South-Vietnamese allies. This is not surprising, since he places himself in the tradition of Barrington Moore (1966) and especially Eric Wolf (1969). Wolf was a well-known adversary of American involvement in Vietnam. He stressed the importance of the (closed corporate) village community in the history of Vietnam. Wolf was evidently inspired by the French éminence grise Paul Mus, author of Viêt-Nam, Sociologie d'une Guerre (1952) and 'The role of the village in Vietnamese politics' (1948), and in the 1960s a visiting professor at Yale University. In his publications, Mus expressed his opinion concerning the preponderant importance of tradition in Vietnam, especially in the countryside. In Mus's view, the rise of the Viêt Minh can only be understood against the background of Vietnamese traditionalism.[5]

It is surprising that Scott makes no mention at all of Paul Mus, though he studied at Yale University and his book was published by Yale University Press. Although he took no courses with Mus, Scott must have been aware of his writing. The reason for ignoring this hitherto most influential scholar on the village community in Vietnam may be attributed to the role which American followers of Mus, notably John T. McAlister, Jr. and Frances FitzGerald, had come to play in the political debate about US involvement in Vietnam. Both authors tried to explain the mysteriously determined resistance of the Vietnamese rural population against American domination by pointing to the role of the traditional village community, just as Mus had argued during the French domination of Vietnam. Quoting the old

Vietnamese saying '*Phép vua thua lê làng*' (The king's authority yields to village custom), they presented a rather mystical image of the Vietnamese village. James Scott apparently did not wish to be associated with such concepts of the Vietnamese village, because he felt that his own concept of the traditional village community was different, and he 'did not think that [Mus] or McAlister had much useful to say'.[6]

Samuel Popkin (1979) is the champion of the political economy approach, and the main critic of the moral economy approach, in particular regarding Vietnam. Popkin squarely associated Scott with Mus, McAlister and FitzGerald, when he criticised them for sketching a falsely romantic image of the traditional, pre-capitalist village. Political economists dispute the existence of a subsistence ethic, the importance of moral arrangements, and the corporate character of the village, viewed as a community. Instead, Popkin considers peasant behaviour as being guided by calculation, aimed at profit maximisation, rather than by moral concepts aimed at risk aversion. Within the village, peasants, landlords and other actors behave in a rational way, i.e., in the interest of themselves and their families. They tend to base their decisions on rational calculations about probable outcomes. This holds true for pre-colonial, 'traditional' societies, where agrarian relations were exploitative rather than harmonious, the village offering hardly any protection for poor peasants. The introduction of the market provided new opportunities for peasants, landlords and entrepreneurs alike, and they invested in new technologies or market opportunities when they felt it would raise productivity and maximise profit.

The political economy approach views peasant *resistance* in the same way. The rational attitude, it is claimed, guides peasants in all their collective actions, be it the construction of a dike or the participation in a rebel movement. They would only join a rebel movement or support a revolution if they felt they would gain by it. They had to believe that such a movement would be successful and that their 'investment' would bear fruit. They would certainly not join a movement out of moral indignation, as testified by the apathy putatively characterising many peasants in the Third World. There must be something in it for them, only to be grasped by joining the movement. This meant that a movement had to be well organised by a leadership that could effectively deal with free-riders. This leadership could be provided by some religious organisation as well as by a political organisation such as the Communist Party.

Scott's claim that he voiced the victim's point of view, as well as his seeming closeness to well-known critics of America's involvement in Vietnam, invested him with a left-wing image. On the other hand Popkin's view remained close to neo-classical theory, which guided American development and nation-building efforts in Vietnam.[7] Of course, there were implicit political messages in both theories. Scott's views stressed the legitimacy of the peasants' claims to subsistence in the face of adverse economic conditions generated by the capitalist market and the modern colonial or post-colonial state, which destroyed the traditional, protective bonds. Their resistance, though based on moral concepts, was utterly rational. It could be deduced from Scott's work, then, that the USA was actually helping the peasants' enemy. Popkin, on the other hand, underscored the opportunities the market presented to the peasants. These opportunities might liberate them from traditional, exploitative bonds. Since peasants rationally calculate in what way they could gain most, they would only participate in a movement if it offered them real advantages. Their participation in rebellions and revolutions had to be attributed to good organisation and cunning leadership. The next step to a theory of the imposition of revolution by coercive organisation is not far away, then. It was here, in this appreciation of rebellion and revolution, that the Scott–Popkin debate was an expression of political conflicts in the USA during and after the Vietnam War.

Part of the theoretical controversy can be attributed to the different research methods they employed. Scott's methodology was primarily historical; he had conducted research in French archives and libraries. This affected the nature of his material, which centred on the rebellions in the Nghe An and Ha Tinh provinces in northern Annam in the 1930s. In these peripheral provinces, poor and densely populated, agriculture was gradually commercialised under the impact of French colonial rule. The French had hardly any direct access to the villages in the area, which appeared to them to be autonomous communities. Popkin, on the other hand, based his book on fieldwork in Vietnam as a counterinsurgency specialist. His research methods were primarily sociological. He interviewed hundreds of peasants and other villagers of South Vietnam's Mekong Delta. The Mekong Delta had been a frontier area where the French established a highly commercialised agriculture. Thus, the delta was integrated into the market from the outset, and had been settled with open, frontier-type villages sharing few of the 'community' characteristics of the villages in Tonkin and northern Annam.[8] Furthermore, Popkin's research in a highly commercialised, politicised and conflict-ridden countryside, where government and army officials had a reputation for being corrupt and indifferent, left him with little room for optimism regarding Community Development programmes, Rural Construction, Cooperation, and other pacification-*cum*-development schemes the US advisors had devised for their South-Vietnamese allies.

The theories put forward by Scott and Popkin constituted clear-cut though conflicting answers to questions which puzzled Americans, regarding peasant rebellion and revolution in Southeast Asia and more generally in the Third World after the Second World War. In a foreword to Gerald Hickey's book *Village in Vietnam* (1964), Paul Mus noted that the recent research by American scholars on Vietnam contributed many new insights in comparison with established French views:

a handful of enterprising young American scholars ... are indubitably adding to our own [French] contribution much that is new and much that is true, as a confirmation of the simple, usually unobserved, yet at times deadly circumstance that the question conditions the answer – and even more, what the questioner makes out of it. The French were in charge, and too often what they finally gathered mirrored their preoccupations and prejudices, so apparent to the observant Vietnamese, in the way we had put our questions.

(Hickey 1964: xv)

This observation, however, applies to the Americans as well. The issue at stake here is: what questions were American researchers asking in Vietnam? What was the context which gave rise to such questions? In order to find these questions as well as the possible answers to them, we may want to look at the vast body of literature on the interrelated topics of peasants, villages, political processes in the countryside, land reform, agricultural development and the like in South Vietnam. These studies, carried out by scientists of various disciplines, were far too numerous to satisfy academic curiosity only. They were intended to satisfy an increasing thirst for knowledge – or better: demand for data – by American policy makers, civil servants, advisors, and especially the American army, on political processes in the Vietnamese countryside. Indeed, such studies were designed, financed, and performed to support the American efforts towards the 'pacification' of the Vietnamese countryside by means of so-called 'counterinsurgency' methods. Applied social science was nothing new, but the scale of 'social engineering' was unprecedented. Before turning to this practice of science at the service of warfare, I sketch the nature of the pacification programmes implemented by various American and South-Vietnamese military and civil agencies.

Pacification: politics and the village

This section deals with the development of American pacification programmes in the Vietnamese countryside. This is not the place to dwell extensively on the history of the Vietnam War and the different counterinsurgency schemes, as this would take us too far from the main focus of this chapter.[9] But for an understanding of the pacification policy, we need to sketch some of the issues and dilemmas confronting the main counterinsurgency programmes. American involvement in Vietnam started as early as 1950, when the French were still waging their Indochina war. Although the US Government had its doubts about French colonial policy, the French did succeed in convincing the US Government to support their struggle against communism. American military support flowed to the French army from 1950 onwards, and by 1954 the USA financed 80 per cent of the French military budget. In return, the French agreed to install a non-communist 'nationalist' government in Vietnam within the framework of the 'French Union'. This government under the emperor Bao Dai was not taken very seriously by the French, the USA, the Viêt Minh and the majority of the Vietnamese population, as the French kept control over key positions and did not cede real power to the 'puppet regime'. The French military and political position became untenable after their military defeat in Diên Biên Phu in spring 1954, just at the time of the Geneva Conference scheduled to settle the Korea and Indochina conflicts. The Geneva Agreements of 1954 provided for a cease-fire and retreat of the Viêt Minh forces north, and French forces south of the seventeenth parallel in anticipation of general elections and subsequent reunification.

The American government and the 'nationalist' government of Vietnam, however, did not sign the Agreements. The Americans, still anxious about a possible Viêt Minh take-over or election victory, used their influence in the former colonial army to install the Diêm regime in South Vietnam. From the outset, American advisors were deeply involved in the creation of the Republic of Viet Nam (South Vietnam). This is exemplified in the role of the famous Colonel (later General) Edward Lansdale, whose team managed, against all odds, to establish Diêm's authority in most of the country (Lansdale 1972; Currey 1988; Kahin 1986: 66–92). In the 1950s the Americans paid little attention to the Vietnamese countryside. Rather, they focused on problems of nation-building, urbanisation, and security affairs, symbolised by the building up of a vast regular army and a politically-oriented police force. Diêm used his army and police to hunt down former Viêt Minh supporters in the villages, and to undo the land reforms that the Viêt Minh had carried through in the Mekong Delta. The landlords regained their land, sometimes even collecting rent over previous years with the help of the police force. The widespread terror and economic setback which this brought forth for much of the peasant population soon triggered off a resumption of the insurgency in the South. Mounting guerrilla activities forced the American advisors to pay more attention to the countryside.

In the late 1950s, the first American researchers set out to conduct field-work in villages. They operated within the framework of the Michigan State University Vietnam Advisory Group which advised the Diêm regime on matters of security, police, intelligence and administration. But what really set the 'machine' in motion was the personal intervention of President Kennedy in 1961 with respect to American policy in countries with insurgency problems. He ordered the coordination of the counterinsurgency efforts of several departments and institutions, including the Department of Defense, the Department of State, the US Agency for International Development (USAID), the US Information Agency (USIA), the Army, Navy and Air Force, the Central Intelligence Agency (CIA), and even the International Voluntary Service (IVS). This resulted in the establishment of the Special Group (Counterinsurgency) within which these organisations were represented. However, the Defense Department continued to play the first and foremost role in this counterinsurgency effort, and from the outset sponsored most social science research on Vietnam and peasant rebellions, if only because it had a sufficient budget to do so.

American efforts in Vietnam centred on the concept of 'pacification'. The military aspects apart, the official US and South-Vietnamese definition of pacification reads like a description of present-day participatory development:

> The military process of establishing sustained local security in the countryside, the political process of establishing and re-establishing local government responsive to and involving the people and the economic and social process of meeting rural people's needs.
>
> (quoted by Grinter 1975: 50)

Until the deployment of American troops in 1965, pacification efforts sought to deprive the guerrilla movement of its rural basis through large-scale resettlement of the rural population. Or, with reference to Mao Zedong's metaphor of the guerrillas moving among the rural population as the fish in the water, the resettlement programmes, modelled after British policy in Malaya, sought to separate the 'fish' from the 'water' by physically separating the peasants from the guerrilla fighters. The scattered population was forced to live in larger units that could be more easily defended. The military aspect was dominant within this counterinsurgency strategy. From 1957 to 1965 a whole range of resettlement schemes were inaugurated, under the well-known Strategic Hamlet programme.[10] The political and social aspects received relatively little attention in the resettlement schemes. It was normal procedure to force the inhabitants of a village to the new camp, and to declare their old lands a 'Free Strike Zone', where the army was allowed to fire at any living creature. If any relief or development aid was provided by the government, the US Army or USAID, it was often partly sold on the black market by corrupt officials. Thus the population had to choose between living miserably in the new hamlets, or living dangerously on their former land, often under the protection of the National Liberation Front (NLF or Viet Cong). Invariably, the resettlement programmes were unpopular with the rural population who considered the new habitats more or less as concentration camps. They turned, therefore, into a political fiasco (cf. Salemink 1991).

Subsequent pacification programmes focused on the political process, in that they sought to install an effective leadership in the villages, loyal to the Saigon Government. They were variously called 'Rural Construction' (1965–1966), 'Revolutionary Development' (1966–1967) and 'New Model' Pacification (1967–1969), and were accompanied by the implementation of many development projects, generously financed by the US Government.

Their aim was to bring about economic development and thus rural support for the government by 'winning the hearts and minds' of the people. However, as these programmes tended to stress the relations between local authorities and the rural population, they only made the population more dependent on the bureaucracy, which already had a solid reputation for corruption. The results were obvious:

> A larger and richer bureaucracy, bolstered by an almost unlimited array of development schemes, and American economic support, did not foster a more acceptable bureaucracy in the eyes of the rural population; all of the public opinion surveys taken in the rural areas tend to stress the fact that to the rural population the government has appeared increasingly unresponsive to rural needs and problems.
>
> (Goodman, in SEADAG 1970: 674)

After the 1968 Tết Offensive of the National Liberation Front, which made a deep impression both in the USA and South Vietnam, the South-Vietnamese government decided to pass a land reform bill ending tenancy, landlordism and consequent exploitation, and giving the peasants title to the land they cultivated. Already before 1968, pressure had been exerted to realise a land reform, notably by the counterinsurgency expert General Edward Lansdale; by USAID, which from 1965 had a permanent representative in South Vietnam; and by the American Congress and public opinion. The unexpected success in the 1968 American pre-elections of senator Eugene McCarthy, a well-known opponent of the Vietnam War, overcame the reluctance of the South-Vietnamese government. In 1970, President Thieu eventually signed the Land-to-the-Tiller Act. US officials hailed the new law as *the* means to beat the NLF politically. At last, social and economic improvements for the peasant population (the third aspect of pacification) had gained priority in US policy.

The new policy, however, was confronted with the consequences of previous schemes. The peasants had not forgotten that after the conquest of an NLF-controlled area the landlords entered their village in US Army trucks to collect rents. Implementation of the land reform was terribly slow, due partly to the landlords' tactics of parcelling out their land to relatives. Other landlords, facing problems with collecting the rent, were only too happy to receive compensation. In the eyes of the peasants the land reform was only a weaker version of the Việt Minh and NLF land reforms in the past. This perception constituted a moral (and therefore political) victory for the NLF. Furthermore, the government destroyed its own rural power base: the landowning class. In short, the US-sponsored pacification programmes were not at all successful. They failed to take into account the effect that the programmes had on the rural population. Furthermore, they were often badly coordinated and poorly implemented, not in the least because of the widespread corruption in the South-Vietnamese administration. The application of the results of social science research was seen to constitute an important tool for improving this situation. Social science was in demand, so the army and other institutions turned *en masse* to social science.

Social science and war

Social science research conducted in support of pacification programmes was grounded in different conceptions, represented opposing interests, and was often conducted by competing agencies. In general, the American intervention was predicated on specific concepts of 'modernisation' and 'development', as propounded by such theorists as Walt Rostow, Samuel Huntington and Lucian Pye, which found their way from the academy into the government (see Gendzier 1985; Hatcher 1990). What is important here, though, is the keen interest of the Department of Defense in understanding 'the' political attitudes of the peasants, and the impact of American policy and military actions. Gradually, the emphasis shifted to more fundamental questions concerning the origins of peasant resistance and insurgency. Interest in the kind of questions addressed by Scott and Popkin gradually developed therefore within the research institutions working for the US Department of Defense.

The Defense Department's interest in social science research was stimulated by the 'Research Group in Psychology and the Social Sciences', established in 1959 at the Smithsonian Institution under Defense contract no. 1354(08), and comprising a number of leading social scientists from American universities under the direction of Dr Charles Bray.[11] The research group comprised sixty-five consultants, including Harry Eckstein, Daniel Ellsberg, Max Millikan, Lucian Pye, and Ithiel de Sola Pool. In 1963, the group published a lengthy study edited by Ithiel de Sola Pool of the Massachusetts Institute of Technology, not incidentally a close colleague of Samuel Popkin. The report stressed the relevance of social science research for an understanding of revolutionary processes going on in the Third World, especially in Vietnam. Science, it stated, could make a substantial contribution to the American counterinsurgency effort, since it would stimulate the use of political methods where military methods did not succeed (quoted by Deitchman 1976: 28–35). One of the papers generated by the Research Group was Harry Eckstein's 'Internal war: the problem of anticipation', which listed the 'frequently stated hypotheses about the preconditions of internal war', as found in the social science literature. Eckstein distinguished between intellectual factors, economic factors, aspects of social structure, political factors, and general characteristics of social process – an outline which would form the basis of Project Camelot's research programme.[12]

The report resulted in an increased recruitment of scholars by the military research institutions for applied social science research in support of the counterinsurgency and pacification effort. Seymour Deitchman, himself an advocate of applied social research, and engaged in its coordination within the Defense Department, has provided a sketch of many of the institutions which commanded and sponsored it. Briefly, counterinsurgency research was sponsored by the Navy's Office of Naval Research (ONR), the Air Force Office of Scientific Research (OSR), the Army's Special Operations Research Office (SORO) of the Department of Defense, the Advanced Research Projects Agency (ARPA), and the Office of the Assistant Secretary of Defense for International Security Affairs (ISA). The research was either performed in-house, or under contract by outside organisations such as the RAND Corporation and the Simulmatics Corporation, by academic institutions like Michigan State University, the Stanford Research Institute, the Massachusetts Institute of Technology, or by individual scientists on a freelance basis. Ideally, all research activities for defence purposes were supervised by the Director of Defense Research and Engineering. His staff, however, dealt primarily with budgetary issues, and was unable to handle the large amount of research activities itself.

In 1964, a Defense Science Board study group evaluated the existing scientific research programmes initiated by the Defense Department and tried to formulate new research directions. A Behavioral Sciences Panel that included Ithiel de Sola Pool was asked to 'conduct a study and evaluation of research and development program and findings related to ethnic and other motivational factors involved in the causation and conduct of small wars among the peoples of Southeast Asia' (Deitchman 1976: 95). The DSB report concluded that the counterinsurgency programmes in Vietnam had been ineffective since they were based on insufficient knowledge of Vietnamese society and especially of the population the programmes aimed at. A large-scale research programme was proposed which could help launch a successful counterinsurgency strategy. The list of research topics included the dynamics of insurgency within the village, its bases of political support, the relations between village elites and the mass of peasants, etc. In fact, it reads like a purely academic programme for peasant rebellion studies (Deitchman 1976: 113).

Hypotheses for a successful counterinsurgency strategy hardly existed – apart from the usual Cold War rhetoric concerning the import and imposition of communism. Research was increasingly channelled along the lines sketched in the DSB report. The three main counterinsurgency projects were Project Agile, CINFAC and Project Camelot. Project Agile was a coordinated research effort concerned with counterinsurgency in Southeast Asia. It was initiated by ARPA which tried to improve American counterinsurgency methods, such as the Strategic Hamlets programme forcing the rural population into 'protected' villages in order to separate the 'fish from the water'. It also studied the impact of the American Special Forces on the attitude of the local population. In 1964, SORO established a Counterinsurgency Information and Analysis Center (CINFAC), which drew upon available studies about tribal groups and social systems in developing societies in general for the benefit of any government agency that needed information on counterinsurgency. The scope of the research effort broadened: the locus of research was extended from Southeast Asia (Vietnam) to worldwide, while the focus of research was also extended, starting from the evaluation of counterinsurgency programmes to include finally the causation of insurgency. This culminated in Project Camelot.

Project Camelot was intended to be a worldwide research effort with a view to generating valid models for predicting the occurrence of 'internal wars', i.e., violent protests against a present regime. From the body of social science literature on social change, consultants employed by SORO had catalogued some 800 hypotheses concerning the causes of internal war, according to the format presented by Harry Eckstein. Almost all of the hypotheses appeared plausible, but many seemed to contradict each other.[13] Research was needed to test these hypotheses in order to construct a model from which 'indicators of internal conflict potential' could be developed (Deitchman 1976: 143).

The counterinsurgency research effort was by no means monolithic. Although there was one basic research problem, the possible outcomes varied according to the perspective adopted in a context of conflict. For the war was not only a conflict between the NLF/North Vietnam and South Vietnam/the USA, but also between protagonists and opponents of the war in the USA and South Vietnam, and between various policy options within the US war effort. This was exemplified in the fate of Project Camelot, which was never to be carried out, since it was increasingly discredited in public opinion and by the academic community. Eventually all social science research for defence purposes came under attack, even in Congress, and the Department of Defense cancelled Project Camelot in order not to endanger counterinsurgency research which was already being carried out in Vietnam. Opposition to the Vietnam War was mounting, and counterinsurgency research in Vietnam by the military was becoming more and more embarrassing, until the responsibility and the means for the sponsorship were partly transferred to USAID, and thus to SEADAG (Southeast Asia Development Agency Group), around 1970. It was evident by then that the US government faced a severe legitimacy crisis, which had its repercussions on research carried out for military purposes.

In the context of early modern European society, Quentin Skinner and James Tully have pointed to the tendency that conflicts, and especially wars, generate globalising theories which are intended to legitimate courses of political action, and thus function as ideologies. Such theories are innovative, but are constrained by the use of the accepted normative language of the era (Tully 1988: 22–25). The same can be said about Project Camelot, which asked the types of questions addressed by moral and political economy approaches. Project Camelot was an effort to overcome the basic uncertainty that guided US actions in Vietnam, by forging a generally valid theory of peasant rebellions and peasant behaviour. This uncertainty was evident in the inconsistency of the US war effort, especially in the US Army counterinsurgency policy, and the apparent failure of the modernisation theory which guided the American intervention. Various policy options competed for primacy, as did the institutional interests they represented. For example, the method used by the Special Forces of trying to gain confidence through partial adaptation to local customs clashed with the nation-building approach of the regular army, symbolised by the forced urbanisation scheme, the establishment of free-strike zones and the use of defoliants. One bombardment or defoliation raid could destroy not only the population's habitat, but also months of careful work by the Special Forces, 'civic action' workers or 'rural reconstruction' cadres trying to win the confidence of the population. This structural inconsistency resulted in a failure to achieve pacification. It led to an ongoing search for new and more sophisticated pacification programmes, as exemplified by their rapid succession.

Every now and then critical reports appeared about the American and South-Vietnamese war effort, admitting that the policy of the National Liberation Front was proving far more effective and attractive for a large part of the rural population. These critical reports were mostly ignored by those in charge. In the same vein, many researchers saw their advice either being ignored or failing, which had a disciplining effect on their work. In effect, research conducted for the American military, by preventing insight into the causes of the conflict, tended to systematically create ignorance in the sense that only conclusions which suited official purposes were accepted, while critical observations were dismissed. Thus, counterinsurgency research contributed to the illusion of a 'scientifically managed' war. The neglect of available bodies of knowledge and insights could have disastrous effects when military interests overshadowed political considerations. This was the case with the army's fixation on acquiring new technologies, advanced weapon systems and more firepower, a fixation that led to an ignoring of the effects of indiscriminate American bombing on the political attitude of rural populations. The war was still perceived as a military struggle rather than a political one, due to American reluctance to see the revolution as home-grown rather than imported and imposed from abroad. Such a realisation could raise doubts as to the legitimacy of US involvement in Vietnam. Communism was straightforwardly equated with evil, aggression and terror. It had to be fought against with every conceivable means, preferably scientifically sanctioned.

This conviction formed part and parcel of the discourse which shaped American policy in Vietnam, and was shared by the majority of the scientists who conducted counterinsurgency research in Vietnam (see Laird 1972; Rostow 1960). This discourse prevented most concerned American researchers from gaining insight into the motivations and attitudes of 'the Vietnamese population', which thus appeared as 'mysterious'. And if they diverged from the dominant discourse, their advice was not heeded (see, e.g., Deitchman 1976, 1978). In this situation of intense conflict and crisis, new generalising theories of peasant rebellion and peasant behaviour were sought within the various agencies doing research for military purposes, as well as in academic circles opposed to the war. Project Camelot was an effort in this direction, but its failure only accentuated the growing crisis in American society. As counterinsurgency research became more suspect, research was increasingly sponsored by civil agencies such as USAID and its more 'academic' branch, SEADAG. SEADAG, however, was more inclined to listen to divergent opinions, certainly after the 1968 Têt Offensive. The two opposing hypotheses concerning peasant rebellions put forward in Project Camelot appeared again in the SEADAG research programmes, eventually taking the form of the moral versus political economy debate.

SEADAG: pacification through development

From 1965 onwards USAID took over most agricultural development programmes from the army. This eventually led to different views being adopted. The change was spurred on by the 1968 Têt Offensive of the South-Vietnamese National Liberation Front (NLF) together with their North-Vietnamese sponsors. Although the offensive, which entailed attacks on most major cities in South Vietnam, including Saigon and Huê, was a military failure, it turned out to be a political success. The NLF showed its strength not only in the countryside but also in the cities, where the regular North-Vietnamese troops were not present. This sudden demonstration of force seemed to contradict all official American claims that pacification was a success and their promises that the war would come to an end soon. After Têt 1968, it was not uncommon for US officials to speak of the lack of 'communication' between the Government of South Vietnam (GVN) and the rural population. Consequently, pacification programmes began to be directed at the removal of the causes for resistance by improving the living conditions of the peasants and improving relations between government and peasants. Researchers believed that one needed only to look at the land policy of the NLF for a model to follow (McDonald Salter, in SEADAG 1970: 724–726).

Suddenly American researchers, USAID officials and others began to show interest in the history of tenancy, rents, landlords, taxation in colonial times, and in Viêt Minh land reform policy (Scott and Leichter 1972; Rambo and Jamieson 1970). Previously, too much interest in 'subversive themes' would have rendered such interests suspicious in orthodox eyes. After Têt 1968, however, USAID became aware of the political value of a land reform in Vietnam, and exerted pressure on other American agencies and on the Vietnamese government to take appropriate measures in this respect. Indeed, in 1970, a land redistribution law was adopted, which was to do away with large landholdings: the Land-to-the-Tiller Act. Financed by the USA, landlords were bought out by the South-Vietnamese government, and tenants received title to a few acres of land. In a June 1973 Report to the Congress by the US General Accounting Office on AID assistance to land reform in Vietnam, it was noted 'that peasants become revolutionary when their conditions of land ownership, tenancy, labor, taxes, and prices become unbearable'.[14] Simultaneously, USAID was carrying out a number of smaller projects in the Mekong Delta, aimed at the development of a commercial, more productive agriculture. Thus the Green Revolution was introduced in the Mekong Delta, along with the credit required for the new technologies needed. The need for mechanisation, fertilisers and pesticides made peasants more dependent on the market for cash. They were transformed into small capitalist entrepreneurs who – like Western farmers – were fully integrated into the market.

USAID officials and USAID-sponsored researchers appeared very optimistic about the prospects for pacification that the land reform seemed to offer. There would be no more exploitation of peasants who achieved a higher standard of living, and finally the much regretted 'gap' between town and countryside, as well as between the government and the rural population, could be bridged. The August 1970 issue of *Asian Survey* contained some of the papers of a SEADAG conference on the Vietnamese land reform which had been put into effect in April 1970. Most of the contributions had an air of optimism and hope: at long last the communists would be beaten on their own turf, i.e., through political means. However, there were some pessimists who doubted the ultimate effects of land reform. After all, it was merely a recapitulation of the policy which the NLF had always propagated and, wherever possible, realised. Furthermore, the new market opportunities and the flow of capital goods donated by USAID would give rise to a higher level of corruption than usual among government officials.

In this context, Samuel Popkin, who had conducted pacification research for the army under a contract with the Simulmatics Corporation, made a comparative study of NLF and GVN performance in the villages. Since the GVN officials and the Vietnamese army officers generally were inefficient, careless and corrupt when compared to communist cadres, he did not expect much from the new development schemes. It was the implementation that mattered. Thus he did not expect a new class of farmers to rise out of the mass of peasants:

> The essence of the conflict is not between a traditional peasant and a modernising state, but between a politically sensitive peasantry and a state that is jealous of its own power and prerogatives.
>
> (Popkin 1970: 671)

It would be hard to ignore the message, which is indeed a forerunner of his later *rational peasant* theme.

Popkin was right in his pessimism. The land reform in the Mekong Delta did not bring the desired political bonus. The objections mentioned above proved to be valid. The implementation left much to be desired, as many landlords circumvented the law by parcelling out their land to members of their families. In fact, for many peasants this was a drawback, as they lost the land they tilled or had to pay rent again. The corruption of the regime prevented a rapid economic development, also because of the lack of necessary capital goods. This was aggravated by the reluctance of the American Congress to allocate more sizeable funds for Vietnam. Another drawback was that the land reform came too late to appeal to the peasants. The American policy of forced urbanisation had been sufficiently 'successful' in relieving the land scarcity which once existed. But in places where peasants did profit from the land reform, they hardly credited the Saigon regime for it, since the NLF had a much longer tradition of land redistribution. Last, in places controlled by the NLF, peasants had more opportunities to acquire necessary capital goods and to market their surplus produce. But at this stage of the war, due to the Têt Offensive and to the so-called Phoenix Program, of killing communist cadres, the NLF guerrilla force had largely been eliminated. The NLF cadres were gradually replaced by regular North-Vietnamese soldiers, to the effect that the guerrilla movement was not as dependent on the local population as before.

In June 1974, a SEADAG seminar was held on 'Peasants, land reform and revolutionary movements'. Both Scott and Popkin contributed papers which subsequently were published in *Comparative Politics*, a reputable political science journal (Scott 1975; Popkin 1976). The April 1976 issue contained most of the other papers presented at the seminar as well. Both Scott and Popkin had been able to work out their theories while receiving grants from SEADAG, which appeared to carry through the job which the Department of Defense had started as Project Camelot. Apart from the models of peasant resistance presented by Scott and Popkin, this issue of *Comparative Politics* contained articles such as 'Adequacy of social science models for the study of peasant movements' by John Powell and 'IRI: a simplified predictive index of rural instability' by Roy Prosterman. The question arises: Why did two opposing explanatory models of peasant resistance emerge in the context of SEADAG, and more generally, of USAID? For an answer we have to turn to the Vietnam War again.

As noted above, the rapid succession of pacification schemes hardly resulted in the desired pacification of the Vietnamese countryside. The Têt Offensive especially had a profound effect on the scientific community, the press and the general American public; it seemed to emphasise the futility of the US intervention in Vietnam. Many researchers who were critical of the American or South-Vietnamese performance saw their advice ignored if it diverged from the dominant discourse on insurgency in Vietnam. The apparent failure of American policy called for a more convincing explanation than the usual 'communist subversion' theme. Some researchers sought the cause of the failure in the discord existing in the American camp, especially in the 'betrayal' by the press and politicians. Others blamed the infamous corruption of the Vietnamese counterpart – the government and army of South Vietnam – for the *échec*. But more relevant to us is the explanation which focused on the mysterious determination of the Vietnamese people to resist foreign intervention. The roots of this attitude were localised in the Vietnamese countryside where tradition still seemed to reign. In the early 1970s this last opinion was translated into sociological theory when John McAlister (McAlister and Mus 1970) and Frances FitzGerald (1972) adopted the analysis by Paul Mus of the traditional Vietnamese village community. Then, after the North-Vietnamese victory in 1975, Scott and Popkin published their books on Vietnam.

James Scott stripped the Vietnamese village of its mystical qualities through the introduction of the concept of moral economy, which purported to show the rationality of traditional arrangements within the village. The destruction of moral arrangements which guaranteed a minimum subsistence level by the introduction of the market economy by the colonial state led poor and middle peasants to resist these outside economic and political forces. In contrast, the political economy approach by Samuel Popkin was a sophisticated critique of 'left-wing' moral economists by intellectuals who supported the American intervention in Vietnam from the outset. Carefully avoiding the jargon about communist subversion and exportation of revolution, Popkin nevertheless shares some basic premises with the theories of Walt Rostow, where his peasants are depicted as *homines oeconomici*. The market metaphor dominates in his description of individual behavioural strategies. The market is considered as beneficial, providing fresh opportunities for all strata of society. As for resistance, this is not generated locally, but can be viewed as profitable by the peasants when there is some strong outside organisation imposing itself on rural society. That is why the Vietnamese peasants were more inclined to support the NLF than the corrupt administration and army of South Vietnam (cf. Moise 1982; Peltez 1983).

In the previous sections I have argued that both theories can be considered as constituting discourses on peasant rebellion which already existed in embryonic form in the Camelot Project, and which were generated within the context of American involvement with Vietnam. It need not surprise us that Popkin, who carried out applied research for the army, shares the basic premises of dominant American discourse legitimising the intervention. His theory, although much more refined than earlier versions, was couched in neo-classical jargon. Scott's approach, on the other hand, can be viewed as a dissident view – the logical alternative in Project Camelot's and SEADAG's predictive models at a time when the pacification programmes were failing. But both approaches have in common the attempt to provide generalising theories about the nature of peasant society and peasant behaviour. And simultaneously, they offered explanations for the American failure to win the war in Vietnam.

Their theories can be considered as globalising theories concerning peasant behaviour. The elements and concepts of both theories were already available, but the way Scott and Popkin combined these provided rallying points for the social science community which had been in crisis over the Vietnam War since the 1960s. The American involvement itself provided the context in which the fundamental question of the causes of peasant rebellion had to be asked and answered. Social science research was to provide the answer to this question, as exemplified by Project Camelot. But Camelot failed, just as the US intervention in Vietnam ultimately failed. Discord between the different institutions of intervention was too wide to be bridged, and the basic discourse on the nature of communism was so rigid as to institutionalise the misapprehensions of Vietnamese society. American society was experiencing a serious political crisis following the defeat in Vietnam and the Watergate Affair. Although Scott and Popkin addressed issues which had to do with Vietnamese society, they also said something about the nature of American society and the legitimacy of the way it dealt with the Third World. They made political statements, which were formulated on the basis of existing and accepted concepts – the normative language – of social science. The Scott–Popkin debate, then, reflects divisions within American society, in particular the social science community, after the traumatic experience of Vietnam. Simultaneously, both theories addressed the basis for outside interventions in developing counties that were mostly peasant societies, not just Vietnam, by analysing the interface between state, market and community.

Back to the future

During the 1980s this theoretical controversy became an important academic debate that was used as textbook material in many social science curricula around the world. Since then, however, both theories have to a large extent been debunked, by feminist scholars, amongst others, who claim that a gender analysis is lacking in both theories and that, within village communities and within families, interests between sexes and the generations do not necessarily converge. So what is the relevance of both theories and their successor theories in this day and age? I would claim that their underlying assumptions about community, market and development still play important roles as the conceptual assumptions underpinning contemporary development interventions. Although both books contained detached, scholarly analyses, the assumptions and conclusions about community, market and development have more practical, development-related implications. Apart from reflecting opposing political stances concerning America's handling of the Vietnam War, the theories of political and moral economy have direct relevance for development policy, SEADAG's (and its main funder, USAID's) first and foremost interest.

Samuel Popkin is outspoken in this respect, warning against false hopes for community development schemes. In his view, high expectations regarding the willingness of villagers to cooperate and participate are mostly unrealistic. Such schemes tend to be coercive and provide a potential for abuse. Popkin asserts that peasants cooperate on the basis of task-specific incentives and calculations, and peasants can benefit from the market much more than they can from bureaucracies (1979: 245–252). In contrast, Scott distrusts the functioning of the market *vis-à-vis* the peasants. He cites the case of the Green Revolution, which offered opportunities to a few rich and middle peasants, but created problems for those who could not cope with the required level of investment, with the risks of crop failure, or for those who were unemployed (1976: 207–212). Implicitly, Scott criticises the kind of market-oriented development that Popkin suggests. In short, where Popkin regards commercialisation as a major contributor to development and peasant welfare, Scott considers it as detrimental to the moral arrangements within the village community and thus to a large part of the peasant population, especially the poorer segment.

This mirrors today's bifurcation of development paradigms, whereby one development approach is epitomised by the structural adjustment policies promoted by the WTO, IMF, the big development banks and many major bilateral donors. This paradigm champions the functioning of the market and the rational actors within the market who try to maximise their profits through competition, not hampered by considerations of 'national solidarity' (through state subsidies) or by notions of responsibility and accountability towards one's own community. Keywords in this development paradigm are economic growth, market reform, free enterprise, rational calculation, profit maximisation, and competition. It is evident that Popkin's political economy theory shares a number of basic premises with this free-market paradigm of development intervention.

Another approach, championed by many NGOs, promotes poverty reduction by self-organisation and empowerment of local groups. Often, these self-styled 'bottom-up', participatory interventions are predicated on the existence of local communities in such approaches as 'community-based natural resource management', 'community health', 'social forestry' or 'community forestry', 'common property regimes' or – in short – community development. Often such development interventions are aided by rapid rural appraisal (RRA) and participatory rural appraisal (PRA) techniques, as promoted by Robert Chambers (1983, 1997), as well as by interventions which are based on local or indigenous knowledge. Such approaches assume the existence of a functioning (moral) community and a degree of solidarity. The parallels with James Scott's moral economy theory are evident. Absent in this simplified dichotomy are micro-finance interventions in the form of micro-credit schemes with revolving loan or savings and credit schemes managed by local groups of mostly women, as originally developed by the Grameen Bank in Bangladesh. This is a mixed form which on the one hand is based on the existence of community solidarity and social cohesion structures among women, but on the other hand aiming at their empowerment and economic enhancement *via* the market, in the sense that the participants are encouraged to invest their credit in productive and commercially viable small enterprises.

Patrick Tierney's (2000) study of Yanomamö research, mentioned in the beginning of this chapter, brings out clearly that research by itself – whether social science research or other research – is an intervention in the life of the group under study. In his study research is portrayed as a direct intervention through the presence of the researchers in the group or community, and indirect because the inner workings of such a group or community are made public knowledge. According to Tierney, the research process itself had direct consequences for the Yanomami. The context of the Scott–Popkin debate reveals that social science research is also an indirect intervention in the lives of people under study and others, no matter what the intentions of the researcher are.

It is unusual that social science research has any serious direct effect on or consequence for the population under study, in the way and degree as reported by Patrick Tierney with respect to the Yanomami – and contested by others. What the Scott–Popkin debate shows, both in its genesis and in its consequences, is that social science theories are formulated and articulated in the context of other interventions in the lives of these people. In extreme cases such as the Vietnam War these are military interventions, but increasingly social science research takes place in the context of humanitarian interventions or peace-keeping operations. More commonly, however, interventions by the state (through laws and policing, education, health, etc.), development interventions, missionary interventions, economic investments by companies and even environmental/ecological investments (e.g., reforestation as part of a carbon sequestration scheme) form both subtext and context for social science research. This is all clear from Patrick Tierney's book about research among the Yanomami (even though this aspect is usually ignored in the responses and critiques of the book), but the same goes for ethnic minority research in, say, Dutch society. Social science theories and statements are not neutral or inconsequential, but tend to legitimise or de-legitimise certain forms of intervention, and privilege some approaches over other ones within such interventions. Whereas social science research usually cannot stop such other types of intervention, it can at least modify somewhat the (discursive) playing field.

What this implies in terms of research ethics is that an ethical code conceived as a series of rules, procedures, prescriptions and especially prohibitions governing the research process is wholly inadequate for the simple reason that it leaves out the context. It leaves out the historical context and the contemporary context of the research process. More importantly, it leaves out the potential futures in terms of consequences, implications or possibilities offered by the research. Anthropology and other social science research is not inherently good or bad, as implied by Tierney's study – or indeed by most existing ethical codes of professional social science associations. Even research which is fully conducted according to ethical codes may have adverse consequences for the research population. Therefore, constant reflection is needed which can only come through transparency and debate rather than through a fixation on rules and procedure – through process-oriented, contextually informed and case-specific *emergent ethics* rather than through fixed ethical codes.

Notes

1 I use 'Vietnam War' for convenience; this war is called the 'American War' by the Vietnamese.
2 A Statement from Bruce Alberts, President of the National Academy of Sciences, 9 November 2000: 'Setting the Record Straight Regarding *Darkness in El Dorado*', http: //www4.national academies.org/nas/nashome.nsf/
3 For Immediate Release, 9 February 2001: American Anthropological Association Launches Formal Inquiry into Allegations made in *Darkness in El Dorado*, http: //www.aaanet.org/press/ ebmotion.htm
4 See Irving Horowitz (1967); Davenport (1985); Fluehr-Lobban (1991); Wakin (1992); Klare (1972).
5 Paul Mus was a famous orientalist who had worked within the framework of the École Française d'Extrême-Orient. From 1944 until 1954 he had carried out secret missions for the French authorities, negotiating with the Viêt Minh.
6 James Scott, personal communication, 24 June 1995.
7 Note, for example, the title of an article by Scott: 'Exploitation in rural class relations: a victim's perspective' (1975). For an idea of the political image of both authors, see Cumings (1981) and Peletz (1983).
8 This qualitative difference between northern and southern Vietnamese villages had been noted early on by Terry Rambo (1973) in his doctoral dissertation. In his 'Protest and Profanation', Scott signals the same difference (1977: 9). Despite the popular dichotomy between North and South Vietnam in the Western imagination, Vietnam has in pre-colonial, colonial and post-colonial times been divided in three main parts (Tonkin, Annam, Cochinchina – or Bac Bo, Trung Bo and Nam Bo) with the period of US intervention as a brief interlude.
9 Solid analyses of the emergence of the concept of counterinsurgency have been provided by Blaufarb (1977) and Cable (1986).
10 They were respectively called Land Development Centres (1957–1960), Agrovilles (1961–1963), or New Life Hamlets (1964–1965).
11 Smithsonian Institution Archives, Record Unit 179, Research Group on Psychology and the Social Sciences Records, 1957–1963.
12 Smithsonian Institution Archives, Record Unit 179, Research Group on Psychology and the Social Sciences Records, box 3.

13 In terms of hypotheses, these were economic theories which stated that internal wars (a) are generated by growing poverty, (b) result from rapid economic progress. Social theories postulated that (a) internal war is a reflection of frustration arising from little social mobility; or (b) results from great social mobility. Political theories stated that (a) internal wars are due to excessive toleration of alienated groups; or that (b) internal wars are responses to oppressive government (Deitchman 1976: 143).

14 US General Accounting Office (1973) *Progress and Problems of US Assistance for Land Reform in Vietnam: Agency for International Development, Department of State (B-159451)*, report to the Congress by the Controller General of the United States, Washington, DC, p. 5.

References

Blaufarb, Douglas (1977) *The Counterinsurgency Era: U.S. Doctrine and Performance*, New York: Free Press.

Brocheux, Pierre (1983) 'Moral or political economy? The peasants are always rational', *Journal of Asian Studies* 42 (4): 791–804.

Cable, Larry (1986) *Conflict of Myths: the Development of American Counterinsurgency Doctrine and the Vietnam War*, New York/London: New York University Press.

Chambers, Robert (1983) *Rural Development: Putting the Last First*, Harlow: Longman.

—— (1997) *Whose Reality Really Counts? Putting the First Last*, London: Intermediate Technology Publications.

Cumings, Bruce (1981) 'Interest and ideology in the study of agrarian politics', *Politics and Society* 10 (4): 467–495.

Currey, Cecil B. (1988) *Edward Lansdale: the Unquiet American*, Boston: Houghton Mifflin.

Davenport, William (1985) 'The Thailand controversy in retrospect', in June Helm (ed.) *The Social Contexts of American Ethnology, 1840–1984*, Washington, DC: American Ethnological Society, pp. 65–72.

Deitchman, Seymour (1976) *The Best-Laid Schemes: a Tale of Social Research and Bureaucracy*, Cambridge, MA: MIT Press.

—— (1978) 'Another step toward Nirvana (response to Murray Wax' review of *The Best-Laid Schemes)*', *Human Organization* 37 (4): 408–412.

Escobar, Arturo (1995) *Encountering Development: the Making and Unmaking of the Third World*, Princeton: Princeton University Press.

FitzGerald, Frances (1972) *Fire in the Lake: the Vietnamese and the Americans in Vietnam*, Boston: Atlantic – Little, Brown and Company.

Fluehr-Lobban, Carolyn (1991) 'Ethics and professionalism: a review of issues and principles within anthropology', in Carolyn Fluehr-Lobban (ed.) *Ethics and the Profession of Anthropology: Dialogue for a New Era*, Philadelphia: University of Pennsylvania Press, pp. 13–35.

Gendzier, Irene (1985) *Managing Political Change: Social Scientists and the Third World*, Boulder/London: Westview Press.

Grinter, Lawrence E. (1975) 'South Vietnam: pacification denied', *South East Asian Spectrum* 3 (4): 49–78.

Hatcher, Patrick Lloyd (1990) *The Suicide of an Elite: American Internationalists and Vietnam*, Stanford: Stanford University Press.
Hickey, Gerald C. (1964) *Village in Vietnam*, New Haven/London: Yale University Press.
Hobart, Mark (ed.) (1993) *An Anthropological Critique of Development: the Growth of Ignorance*, London: Routledge.
Horowitz, Irving L. (ed.) (1967) *The Rise and Fall of Project Camelot: Studies in the Relationship between Social Science and Practical Politics*, Cambridge, MA: MIT Press.
Kahin, George McT. (1986) *Intervention: How America Became Involved in Vietnam*, Garden City, NY: Anchor Books.
Keyes, Charles F. (ed.) (1983) 'Peasant strategies in Asian societies: moral and rational economic approaches – a symposium', *Journal of Asian Studies* 42 (4), special issue.
Klare, Michael T. (1972) *War Without End: American Planning for the Next Vietnams*, New York: Random House.
Kleinen, Johannes (1988) *Boeren, Fransen en Rebellen. Een studie van boerenverzet in een Midden-Vietnamese regio (1880–1940)*, doctoral dissertation, University of Amsterdam.
Laird, Melvin R. (1972) *The Nixon Doctrine: a Town Hall Meeting on National Security Policy*, Washington, DC: American Enterprise Institute for Public Policy Research.
Lansdale, Edward (1972) *In the Midst of Wars: an American's Mission to Southeast Asia*, New York: Harper and Row.
McAlister, John T. Jr and Paul Mus (1970) *The Vietnamese and their Revolution*, New York: Harper Torchbooks.
Moise, Edwin (1982) 'Review of *The Rational Peasant* – the political economy of rural society in Vietnam', *Bulletin of Concerned Asian Scholars* 14 (1): 72–77.
Moore, Barrington Jr (1966) *Social Origins of Dictatorship and Democracy: Lord and Peasant in the Making of the Modern World*, Harmondsworth: Penguin Books.
Mus, Paul (1948) 'The role of the village in Vietnamese politics', *Pacific Affairs* XXII (9): 265–272.
—— (1952) *Viêt-Nam, Sociologie d'une Guerre*, Paris: Editions du Seuil.
Peletz, Michael G. (1983) 'Moral and political economies in rural Southeast Asia', *Comparative Studies in Society and History* 25: 731–739.
Pool, Ithiel de Sola (ed.) (1963) *Social Science Research and National Security*, Washington, DC: Smithsonian Institution, under Office of Naval research contract 1354(18).
Popkin, Samuel L. (1970) 'Pacification: politics and the village', *Asian Survey* X (8): 662–671.
—— (1976) 'Corporatism and colonialism: political economy of rural change in Vietnam', *Comparative Politics* 8 (3): 431–464.
—— (1979) *The Rational Peasant: the Political Economy of Rural Society in Vietnam*, Berkeley: University of California Press.
Rambo, A. Terry (1973) *A Comparison of Peasant Social Systems of Northern and Southern Vietnam: a Study of Ecological Adaptation, Social Succession and Cultural Evolution*, Carbondale: Center for Vietnamese Studies, Southern Illinois University.

Rambo, A. Terry and Neil L. Jamieson III (1970) *Cultural Change in Rural Vietnam: a Study of Long-Term Communist Control on the Social Structure, Attitudes, and Values of the Peasants of the Mekong*, New York: Asia Society, SEADAG paper no. 73(4).

Rostow, Walt W. (1960) *The Stages of Economic Growth: a Non-Communist Manifesto*, London: Cambridge University Press.

Salemink, Oscar (1991) '*Moïs* and *Maquis*: The invention and appropriation of Vietnam's Montagnards from Sabatier to the CIA', in George W. Stocking Jr (ed.) *Colonial Situations. Essays on the Contextualization of Ethnographic Knowledge (History of Anthropology 7)*, Madison: University of Wisconsin Press, pp. 243–284.

Scott, James C. (1975) 'Exploitation in rural class relations: a victim's perspective', *Comparative Politics* 7 (4): 489–532.

—— (1976) *The Moral Economy of the Peasant: Rebellion and Subsistence in Southeast Asia*, New Haven: Yale University Press.

—— (1977) 'Protest and profanation: agrarian revolt and the little tradition', *Theory and Society* 4: 1–38, 211–246.

—— (1985) *Weapons of the Weak: Everyday Forms of Peasant Resistance*, New Haven: Yale University Press.

Scott, James C. and Howard Leichter (1972) *A Bibliography on Land, Peasants, and Politics for Viet-Nam, Laos, and Cambodia*, Madison, WI: University of Wisconsin Land Tenure Center, Contract AID/csd-2263, project 931–11–120–111.

SEADAG (Southeast Asian Development Agency Group, USAID) (1970) 'Politics, land reform and development in the countryside, A SEADAG conference', *Asian Survey* X (8): 627–764.

Skinner, Quentin (1978) *The Foundations of Modern Political Thought* (Volumes 1 and 2), Cambridge: Cambridge University Press.

Tierney, Patrick (2000) *Darkness in El Dorado: How Scientists and Journalists Devastated the Amazon*, New York/London: W.W. Norton and Company.

Tully, James (ed.) (1988) *Meaning and Context: Quentin Skinner and his Critics*, Cambridge: Polity Press.

Wakin, Eric (1992) *Anthropology Goes to War: Professional Ethics and Counterinsurgency in Thailand*, Madison: Center for Southeast Asian Studies, University of Wisconsin.

Wolf, Eric R. (1969) *Peasant Wars of the Twentieth Century*, New York/London: Harper and Row.

Wolf, Eric and Joseph Jorgensen (1970) 'Anthropology on the warpath in Thailand', *New York Review of Books* 15 (19 November): 26–35.

Chapter 9

Anecdotes, situations, histories

Varieties and uses of cases in thinking about ethics and development practice[1]

Des Gasper

What can we do with cases in development practice?

Pim de Graaf, now a Médecins Sans Frontières manager in Amsterdam, earlier worked as a doctor in an area in Southern Tanzania. Most 8–12-year-old children in this area had bilharzia and hence sometimes urinated blood. Those who did not pass blood were considered sick and were treated by traditional doctors. At a conference (NVCO, Soesterberg, 1997) de Graaf recounted how he decided not to intervene or even seek to dispel the beliefs. He feared he would make the majority of the children feel ill and their parents feel guilty, in circumstances where a sustained supply of anti-bilharzia drugs could not be expected.

Two opposed responses to de Graaf's story emerged. Group A held that he should have supplied medical information, to open a dialogue and permit people to make better-informed choices; not to do so was to treat them as moral infants. Group B held that local practices must be presumed appropriate. They argued that Western medical practices should not be promoted, being often deeply flawed or inconsistent with local resources and culture, which must instead be strengthened and built upon. De Graaf himself in effect formed a Group C, which abstained from intervention not because of doubts about Western medical knowledge but because of a perceived dilemma between giving people more awareness and choice and leaving them more happy. The case served well in surfacing profound disagreements about medicine, 'communities' (a favourite category in Group B, suspect in Group A), and 'development' (a term discarded by Group B, retained in Group A). It contained no easy route to reducing the disagreements.

Case material is vital, but can be random, casual, or bewildering.[2] I will consider the roles and limits of various types, including case studies proper, anecdotes and abstracted choice situations, in improving understanding of ethical tensions, conflicts and choices, with special reference to development practice and emergency relief.[3] The focus on 'development' brings characteristic inter-cultural, inter-national, inter-income strata and inter-generational concerns; but most of the chapter is relevant for other contexts too. The discussion will centre on types of cases and general issues in their use, not on drawing substantive conclusions about the examples presented. Where comments are given, these are either views of the authors cited or are there to add flavour and suggest ingredients and issues in deciding in and from cases, not more than that.

I take as starting point that development is 'a multi-faceted, multi-vocal process, and a complex site of contestation', beyond any one agent's powers to foresee and control (Grillo and Stirrat 1997: vii). In such contestation and vocalising, agents seek to define and defend themselves and influence others through language, including ethical statements and systems.

We are often regaled with anecdotes of the invincible horrors, hyper-complexity, hypocrisy, and unintended negative effects of development interventions; or – now less frequently than earlier – of the reverse. Anecdotes can serve to give us questions, and to convey some aspects and varieties of experience. But they lack depth, a systematic basis of comparison and, often, a sense of inquiry.

Analytically inclined philosophers reflect on simplified abstracted situations of moral tension and choice, which can serve to sharpen and organise some concepts and intuitions. When one reads the work on ethics by many (not least Anglo-American) philosophers, and indeed some Northern social scientists, one is liable however to weary of their narrow, and often only implicit, sets of experiential source materials.[4] Anthropologists, on the other hand, provide extended case histories – of policies, projects, organisations or individuals – which sometimes go further than do anecdotes and abstraction and can deepen their inheritance of questions and concepts. When one reads these richer case studies one must ask however not only how valid is the account, but how good is the sample and how we can make case studies into more than lengthy anecdotes.

One theme in the chapter, already apparent and to be discussed in the following section, concerns the different predilections, contributions and limitations of various disciplines and professions. A second theme, to be discussed in the subsequent section, concerns the choice between richer cases and more selective ones, between thicker and thinner, and the underlying differences in philosophy or purpose. A supportive theme is how considerations distinctive to normative argumentation sometimes justify different use of cases compared to when purposes are descriptive or explanatory. For example, not only is more information sometimes unnecessary, certain types of information can be undesirable as they could bias decision makers.

A last theme is that use of a wide range of types of case is in large part justifiable, for practical action and associated analysis call for a mix of types of thinking and feeling and willing. Notwithstanding the differences between philosophies, all the styles that we will see can be legitimate when in an appropriate niche or role. Ethics and reflective action involve a set of distinct arenas, marked by distinct purposes and correspondingly different methods and use of cases. For mobilisation of attention, concern, sympathy and energy, particular types of case serve well, often somewhat simplified but showing real people. Second, the choices thrown up by cases are tackled using whatever resources of thought and emotion are mobilised and found relevant. Where people find these resources insufficient or in conflict they may turn to explicit theorising. Depersonalised cases, simplified more drastically, may be used to help here. When we try to apply theories to complex real situations, we need further skills in selecting, adapting and combining ideas from theory, in facing and working with real people, and of practical idealism; and can strengthen these by reflection on rich, real cases.

Varieties of 'case' or example

Let us consider types of case or example under six headings: (1) thick case studies; (2) thin case studies; (3) real life choice situations; (4) real life anecdotes and other illustrations; (5) conceivably true fictions; and (6) impossible fictions. We begin with the traditional ideal amongst anthropologists, the thick case study.

Thick case studies: standard research advice and beyond

A *thick* case study is holistic and includes distinctive, even idiosyncratic, situations and details, people and cultures, and treats them in their contexts, technical and institutional, local and beyond. Criteria for 'thickness' are thus: first, broad scope, provided to 'situate' a case, contextualise it, and view it holistically; second, degree of detail, notably case-specific, person-specific detail; and third, penumbrally, use of a plurality of methods, perspectives and voices.

Thickness is characteristically but not exclusively anthropological. The respective strengths and weaknesses of holistic and analytic approaches in descriptive and explanatory studies, and their potential complementarity, are well known.[5] Larger samples normally bring a narrower scope of investigation and much greater non-sampling error. Single case studies cannot sustain generalisations, but provide insights and hypotheses as well as some understanding about those specific cases. They are often stronger in 'bandwidth', 'providing answers to a wide array of questions rather than [precise information on a] single question' (Shadish *et al.* 1991: 310). In fact, for evaluation of ongoing or completed programmes, Stake and others call for priority to be given to 'bandwidth', broad-ranging observation, and hence rich, open-ended case studies.[6] This allows one to be rough but relevant, rather than sticking to a flawed pre-set observational frame, typically given by pre-set programme objectives. Stake argues that even if case studies are weak on generating law-like explanations, they are strong 'When the aims are *understanding, extension of experience, and increase in conviction in that which is known*' (1978: 7; emphasis added; 'understanding' refers here to grasping participants' interpretations, motives and actions). All three roles are vital in ethics, as we will see.

In a study of 1980s literature relevant to the ethics of development aid, I suggested that 'some readers may well feel, at least on first examination, that the most rewarding pieces. ... were those – such as the books by Shawcross [a journalist, on relief to Cambodia in 1979–1983; *The Quality of Mercy* (1984)] and Harrell-Bond [an anthropologist, on aid for Ugandan refugees in Sudan in 1980–1985; *Imposing Aid* (1986)] – not written by philosophers or economists!' (Gasper 1997: 41). Often far richer experience is drawn on: 'From the urgency of the events it describes, much of the literature from [emergency] cases like Ethiopia, Cambodia and Rwanda has been pointed and holistic; not formal examinations of dense but narrow data, but thought-provoking accounts of decision making done with poor information and under pressure' (Gasper 1997: 39).

The best thick case studies are not necessarily the most detailed. Those sometimes provide merely the raw materials for a good – enlightening, connections-revealing – study. Many historians argue that since selections are inevitable they should be explicit, systematic and purposeful (e.g., Stretton 1969). There should be a guiding set of questions (though indeed not only or necessarily the ones with which the historian began) which turn an account into a meaningful case, a study of something, not a doomed effort to recount everything. Lisa Peattie's streamlined *Planning – Rethinking Ciudad Guyana* (1987) about the planning and growth of a new city in Venezuela from the 1960s to the 1980s, is at least as useful as the more congested project histories in Doug Porter *et al.*'s *Development in Practice* (1991) (on an Australian-aided resettlement project in Kenya, 1973–1989), or Norman Uphoff's *Learning from Gal Oya* (1996) (on a decade of irrigation organisations on a scheme in Sri Lanka). But each is of exceptional quality, drawing insights through its multidisciplinarity and greater spread of years than in most evaluations.

Thin case studies

Many studies which have sufficient depth and investigative character for the title 'case study' nevertheless use a rather limited and pre-set range of questions and methods, and hence may be called 'thin'. They are not holistic. When well done, they can be extremely incisive and helpful; for example the studies in Sen's *Poverty and Famines* (1981), of the famines in 1940s Bengal and 1970s Bangladesh, Ethiopia, and the Sahel.

What makes a thin case study 'well done', or productive? Consider three examples. Nussbaum and Glover's collection *Women, Culture, and Development* (1995) opens with a case study by Marty Chen that presents obstacles to obtaining paid employment which have been faced by many rural women in northern parts of the Indian subcontinent: disapproval and obstruction by their (extended) families and dominant sections in local 'communities'. A digest of other work, including her own, this thin case study has only one consistently heard voice, Chen's, and focuses only on simpler situations, where women actively seek external employment and yet are obstructed. But these situations remain real and the study informs and enriches several subsequent chapters which refer to it when assessing Sen's or Nussbaum's capabilities approach.

Many of Robert Chambers's cases in *Whose Reality Counts?* (1997) appear rather as anecdotes, brief illustrations of a pre-formed conclusion. But some are quite extensive and analytical, draw on work by many others, and can be placed here, notably his cases of 'massive error' and failure to learn from experience, which concern three myths of the 1980s: huge post-harvest losses, catastrophic deforestation by local populations, and success (somewhere) with animal-drawn tool-carriers.

Using a text-based approach, Keith Tester's *Moral Culture* (1997) looks at reactions to, and subjective involvements in, various mid- and late-twentieth-century massacres and genocides. His only case study in my sense is of My Lai, where American troops shot dead at least 347 Vietnamese villagers – virtually all of them old, women, or children – in a few minutes one morning in 1968. Here Tester mainly applies a theory rather than examining the Americans or the villagers in personal detail. Like Sen, Chambers, and Chen, Tester piggy-backs on previous work on his case, and then usefully connects it to related broader theorising.

An effective thin case study could thus be one which builds on previous thicker work on the case, and starts to identify or posit key aspects and relate the case to other instances and relevant theory. The intention can be to illuminate and/or draw conclusions about the case, or to identify principles relevant to a range of cases. Clarifying and assessing posited principles might require a move to a more abstracted mode, as we discuss later.

Real-life choice situations – with or without advice

Some discussion cases are presented in a more or less neutral fashion, giving a situation and a choice arising, followed by a request for the reader to make an argued choice, and/or by presentation of the author's view. Such choice situations can be written thickly or thinly. Usually they are towards the thin side, as in many public and business administration exercises, since the intention may be to ensure space for interpretation, arguments, and mobilisation of readers' own experience and insights. Scenarios used for instruction in other professional fields – or in religion – often share this format.

In his lucid and helpful 'Doing the right thing: relief agencies, moral dilemmas and moral responsibility in political emergencies and war' (1997), Hugo Slim presents four 'scenarios'. They have this concern: what ethical compromises are acceptable when trying to do good? The cases while real are very schematic. Each is stated in about 200–300 words, to describe a choice that has faced relief agencies. Slim then expounds his recommended responses in about 500–800 words per case.

Let us look at the first scenario. It asks whether relief agencies should have supplied the Rwandese refugee camps in Zaire in 1994–1996, despite knowing that the camps were dominated by Hutu forces who had been involved in the preceding genocide of Tutsis (and of Hutus willing to work with Tutsis to implement the 1993 Arusha peace agreement), and who were continuing in armed conflict in Rwanda and preparing for a re-invasion to complete the genocide. (Not mentioned by Slim but known amongst some agencies, the Hutu forces also continued with killings in the camps and environs.) Slim advises that any future mis-deeds by Hutu forces coming from the camps would be their own responsibility, not those of agencies who had supplied them with non-military material; the responsibility of relief agencies is instead to supply food and other necessities to people in distress.

Slim presents difficult choices, different responses, and his own argued recommendations. He does not discuss the cases with a depth or tone intended to further other interpretations. The relief community and some of its agencies and their members were torn apart by the stress of choices faced in Rwanda, Zaire, Sudan, Bosnia and elsewhere. One role of his scenarios seems to be to strengthen morale, provide simple workable guidelines, and help staff sleep at night. He uses the format of the sermon, and subordinates case detail to moral theory. However, he gives sufficient materials to provoke reflection and possible alternative responses.[7]

De Graaf's Tanzania bilharzia story at the start of this chapter is another case of a real choice, with a more anecdotal personal element. Its very lack of detail makes it a Rohrsach test for drawing out people's presumptions. Before taking a stance should one not know something about the nature of bilharzia and its effects in the locality concerned, the effects of the treatment given by traditional doctors to those children who in reality do not have bilharzia, and the range of other possible treatments?[8] Yet battle lines are often drawn in advance and lead to a re-run of old conflict scripts, as at the conference where de Graaf spoke.

Real-life anecdotes

Cooper and Packard note that 'Template mechanisms are preconstructed frameworks which are used to simplify and control complex environments. One such mechanism is the "case", reducing a complex instance to a single useful message' (1997: 24). Within organisations, many cases are reduced to simple warning plaques: 'Remember the case of Munich 1938/ Rwanda 1994/...'. Given that there are richer types of case, this reduced notion of a 'case' matches what we will call anecdotes.

Anecdotes are typically superficial and relatively short stories that serve to illustrate a point. They lack the more exploratory investigative character and usually also the depth of the case study proper. Frequently the point is pre-selected. Robert Nozick's (1974) example of the riches accruing to a famous sportsman through gladly made payments by myriad fans asserts the unquestionable rightness of the idol's immense wealth and his uninfringeable claim to it all. He does not probe real cases further.[9] Closed rather than open use of a case is common; for example, most of the cases in Caufield's (1998) disturbing history of the World Bank or in Chambers's *Whose Reality Counts?* (1997). This is not necessarily a criticism: Caufield's and Chambers's illustrations seem powerful and convincing. Sometimes anecdotes serve as vectors of insights. However, many cases Chambers describes involve the use by others of anecdotes and illustrations to re-endorse a misguided pre-fixed position. Fairhead and Leach (1997) give a fuller exposition of one example, the 'evidence' claimed for progressive deforestation in Guinea even when masses of villagers and photographs indicated the opposite.

Anecdotes frequently function as put-downs, illustrations of the absurdity, sub-humanity and otherness of 'them'. Such anecdotes flourish in everyday talk, low-grade journalism, and the travelogue. Talented exponents have included Evelyn Waugh, Paul Theroux and the Naipauls.[10] The anecdote is a natural partner also of international aid and the quick visits and existential distances common in 'technical assistance'. Leonard Frank's 'The development game' (1986), a short story about an anomic multi-national UN project identification mission in the frontier province of Pakistan, is itself an extended, depressing, anecdote. Though fictional it apparently derives closely from experience.

Conceivably true fictions

Anecdotes dispense with information about situations when it is incidental or inconvenient for their message. Armchair philosophy, like neoclassical economics, has tended to dispense with real situations altogether, finding them inconvenient for analysis, clumsy, too complicated. It prefers fictions – some conceivably true, others conceivable but impossible – so that it can focus precisely on one or two issues at a time. This artificial style has thrived in analytic philosophy with a predominant contemporary Anglo-American middle-class range of references and cast of characters. Its limitation lies not in the attempt to hone concepts and formulate issues, but rather when such work seeks to draw conclusions in advance of exposing its constructs to real and more varied experiences.

It is worth remembering that fiction, hopefully in realist mode, enters all appraisal and evaluation: the specification of a counter-factual case to represent what would (have) happen(ed) without the intervention that is under assessment. However well we try to simulate, comparison cases in social science always differ from the intervention case in ways other than not having had the intervention, so we require supportive arguments to justify them as good enough representatives of the fictional, counter-factual case (Deming 1975).[11]

Hypothetical, but possible, cases of other types figure importantly in ethics. Their force typically rests on being possible, for they are to make people consider their own and others' feelings in or about cases which they can vividly envisage, or 'feel themselves into'. Much of Martha Nussbaum's work tries for this reason to enrich ethics and social philosophy by examination of fiction (e.g., Nussbaum 1997). Here we will look at some more schematic examples.

American philosopher Thomas Nagel (1994) contends that *ethical* arguments cannot be *based* on self-interest alone (though self-interest can often be *concluded* to be ethically valid), nor on appeal to authority (e.g., religious). Those are different types of argument. A distinctively ethical approach is seen if one reviews one's opinions, arguments and feelings about fairness in respect to oneself, and draws out the implications for one's relations with others. If your umbrella has been stolen at a restaurant, you might well feel resentment, not just annoyance, and that *nobody should* do that to anyone else. Therefore, says Nagel, you can (if not a very small child or psychologically damaged) be led to see that *you* should not do the same to anyone else. This is the line of reflection: 'How would *I* feel if you/they did that to me?' A partner line involves thinking about how others would feel in the situation that you would resent: 'How would they *feel* if you/I did that to them?' This may alter one's own feelings about the action; one then tries to make one's whole set of beliefs consistent. Nagel's examples remain from restricted milieux but are legitimate and effective for his main audience (another example is: should one steal a library book, for one's 'important' work?); and the lines of argument can readily fit development intervention cases.

In discussing the (in)justice of women's positions, I found it helpful to construct hypothetical cases of consent where women accept subordinate roles (Gasper 1996: 654–655). In Case 1 the women have no real alternative. So their acceptance will not satisfy Onora O'Neill's conditions for a choice which should be acceptable to others: that it was under conditions of no deceit, no fear of victimisation, adequate awareness, and ability by all to reject or renegotiate (O'Neill 1991). In Case 2 they have real alternatives, but without adequate education or sufficient awareness and information about the alternatives; this too fails to meet the requirements. In Case 3 they have real alternatives, thorough awareness, and no cultural and psychic moulding into accepting subordinate roles. Their acceptance is then fully valid according to O'Neill's criteria, even if unexpected. In one variant (3i) the women have never been moulded into any roles – but that takes us into the realm of impossible fictions. In another variant (3ii), they have been de-moulded, by education and reflection, but accept one or more arguments for their subordinate role. This is possible, but certainly not true for all cases of consent. More prevalent may be Case 4: the women have real alternatives and reasonable awareness of them, but are culturally and psychically moulded into accepting, and perhaps relishing, (mainly) subordinate roles. O'Neill's criteria do not query this acceptance, only require that women continually have the alternatives and (access to) a good awareness of them – even if these two conditions go against local culture. If such an awareness generates dissat-isfaction by women with their culturally given roles, then we are no longer in Case 4, and O'Neill's criteria imply that the roles are not acceptable.

The cases are presented in hypothetical form ('imagine a case in which ...'), though real counterparts are posited for Cases 2 and 4;[12] and real examples can be found for Cases 1 and 3(ii). Case 3(i) is dismissed as incon-sistent with firm knowledge (that those not moulded within a society remain sub-human, like 'wolf-children'). This type of argumentation in hypothetical mode thus relies on empirical knowledge from other contexts. Some other hypothetical argumentation draws insights from cases which we believe to be impossible.

Impossible fictions

O'Neill was led to consider which hypothetical cases are relevant, from reflection on the approach of John Rawls (1971). Rawls's 'original position' and its 'veil of ignorance' provide the classic modern examples of influen-tial, impossible fictions in philosophical ethics. In the 'original position' all protagonists know the range of possible outcome positions for individuals that corresponds to each possible set of rules for their society, but not which positions they personally would occupy. They are then required to agree a set of rules. Protagonists are expected to be risk-averse, personal-utility maximisers, and hence to adopt a maximin strategy and agree on rules that will do best for the bottom group in the society. Amongst numerous objec-tions raised against Rawls, some queried this notional situation, arguing that it did not and cannot exist, people cannot shed their identities and it is farcical to premise that they should.

One cannot merely object that Rawls (1971) considers a case that cannot exist: philosophers have always used this method. Nussbaum presents clas-sical Greek analyses of human-ness, which compare humans with notional beings who lack some of our attributes (e.g., lack mortality, as a god), in order to clarify our attributes and their implications. Any objection would have to concern Rawls's particular assumptions relative to the purpose of his analysis. O'Neill agrees with the necessity and desirability of abstraction – ignoring some features of a situation – but stresses that it can be done unac-ceptably, leading to idealisation: ignoring vital relevant features about the agents involved and/or making excessive presumptions about them (e.g., perhaps, that they are only risk-averse, selfish maximisers). Jamieson (1991) adds warnings about science-fiction/fantasy cases in moral philosophy. Reactions we give to any particular proposed implications of the posited differences (of technology, laws of nature or whatever) will not be reliable, because we will not know enough about their other implications for a way of life. In contrast, in imagined but possible cases we can know by experience enough about the context to provide worthwhile reactions.

In discussing impossible fictions have we gone beyond the domain of ethically puzzling cases in or about development *practice* where people ask: which other cases are relevant to compare with, and which principles should we use to help us think about our *choices*? Have we entered the domain of cases used in philosophical *theorising* to try to construct and choose between moral *principles*? It would not be a problem, for this chapter aims to clarify the range of types of case we encounter; rather it provides instructive contrast. Further, there is no tidy gap between examination of real cases and ethical theorising. Argument about disputed real cases rapidly takes us into theorising, and not only when the argumentation is by philosophers.

> In real life it is common for people to apply role reversal tests, to appeal to possible outcomes of actions or policies, or to point to special responsibilities and obligations. ... When we ask why we should be moved by such considerations, or we test them in order to see whether they hang together with other beliefs and commitments that we have, we are engaging in moral theorising. Generally we are pushed into theorising by pragmatic considerations. ... [The] distinction between moral theorising and moral practice is an untenable dualism. Moral theorising is part of moral practice.
>
> (Jamieson 1991: 479)

Anyone familiar with current debate on the ethics of humanitarian relief, for example, will recognise this. In disputes about burning current or recent cases, practitioners and policy makers (not only philosophers) bring forth general principles and offer arguments for them, including reference back to earlier cases and to hypothetical situations.

Refinement of the classification?

The classification used above – six types of 'case', real or imagined – is imperfect, yet gives some feel for the relevant range of types.[13] It concentrates on two dimensions of variation: (i) thickness–thinness; and (ii) real–imagined. Table 9.1 summarises the six types of treatment of cases that we examined, with a little elaboration especially for the imaginary cases, where it employs the further dimension: (iii) possible versus impossible.

	Thick Reports	Intermediate	Thin Reports
Real situations	1 – The anthropological case study	2 – The thinner real case study	4a – Thin anecdotes from real life
	4b – Thick anecdotal accounts	3 – The thinner real choice situation, with choices highlighted and kept separate from advice	
Imagined situations	5a – Conceivably true thick fictions	5b – Conceivably true thinner stories or situations	5c – Conceivably true but fabricated thin anecdotes
	6a – Impossible imagined thick stories and situations	6b – Impossible imagined thinner tales and situations	6c – Impossible imagined fragmentary aspects

Table 9.1 Types of reports of situations

A number of other dimensions emerged: (iv) open-minded/inquiring versus closed/concerned only to convey a set conclusion; (v) whether evaluative criteria and judgements are built in or as far as possible separate and explicit; (vi) whether evaluative conclusions/advice are provided or not. We used criterion (iv) to distinguish 'case studies' from anecdotes, the latter being short of openness and inquiry, not only of words. Anecdotes were taken to be typically thinner, but not necessarily so; we can have long thick anecdotes or series of anecdotes, as in much travel writing. Similarly, one can have thick, but closed, case studies, as in some autobiography and historiography.

Highlighting these dimensions, and no doubt there are more, helps us to see additional possibilities. In the 'thin' column we could add: real, thin, statistics; real, solitary, visual images; and fabricated images. De Waal (1997) makes a fierce assault on the abuse of images and statistics by Northern media and NGOs with respect to famines in Africa, real or feared.

If we add a time dimension we can distinguish 'snapshot' cases from those with a story-line. Stories are the characteristic mode for understanding interrelations of specific people who think, feel and choose in complex ways. Emery Roe warns us of the disturbingly simple story structures that underlie much development planning (Roe 1989).

Thick–thin, open–closed, and possible–impossible constitute dimensions of contrast, not binary pairs; likewise the divisions between descriptive cases and 'choice situations' and between explicit and immanent values. Further, a plurality of criteria which can move independently of each other, as mentioned for 'thickness', means there exist many 'grey' intermediate possibilities. We might be led to seek a more complex set of categories.

Such extensions are unnecessary for the present purpose: to show that there is a range of types of reference to cases, each with its strengths, limitations and distinct role or roles in normative argumentation and practice. Having established the presence of a range, the second half of the chapter examines more closely strengths, limitations and roles.

'Thick' versus 'thin': what makes cases relevant, and for what?

In this section we consider the complementary virtues of including a lot (being thick) if it really is relevant, and of leaving out a lot (being thin) if it really is irrelevant, in discourse oriented to making or assisting ethically charged choices. We will see how different philosophies can lead to the choice of thicker or thinner cases, but will also note scope for coexistence. Different purposes and occasions will justify different styles.

We look first at the functions of concrete examples: to convey patterns in a flexible and vivid way, and to offer vicarious experience. While thick description can do this, there are misunderstandings about its power and priority in moral argument. Out of presumptions of harmony and consensus comes a questionable communitarian claim that moral choices within societies can and should be settled by detailed description of 'the culture'. This approach will be contrasted with ideas about the role of well-selected exclusions in ethical argumentation: vital features must not be left out, but nor must irrelevant ones be included. And since ethics have to be more than an intellectual exercise alone, we consider the further role of moral exemplar cases in strengthening motivation. The final section of this chapter will integrate these ideas into a picture of linked stages in work in ethics.

The importance of being concrete and thick? I: Exemplars and vicarious experience

> This exemplar is and remains a particular that in its very particularity reveals the generality that otherwise could not be defined. Courage is like Achilles. ... The example is the particular that contains in itself, or is supposed to contain, a concept or a general rule.
>
> (Arendt 1982: 77, 84, cited by Tester 1997: 55)

What do cases do and examples exemplify, and how? They convey patterns; thick cases can also provide vicarious experience.

As Thomas Kuhn (1977) emphasises, an *exemplar* is a specific instance which embodies and illustrates ideas that are not easily or satisfactorily formalisable. For Kuhn this was the prime meaning of 'paradigm': a concrete model of practice which conveys how to 'see' situations and decide which method or formalisation should be applied and how, and which helps one to anticipate and avoid various pitfalls. Although 'paradigm' originally means exemplar, a second sense used by Kuhn crowded out the original and more profound sense, to his regret. This was 'paradigm' as disciplinary matrix: the set of basic commitments, notably the set of approved exemplars, shared by a group of scientists. Why is the exemplar sense more profound? Because exemplary instances are many and multi-faceted, and the definitions and rules and advice which we impute from them are more subtle and fluid – yet exist. The advice on patterns is absorbed sub-consciously so we can apply it without delaying for conscious reflection; and it comes embodied in a vivid real example that aids recall.

We learn our first language in this manner. Similarly, training in 'disciplines' and professions includes absorbing skills and values from tales of good/bad/typical practice. Benner (1991) identifies types of 'learning narrative' in the caring professions, based on her interviews with nurses: (1) stories that show the importance of remaining open to experience and not prejudging cases; (2) stories that convey how to better judge appropriate degrees of involvement with patients and their families; (3) stories that reveal the limits to our understanding and control: 'narratives of disillusionment'; (4) stories about coping with suffering and death; and (5) stories about dealing with colleagues, systems and cultures (such as arrogant doctors, male chauvinists, biases against showing concern, etc.).[14] The stories may bring associated emotions that enter the memory too and help to motivate action later. Each area of practice has its own sorts of stories. Far from all such exemplars are strongly culturally relative. The same applies for exemplars that promote ethical motivation rather than skills for acting once we are motivated.

Practice stories and inspirational exemplars are typically not only concrete but thickly textured too, and work by providing vicarious experience.

> Direct personal experience is an efficient, comprehensive and satisfying way of creating understanding, but a way not usually available to our evaluation-report audiences. The best substitute for direct experience probably is vicarious experience – increasingly better when the evaluator uses 'attending' and 'conceptualising' styles similar to those which members of the *audience* use.
>
> (Stake 1980: 83; emphasis added)

Vicariousness helps through 'adding to one's experience and re-examining problems and possible solutions intuitively. ... [We recommend that] program evaluation studies should be planned and carried out in such a way as to provide a maximum of vicarious experience to the readers who may then intuitively combine this with their previous experiences' (Stake and Trumbull 1982: 2). Intuitive re-examination and revision works because so much of our thinking is in terms of tacit and evolving patterns, not explicit rules.

A rare example of a case study by a social scientist which is rich enough to convey in addition to 'thickness' – a sense of a whole context and real lives – a vicarious feeling of having met particular individuals, been in specific locales, observed actual meetings, is – surprisingly – by a development economist *cum* policy analyst, Robert Klitgaard's *Tropical Gangsters* (1991). Klitgaard's account of his work in the late 1980s as an advisor in Equatorial Guinea is partly autobiographical: so it describes real people and places, not only themes.[15] Furthermore, his style is novelistic, albeit a thinned-down man-abroad Hemingwayesque style: he relies on directly reported speech not only on paraphrases, and he treats aspects of individuals, occasions and routines that do not enter even many anthropologists' reports. The style conveys a sense of engagement with people as people, rather than as imperfect embodiments of social science categories or as (un)friendly aliens. And it is integral rather than incidental to his argument, that an effective economic programme can stem only from locally based (not Washington-based) analysis, commitment and 'ownership'; that to externally facilitate and strengthen these requires a collegial interaction, which in turn requires from facilitators a combination of courtesy, curiosity, openness, and vivacity – in each case both intellectual and interpersonal – and thus a capacity and desire to deal with others as people, not just as counterparts or clients or other.[16]

De Waal's *Famine Crimes* (1997) recounts a comparable example: the contrast in style between Mohamed Sahnoun, the UN special representative in Somalia in 1992, and his successor Ismat Kittani. Sahnoun argued against and was building alternatives to the disastrous US-led, UN-mandated military intervention which Kittani then helped to precipitate and administer. While unusually pointed in giving attention to individual officials and their styles, De Waal's brief treatment remains anecdotal and more forgettable, without the 'bite' that the details and intimacy of vicarious experience can give.

Klitgaard's (1991) case study matches an expectation that vicarious experience is usually best obtained through an intermediate level of thickness. The precise level depends on the audience, but great thickness (in using the style of those being described) may well be impenetrable to the audience, while thinness can fail to establish credibility and empathy.

Vicarious experience is important within as well as across cultures, as suggested earlier by Thomas Nagel's (1994) examples. For cultures are not well-defined, clearly separate, unities that exist fully programmed into 'their' members' minds. Vicarious experience across cultures tends to be thinner; but some examples transcend boundaries. Let us take a longer case.

Øyhus on the ethics of transfer of ox-cultivation to the Toposa

The Toposa are a small group of semi-nomadic pastoralists in Eastern Equatoria, Southern Sudan. The men herd cattle, either their own or if they are poor someone else's, and live in camps a few days' walk from more central settlements, where women, children and the elderly spend most of their time. The women cultivate sorghums around these settlements, but most move to the camps in the dry season, when cattle products become the main food. Until fairly recently, cattle belonged to the men's world, farming to the women's. Farming technology was at the level of hoe cultivation, so yields were low despite use of fertile (but heavy – mostly black cotton) soils. Enormous disparities in wealth are present: some own huge herds, some little or none. Øyhus (1998) recounts how from around the mid-1960s rainfall became more erratic and on average lower. Together with the introduction of automatic guns, this brought escalation of the traditional cattle-raiding between the Toposa and groups such as the Turkana and Dinka, such that it is now 'quite similar to regular warfare' (Øyhus 1998: 10). By the late 1970s, substantial numbers of Toposa had lost their animals due to drought, disease or raiding, and serious malnutrition was widespread.

In the early 1970s, at the end of one civil war in Sudan, a Norwegian NGO started relief operations in Eastern Equatoria. In the early 1980s it began work with the Toposa, in response to the famine situation in their area, and decided to promote quick-maturing grains, root crops, and ploughing with oxen. However, it was aware that 'oxen were "sacred" for the Toposa men' (Øyhus 1998: 13). Therefore the proposed innovation was presented to the local councils of (male) elders, who led a series of lengthy discussions. Was ox cultivation compatible with *nyepite kangi Toposa*, the Toposa's system of norms, values and beliefs – especially given that it would be a novelty whereas *nyepite* is, in Toposa eyes, eternal and unchangeable? After two or three months, the answer was yes. Within the treasures of *nyepite*, suggests Øyhus, the elders could feel that they had identified ox cultivation as a dormant practice, approved but not yet used because not previously needed.

Crop production in this semi-desert savannah was a response to a crisis, but brought new hazards. Not only do crops fail totally in some years, intensified settlement and grazing around the centres risk erosion and offer a greater target for raiders. In Øyhus's view, 'the elders ... in reality, did not know what they were doing ... it was far beyond their capacity to perceive the consequences of applying the technology. It was therefore, in reality, the outside expert who made the decision' (1998: 15). This may seem strange to the elders, who were capable of saying no, as we will see, and unlikely to agree that an outsider was any more able to predict the consequences.

The NGO knew that oxen were part of the male economy and arable farming part of the female economy. It decided initially that ox cultivation would be more easily accepted via increasing entry of men to cropping rather than by entry of women to animal husbandry. However, as the ox cultivation programme expanded, the NGO became concerned at the unintended effect of the exclusion of women, whom they feared would lose their status in farming and their autonomous place. A proposal to let women plough was brought to the councils of elders – and clearly rejected, as against *nyepite*. However, amongst the Toposa the elders can condemn, shun and shame, but have no power to forbid or prevent people in other families. The NGO decided to offer ploughing training to women. Some came forward from the start, mostly socially marginal widows and orphans from a mission station. Later, many other Toposa women applied for and received training.

The whole experiment was terminated in 1985 when rebel forces in the new civil war entered the area. The Toposa dispersed to their cattle camps. For the elders, suggests Øyhus, this disaster could be interpreted as the consequence of a break from *nyepite* inherent in women working with cattle. Others though, one could posit, could equally claim it as the heavens' reply to introduction of ox cultivation, or to doing so first without women.

Øyhus's case study does the following, hopefully evident even from a summary at a fraction of its length.

- It shows profound value conflicts and corresponding areas for examination and choice.
- It suggests the pervasiveness and centrality of unintended and indirect effects (such as a possible clash between elders and women over who 'owns' 'the culture', who defines what it will include). They reflect the interconnection of multiple arenas, beyond the powers of foresight of those present.
- It brings these issues to life, to an extent and with a richness likely to be absent from generalised reference: its review of conditions and events is holistic, and contextualises and provides culture-specific details, though it lacks individual persons and voices.
- It sows some seeds for an answer to 'why should we be concerned?' The exposition of the Toposa's complex adaptation to a difficult environment, new hardships arising from external forces, the threat of an undeserved decline in women's position, the careful deliberations of the elders (and the NGO), the decision of some women to ignore the elders' ruling, may establish a basis of sympathy and for external response of some sort.

• Like De Graaf's bilharzia case, the case study does not provide an answer for what such a response should be.

The importance of being thick? II: A communitarian claim

In situations marked by ethical challenges, how far will thick descriptions help? How could one pursue this Sudan case on oxen ploughing, or the bilharzia case from Tanzania? Intuitions manifestly differ between people. One can try to identify local traditions in more detail, but these can be interpreted and valued differently by different local residents. Dominant groups might for example downgrade the concerns of women and children. Who represents the children whose lives could be damaged in the bilharzia case?

Clifford Geertz used the adjective 'thick' for a type of *description*. We need thick descriptions of cultures and actions within cultures because they are subtle, complex, and contextual. Michael Walzer's *Thick and Thin* (1994) has taken the term 'thick' instead for a style of *moral argumentation* which is 'richly referential, culturally resonant, *locked into* a locally established symbolic system or network of meanings' (1994: xi; emphasis added). A link between the two usages is provided by the idea (though it is not necessarily Walzer's) that moral argument largely or even solely reduces to finding the culturally authentic description of an action, which will itself contain or imply an evaluation.

Walzer holds that moral argument within a society is and should be 'thick', whereas moral argument between societies is 'thin' ('simply the contrasting term'), derived from the thick domestic discourses by reduction and simplification to find common denominators, and thus relatively weak and limited. But we can put this more favourably: if thin argumentation fits one type of context and thick another, then being thin is not automatically inferior.

The view that intra-societal moral thinking works through thick, culturally specific descriptions has several limitations. Much intra-societal moral argumentation is thinner: 'intelligibility and abstraction are in fact close and necessary allies rather than antagonists' (O'Neill 1996: 69). Thickness is not always necessary. Nor is it always sufficient: while sometimes finding an agreed thick description of an action suffices to produce a moral judgement, since the action appears 'so unambiguously desirable or deplorable ... different examples would show that even the finest-grained agreement on the appropriate articulation and description of cases may leave us uncertain how to act' (O'Neill 1996: 87). This might well apply for Slim's (1997) emergency relief cases or the bilharzia case. Thickness is not necessarily more meaningful, even for insiders. Cultures are more internally plural, underdefined, and internally contradictory and contested than suggested in communitarian discourse. In addition, much thinking and communication, including cross-cultural, proceeds with considerable effectiveness in terms of concrete, non-written examples. Their openness of texture and meaning, and ability thus to evolve in significance, further weaken claims that 'here', 'in Rome', 'our' given and determinate moral language settles the ethical assessment of cases. Ironically, the 'thick' communitarian position itself rests on what Sherry Ortner (1995) calls 'ethnographic thinness', a failure to closely observe.

The virtues of slimming – O'Neill on excluding irrelevant details when assessing justice

As in law, so in ethical argumentation, a great share of attention goes into deciding what type of case one is dealing with, and correspondingly which criteria should be adopted. Is ox cultivation primarily a livestock use issue or a cropping issue? Does Toposa men's exclusive world end at the cattle camp or extend wherever cattle go? O'Neill argues that classification of cases must be by justifiable rules. Rather than relying on intuitions or traditions, the rule we advocate should be one that others could, after thorough unforced consideration, accept and adopt. This is a sterner requirement than that our rule for others be one we would accept for ourselves, for such a rule could be specially advantageous to us. Even that alternative requirement would often be demanding. In the Tanzania bilharzia case, would Group B, who advocated not querying local practices, accept that, say, a foreign doctor with superior knowledge who visited Europe during the centuries when bleeding the sick was common practice there should have stayed quiet to avoid disturbing the locals? Would they agree that they themselves should not be informed if, say, a Tanzanian doctor visiting the Netherlands observed that Dutch alternative pharmacists appeared to have misclassified and misprescribed Tanzanian remedies? (Here we use Type 5 cases, imaginary but not impossible.)

Let us consider O'Neill's own principle: a Kantian 'requirement of acting only on principles that can be acted on by all' (O'Neill 1995: 147). Rules of justice for a particular context have to be acceptable to all involved, in conditions of no deceit, no fear of victimisation, and ability by all to reject or renegotiate. Agreement given in conditions of unjust domination is not sufficient. O'Neill argues that building such agreements requires abstraction without idealisation, and context-sensitivity without pure relativism (1991, 1996). We must not omit essential features from our analysis, nor must we include incidentals or biasing premises.

Since each case has some unique features, abstraction is essential in any practical (i.e., choice oriented) reasoning which has to apply to more than a single case – for example to a varied range of agents (O'Neill 1996: 61). For example, sometimes sex is a relevant distinguishing feature: we should know sexes if we want to judge medical needs; in some other cases knowing sexes is not relevant and might only bias choice (Gasper 1996). But while abstraction, thinning-out of case details, is required for understanding and judgement, it can go too far: exclusion of (morally) important differences is a danger. Conversely, context-sensitivity is required to include those relevant differences; but reference to the thick particularity of cases can degenerate into communitarian relativism, where too many particular local features, conventions and traditions, including prejudices and unjustified discriminations (e.g., that widows, or women in general, have no right to employment outside the home), are treated as defining relevant differences (Gasper 1996: 652).

The importance of being concrete and thick? III: Moral exemplars and moral motivation

The basis for morality is a willingness to consider other people's costs and benefits. 'How would they *feel?*' arguments fail if some people lack that willingness to empathise. The 'How would *I* feel?' argument might sometimes still have effect: reasoning from and tidying up one's own feelings. It leads us to see a likely inconsistency (when I resent the theft of my umbrella as *unfair*, and not only because it has been done to *me*, yet want to do the same to someone else). But it does not tell us how such an inconsistency should be altered (whether by no longer feeling resentment at the theft, or by no longer wishing to take someone else's umbrella); nor does it ensure the motivational basis for doing anything about the inconsistency. Thus we require attention both to feelings and reasoning.

While feelings alone may be inconsistent and unreasonable, reasoning alone gives us insufficient direction or motivation. Possibly the feeling/reasoning dichotomy is overdrawn (Nussbaum 1995, 2001). Could one ever think of aesthetic judgement as something divorced from feelings? So why should one for ethical judgement? We could think rather of training moral intelligence, in which cultured feelings are inherently a part; and we can link to virtue ethics, which focuses on character. Given that, as parents know, 'morality requires the development of the moral emotions' (Held 1994: 169), how does one foster them?

Benner describes, besides 'learning narratives', another type of storytelling by professionals. Constitutive or sustaining narratives 'exemplify positive notions about what is good' (1991: 2), as the necessary complement to skills about how to promote it. They convey core values about why one is a professional (a nurse/relief worker/policy adviser/teacher/ ...), including 'essential embodied human distinctions of worth, such as honor, courage and dignity' (Benner 1991: 4); and sustain one in difficult times.[17]

To promote fellow-feeling and motivation, moral exemplars – inspirational cases and persons – can help, besides more general study, exposure, and reflection on stressful choices. Singer (1997) and Tester (1997) discuss heroic individuals from the Holocaust, to show the reality of alternatives to participating in genocide. But these cases set such demanding standards that their impact might well be slight.[18] Slim cites therefore a variety of exemplars in relief and development work: not only epic, faraway figures – nineteenth-century Europeans such as Henri Dunant; twentieth-century Southern leaders such as Chico Mendes and Steve Biko – but especially from within the suffering groups themselves.

> While the moral imagination of most international relief workers is still primarily conditioned by the traditional Western humanitarian role model of the heroic intervenor, the great majority do also speak of encounters with impressive moral role models from inside the emergency. ... Many individual aid workers do indeed carry with them the memory of the suffering and moral courage of a particular person or incident which sustains their own personal conviction as a relief worker.
>
> (Slim 1997: 11)

Away from the field, fiction and biography can give vicarious experience of others' joys and tragedies, and their responses, strength, skills and commitment. The literature of the struggle against apartheid is one rich school. At a lesser pitch, the sorts of biographies in Johnson and Bernstein (1983; on a range of Southern poor), Naipaul (1990; on varied Indian individuals and families), Leonard (1991; on notable Kenyan civil servants), and George (1997; on around a hundred Southern professionals) offer something valuable. The lives need not be dramatic nor the cases long. They do their 'thick' work by being holistic, contextualising, adding personal flavour and extra perspectives.

Varieties of task and arena

Cases have become central in recent ethics. Ethical theory does not give a master mechanism for making decisions; its role is more supplementary. Theories here give categories and tests for examining cases, not laws for settling them. Nor is 'culture' an all-purpose problem solver, as we have seen. Existing moral languages within communities (a category equally imprecise) are not sufficiently comprehensive, clear, cogent and consistent to do more than provide resources for facing cases. Thus philosophers increasingly speak of 'practical ethics' not 'applied ethics'. This final section presents a tentative framework that indicates distinctive places in practical ethics for different styles of case-use and argumentation.

Table 9.2 summarises our findings about the range of types of case-example and about different moments in thought, marked by different purposes. One might distinguish more or fewer moments or stages, depending on context; they do not form a fixed sequence – many starting points, paths and feedbacks are possible; and sometimes a case will be helpful at more than one stage.

	Stage / focus of ethical / practical discourse	Roles of cases / examples	Features of typical cases / examples
Cases/Examples	Exposure	Cases can *sensitise and motivate*: Sensitise to situations, issues, ethical claims; build fellow-feeling; and convey notions about what is good.	Vivid, engrossing. About real people. Some thin, some thick, but especially intermediate. Including anecdotes, choice situations, 'constitutive narratives', personal exemplars.
	Everyday analysis of a real problem case	Reference to other cases/examples *exemplifies patterns and possibilities*, and so aids analysis of real cases faced.	Striking paradigm cases. Anecdotes and 'learning narratives', including about stances, options, limits.
	More formal theorisation (when required)	Cases here should *deepen and systematise analysis*: Help to clarify and discipline ideas; and test the coherence of candidate theories.	Clear, sharply focused. Not about real people. Thin. Including choice situations and impossible scenarios.
	More theorised analysis of a real problem case (when required)	Reference to other case-situations is to *support choice-making* and future observation and theorising. To help show which theories are relevant to a problem context. To test relevance and realism of candidate theories.	(1) In training: rich real practice cases; and well-theorised (often thinned) cases. (2) In practice: comparison with well-theorised (often thinned) real cases.
	Negotiation, decision, compromise Action	*To support practice* Including: to help to build and maintain attitudes, character.	'Learning narratives', including about relationships, stresses, tactics. Thick or intermediate. Personal exemplars.

Table 9.2 Different stages of practical discourse have different roles, and types of, cases

Sensitisation involves drawing and giving attention to situations, cases, issues, claimed ethical principles and formats. Its roles include: to broaden the range of concerns, to counter selfishness and myopia, mobilise emotions and motivation, raise doubts; to see, compare and feel. Its case examples should be vivid and involving, and preferably concern real people. They can be simple or rich, but not too rich for absorption. Simple cases without much information have a special role in drawing out commentators' presumptions. Anecdotal and thicker practice stories fit here too, for providing vicarious experience is vital. This sensitisation stage thus matches one role Goulet (1995) emphasises for development ethics: to offer grounded existential witness. He stresses phenomenological study to reveal and clarify values and value-choices encountered in a situation. As this work becomes more analytical it merges into the following stages.

Analysis of a problem case seeks to build on prior awareness and concerns, and to discipline emotions and argumentation. It may lead into theorisation, to clarify and also add and revise concepts and frameworks, strengthen and extend logic and consistency, compare systems of values. Cases here must be clear and purposeful: giving a sustained focus, identifying which are relevant differences, which irrelevant, and so on. They should probably not concern real people, for that can bring distraction by extraneous and opportunistic considerations.

Practice must draw on other stages as required, while recognising the inevitable limits and simplifications of one's claimed experiential base and theoretical equipment. One is particularly interested to see where different metaphysical starting points and theoretical routes lead to the same recommendations. Case-thinking helps to inform and complement proposed policies, principles, guidelines and codes. The cases referred to must (again) be rich and real. They can help give a feel for contexts and thus some ability to judge when particular conceptualisations and models fit. The cases should include 'practice stories', and convey something about the attitudes, character(s) and skills helpful in dealing with complexity, uncertainty, limits of theory and plurality of viewpoints, stress, and the need for choices, negotiation, compromises and creativity. The experience from practice must feed back into the scanning for evidence and into re-conceptualisation and theorising.

Overall, we have seen a variety of modes of recourse to cases and illustrations in practical ethics and development practice, each with pros and cons; that distinctive considerations arise in normative argumentation, justifying this separate discussion; and that to a significant extent different stages of work involve different types of use of cases. My pictures of each aspect can be improved. I hope though to have given a usable introduction.

Notes

1 A revised version of a paper which appeared in *Development and Change* 31 (5); published here with the permission of the editors of *Development and Change*.

2 'Case' can mean an instance (a situation/event/person/...) *or* a representation of an instance. In referring to the latter, we reserve the term 'case study' for representations with some depth. In literature on qualitative research methods the term can be further restricted, to study of a system 'bounded in time or place' (Creswell 1998: 40), such as an organisation, project, policy, decision or whatever. The case-study tradition so defined overlaps with but is distinguishable from other qualitative research traditions such as biographical study, phenomenology (investigation of the meanings of a phenomenon for participants), and ethnography (a portrait of a broad cultural system; Cresswell 1998). However, in this chapter all may be called case studies.

3 Not only North–South development cooperation is 'development intervention'. For background on development ethics, see, e.g., Crocker (1991), Gasper (1997).

4 When the materials are less narrow they have sometimes been questionably derived. Ernest Gellner complained of 'scandalously irresponsible, scissors-and-paste, selective use of ethnographic material' by Northern philosophers seeking self-sufficient moral communities in the South (1974: 145).

5 See, e.g., Bulmer and Warwick (1983); Patton (1997).

6 See, e.g., Stake (1995); Richards (1985); Padaki (1995).

7 Gasper (1999a) critically discusses Slim's cases and the idea of narrow zones of responsibility and accountability for aid and relief agencies.

8 Bilharzia particularly affects children of a certain age since it is contracted by bathing and drinking in infected rivers. Younger children are less exposed; older children in general acquire resistance and hence stop passing blood. Treatments can include – when funds and supplies permit – drugs, or elimination of the freshwater snails that carry the larvae of the bilharzia worms, or elimination of carriers outside water such as rats; or change in patterns of bathing and drinking if alternatives are possible and acceptable.

9 Nozick referred to a real person but without examination of societal and historical context. While a fictional example could have been used, reference to a historically unique, sympathetic figure – Wilt Chamberlain, perhaps the first black American basketball super-star – added a special pitch to his attempt to mobilise assent to an absolute right to retain all of whatever one receives by legal means in the market (see Gasper 1986).

10 In 'The not so gentle art of the development anecdote', I disputed not 'whether the Naipauls offer particular insights but the quality of their involvement and hence of their overall understanding and impact ... [and how their] anecdotes – inevitably fragmentary – about individuals lead into judgements about nations plus proffered development prescriptions' (Gasper 1986: 180–181). V.S. Naipaul has however later appeared also as a practitioner of thick-ish life-story social history (Naipaul 1990).

11 Fictions in fantasy mode – impossible or implausible visions of project performance – also play a role, as inspirational and legitimating 'myths' in planning and implementation, to call forth effort and support for enterprises with uncertain and delayed benefits. Such visions better fit our next category, 'impossible fictions'.

12 For Case 2, I referred to, for example, Li (1995) on women in pre-1990s China, and for Case 4 to studies of contemporary Kerala.

13 The classification is already more refined than that in Jamieson's survey article on method in moral philosophy (1991), which modifies O'Neill (1986). Jamieson

has only one category ('ostensive', that is, taken from real life) to cover my first four.

14 See also Forester (1993) on 'practice stories' in urban planning.

15 The names in *Tropical Gangsters* are usually amended, but in general the persons will be recognisable to others who have worked in the same organisations. They are not composite characters, unlike the 'devil's advocate' entitled The Reasonable Social Scientist in Howard Richards's *The Evaluation of Cultural Action* (1985), another study concerned to provide vicarious experience. Richards describes a community development programme in Chile and his experience in evaluating it. Seeking to change a specific methodology, not only a mind-set, Richards aims to persuade primarily through general arguments which are given extensive illustration, rather than primarily through Klitgaard's approach of conveying lessons by a story.

16 Not only may one doubt how widely these requirements for effective facilitation can be attained and sustained, facilitation is not a substitute for structural changes in institutions, capacities, and so on. Klitgaard would agree, yet stress the potential – and duty – for well-directed facilitation to contribute towards such changes. See Gasper (1999b) for further discussion.

17 From nursing, Benner cites narratives of (1) the joy of healing and transcendence (especially if unexpected); (2) heroic rapid skilled intervention; (3) the growth of caring feelings, e.g., between patient and family; and (4) endurance and communication in the face of extreme suffering.

18 In a famous attack on the desirability of 'Moral Saints', Susan Wolf (1982) goes further; but rather than studying real exemplars she stays with hypothetical cases of individuals who devote themselves overwhelmingly (and, she presumes, directly) to the good of others (the less important variant she emphasises) or to the overall good of society (which also includes their own good). In contrast, Lawrence Blum (1988) studies a series of real figures, to identify a variety of styles of morally exemplary figure, not a single 'saint' model. O'Neill (1996) notes many relevant virtues, certainly not only the supererogatory (beyond duty) virtues of moral heroism. See also the sections in Gasper (1986) on 'Degrees of Obligation' and 'Ethics and the Art of the Possible'.

References

Arendt, H. (1982) *Lectures on Kant's Political Philosophy*, Chicago: University of Chicago Press.

Benner, P. (1991) 'The role of experience, narrative and community in skilled ethical comportment', *Advances in Nursing Science* 14 (2): 1–21.

Blum, L. (1988) 'Moral exemplars', *Midwest Studies in Philosophy* XIII: 196–221.

Bulmer, M. and D. Warwick (eds) (1983) *Social Research in Developing Countries*, Chichester: John Wiley.

Caufield, C. (1998) *Masters of Illusion: the World Bank and the Poverty of Nations*, London: Pan.

Chambers, R. (1997) *Whose Reality Counts?*, London: Intermediate Technology Publications.

Cooper, R. and R. Packard (1997) 'Introduction', in R. Cooper and R. Packard (eds) *International Development and the Social Sciences*, Berkeley: University of California Press, pp. 1–41.

Creswell, J. (1998) *Qualitative Inquiry and Research Design: Choosing Among Five Traditions*, Thousand Oaks: Sage.

Crocker, D. (1991) 'Toward development ethics', *World Development*, 19 (5): 457–483.

De Waal, A. (1997) *Famine Crimes: Politics and the Disaster Relief Industry in Africa*, London: James Currey.

Deming, W.E. (1975) 'The logic of evaluation', in M. Guttentag and E. Struening (eds) *Handbook of Evaluation Research*, Newbury Park: Sage.

Fairhead, J. and M. Leach (1997) 'Webs of power and the construction of environmental policy problems: forest loss in Guinea', in R. Grillo and R. Stirrat (eds) *Discourses of Development: Anthropological Perspectives*, Oxford: Berg, pp. 35–57.

Forester, J. (1993) 'Learning from practice stories: the priority of practical judgement', in F. Fischer and J. Forester (eds) *The Argumentative Turn in Policy Analysis and Planning*, Durham, NC: Duke University Press, pp.186–209.

Frank, L. (1986) 'The development game', *Granta* 20: 229–243.

Gasper, D. (1986) 'Distribution and development ethics', in R. Apthorpe and A. Krahl (eds) *Development Studies: Critique and Renewal*, Leiden: Brill, pp. 136–203.

—— (1996) 'Culture and development ethics: needs, women's rights, and western theories', *Development and Change* 27 (4): 627–661.

—— (1997) 'Development ethics: an emergent field?', in C. Hamelink (ed.) *Ethics and Development: On Making Moral Choices in Development Cooperation*, Kampen: Uitgeverij Kok, pp. 25–43, 182–185.

—— (1999a) ' "Drawing a line": ethical and political strategies in complex emergency assistance', *European Journal of Development Research* 11 (2): 87–115.

—— (1999b) 'Ethics and the conduct of international development aid: charity and obligation', *Forum for Development Studies* (Oslo) 1: 23–57.

Gellner, E. (1974) *Legitimation of Belief*, Cambridge: Cambridge University Press.

George, S. (1997) *Third World Professionals and Development Education in Europe: Personal Narratives and Global Conversations*, New Delhi: Sage.

Goulet, D. (1995) *Development Ethics*, London: Zed Books.

Grillo, R. and R. Stirrat (1997) Preface, in R. Grillo and R. Stirrat (eds) *Discourses of Development: Anthropological Perspectives*, Oxford: Berg.

Harrell-Bond, B. (1986) *Imposing Aid: Emergency Assistance to Refugees*, Oxford: Oxford University Press.

Held, V. (1994) 'Reason, gender and moral theory', in P. Singer (ed.) *Ethics*, Oxford: Oxford University Press, pp. 166–169.

Jamieson, D. (1991) 'Method and moral theory', in P. Singer (ed.) *A Companion to Ethics*, Oxford: Blackwell, pp. 476–487.

Johnson, H. and H. Bernstein (eds) (1983) *Third World Lives of Struggle*, London: Heinemann.

Klitgaard, R. (1991) *Tropical Gangsters*, London: I.B. Tauris and Co.

Kuhn, T. (1977) *The Essential Tension*, Chicago: University of Chicago Press.

Leonard, D. (1991) *African Successes: Four Public Managers of Kenyan Rural Development*, Berkeley: University of California Press.

Li, Xiarong (1995) 'Gender inequality in China and cultural relativism', in M. Nussbaum and J. Glover (eds) *Women, Culture, and Development*, Oxford: Clarendon Press, pp. 407–425.

Nagel, T. (1994) 'The objective basis of morality', in P. Singer (ed.) *Ethics*, Oxford: Oxford University Press, pp. 155–158.

Naipaul, V.S. (1990) *India: a Million Mutinies Now*, London: Heinemann/Minerva.

Nozick, R. (1974) *Anarchy, State and Utopia*, New York: Basic Books.

Nussbaum, M. (1995) 'Emotions and women's capabilities', in M. Nussbaum and J. Glover (eds) *Women, Culture, and Development*, Oxford: Clarendon Press, pp. 360–395.

—— (1997) *Poetic Justice: Literary Imagination and Public Life*, Boston: Beacon Press.

—— (2001) *Upheavals of Thought – The Intelligence of the Emotions*, Cambridge: Cambridge University Press.

Nussbaum, M. and J. Glover (eds) (1995) *Women, Culture, and Development*, Oxford: Clarendon Press.

O'Neill, O. (1986) 'The power of example', *Philosophy* 61: 5–29.

—— (1991) 'Justice, gender and international boundaries', *British Journal of Political Science* 20: 439–459.

—— (1995) 'Justice, capabilities and vulnerabilities', in M. Nussbaum and J. Glover (eds) *Women, Culture, and Development*, Oxford: Clarendon Press, pp. 140–152.

—— (1996) *Towards Justice and Virtue: a Constructive Account of Practical Reasoning*, Cambridge: Cambridge University Press.

Ortner, S. (1995) 'Resistance and the problem of ethnographic refusal', *Comparative Studies in Society and History* 37 (1): 173–193.

Øyhus, A.O. (1998) 'Universal soldiers: the developers' paper to conference on Ethics and Development', Norwegian Association for Development Research, Skjetten, 5–6 June.

Padaki, V. (ed.) (1995) *Development Intervention and Programme Evaluation*, New Delhi: Sage.

Patton, M.Q. (1997) *Utilization-Focused Evaluation*, 3rd edition, Thousand Oaks, CA: Sage.

Peattie, L. (1987) *Planning – Rethinking Ciudad Guyana*, Ann Arbor: University of Michigan Press.

Porter, D., *et al.* (1991) *Development in Practice*, London: Routledge.

Rawls, J. (1971) *A Theory of Justice*, Cambridge, MA: Harvard University Press.

Richards, H. (1985) *The Evaluation of Cultural Action: an Evaluative Study of the Parents and Children Program (PPH)*, London: Macmillan.

Roe, E. (1989) 'Folktale development', *The American Journal of Semiotics* 6 (2/3): 277–289.

Sen, A. (1981) *Poverty and Famines*, Oxford: Oxford University Press.

Shadish, W.R., T.D. Cook and L.C. Leviton (1991) *Foundations of Program Evaluation: Theories of Practice*, Newbury Park: Sage.

Shawcross, W. (1984) *The Quality of Mercy: Cambodia, Holocaust and Modern Conscience*, London: André Deutsch.

Singer, P. (1997) *How Are We to Live? Ethics in an Age of Self-interest*, Milsons Point, NSW: Random House Australia.

Slim, H. (1997) 'Doing the right thing: relief agencies, moral dilemmas and moral responsibility in political emergencies and war', Studies on Emergencies and Disaster Relief no. 6, Uppsala: Nordiska Afrikainstitutet.

Stake, R. (1978) 'The case study method in social inquiry', *Educational Researcher* 7: 5–8.

—— (1980) 'Program evaluation, particularly responsive evaluation', in W.B. Dockrell and D. Hamilton (eds) *Rethinking Educational Research*, London: Hodder and Stoughton, pp. 72–87.

—— (1995) *The Art of Case Study Research*, Thousand Oaks: Sage.

Stake, R. and Trumbull, D. (1982) 'Naturalistic generalizations', *Review Journal of Philosophy and Social Science* 7: 1–12.

Stretton, H. (1969) *The Political Sciences*, London: Routledge and Kegan Paul.

Tester, K. (1997) *Moral Culture*, London: Sage.

Uphoff, N. (1996) *Learning from Gal Oya*, London: Intermediate Technology Publications.

Walzer, M. (1994) *Thick and Thin: Moral Argument at Home and Abroad*, Notre Dame, IN: University of Notre Dame Press.

Wolf, S. (1982) 'Moral saints', *Journal of Philosophy* 79: 419–439.

Chapter 10

The virtual reality of Protestant development aid in the Netherlands

Els Scholte[1]

Introduction

Is there such a thing as authentic communication about development? And if so, what does it mean? What constraints and opportunities are involved in the effort to communicate authentically about issues of development to an audience in the West? In this chapter I reflect on these questions on the basis of my experiences as communication officer for a large Dutch Protestant church during the past four years. The data emerge from these concrete experiences. The chapter is not the outcome of detached research. On the contrary, it intends to give a glimpse 'from within' of some of the participants' points of view and modes of communicating. I also make references occasionally to experiences of fellow agencies.

For a number of years I have been engaged in providing information to the public. It is my task to inform local members of the church. This information must enable local churches to give substance to their international responsibilities. These broader tasks of communication have traditionally received a central place in the church. This reflected the theological view that local churches, not experts or professionals, are responsible. These views have a long tradition. Communication is thus deemed to be of vital importance. It is part and parcel of the broad 'missionary calling' of the churches. Of course it serves more restricted financial interests too. The goal of income generation is traditionally linked to provision of information to the church. Communication serves different interests: it must help the churches to be true to their calling. And it must secure funding.

These tasks are not a straightforward, unambiguous and unproblematic whole. The daily responsibilities of a communication officer are more complex (more appealing as well as demanding) than that. In my daily work I have to deal with a number of contradictions and constraints. These engender unexpected problems. The core of these problems emerges from a deepening gap between the 'demands' made by the Dutch public and the changing definitions of responsibility emerging in the domains of international collaboration.

There is a growing contradiction between demand and the supply sides of information. An increasing gap can be discerned between the demands made in the Dutch scene and in the international domains. Yet, we are assigned to mediate and bridge the gap. How can we bridge a divide when the demands for information are so diverse? The problems are not primarily technical; conflicting needs for information confront me with a serious moral problem. One thing is certain: I can never do a perfect job. Conceiving of professional communicators as bridge builders between different worlds may be a bit too nice, but may help to make my point. When we do our job we often end up losing sight of one end of the bridge. Or even of both. How then, could we achieve a crossing?

Inherent contradictions: defining the problem of authenticity

Why is the task of communicating and bridge building between the local and the international domains becoming increasingly problematic? Changing needs and demands confront us in each of the two domains.

People within as well as outside churches increasingly wish to be re-assured that the concrete work – projects – 'fit' their own views and inclinations for solidarity. Charitable inclinations increasingly depend on such a direct link. As communication officers we must cater for these needs. The point is not so much that these demands lead to Euro-centric views of development. Of course they do, much in the same way as missionary responsibilities in the past reflected specific Dutch views. However, the concrete forms of Euro-centred charitable inclinations are changing. A direct link must be forged. The people wish to 'feel good' and be reassured that they 'do good' at the same time. The information about activities overseas must nurture the 'feeling good' of the constituency increasingly 'now'. There is a demand for instant gratification among the Dutch public. More encompassing theological frameworks are losing their long-term and more general appeal among church members. As a result, communication officers tend to follow the trend. As marketing experts they tend to focus on gratifying donor needs.

But this may lead to communication becoming encapsulated in a donor's world, divorced from needs and views expressed in the international community. If this process goes on unchecked 'the South' is diminished, as it were, becoming an 'object', a setting for gratifying donor needs, a particular stage set up for catering for an increasingly erratic Western public. The South is thus robbed of its own distinctive voice. The views of partner churches in other parts of the world become subordinated to the needs of a Dutch public. These partners may so be reduced to being a source for 'info-tainment'.

There are serious problems involved. The tendency to emphasise communication as a commercial and professional domain is in stark contradiction with values of partnership, which have become vitally important to the churches in the last decades. These values emerged after the Second World War. The values of partnership between the churches constituted a critical response to earlier colonial donor-centric practices. Western churches became severely criticised as a result. Thus the churches engaged themselves in a process of de-colonisation. Notions of partnership took centre stage. Official missionary and developmental engagements reflect these views. The churches fully endorsed ideologies of partnership and shared responsibilities (Enklaar 1968: 19). It was widely accepted that Western dominance should be rejected. One striking example may illustrate the struggle for correcting Western predominance in the international missionary scene.

In 1971 John Gatu, general secretary of the Presbyterian Church in East Africa, demanded a moratorium on aid. He advocated a temporary stop to all Western support. Aid, he said, primarily reflected donor views and donor needs. It prolonged the dependencies that existed between North and South (van der Poort 1989: 146). Although this moratorium never actually happened, Gatu's call had a tremendous effect on all churches. Intense efforts were made to disengage mission and development from regimes of domination. The conference of the World Council of Churches in 1968 marked this change of focus. The slogan of the conference 'justice instead of charity' gave rise to a new view on mission and development (Enklaar 1968: 28).

It has proved difficult to establish a truly equal relationship between development agencies and their partners in developing countries. But in the last decades Western agencies have made a serious effort. They have gradually changed their policies as a result of the criticism. The churches now subscribe to values such as dialogue, sustainability, respect for the local culture and participation. Many agencies formulated ethical guidelines. Preventing aid from becoming 'top down' and negligent of the views of partners and 'local' traditions has become a central concern.

Thus communication must deal with contradiction. International solidarity, equal partnership, and respect for the other became the core of the international agenda. Yet, in recent years the Dutch public has generated different concerns. Communication must heed the concerns with respect for overseas partners. Yet, a constant attention to the changing needs and views of the Dutch constituency is inevitable too. In my work my colleagues and I deal with this contradiction. In what ways?

Coping with the constraints

Coping with these constraints set to communication is an elusive task. One thing remains certain: the job can never be done 'properly'. Two brief examples may clarify how agencies cope with this issue. The first involves 'Plan International' (PI), an international development agency for children's aid. PI experienced a rather heavy criticism during the 1970s and 1980s. The criticism was aimed at its strategy of making people in the West financially adopt as 'foster parents' one or more children in a developing country. PI catered for the need for a direct, straightforward link between the two worlds. PI allowed foster parents to enable 'their' foster child to go to school, have sufficient food, clothing and shelter, etc. The approach appealed to many people in the Netherlands. It met with criticism, however. It was said that the programme increased inequality within the local communities with some children receiving substantial financial support while others received none. As a result of the criticism Plan International gradually changed its policy. It started to focus on improving living conditions in the village. It stopped supporting individual children and their families. Agricultural extension work or community development, for example, became part of its policy overseas also.

However, the communication strategy of Plan International to the Western donors remained more or less the same. In its marketing PI continued to advocate adoption of individual children by so-called 'foster parents'. This image aimed at securing the willingness to support PI, even as it no longer reflected the work carried out internationally (*Trouw* 1998: 1). One would expect PI to adjust the content of its communication to Dutch foster parents, reflecting the greatly changed practices of development. But for many foster parents the image of directly helping children remained very appealing, though some started to realise that image and 'reality' did not fully match anymore. PI's commercial strategy continued to work very well: a lot of funding was generated. So the two worlds in which PI was active: of Western fund raising, and of community organisation in the Third World, gradually drifted apart. Meaningful connections between the two became increasingly illusory. PI was trapped in the contradiction. A lot of harm was done. Angry cries of disappointed foster parents, who discovered that their foster children were no more than a virtual reality, could be heard from time to time. For PI this caused much public embarrassment as journalists were glad to expose the myths of foster parenthood. Many parents felt that they were being cheated. Some had travelled long distances to meet with 'their' foster children. But when they came to the villages they discovered none. Public exposure was very painful and came at great cost. A highly successful commercial marketing strategy had lost meaningful linkages to the concrete programmes overseas. The demands by the two domains had visibly publicly collided.

As communication officer of the development agency of the Dutch church I confront quite similar dilemmas. The problem at hand is not of PI's making at all. All agencies face similar problems, though their responses may differ. The Dutch churches took a somewhat different course of action in dealing with the issue. Another case may indicate how they coped with the dilemma. The Dutch churches experienced major transformations in their international engagements. Since the Second World War new agencies have been set up expressive of a need for new forms of partnership. Next to missionary activities, organisations for Christian aid and development were set up. In the late 1980s some of the Protestant churches felt, however, that the distinctions between these kinds of work had lost significance. As a result, Christian aid and development missions were placed under one encompassing institutional roof. The distinctions between missionary and developmental activities of the churches had become increasingly anachronistic in the international domains.

The response of the churches to the blurring of these distinctions in the international scene was twofold: first, the international operations were integrated. A second response is of great importance as well. Communication was centralised also. It became now an independent central unit, responsible for communicating about all international activities to the local churches. The centralisation had major effects. Before centralisation, the tasks had been carried out by the operational departments of mission, development and Christian aid. But now a new institutional divide came about: international work was segmented from communication. Each now started to exert themselves in more distinctive ways.

The institutional centralisation had unexpected outcomes for the professionals responsible for communication. They were now fully confronted with contradictions in the interfaces between the different domains of their church – local and international. The dynamics in each of the two domains are quite different. As has been stated already, distinctions between mission and development blurred in the international domain. Yet, these very distinctions were often firmly upheld within the Dutch scene. Local views clearly had their own dynamics and differed from international priorities. Specific local preferences became evident. Some church members are willing to support the international work of the churches only if it does not include missionary activities. It seems that the mission still copes with the rather inaccurate, yet hard to eradicate image of providing bibles to the hungry instead of bread. Others, on the other hand, continue to believe that the preaching of the gospel is the all-important task of the churches. Thus any extra money they are willing to give is earmarked for these activities. The communicators had not been exposed fully to these contradictions. Before the process of separating communication from international relations they had to deal only with some segments of the church's constituency. Now they confronted a much broader spectre. The problems of coping with contradictions between the demands from each of the two domains intensified. And as a result the issue of authentic communication arose for the communication officers. They had to make choices and face the consequences.

Among the staff members of the central communication department the inclination to comply with local distinctions intensified. Separate images of missionary work and development aid were produced. This increased the commitment and feelings of responsibility at the local setting. The tendency to heed the local views of the Dutch public became stronger in the last decade for another reason too. The centralising of its communication confronted the Dutch church increasingly with the fact that it was in competition with other donor agencies. A marketplace of good intentions gradually emerged. While the churches did not take an active role in this emerging market, they could not escape its consequences altogether. Income generation became an increasingly important issue. As the ties between the operational departments of the churches and communication were loosened, communicators became more exposed to the demands made at the local scene in the Netherlands.

The transformation is still much more muted when compared to some of the other development agencies. The demands made by international partners are still taken very seriously. But still, a new beginning has been made. The balance between the two domains is not stable. The communicators cannot escape dealing with the shifts.

The communication department started to 'ignore', as it were, to a large extent the merging of the various international practices of mission, development and Christian aid. They chose to stick to the distinctions which are still taken very seriously by the local Dutch constituency. Information is 'constructed' with an eye on catering for the rather diverse local perspectives. The religious diversity of the church's constituency is very much taken into account. The myth that all churches share one view and have the same need for information is rejected. That would be a very biased view for any communication officer. Communication thus continues to take the established distinctions between mission and development very seriously. The fact that these distinctions are becoming an anachronism internationally is not fully acknowledged. Instead a 'professional' choice is clearly made.

As noted, these problems of ambiguity and separation are not specific to one agency or another. They are not exclusively Plan International's, nor the churches' problems. All development organisations must confront the double-edged character of communication. What differs is the manner in which the different agencies cope with the problems. Communication within the churches has been increasingly pressured by the demands of modern commercial marketing strategies. That has meant that a price is exacted, namely of informing. Communicators have established separate direct lines between their specific 'products' and 'consumer groups'. These lines service 'religious niche markets'. Several 'brands' of international practices are distinguished. Each of the brands is communicated to a distinctive Christian constituency. While this strategy may be commercially interesting, the success comes at a price: to a certain extent the features of the messages are invented by the communications department. The messages do not primarily reflect the knowledge about the international scene. Does this affect the credibility of the agencies, or the authenticity of communication?

For some of the professionals involved, this process of 'virtualisation' is hard to understand. They feel that it is strange to sacrifice the goal of providing the best possible information coming from the international domains. Is meaningful communication between the international partners and local churches in the Netherlands not being sacrificed only for selfish reasons? They argue that the attention to funding has become the master of our minds. For some, a painful issue of authentic communication arises. More than a few feel increasingly alienated.

These moral concerns are entirely to the point. But what can we say to these people? How to judge the transformations that are taking place? Maybe we must start acknowledging that the job cannot be done in an unambiguous way. It is important not to make a judgement too quickly and not – indeed not – to romanticise past practices.

In the next paragraph I reflect upon some of my recent experiences when engaging in the commercial domains of communication. I argue that the all out effort to be 'effective' when promoting the international engagement of the church exacts specific prices. But what are these? And are the prices that we are asked to pay fair? Is there an alternative to this messiness of communication? Must we perhaps learn to better distinguish between more and less acceptable bodies of 'messy information'? The next story tells us of the boundaries of our engagement of communication both in a literal and a metaphorical way.

Communication: how to be authentic at the border

In March 1999 the situation in the Balkans – and especially Kosovo – got out of hand. Immediately after the bombing by NATO started, thousands of Albanian Kosovars fled the country. The media brought the latest news about the crisis. The first preparations for emergency aid began. My agency *Kerken in Aktie* collaborated with a strong local partner in Macedonia already active in sheltering refugees who have crossed the border. The department of communication of *Kerken in Aktie* felt that it must try to attract media attention to the work of this local partner. It felt that this might be achieved by sending a Dutch communication officer to meet with the Dutch national press which was gathering at the Macedonian border.

On 1 April I left for Kosovo. It was my task to inform the Dutch public through the media about our work in the emergency area. I have never felt so acutely the weight of mediating between a project in the field and the public (as represented by the national press). Our Macedonian partner organisation pressed me to explain the difficult situation it confronted within Macedonia. But the press was not interested in that. Reporters kept asking for figures: how many deaths, what are the casualties, how much bread has been distributed? The message that *Kerken in Aktie* was actively supporting the Kosovan refugees through a Macedonian aid organisation was not welcome. It seemed too complex. I explained over and over again that the Dutch churches provided assistance by funding local Macedonian organisations and not by setting up its own operations. But this was 'beyond' the Dutch press. They wished to speak to Dutch aid-workers. Our local partner may have been one of the most active relief organisations in Macedonia, but most journalists found that unimportant. When I informed them of the sponsoring by our churches, one reporter wrote that 'only local organizations are doing effective work here'. Neither the local organisation nor our Dutch support was mentioned. When *Kerken in Aktie* joined in the preparations for a national Dutch fund-raising event on television, we were told that our Macedonian partner could not appear on television, because he was 'not Dutch enough'. A major Dutch newspaper published an overview of the activities of the Dutch aid organisations. It reported that *Kerken in Aktie* was doing practically nothing (it has sent one person – me – with one mobile phone, 'no food, no other goods'). End of story. In other words, my message that *Kerken in Aktie* was active in the region was left hanging. There was no other side to the bridge. For the large majority of the press the mere fact that the relief activities were not run by the Dutch meant simply that they did not exist. It was not that the press transformed or distorted my reality. The press actively created a reality of its own, to which my 'information' was quite irrelevant. It seems that we were engaged in two unrelated monologues.

Suddenly, I thought of some of my own colleagues from the projects' department in the Netherlands. I recognised their frustration when they had told me their stories about the international work they are related to. Had they not shown a similar frustration when I needed a story for my own work of informing the Dutch public? Had I myself not heard before that I was quite unable to listen to and grasp their messages, being too preoccupied with my own public? It became clear to me that making a quick judgement is no solution.

At the Macedonian border I realised that being 'there', 'on the spot', was an engagement in emptiness. Yet, it also provided an opportunity to wield tremendous power. In my role as a public relations officer I could relay powerful images and construct a new reality. But only if the journalists felt that I could conform to their expectations and 'needs'. Here I stand, in front of the CNN cameras. I am one of the few at the border who have actually crossed it. I have even talked to some real life refugees. Suddenly, everyone decides I may be very interesting stuff. If I make the kinds of statements which are regarded as 'news' I may have an impact. Shall I say something really terrible about the UNHCR, or even about the High Commissioner? Such a statement would most probably be broadcast world-wide. I know of the subtle or not so subtle effect of bold statements.

Perhaps I should 'inform' the reporters that I have heard 'rumours' about five people dying on the other side of the border. That message might become the gospel truth the next day. People with political power may watch CNN that night, and respond in some way or another. Many people could become angry with the Macedonian government. I can already hear the angry cries: 'how can they let these people die, it is a crime against humanity to keep this border closed'.

These thoughts came to mind when I faced the cameras. How powerful I could be. How helpless I actually am when I try to get across my own message, the story about my Macedonian partners, about the seemingly futile support provided by my own church. But I realise that while 'reality' may be a complex and slippery notion, I must still honour it. Communication surely deserves careful treatment. Yet I do not always know what that means. What indeed is authentic communication? For some time I was out there, 'on the spot', as CNN calls it. However that may be, I was at the borderlines of authentic communication.

Communication at the institutional borderlines

The encounters at the border make the contradictions clear. The stubborn unwillingness of most reporters to actually listen to me after asking for information does not reflect journalistic practices only. There is more to it. The contradictions are manifest at all borderlines, geographical and institutional. They also affect the dynamics of communication within the development agencies themselves. I shall make some comments on the changing networks of communication. In order to grasp the issues of contradiction we must understand how they manifest themselves in the networks that have so deeply transformed in the last decades.

The institutional setting in which communication tasks are performed has changed. The transformation has been described as the emergence of a new profession, with a special more-or-less technical expertise in getting messages across. Much has been written on the Western context. I wish to mention a few aspects of the transformations in the international contexts in which our churches operate. Transformations that created a need for special communication officers started to arise.

Whose tasks are the new professionals taking over? A few observations can be made. In the not-too-distant past the churches could make use of highly visible networks of missionaries. The churches could thus give 'face' in a literal sense to their responsibilities. Making mission work visible was no big problem. Concrete Dutch faces could be linked to the various kinds of work in other countries. To the questions asked at the border (of Macedonia or Indonesia or elsewhere) it was possible to reply: 'look here is the Dutch guy', woman or man, 'that' is what we are talking about. It was clear that expatriates – the Dutch – played an important role in communication. This was good for fund raising; the linkages between the 'feeling good' and the 'doing good' were relatively clear and unambiguous. Concrete faces were expressive of the responsibilities of the churches.

But there was a problem to this. The direct and unambiguous links constituted a closed circuit. After the Second World War it became clear that this smooth-running communication came at great cost. The churches increasingly realised that their partner churches were marginalised from the circuits of information. It was a donor-centred affair. At the time the notion of colonialism was attached to it. As we have mentioned above, the churches took the criticism seriously. The role of the expatriates gradually diminished. But how were these vital tasks of communication taken over? Gradually the need for special communication officers became more intense. It reflected among other things the need for more equal partnership at a global level.

Project officers were the first to take over the tasks of communication. In the last decades, they became key sources for good information. They were in almost daily contact with their partners overseas. They had the best access to information about partner churches, special issues or projects carried out elsewhere. Within this context regular calls for financial support were still relatively unproblematic. Project officers were trusted sources of information. The regional and thematic offices of international collaboration now provided the vital links between the international and internal domains.

The advent of the new media changed the institutional landscape. Established routines collapsed. Suddenly the distance between the churches 'out there' and 'here' almost disappeared. The need for mediation and information was greatly affected. Access to information about the Third World proliferated immensely on television and the Internet. International travel increased. Access to information about other countries, cultures and religions proliferated. What need was there for institutional mediation between the different worlds? 'Expertise' was no monopoly anymore of the institutions. The expertise of regional officers in the church agencies suddenly became much less vital. The rank-and-file of the church now had a range of options for getting information themselves. The information produced by the project officers of the church agencies almost drowned in an ocean of images generated daily about the Third World. Who needed their specific expertise for the time to come?

Communication became highly problematic as a result. The public now gained direct access to a wide range of sources of information. For the churches the tasks of communication transformed considerably. The information provided by the different agencies was much less in demand. Scarcity of information had disappeared. The churches now had to make an extra effort for their voices to be heard. Their role was affected in other ways also.

Increasingly they were confronted with newcomers in the field. Since the nineteen sixties a great number of development agencies came about, private or semi-public. The domains of international development cooperation expanded. Plan International and *Médicins sans Frontières* are well-known newcomers, for instance. They created a new market for a Dutch public that was willing to make charitable contributions in the domains of development and international collaboration. As newcomers they had to create their own constituency within Dutch society. Thus marketing and fund-raising techniques became a very important engagement to the newcomers. Their messages to the Dutch public did not come from existing institutions, such as the churches. A willing, yet demanding Dutch public required special attention. Special marketing departments and techniques emerged. These marketing staff became increasingly important. Communication sometimes became the core business itself.

But again the successful marketing of 'solidarity' among the Dutch came at a cost. The distance between the two domains increased. The two sides of the bridge of communication started to drift apart. While in the various agencies the communication departments exclusively catered for the charitable needs of the general public, project officers took care of international cooperation. Increasingly closed circuits were the outcome of this transformation. The examples about Plan International and the Dutch churches I provided at the beginning of the chapter indicate that. The circuits of communication by the Dutch for the Dutch closed again. Again, also, partners overseas remained the outsiders. They were to a large extent marginal, or provided the stage for a Dutch play to be performed. This closing of the lines of communication caused tensions. First of all, tensions between the offices of communication and the departments engaging in the international affairs. These became almost a daily routine. The different worlds drifted apart not only along the geographical borderlines, this occurred also at the institutional borderlines within these very organisations. Mintzberg (1979) has provided us with a telling concept for understanding what happens at the institutional borderlines. Segmentation takes place; it seems anywhere, in any meeting of the different lines of communication. Perhaps foreseeing our futile encounters with the world press at the Macedonian border he gave the process of estrangement within communication an appropriate name: 'Balkanisation'.

In search of authenticity in communication: concluding remarks

What does authentic communication mean? We must return to the question I raised at the beginning of the chapter. Charles Taylor (1991: 16) defined authenticity as 'the moral ideal of being true to oneself'. He wrote these lines with a particular purpose, that is, to combat the Western inclination to restrict the notion of morality to the domain of 'care for the other'. He confronts the notion that 'care for the self' is of lesser moral significance. He wishes to correct this impression. Hence his use of the powerful moral image of 'authenticity' of being true not for care of the other but for care of the self. As Taylor shows, care for the other is closely connected to our search for authenticity. He does not plead against any form of Western self-centred forms of autism. Charles Taylor thus makes it clear also that authentic communication implies the search for an appropriate linking of these two responsibilities. While he emphasises that we have lost sight of a moral view of the self in the 1980s, he advocates the need to link the two in a morally acceptable way.

This is part of the task which I set myself here. Time and again I have suggested in my case material the need to understand communication as a balancing act between these two responsibilities. Taylor substantiates this view. But there is more to it. While Taylor sets an important agenda, for understanding and transforming our practices of communication we must do more. This is a formidable and difficult task. Baudrillard (1995: 81) suggests that in our post-modern world we have lost sight of any reference point of communication. It is not linked to any care, not for the self, nor for the other. Baudrillard writes: 'representation bears no relation to any reality whatever, it is its own pure *simulacrum*'. In my descriptions I have used the metaphor of communicators as bridge builders between different worlds. They provide reliable, 'true' information. But each time I asked for attention to the fact that being effective providers of linkages came at a high price. The job could not be done properly. The linking and the drifting apart go hand in hand. The one cannot be separated from the other. And as Baudrillard writes, we often end up creating images that no longer have any reference point. The bridge may just hang in the air. He provides us with a powerful insight into the nightmare of moral emptiness which results from this. I have given some examples about the processes of social closure and the loss of meaning. We are regularly losing our reference points at the borderlines of communication. I suggested that a much more general use be given to the concept of 'Balkanisation'. The concept may provide us with a key to understanding what actually goes on in communication, first of all its contingencies.

While Taylor urges us into a search for authenticity, Baudrillard informs us that these very quests for authenticity are contingent and problematic. They may very well fail. It goes beyond the remit of this chapter to argue what this insight means in practical terms. However, let me finish by saying that I feel that these insights are of the greatest practical significance. They may lead to an awareness of communication as a contingent practice, allowing us the space – the insight as well as the courage – for new concrete forms of moral engagement. I hope that the Dutch churches and the other agencies bearing responsibility in a global perspective will take up this call. A lot is to be gained in a moral as well as a practical sense.

Note

1   This contribution could not have been written without the strong and ongoing
    support of Ananta Giri and Philip Quarles van Ufford. I owe them my sincere
    appreciation.

References

Baudrillard, Jean (1995) 'The map precedes the territory', in Walter Truett Anderson
    (ed.) *The Truth about the Truth: De-confusing and Re-constructing the Postmodern
    World*, New York: Jeremy P. Tarcher/Putnam, pp. 79–81.
Enklaar, I.H. (1968) *Onze blijvende opdracht*, Kampen: J.H. Kok.
Mintzberg, H. (1979) *The Structuring of Organizations: a Synthesis of the Research*,
    Englewood Cliffs: Prentice-Hall.
Taylor, Charles (1991) *The Ethics of Authenticity*, Cambridge, MA: Harvard Univer-
    sity Press.
Trouw (1998) 'Geld voor adoptiekind gaat in de praktijk "zelfs naar bruggen" ',
    Trouw, 22 December, p. 1.
van der Poort, Kees (1989) 'Moratorium-discussie achterhaald?', *Wereld en Zending*
    18 (2): 146–152.

Chapter 11

What are we in fieldwork for?

Albert E. Alejo, SJ

> With my own background I am unable to do what so many researchers do
> – just study and leave.
>
> (Alting von Geusau 1985)

The practice of ethnographic fieldwork is first experienced as a social intervention before it is transformed into a textual invention. Fieldworkers do
not only work in the field, however the field is understood; they also *work* it.
In the process of inserting themselves into a community or accompanying a
group in their movement they also encounter, delight in, collide with, adjust
to, miss or misunderstand other people's actions and reactions. They impact
on the lives of the people involved in their study perhaps as much as those
people transform the researchers' views of things.

Fieldworkers move almost inevitably from the already complex participant observation to an even more entangled, often multi-stranded, partisan
participation (Gupta and Ferguson 1997; Marcus 1995). This seems especially true in studying nascent social movements in the context of contested
development projects (Gardner and Lewis 1996; Albert 1997) as the
following reflection on a Philippine case wishes to show.

From Narmada to Apo Sandawa

This reflection on the political and practical dimensions of fieldwork started
when I met Medha Patkar who was the leader of the Narmada Bachao
Andolan in India. From London, I took a short one-month visit between
July and August in 1994 to the area of the Bhils who were among those
affected by the Narmada Dam Project. Medha Patkar's position posed a
challenge to me. Exploring her Hindu and Gandhian tradition, she moved
among the tribal groups as speaker and chanter, sometimes as cook and
counsellor, as trainer and translator. Among those supporting the movement
were book writers, some of whom were themselves vending their own books
on top of cars during rallies.

I thought that there must be a way of doing research without always
having to draw a very sharp line between academic rigour and social rele-

vance, and that if pressed to make a preference, one could go further by considering a legitimate people's movement more important than one's research. As Medha Patkar argues, the general writing on paradigms of development, even alternative development, would not change the world and the exploited systems. The necessary thing to do was to commit oneself to a real community, 'like staking a territory as your own by planting your flag there, by capturing a symbol and shaking it for all its worth' (Patkar 1992: 278).

In the Philippines, Virgilio Enriquez (1994) pioneered a search for an ethical, relevant and culturally appropriate approach to social science research. One can argue that his call for a 'liberating' research practice (Enriquez 1992) ran the risk of equating the social with the national project (Pertierra 1997: 11–12.20; Enriquez 1992: 43). But I resonate with the way he stretched the meaning of 'indigenous facilitation research'. Whereas participatory research assumes equality between the researcher and the researched, indigenous facilitation research 'goes farther by recognising the superior role of the participant or the culture bearer as the one who determines the articulated and implied limits of the research enterprise'. In this framework, the facilitative researcher becomes more of a 'morale booster, networker, or at most a consultant who confers about the research problem with the community who are, in this case, the real researchers' (Enriquez 1994: 59).

Just before going to the Philippines to start my fieldwork in 1995, I visited a Dutch anthropologist in Chiang Mai. Leo Alting von Geusau has built up a library on the Akha. In the short weeks that I spent with him, I learned how, along the way, his scholarly work had become inseparable from his commitment to the people he studied. He explained, 'I discovered on the one hand, a wealthy, enormous complexity of the Akha culture. On the other hand, I discovered the many problems they have. I felt committed, "very involved"' (Alting von Geusau 1985: 44).

This involvement resonates with the words of Dell Hymes, who recognised that 'by virtue of its subject matter, anthropology is unavoidably a political and ethical discipline, not merely an empirical speciality' (1972: 48). Our simply being there among the people we study already has consequences, over and above the textual production that results from that experience. Nancy Scheper-Hughes puts it more emphatically. 'We cannot delude ourselves into believing that our presence leaves no trace, no impact on those whose lives we dare intrude' (1992: 25). So, for better or for worse, wittingly or unwittingly, the practice of fieldwork places the ethnographer in relative position of power, the handling of which calls for an ethical and disciplinal reflection (Gledhill 1994: 217).

Anthropological reflections in the 1980s promised to provide insights on this notion of practice (e.g., Ortner 1984; Marcus and Clifford 1986). The general impact of this reform movement, unfortunately, was limited to 'ethnographic writing only' (Marcus 1999: 10, note 4; cf. Fardon 1990; Pels and Salemink 1994: 5.16ff). Apparently, the new ethnography neglected the 'social and political processes almost completely, not necessarily by denying them salience, but by backgrounding them to questions of representations, construction and deconstruction' (Gledhill 1994: 225; see also Scheper-Hughes 1992: 24). The concept of practice as a set of activities, strategies and social intervention was 'relegated to the back burner' despite its relevance to issues of development and social movements (Gardner and Lewis 1996: 40).

Recent studies call for flexibility in diversifying our knowledge from different field positions (Giri 1998; Gupta and Ferguson 1997; Clifford 1997; Hastrup and Fog Olwig 1997). They call, too, for reflexivity and 'self-aware-ness' (Pels and Salemink 1994) in the ways we as fieldworkers 'follow' our subjects and their movements (Marcus 1995), or 'tame' them to become good informants (Hobart 1996). Finally, they call for 'reflection' on what our field-work relationship means to our research subjects (Paine 1998: 134; Ginsburg 1997: 140, 123). All this suggests that anthropology stands to gain by seeking to combine reflexivity and relevance in making fieldwork itself as a time, space, and infrastructure for people's self-assessment and empowerment.

I carried similar ideas and models of solidarity during my own fieldwork in Mount Apo Sandawa, site of the geothermal power plant that was constructed by the Philippine government and was opposed by environmen-talists and advocates for the indigenous people's rights. Although I was in contact with the protesters as well as the government, I found myself studying and working with a small Manobo social movement that was crit-ical of both camps. My Manobo hosts became key figures of this new indigenous movement. The group, called *Tuddok*, wanted cultural regenera-tion and to claim an ancestral domain. And for this aim, they saw my research as a possible ally. Without formal contract, but with constant assessment of our roles, a partnership developed between my cultural research and their cultural movement. My research then served as a resource for the movement just as the movement provided substance for my research. To understand this, we need a general background on how the Mount Apo environment has been politicised.

Geothermal project and political protest

Burdened with debts and wanting to catch up with Asian tiger economies, the Philippine government decided to speed up the exploration of its indige-nous sources of energy. In 1987 the government-owned Philippine National Oil Company (PNOC) drilled two exploratory wells for the 250 MWe Geothermal Project at the heart of the remaining rain forest of Mount Apo, the highest mountain in the Philippines. This home of the endangered Philippine Eagle is included in the 1982 United Nations List of National Parks and Equivalent Reserves, and is listed as one of the heritage sites of the Association of Southeast Asian Nations. More importantly, perhaps, Mount Apo is considered the ancestral territory of the Manobos and the Bagobos.

A wave of protest emerged, starting from a small tribal organisation and from individual government officials. The protest intensified with the participation of big environmentalist groups and Catholic and mainstream Protestant church activists, supported by advocates not only in Manila but also in Britain, the Netherlands, Japan, and the USA. This led to a decade of debate on issues ranging from the legal status of the project to its environmental consequences and its cultural impact on the resident tribes who claim Mount Apo as their ancestral domain (Broad and Cavanagh 1993; Mincher 1992).

In 1989, twenty-one *Datus* from nine tribal communities around Mount Apo performed a *D'yandi*, a historic blood pact, vowing to 'defend Mount Apo to the last drop of our blood'. A counter ritual called Pamaas, sponsored this time by PNOC, to dispel the cosmic effect of the Dyandi curse, followed this. This conflict of rituals dramatised the violent exchange between the government military and the Communist New People's Army, that claimed lives from both camps. A huge multi-sectoral coalition, called Task Force Apo Sandawa (TFAS), spearheaded the fight against the PNOC's 'development aggression' (Rodil 1993; Broad and Cavanagh 1993; Durning 1992: 5).

As a result, PNOC operation was temporarily suspended. The World Bank and the ExIm Bank of Japan withdrew their funding commitments. PNOC staff had to re-examine the company's policy and improve its technology. In 1991, PNOC submitted a comprehensive 10-volume Environmental Impact Study which included a module on the socio-cultural dimension of the project. This won for the company the much-coveted Environmental Compliance Certificate (ECC).

Other factors also led to the granting of the ECC. Extreme droughts rendered the existing hydroelectric power plants incapable of supplying enough energy, resulting in long months of daily 8-hour power outages. The Gulf War also triggered insecurity on the part of government planners who warned against too much dependence on the Arab oil-producing countries (Lamberte and Yap 1991).

Appeals against the granting of the ECC were dismissed by the Supreme Court. A special Presidential Proclamation carved out from the 72,000-hectare national park the 701 hectares of the project as geothermal reservation. In 1992, President Ramos signed the Memorandum of Agreement between the government and the representative organisations of the affected communities, thus sealing the legal status of the project.

But national and international advocacy against the power project, especially in London and the Netherlands, continued even up to the mid-1990s (e.g., Philippine Resource Center 1994; Broeckman *et al.* 1996). In

Mindanao, the local Catholic clergy kept up the fight by continuing to denounce the project in its pastoral messages and radio homilies. The annual commemoration of the Dyandi blood pact dwindled in attendance, but a significant number of protest groups still maintained the hard-line stance of 'no compromise' with the power company.

Existing researches and documents tended to reduce the actors in the field to two: the project proponent, and its loyal opponent. Those who did not fall within these categories were not considered actors. This was clear, for example, in the thesis written by a PNOC manager who studied in Britain. Castro, who helped create the PNOC office for 'dealing with public opposition', did not discuss those who were in-between 'since we do not expect severe complications' from them (Castro 1996: 11). Castro's analysis is valuable for the understanding of the company's discourse and practice. Her lack of fieldwork, however, prevented her from seeing other contextual actors who might not be as 'disturbing' as the project protesters, but who would later become quite crucial in their emergent roles.

(En)countering culturelessness

From initial readings, I expected that the controversy surrounding the Mount Apo Geothermal Project would make it difficult for me to enter the village. So armed with permits from the Provincial Governor, the Office of Southern Cultural Communities, the Municipal Mayor, and the Chief of Police, I approached the Barangay Captain. While he appreciated my research, he asked me to explain my purpose to the Barangay Council the following week. The Barangay Council expressed fears regarding my stay in the village. It asked me to come back the following week to face the Tribal Council. The Tribal Council, which included the resident Protestant pastors and the paramilitary personnel, also raised a number of issues attendant to my proposed residence in their area. Later, the Tribal Assembly was convened. They decided that I could be a visitor but not a villager, for the following reasons.

First, being a priest, I was automatically identified with the activist local clergy that had been at the forefront of protest against the state-owned power project. Since the protest movement was associated with the Communists, they feared that if I stayed in the area, the place might become militarised again.

Second, being a Catholic priest, my presence could be divisive for the village, which was predominantly under evangelical Protestant churches. The stigma of being a harbinger of the fatal '666' from the Book of Revelation had never been totally erased, even by this time.

Third, being a Tagalog from Manila, I could also end up getting their lands, as the settlers from the north had supposedly done since the war. The fact that I was born on the same island of Mindanao did not help.

Finally, what do people get from researchers, anyway? They take pictures, interview old men, and report about them to far-away places. Apparently, they had had bitter experiences with researchers, both from the supporters of the project as well as from its opponents who used them solely to further their own agenda.

In the process, I got to learn about their political institutions and practices. Their questions revealed their fears, which in turn gave hints about their history.

The most disturbing question, however, came from the sidelines. 'But Father', asked Apo Ambolugan, a gentle elder in the village, 'why do you still want to study us? We have no more culture here.' This question really hit me hard. It betrayed the state of collective low self-esteem of the tribe. He continued: 'Why us? Why not the T'boli of Lake Sebu? Or the Matigsalug of Bukidnon? They still have *agong* there. They still dance. And they still wear our native clothes. We have nothing left here.' This avowal of what may be called 'culturelessness' (cf. Rosaldo 1988, 1989: 197; Fallows 1987) haunted me for the rest of my fieldwork.

Apo Ambolugan's statement could just have been an oblique way of driving me away. But he was not alone in harbouring this feeling. There was, indeed, a prevailing feeling of '*kahiubos*' or collective low self-esteem among the Manobos, not simply in relation to the Visayan settlers but to other tribes as well. Part of this feeling of marginalisation is due to the marginality of the land itself. The terrain is mostly steep and sloping. The climate is too cold for lucrative fruit crops such as durian and marang. Bananas are plagued by many forms of disease. Other possibilities such as strawberries and cut flowers are still at the experimental stage. The only regular source of income is soft broom production, using tiger grass or *tahiti*. Coffee would have been good if it had not been abandoned in favour of PNOC employment. The PNOC road promised access to big markets for the natives' products, unfortunately more goods come up to the village than make it downtown.

The original centre of the tribal community, an open space that served as a basketball court and cultural arena, was abandoned when the new PNOC road was constructed. Many houses were moved to the side of the new road, thus symbolically and literally splitting the village to make way for the huge trucks that connect the geothermal plant to Kidapawan Poblacion.

In the genealogy of the Apao, the first ancestor remembered by the local people was himself a poor man. He was so poor he had to borrow garden tools from the Tagabawa on the Davao side of Mount Apo. The name Apao itself meant 'a tiny flea'. Apao left no legacy of handicrafts or huge dwellings. But Apao had at least five wives and many descendants. And they liked talking together and they had dreams. For at least two people, this was enough to start to regenerate their culture. And for academic as well as personal reasons, I decided to share my research with their project.

Simple steps, complex moves

I had the courage to say to Apo Ambolugan that I knew that all cultural energy was not yet lost, because on 5 October 1995, on my very first visit to Sayaban, I met the two would-be leaders of a gentle cultural regeneration of the tribe. They were cousins Beting Umpan Colmo and Pastor Tano Umpan Bayawan. Even before I arrived, they had already dreamt of 'regenerating' their culture.

'We start with a family reunion', Tano and Beting explained. 'We envision a lively tribal culture. But since we are not in any influential position to do so – we are not the *Barangay*, we are not *Datus*, we are not wealthy – we will start with our family or clan. The Umpan clan. If we could bind ourselves together, and then later play the *agong*, and dance as a family, then we can perhaps be the model for the rest of the clans to follow.'

It sounded extremely modest. But considering the entropic situation as I was beginning to understand it, it made realistic sense. My instinct told me that this was the kind of movement I was looking for. In the midst of a general social paralysis, here was a source of energy. They told me they did not want to become involved with and be manipulated by NGOs who presented themselves as an alternative to the powerful government and development projects. They wanted a movement of their own, addressing the tribal situation according to their own analysis and interpretation. Theirs would not be an action directly or primarily against PNOC, although it might have to reach that point later. It would have something to do with their dignity as a people. It would touch on the land issue but the strategy would be to work on culture.

Tano and Beting came from slightly different backgrounds. Tano Bayawan, in his late thirties, was a pastor of the Church of Christ. His work as a Bible translator under the Summer Institute of Linguistics (SIL) was for him a spiritual devotion and a service to his tribe. But SIL was not addressing the development of their culture, to which he was equally committed. He wanted a book written on their tribe.

Like Tano, Beting was also in her thirties. But unlike her cousin, Beting had lived apart from the tribe for many years. Her Visayan father already had children when he settled in the nearby Muaan. Her Manobo mother died when she was six. She was reared by her Visayan half-sisters who, aside from inheriting more lands, attempted to instil in her disgust for her own tribe. Her other sister by her native mother, who had more experience with the tribals, later became an outspoken opponent of PNOC. Beting worked with a human rights law office and with a foundation for child victims of war. She received a German scholarship towards a college degree in psychology. Seeing the ways of NGOs, and the situation of her fellow natives, she decided to go back to her tribe. It was timely that I met her accidentally on my first visit to the place. She was very articulate in Visayan, Tagalog and English. She needed, however, to brush up her Manobo.

When the Tribal Assembly rejected my stay, I decided to concentrate on their movement. They welcomed my research, in return, as possible assistance to their cause. In what follows, I shall offer some instances illustrative of the overlapping projects of research and movement during fieldwork. Like Ginsburg, I want to present this 'not as self-justification but as part of perennial discussion of the role of scholarship in processes of social transformation' (Ginsburg 1997: 140).

Family movement and ironies of fieldwork

From the time we decided on a kind of partnership, Beting and Tano started listing their relatives. The process so excited their relatives that, to their surprise, the planned clan reunion was held within three months rather than two years.

There was one problem, though. Since they had no single percussion instrument left, I was asked if I knew anyone who could lend them an *agong* and a set of *kulintang* (brass drums). Because I was not allowed to live in the village, I had to stay in the parish at the town centre. And through my new contacts in the parish church, I was able to convince a Manobo family, already residing in the lowland, to lend their heirlooms.

On 5–7 January 1996, the whole clan of Ayon Umpan gathered in Muaan, the legendary origin-centre of migration for the tribal communities in Kidapawan. It broke the ice of lethargic existence. They revived an old ritual called *Pakaa't Kallo*, which literally meant feeding the tools of the farm. A number of young Manobos recited their poems in the vernacular. These poems were created during a poetry workshop we held a few days before the reunion. The family marked the grave of two relatives who had drowned in the river. They also invented a new ritual of giving native names to those who had only 'Christian' names. A guest priestess improvised the naming ritual out of traditional elements such as bamboo, water, flower and comb. And where did they get their native names? From our unfinished genealogy that Beting presented on the table. The presence of the musical instruments spelled a big difference. They were surprised to recall the many tunes they feared they had forgotten. There was joy in being able to dance again. Then the children took over the drums when their elders got tired. Towards the end of the *Kalivungan* (celebration), they selected officers for the new organisation, called *Tuddok to Kalubbaran ni Apo Ayon Umpon* (Pillars of the Descendants of Elder Ayon Umpan). Beting, my research partner, was appointed leader of the Tuddok. Then they formed committees to handle concerns such as financing marriages, assisting the sick members of the family, establishing communal farming, and sending children to school.

They also created a special committee to work for their ancestral domain claim. The committee reflected a recent concern. They argued that regenerating their culture meant, among other things, the revival of dancing. But how could they continue to dance if they were not secure in their land?

Legally, there was an opening for this plan. They had heard of the Departmental Administrative Order No. 2, which provides a detailed procedure whereby a tribal community can present a claim to their ancestral domain. Once the claim has been validated, the government can grant a certificate of its recognition. The Tuddok started working for this recognition.

Some leaders of the protest groups dismissed the Tuddok initiative as being 'clannish'. They wanted to 'help' them so that their 'narrow' vision of the Mount Apo problem could expand to include the 'bigger' issues of 'development aggression', 'biodiversity', and 'ethnocide'.

Tuddok leaders argued, however, that the issue-based protest campaign against the powerful geothermal project had done nothing to stop it. That type of movement had not improved the lives of the affected tribal community. They wanted to assert their self-determination not only in the face of the PNOC geothermal company, but also of the NGO community. In her written reflection, Beting said that the Tuddok aimed to explore a path of development that was an 'alternative to the alternative'.

At this point, it was clear how the new group was opening up a new space for their participation in the making of their contribution to their history. The consolidation of the clan, the marking of places for the living and the dead, the invention of a naming ritual, the resourcing of their genealogy for the new generation, the re-playing of the *agong* and the re-animation of the body in dancing – these were all micro-processes charged with the Manobo agency.

In this light, would the fieldworker's facilitation in the loan of musical instruments be considered a breach of professional standards of objectivity or a form of militant interventionism? If in earlier fieldwork, extracting artefacts – by buying or borrowing or simply receiving gifts – was considered part of fieldwork practice, would putting in cultural symbols in response to local requests be dismissed as problematic practice?

Mobilising bloodlines

The movement that chose to start from the family and the body had to encounter a trial precisely there – in the weak family attending to a sick body. Ettok, the seventeen-year-old poet-artist, was sick. He worked part-time with the geothermal company to earn an allowance for his secondary education. But he came home one day with infected marrow in his left thigh. After long deliberation over whether it was caused by mountain spirits or by company chemicals, they finally decided to take him to hospital – in far away Davao City.

Ettok's case became complicated. He had to undergo two operations. His daily antibiotics and food alone cost the equivalent of one week's family income. Ettok's father thought of selling a piece of land. In the midst of their struggle to claim their ancestral domain, they were sometimes pressured to do what they hated most about their forefathers' mistakes.

My fieldwork identity also had to be reshaped. At one point, the PNOC Community Relations Officer needed a priest to 'bless' their new office building inside the power plant. Most of the employees, he argued, were Catholics. The parish priest found different alibis to evade it. The task fell to me because, as a researcher, I was supposed to be in a 'more neutral position'. But what could blessing the PNOC premises 'mean' to NGOs, to activist clergy, and to Tuddok members themselves? With the consent of my Tuddok friends, however, I agreed to perform the rite and even managed to drop a line during my homily which, according to some employees, 'disturbed some company personnel'. After presiding at the liturgy, I brought the collected money to Ettok. The managers assured me that the money did not come from the company but from the Catholic employees themselves. The gesture was to save me from possible rumours.

On another occasion, Beting and I decided to approach the manager of Oxbow, the Canadian company constructing the power plant for the PNOC. The Canadian manager twice visited me in the parish church and I remembered that he had offered to help the tribal people in the area. Beting knew that the opposition groups, her sister included, would not have approved of asking for help from the 'enemy'. But the donation from the Oxbow manager – who said he had 25 per cent Indian blood – supplied Ettok's medicine for a precious few days.

Ettok's importance to the new cultural movement could not be measured. Although he would not normally be considered a movement entrepreneur, his attitude towards his sickness, not to mention his artistic gift itself, inspired its leaders. Beting, for example, almost left the Tuddok movement during one of her deliberations on the value of their cultural struggle. 'Was it worth her sacrifice of personal search for a stable relationship?' During one telephone conversation, she confessed that the sight of Ettok sketching Manobo scenes in the Davao hospital 'energised' her. Ettok once borrowed a wheelchair and started roaming around the hospital, talking to fellow patients and their nurses. People flocked to his drawings. Manobo old folks playing the traditional musical instruments stood out as features of his drawings. Beting realised, 'how silly of her to brood over petty things'. There was Ettok, the supposedly lame man, arousing in people new reasons to go on.

Ettok's hospitalisation had certainly sharpened the Manobos' sense of financial poverty, but at the same time it dramatised their capacity for cultural integrity.

I had scanty notes on these episodes because I was not certain during fieldwork whether they were just time-consuming, altruistic, emotionally draining distractions from the 'real' research (cf. Gardner and Lewis 1996; Gledhill 1994: 218). I include these details, however, to point out that social movements or, better still, cultural struggles *vis-à-vis* development involve not only big mass rallies, but also minute practices and processes of almost invisible self-assertion, improvisation and production of meanings (Escobar 1992). In these micro-processes and micro-spaces, even the 'non-entrepreneurs' of the movement play significant roles. They also reveal that neither disciplinary distancing nor principled militancy suffice to explain the formation of the research relationship or the direction, meaning, intensity or pacing of a movement.   •

Rootworks and paperworks

The more visible struggle of claiming ancestral domain kept the Tuddok busy during most of the succeeding months. In claiming a portion of Mount Apo National Park, the Tuddok had to contend with a rival Manobo claimant from a neighbouring village. The contest on the rightful land claim required the Tuddok to present more convincing local history and ethnographic evidence than had been submitted by the other *datu*. The rudimentary history and fragmentary genealogy of the resident clan taken so far from individual interviews had many 'gaps'. They were worried that the stories of the elders would not be coherent when the time for public hearing came.

Remembering what I had picked up from the Obo-Manobo Phrasebook published by the Summer Institute of Linguistics, I explored the use of the word *kodpotongkooy*. *Kodpotongkooy* simply means 'talking to one another'. Such informal discussion could range from visiting kin to sharing *itulan* (history which is true) to *ponguman* (legends and therefore not necessarily true) and to *kolivuungan* (celebration). I asked whether it could also be used to check genealogies and 'collate' historical accounts. That discussion itself became a *kodpotongkooy*. They then thought of gathering all the elders who had been interviewed already, plus others who had not been consulted. To attract as many participants as possible, they paged Apo Salumay, via the provincial radio station public service, to lead their series of *kodpotongkooy*.

Apo Salumay, a highly respected former village chieftain of Sayaban, who had, however, been away for the past twenty-seven years, became the primary historian of the group. It has since then become customary to call *kodpotongkooy* whenever the group wanted to discuss a problem or make any decision. This to my mind was one of the most important sequences during the research–movement partnership. Not that *kodpotongkooy* had not been there before. As a matter of fact, this informal way of discussion constituted the most common way of exchanging views and making collective decisions. But its new application in what could be called a 'discourse formation' was, according to Datu Atawan, a source of *konokkaan*, or strength. From casual conversations with people on the road, to visiting relatives and feeling deeply for them, to extremely formal meetings of elders, people could derive strength. They could speak, they could discuss, they could debate, they could argue. Somehow the planning for the family reunion and the listing of the genealogy paved the way for the formation of a local discourse, an alternative to the government rhetoric and especially to the silent transcripts of the tribal people themselves.

In *kodpotongkooy*, speaking out and talking together, in opening spaces for a new discourse to develop, the tribe comes to life again. This is where the old men are given importance. This is where dreams are accepted as a source of knowledge. This is where plans are made real. This is also an occasion for bodily performances as well as the school for audienceship. This is where the tribe is very much itself (cf. Racelis 1999).

In contrast, so much in the process of development conspires to silence them. Authentic assistance, it appears to me now, will have to touch on the multiplication of space for the blossoming of their local discourse 'facilitating in finding their voices, rather than speaking on behalf of them' (Gardner and Lewis 1996: 47–48). To some extent, this ethnography shares in the search for *konokkan* (strength, energy) by entering into intimate *kodpotongkooy* with the actors in the field as well as in this text. This upbeat assessment of collective discourse formation, however, should be tempered by the complexity of local politics.

When the Tuddok land claim was gaining momentum, some local managers of the power company called the village officials to a secret meeting. As a result, a local leader took some of our documents without permission. The Tuddok had to send a formal complaint to the PNOC office in Manila to stop the secret company intervention in the legal process.

Towards an alternative to the alternative movement

The Tuddok's assertion of self-determination was put to the test when it expanded in numbers as well as in activities. Their meagre finances, reinforced only by my tight research budget, could not cope with their growing needs, even just to provide coffee for increasingly frequent meetings. I broached the idea of opening their movement to some potential 'supporters'. Their initial vehemence to the idea made me feel guilty for introducing the topic. They did not want to have anything to do with NGOs and other funding agencies.

Beting explained this stance in an abridged article sarcastically entitled 'Our Simple Story' that she published ironically in the newsletter of the protest. 'We were considered and looked upon as powerless beings. The people in the alternative movements, therefore, saw that we were in need of their liberating development plans, strategies and projects. Ironically, in this move, we were not viewed as partners but plain "beneficiaries". ... We may want to correct the misrepresentation of our voices but how can we offend our saviours?'

These sharp words find kindred spirit in contemporary literature articulating similar sentiments both at home (cf. Tauli-Corpuz 1993) and abroad (cf. Warren 1997; von Benda-Beckmann 1997). Upon serious consideration of the actual predicament, however, the group picked up the suggestion of accepting assistance from outsiders, but only under certain conditions. I summarise these conditions here based on Tuddok documents and practice.

1   Donors should not give huge amounts of money. Tribal leaders can be corrupted by money. They believed they were not exempt from this weakness.

2   Donors should not visit them in the area unless formally invited. The presence of outside donors in the area triggers the suspicion that the leaders of the movement are getting a lot of money.

3   Donors should not give them seminars. The Tuddok leaders insisted that they were still trying to discover what they knew. Seminars generally created the impression that the speakers knew what was best for the group. It would be difficult to reject the teachings of the seminar teachers if they happened to be their aid-givers, too.

4   Donors should not invite them to join coalition groups. These big coalitions generally tended to be dominated by strong groups with political or ideological agendas. The whole network then would be forced to agree to big statements, which the likes of the Tuddok could not maintain or understand.

5   The Tuddok did not want to use or be used by media. They wanted to have control of the representations made of them. Since the media had its own priorities, they refused to accept being objects of advocacy using TV or radio broadcast, or even print media. Along this line, the Tuddok also harboured deep suspicion against researchers who needed the people only for data gathering but had no place for them in doing analysis.

They admitted that these were extremely stringent rules. They begged, however, for a genuine trust in their capacity to discern what they could do by themselves with some help from friends.

An enterprising NGO accepted the challenge. A friend of mine, working for a research NGO, came for a visit. Her visit coincided with celebration for the return of the tribal culture through their newly bought *agong*. When she returned to the city, she recommended to her NGO to consider assisting the Tuddok in its continuing cultural movement and research, but under the Tuddok's own terms. Her NGO, the Alternate Forum for Research in Mindanao (AFRIM), adjusted its policies and practices to absorb the conditions of the Tuddok movement seriously. In time, the Tuddok also appreciated AFRIM's assistance and formally welcomed it in the community through a simple ritual.

From January 1997 up to the present, AFRIM and Tuddok have been experimenting with this new type of relationship between an extremely sensitive people's movement and an understanding NGO. The result seems good so far. In November 1997, the expanded Tuddok movement filed its petition for its ancestral domain claim covering some 20,000 hectares of forest and farmlands within the Mount Apo National Park and including the 701 hectares already occupied by the PNOC. While the PNOC project remains in the area, the Tuddok now have achieved, in less than three years, a better bargaining position for the people most directly affected by the project – something the protest intervention never quite achieved in a decade.

Fieldwork and the uneasiness of research practice

The following sequence reveals other aspects of the researcher's positionality in the 'field' and how learning from the field could be applied to fieldwork itself.

The geothermal company, in its desire to understand the indigenous culture around the project and its future sites, commissioned a multi-disciplinary socio-cultural study of ten indigenous cultural communities around Mount Apo (Gloria 1997). A group of consultants from different universities gathered together, but the contract was signed by the president of Davao University, run by my fellow Jesuits. The research team leader invited me to attend the presentation of the initial result. The venue was the most luxurious island resort in Davao City. I was grateful for being asked to join the privileged group of government policy makers and academic consultants. But I also had to ask whether they had invited anyone from the ten communities who were the subject of the multi-million-peso study. They had not. I was told that the research result was strictly for those who would make use of it in policy and planning.

Beting and Tano did all they could to be given a place during the consultation. They even sent a fax message to the Manila office of the PNOC. Frustrated, they had to rely on me to tell them about the controversial conclusions and methodology of the commissioned research. The ironic twist was that Tuddok leaders also implicated me in the PNOC research because I was associated with the Jesuit University that conducted the research.

Several months later, in October 1996, it was my turn to present a paper about my ongoing fieldwork to the annual conference of UGAT. Having learned from the PNOC experience, I asked the conference organiser to allow Beting and Tano to attend the discussion, which was focused, propitiously, on 'Indigenous Peoples: Knowledge, Power and Struggles'. At the opening session, Beting took the microphone, and after introducing herself she said: 'I come here to study how you study us.' From then on, almost no discussion was closed without Beting's views being heard.

More than a year after I 'left the field', I felt a consultation session with Tuddok was in order. In April–May 1998, I went back to the Philippines aiming to meet not only the Tuddok leaders but also those who had initially had problems with my stay in Mount Apo. Contrary to my expectations, my Tuddok partners felt very awkward with my presence. They also had to meet me in Davao City and not in Mount Apo, because the old accusation of a priest being behind their movement had re-emerged together with the formation of a new faction within the village. The NGO partner, however, was already accepted in the village. It would not be helpful to the movement if the NGO became associated with the priest. The group also had serious division within. I came out of the whole exercise with a more pragmatic, but still realistically hopeful view of the ethics and politics of social research on social movements.

Between and beyond objectivity and militancy

My own experience and that of others suggests that doing fieldwork today, especially in a contested development process and people's struggles, requires ethnographers to be 'fieldworkers' as well. As such, fieldworkers play different roles, including some not often associated with professional practice. They shift positions at the risk of being haunted by 'methodological anxieties' in producing knowledge based on 'varying intensities and qualities' (Marcus 1995: 100; cf. Clifford 1997: 219, note 3; Gupta and Ferguson 1997: 37).

This thrust should not be associated necessarily with political or ethical militantism. Marcus calls it 'circumstantial activism' (1995). Bruce Albert (1997) supplies a more experiential clarification. In the process of studying the people's struggle for *ethnogenesis* and access to resources, the researchers also get recruited to serve in various other activities such as mediation, documentation, action-oriented research and didactic ethnography. In this context, the anthropologist's 'observation' is no longer merely 'participant'; his social 'participation' has become both the condition and the framework of his field research (Albert 1997: 57–58). That is how they can go on doing their research, especially within a community that has grown more sensitive to the politics and ethics of being researched.

Both Burdick and Albert are careful enough not to totally conflate the project of the researcher and that of the people they study. Burdick stresses the critical function of the fieldworker within the movement. He also includes in the practice the 'relativization of the ethnographer's voice' (Burdick 1995: 374). Albert advocates a kind of 'critical solidarity' that does not limit professional practice to 'a mere reproduction' of the host's 'ethnic discourse' (Albert 1997: 58–59). Overlapping of projects does not mean a total congruence of concerns and interests.

What most of these discussions seem to miss is the glaring reality that the personality of the researcher matters a lot during fieldwork. I do not mean to talk about gender or class or geopolitical origin, hybridity of identity, threshold for trauma, sexual orientation, technical skills, wealth, and political or religious affiliation *per se*. While they may all be potential sources of tension, creativity, and involvement, it remains to be discovered and negotiated which of these aspects of the fieldworker's subjectivity would be contextually relevant.

In this case, I was supposed to be going smoothly in my fieldwork because I was 'at home' in my country. But I was not allowed to reside in that Protestant tribal village partly because of my being a Catholic priest. 'Wherever there is a priest, there is conflict', many would say. The fact that I was also a Christian or that I was born on the same island did not matter in that particular milieu. My position as a priest, however, provided my 'host family' with external contacts which facilitated the hospitalisation of a young tribal artist who, in turn, inspired the depressed leaders of the new social movement by the way he produced paintings, poetry and pottery in spite of his sickness.

This sensitivity to the ground-level complexity of the fieldwork identity of the researcher challenges the traditional notion of professional anthropological practice. In the field, professional anthropologists cannot be and are not only professional anthropologists. Robert Paine realises its importance to the discipline: 'It surely matters personally to most of us what "they" think of us (and that likely influences our research and its "objectivity")' (1998: 134).

Once in a while, too, anthropologists are called to respond to life situations according to their temper and even passion. This is not bad news to the discipline. Being human in the field should not be considered as a hazard to the study of fellow human beings. In fact anthropology should include in its ragbag repertoire even the human failings of the researcher. Rosaldo (1989: 173) argues, quite passionately, that 'human feelings and human failings provide as much insight for social analysis as subjecting oneself to the "manly" ordeals of self-discipline that constitute science as a vocation. ... Why not use a wider spectrum of less heroic, but equally insightful, analytical positions?'

Conclusion

My title 'What are we in fieldwork for?' alludes to a common idiom 'What are we in power for?' I assume here that doing fieldwork, especially in the context of a contested development initiative, is, to some extent, an exercise of power. The ethnographer *qua* ethnographer is not a powerful political actor. It remains true, however, that in some cases, in the field, prior to the packaging of the research result, the fieldworker might have some power –

if only the capacity to do harm. It remains equally true that we can take the opportunity of fieldwork to give due 'recognition' of each other as 'persons'. Persons, to use Hobart's words, are 'non-unitary and complex beings, who are each grappling with very different life circumstances and dislocations' (1996: 32). Hobart, however, should expand this notion of recognition to include the actual practices of fieldwork which he tends to lump into the penal gerund of 'disciplining'. But 'seeing, listening, recording,' as Scheper-Hughes (1992) asserts, 'can be, if done with care and sensitivity, acts of fraternity and sisterhood, acts of solidarity. Above all, they are the work of recognition. Not to look, not to touch, not to record, can be the hostile act of indifference.'

To this struggle for mutuality and solidarity, anthropology itself as a discipline is called upon to participate and its practice changed. As Dell Hymes (1972: 54) appealed a couple of decades ago, 'anthropology must lose itself to find itself, must become as fully as possible a possession of the people of the world', for otherwise, 'our work will drift backward into the service of domination'.

References

Albert, Bruce (1997) ' "Ethnographic situation" and ethnic movements: notes on post-Malinowskian fieldwork', *Critique of Anthropology* 17 (1): 53–65.

Alejo, Albert E. (2000) *Generating Energies in Mount Apo: Cultural Politics in a Contested Environment*, Quezon City: Ateneo de Manila University.

Alting von Geusau, Leo (1985) 'A dedicated anthropologist', *Living in Thailand* December: 44–45, 83.

Broad, Robin and John Cavanagh (1993) *Plundering Paradise: the Struggle for the Environment in the Philippines*, Berkeley: University of California Press.

Broeckman, Corinna, Mary Ann Fuentes, Ma. Theresa dela Cruz-Jabon, Joachim Stekeler and George Maue (1996) *Under the Grid: the Energy Situation in Mindanao*, edited by Roberto Verzola, Davao City: Kinaiyahan Foundation, Inc.

Burdick, John (1995) 'Uniting theory and practice in the ethnography of social movements: notes toward a hopeful realism', *Dialectical Anthropology* 20: 361–385.

Castro, Esperanza Carreon (1996) 'Opposition to the Mt. Apo Geothermal Project: understanding the parties in conflict', unpublished thesis, MSc in Economics in Social Development Planning and Management, University of Swansea.

Clifford, James (1997) 'Spatial practices: fieldwork, travel, and the disciplining of anthropology', in Akhil Gupta and James Ferguson (eds) *Anthropological Locations: Boundaries and Grounds of a Field Science*, Berkeley: University of California Press.

Denzin, N. 'Epistemological crisis in human disciplines: letting the old do the work of the new', in Richard Jessop, Anne Colby and Richard A. Shrewder, (eds), *Ethnography and Human Development: Context and Meaning in Social Inquiry*, Chicago and London: The University of Chicago Press.

Durning, Alan Thein (1992) *Guardians of the Land: Indigenous Peoples and the Health of the Earth*, World Watch Paper 112.

Enriquez, Virgilio G. (1992) *From Colonial to Liberation Psychology: the Philippine Experience*, International Edition, Manila: De la Salle University Press.
—— (1994) *Pagbabagong-Dangal: Indigenous Psychology and Cultural Empowerment*, Quezon City: Akademya ng Kultura at Sikolohiyang Pilipino.
Escobar, Arturo (1992) 'Culture, practice and politics: anthropology and the study of social movements', *Critique of Anthropology* 12 (4): 395–432.
Fallows, James (1987) 'A damaged culture', *Atlantic Monthly* November: 49–58.
Fardon, Richard (ed.) (1990) *Localizing Strategies: Regional Traditions of Ethnographic Writings*, Edinburgh: Scottish Academic Press.
Gardner, Katy and David Lewis (1996) *Anthropology, Development and the Post-Modern Challenge*, London: Pluto Press.
Ginsburg, Faye (1997) 'From little things, big things grow', in Richard Fox and Orin Starn (eds) *Between Resistance and Revolution: Cultural Politics and Social Protest*, New Jersey and London: Rutgers University Press.
Giri, Ananta Kumar (1998) *Global Transformations: Postmodernity and Beyond*, Jaipur and New Delhi: Rawat Publications.
Gledhill, John (1994) *Power and Its Disguises: Anthropological Perspectives on Politics*, London: Pluto Press.
Gloria, Heidi (1997) *A Baseline Study of Ten Indigenous Cultural Communities Around Mt. Apo. Final Report*, 8 vols, Davao City: Philippine National Oil Company.
Gupta, Akhil and James Ferguson (eds) (1997) *Anthropological Locations: Boundaries and Grounds of a Field Science*, Berkeley: University of California Press.
Hastrup, Kirsten and Karen Fog Olwig (1997) *Siting Culture: the Shifting Anthropological Project*, London: Routledge.
Hobart, Mark (1996) 'Ethnography as a practice, or the unimportance of penguins', *Europea* 2 (1): 3–36.
Hymes, Dell (ed.) (1974) *Reinventing Anthropology*, New York: Pantheon Books.
Lamberte, Mario B. and Jose T. Yap (1991) *The Impact of the Gulf Crisis on the Philippine Economy*, Working Paper Series No. 91–03, October 1991, Makati: Philippine Institute for Development Studies.
Marcus, George (1995) 'Ethnography in/of the world system: the emergence of multi-sited ethnography', *Annual Review of Anthropology* 24: 95–117.
—— (ed.) (1999) *Critical Anthropology Now: Unexpected Contexts, Shifting Constituencies, Changing Agencies*, Santa Fe, New Mexico: SAR Press.
Marcus, George E. and James Clifford (eds) (1986) *Writing Culture: the Poetics and Politics of Ethnography*, Berkeley: University of California Press.
Mincher, Paul (1992) 'The Philippine energy crisis', *The Ecologist* 23 (6): 228–233.
Ortner, Sherry (1984) 'Theory in anthropology since the sixties', *Comparative Studies in Society and History* 26 (1): 126–166.
Paine, Robert (1998) 'By chance by choice: a personal memoir', *Ethnos* 6 (1): 134–154.
Patkar, Medha (1992) 'The strength of a people's movement', in Geeti Sen (ed.) *Indigenous Vision: Peoples of India Attitudes to the Environment*, New Delhi: Sage Publications; New Delhi: India International Centre.
Pels, Peter and Oscar Salemink (1994) 'Introduction: five theses on ethnography as colonial practice', *History and Anthropology* 8 (1–4): 1–34.
Pertierra, Raul (1997) 'Culture, social science and the conceptualization of the Philippine nation-state', paper presented at the European Conference on the Philippines, Aix-en-Provence, February.

Philippine Resource Center (1994) *Making a World of Difference: an Information and Action Pack on Indigenous Peoples in the Philippines*, London: PRC.

Racelis, Mary (1999) 'Anthropology with people: development anthropology as people-generated theory and practice', *Development Anthropologist* 17 (1–2): 72–78.

Rodil, B.R. (1993) *The Lumad and Moro of Mindanao*, London: Minority Rights Group.

Rosaldo, Renato (1988) 'Ideology, places and people without culture', *Cultural Anthropology* 3 (1): 77–87.

—— (1989) *Culture and Truth: The Remaking of Social Analysis*, London: Routledge.

Scheper-Hughes, Nancy (1992) *Death Without Weeping: the Violence in Everyday Life in Brazil*, Berkeley: University of California Press.

Tabak (1990) *Apo Sandawa: Sacred Mountain*, 15-minute documentary film, Frontier Productions, London.

Tauli-Corpuz, Victoria (1993) 'An indigenous peoples' perspective on environment and development', *Indigenous Affairs* 1/93: 3–17.

von Benda-Beckmann, Keebet (1997) 'The environmental protection and human rights of indigenous peoples: a tricky alliance', *Law and Anthropology* 9: 302–323.

Warren, Kay B. (1997) 'Narrating cultural resurgence: genre and self-representation for pan-Mayan writers', in Deborah Reed-Danahay (ed.) *Auto/Ethnography: Rewriting the Self and the Social*, Oxford and New York: Berg.

Chapter 12

Reconstituting development as a shared responsibility

Ethics, aesthetics and a creative shaping of human possibilities

Ananta Kumar Giri and
Philip Quarles van Ufford

> When the horizon of meaning shrinks, when the process of knowledge disintegrates, and when the passage of time would seem to have changed directions, modern man seeks refuge within a shell of ignorance and denial. To break this shell is what is required today.
>
> (Binde 2000: 55)

> In the labor of caring there is first of all a skilled activity, often time consuming and involving great bodily exertion. But there is skill and adaptability here such that one has an experience of growth in the art of nurturance. ... Caring is a manifestation of love and concern; one feels deeply for what one cares about. ... The object of our care is, at the moment of our care a source of value and very often of intrinsic value. In caring therefore there is a commitment to the wellbeing and flourishing, a joy in its perfection and sorrow in its stresses and strains. And lastly, caring gives us a unique mode of access, a kind of knowing which may be called knowing-with.
>
> (Sunder Rajan 1998: 78)

The present volume has shown us how we are at a crossroads now in our vision and practice of development. Many of our difficulties here relate to our inability to look at and participate in the field of development as a field of relationship and as a quest for a shared responsibility which brings the self and other together. Half a century ago, development began as a hope for a better human possibility, but in the last fifty years, this hope has lost itself in the dreary desert of various kinds of hegemonic applications. But at the turn of the millennium there is an epochal challenge to rethink and reconstitute the vision and practice of development as a shared responsibility – a sharing which binds both the agent and the audience, the developed world and the developing, in a bond of shared destiny. This calls for the cultivation of an appropriate ethical mode of being in our lives which enables us to realise, be prepared for and be worthy of this global and planetary situation of shared living and responsibility (Apel 1991, 2000). As Habermas tells us, 'The moral or ethical point of view makes us quicker to perceive the more far reaching, and simultaneously less insistent and more fragile, ties that bind the fate of an individual to that of every other – making even the most alien person a member of one's community' (Habermas 1990: 20). But the self-confidence that Habermas poses in the ability of an ethical perspective and ethical engagement to help us perceive and be prepared for our shared responsibility may be difficult to proceed with in its entirety as a guide to ethics and development. For many critical commentators and interlocutors, an ethical agenda has almost always implied an agenda of the care of the other in a hegemonic manner where what is good for the other has already been defined by the benevolent self. In fact, the problem with the practice of development in the last fifty years has been precisely with such an ethical agenda which has been an agenda of hegemonic application of *a priori* formulations in which the objects of development do not have much say in defining and shaping the contours of their development (Carmen 1996). Such an agenda makes development an other-oriented activity where the actors of development do not realise that the field and the practice of development provides, and ought to provide, an opportunity for learning (cf. Nederveen Pieterse 2001), self-development and self-transformation, both for the object and the subject of development. In this context, there is a need to rethink development as an initiative in self-development on the part of both the subjects and objects of development, and ethics not only as an engagement in care of the other but also as an engagement in care of the self. Such a redefinition and reconstruction of both ethics and development is a crucial starting point for a new understanding and reconstitution of development as a shared human responsibility, and as a shared human possibility.

Rethinking development from the vantage point and practice of self-development urges a shift in perspective from us: a shift from looking at development as ameliorating the condition of the other to looking at it as an initiative in self-development. Self-development here refers to the self-development of both the agents of development as well as subjects, the so-called target groups of interventions. In contemporary rethinking of welfare and well-being in advanced industrial societies, we are told that without the development of an '*autotelic* self' which takes upon itself the responsibility for one's development and for taking oneself out of the trap of poverty and unfreedom, no amount of development intervention and welfare work can help alter the initial situation of poverty and helplessness (Giddens 1994, 1999). At the same time, those who are engaged in developing others and creating a more capable and functioning environment have a need to develop themselves. Although in the contemporary late-capitalistic, neo-liberal redefinition of welfare, emphasis on self-development has many a time manifested itself in a politics of irresponsibility (cf. Bauman 2001), of blaming the victim for his/her failure, this particular manifestation should not deter us from realising the potential that a quest for self-development today has in transgressing the boundaries between self and other, subject and object in interventions of welfare and initiatives of development. Fortunately for us, there have taken place important movements in the development field, such as Swadhyaya and Sarvodaya, which reiterate that development is not only meant for the other, it is also meant for the self and in development, both the development of the other and development of self should go hand in hand (Roy 1993; Sheth 1994).

Towards an aesthetic deepening and broadening of the agenda of ethics: aesthetics and the calling of care of the self

The emphasis on self-development in the field of development practice is accompanied by an aesthetic deepening of the agenda of ethics where care of the self as an artistic work *par excellence* becomes the heart of ethics. Traditionally, we look at ethics as being concerned with the consequences of one's action for the other. But ethics as care of the self urges us to realise that our action also affects ourselves, and through care of the self, we are able to become worthy helpers and servants of the other. Such a deepening of the agenda of ethics draws its most immediate inspiration from Michel Foucault, who urges us to realise that 'the search for an ethics of existence' must involve an 'elaboration of one's own life as a personal work of art' (Foucault 1988: 49). Foucault's agenda of an aesthetic ethics is developed in the context of his discussion of ethical life and ethical ideals in antiquity. But this is not meant only to be an archaeology of the past, but also to suggest a possible mode and ideal of ethical engagement for the present and the future. For Foucault, in antiquity, 'the search for an ethics of existence' was 'an attempt to affirm one's liberty and to give to one's life a certain form in which one could recognize oneself, be recognized by others, and which even the posterity might take as an example' (1988: 49). For Foucault, life as a work of art involves care of the self, a conversion to self, an intense relation with oneself. While ethics is usually conceived as care for the other, for Foucault, ethics at the same time must help one to 'take oneself as an object of knowledge and a field of action, so as to transform, correct, and purify oneself, and find salvation' (1988: 42). Furthermore, aesthetic ethics as care of the self involves the cultivation of appropriate values in the conduct of life. The most important task here is not to be obsessed with exercising power over others and to be concerned with discovering and realising 'what one is in relation to oneself' (1988: 85).

Foucault's call for self-restraint *vis-à-vis* one's work of power is particularly salutary in the field of development where agents of development have sought to impose their own will and models on the targets of development interventions. Through development of self-control the actors of development can resist the temptation to unnecessarily meddle in the lives of those with whom they are in interaction, and thus facilitate their self-flourishing and self-unfoldment. For Robert Chambers, 'it implies that uppers have to give up something and make themselves vulnerable' (Chambers 1997: 234). An engagement in self-control also enables actors of development to be aware of the hegemonic implications of a project of ethics which is primarily prescriptive. It enables them to continuously seek to transcend the world of separation between the creators of development and the beneficiaries of such a creation. Recently Majid Rehenema, who has applied Foucault's insights in going beyond the impasse of contemporary development interventions, has called for a 'bottom up aesthetic order' in development at the heart of which lies a desire on the part of the actors to be true to themselves and develop their 'inner world' and challenge the distinction between the makers of the worlds of beauty, truth and goodness and those who enjoy their benefits. In such a bottom-up aesthetic reconstruction of development, 'Right action involving others starts always as a personal work on oneself. It is the fruit of an almost divine kind of exercise, which usually takes place in the solitude of thought and creation' (Rehenema 1997: 401).

Creativity and the 'concrete shaping of freedom' are at the heart of the Foucauldian aesthetic ethics. Such an aesthetic inspiration encourages actors of development to be creative, and discover and foster creativity in the lives of others (Osborne 1997: 131). It also encourages them to produce 'togetherness in different contexts' rather than 'assert any founding principle of social order' (1997: 131).

From mimetic to aesthetic representation: the calling of aesthetic politics

Like Foucault, in recent times, philosopher and historian Frank R. Ankersmit has also urged us to be aware of the dangers of an agenda of prescriptive ethics by presenting us with an alternative proposal of what he calls 'aesthetic politics' (Ankersmit 1996). For Ankersmit, while 'ethics makes sense on the assumption of a (Stoic) continuity between our intentions, our actions and their results in the socio-political world', aesthetics draws our attention to the gaps and discontinuities among them. For Ankersmit, aesthetics originates in the gap between representation and the represented and it is important to develop an appropriate style of life and responsibility in this gap by first acknowledging that there is a gap. The problem with the ethical agenda of modernity, for Ankersmit, is that it has tried to sweep this gap under the carpet in the name of an ideal model of unity. Ankersmit makes a distinction between mimetic representation, which denies this gap between representation and the represented, and aesthetic representation, which acknowledges this gap and builds on it. For Ankersmit, mimetic representation is against representation itself as 'representation always happens, so to speak, between the represented and its representation; it always needs the presence of their distance and the ensuing interaction' (Ankersmit 1996: 44). The problem with modernist politics for Ankersmit has been that it has been a hostage to the politically correct ideology of mimetic representation where political representatives are required to mirror the expectations of their constituency. This creates a compulsion for politically correct mimetic representation rather than a representation which is based on one's autonomous self-identity and negotiation between this identity and the aspirations of the represented. For Ankersmit, acknowledgement of this gap becomes an aesthetic work *par excellence* where actors learn to develop an appropriate political style in the midst of fragmentation rather than with a valorised united whole, which does not exist any more. Aesthetic political representation urges us to realise that 'the representative has autonomy with regard to the people represented' but autonomy then is not an excuse to abandon one's responsibility. Aesthetic autonomy requires cultivation of 'disinterestedness' on the part of actors, which is not indifference.[1] To have disinterestedness, that is, to have 'comportment towards the beautiful that is devoid of all ulterior references to use – requires a kind of *ascetic* commitment; it is the "liberation of ourselves for the release of what has proper worth only in itself"' (Osborne 1997: 135).

In aesthetic politics, the development of appropriate styles of conduct on the part of the representatives is facilitated by the choice and play of appropriate metaphors. For Ankersmit, in the development of an appropriate style of conduct for a representative the metaphor of a 'maintenance man' or woman is more facilitating for self-growth than that of an architect. While the architect thinks that s/he is designing a building of which s/he is the creator, a maintenance person has a much more modest understanding of his/her role and does not look at his/her effort as creating a building out of nothing, rather as continuing a work to which many others have contributed. Such a metaphor of 'maintenance man' can provide a new self-understanding to actors, in the fields of both politics and development, where we do not have any dearth of actors, institutions and worldviews that attribute to them the role of the original creator, the architect, the god. But such a self-understanding of ourselves as architects leads to arrogance and dominance.[2] In this context, there is a modesty in the metaphor of the 'maintenance person' which is further facilitated by the choice of the metaphor of the captain of a ship. It is not enough for a captain to have only an *a priori* plan; s/he must know how to negotiate between *a priori* plans and the contingent situations on the ground. Such a capacity for negotiation, which is facilitated by one's choice of an appropriate metaphor such as captain and 'maintenance person', is crucial for the development of appropriate styles of conduct on the part of the actors in the fields of politics and development. In developing his outline of aesthetic politics, an outline which has enormous significance for reconstituting the field of development as a field of artistic rather than mimetic representation which in turn calls for the cultivation of an appropriate style of life on the part of the actors of development, Ankersmit writes: 'when asking himself or herself how best to represent the represented, the representative should ask what political style would best suit the electorate. And this question requires an essentially creative answer on the part of the representative, in the sense that there exists no style in the electorate that is quietly waiting to be copied' (1996: 54). For Ankersmit, 'aesthetics will provide us with a most fruitful point of departure if we desire to improve our political self-knowledge', and in this self-knowledge, autonomy of actors, units and institutions has a crucial significance. In fact, nurturing the autonomous spaces of self, institutions and society itself as spaces of creative self-fashioning and development of creative styles of action becomes an aesthetic activity *par excellence*. Of course, autonomy here is not meant in a defensive sense, of preserving the established structures rather than transforming them in accordance with the transformative imagination of actors and a democratic public discursive formation of will (Giri 1998a; Habermas 1995).

Ankersmit's application of the perspective of aesthetics in the field of politics has important lessons for us. First, it is an attempt to reverse the contemporary tendency to evade our political responsibility in the name of an aesthetic care of the self. Aesthetic ethics to Ankersmit involves an effort to 'improve our political self-knowledge' which brings work on self-improvement and self-development much more closely to the public sphere than the Foucauldian care of the self which, as we shall see shortly, is sometimes not sufficiently aware of its responsibility to the public domain. The aesthetic politics of Ankersmit also presents an alternative to the dominant mode of aestheticisation of politics which has expressed itself in what David Harvey (1989), giving the example of the Nazi effort to aestheticise politics, calls 'aesthetics of empowerment'. But the aesthetic politics in Ankersmit is not geared to a will to power but inspired by a will to political self-knowledge and the will to develop oneself as a 'maintenance man'. As against the tyranny of unity in certain strands of German aesthetics such as Schiller's, Ankersmit's aesthetics celebrates and works 'within an irrevocably broken world' (Ankersmit 1996: 53), but the brokenness of the world is not an excuse to abandon one's responsibility.

Towards a broader view of aesthetics: aesthetics as justice and respect for difference

Ankersmit helps us to unbound aesthetics itself from its narrow conceptualisation as only art, and in the process to deepen and widen it. In order to come to terms with the predicament of development as we seek to reconstitute it with new possibilities from both ethics and aesthetics, it is important for us to have intimations of such a broadened view of aesthetics. In his important work, *Undoing Aesthetics* (1997), Wolfgang Welsch provides us with such a view. In preparing an outline of his agenda of what he calls 'Aesthetics Beyond Aesthetics', Welsch presents an aesthetic or elevatory imperative: 'in perceiving, keep yourself free of sensuous sensation ... don't just heed primary vital pleasures, but also exercise the higher, peculiarly aesthetic pleasure of a reflective delight' (Welsch 1997: 63). For Welsch, an aesthetic sensibility enables us to appreciate the significance of difference while not evading our responsibility to it. Urging us to realise that aesthetics has 'an ethico-moral radiance', Welsch (building on Adorno) argues that it is 'only in aesthetics that justice can be spoken of at all, not in the policies for the realization of the idea of justice' (1997: 71). While political justice, being based on 'the principle of formal equivalence', causes differences to disappear and exercise power over them, aesthetic justice acknowledges the differences and suggests a way out of the 'machinery of domination' in which political justice remains imprisoned (Welsch 1997: 71; see also Scarry 1999). Welsch discusses in details the ethical implications and consequences of contemporary aesthetic awareness, and some of these are as follows: an awareness of specificity, an awareness of particularity, vigilance, attentiveness, tendency to acknowledge and tendency to justice (Welsch 1997: 73).

Welsch helps us to understand how the establishment of a non-domineering relationship between self and other is at the heart of aesthetics. We get intimation of such a perspective on aesthetics also from philosopher Seyla Benhabib. What is crucial to her perspective is a respect for difference and cultivating an appropriate relationship to difference – neither hegemonic universalism nor relativistic withdrawal – which leaves differences to their own fate, and eschewing any notion of responsibility on the part of the self, becomes an aesthetic work *par excellence*. Building on Adorno and Horkheimer, Benhabib, like Welsch, provides us with a much broader agenda of aesthetics. Benhabib urges us to understand aesthetic engagement as recognising the face of the other and then establishing a non-repressive solidarity with him/her. Such an engagement can nurture new hopes within us for a new relationship between the self and the other. In the evocative words of Benhabib:

> The overcoming of the compulsive logic of modernism can only be a matter of giving back to the non-identical, the suppressed, and the dominated their right to be. We can invoke the other but we cannot name it. Like the God of the Jewish tradition who must not be named but evoked, the utopian transcendence of the compulsive logic of enlightenment and modernism cannot be named but awakened in memory. The evocation of this memory, the 'rethinking of nature in the subject' is the achievement of the aesthetic.
>
> (Benhabib 1996: 333)

Here, 'The aesthetic emerges as the only mode of expression that can challenge the compulsive drive of Western reason to comprehend the world by
making it like itself, by supplementing it. ... The aesthetic intimates a new
mode of being, a new mode of relating to nature and to otherness in
general' (Benhabib 1996: 333). Benhabib urges us to realise that 'the
aesthetic negation of identity logic also implies an ethical and political
project' and has within it the seeds of a new utopia, a utopia 'not of
appeasement and rest, but of constant integration and differentiation' (1996:
338). What Benhabib writes deserves our careful attention:

> The utopian content of art heals by transforming the sensibilities of the
> modern subject: art as utopia, art as healing, but as an ethical and polit-
> ical healing which teaches us to let otherness within ourselves and
> others be. Art releases the memories and intimations of otherness which
> the subject has had to repress to become the adult, controlled, rational,
> and autonomous self of the tradition.
>
> (Benhabib 1996: 336)

Aesthetics and the quest for authenticity

Welsch urges us to realise that aesthetics is not simply a category of perception, it is also an aspect of our knowledge. Epistemology has an aesthetic
dimension too. This point of Welsch's is illuminated by Habermas's recent
discussion that there may be modes of knowledge and expression where one
wishes to be authentic, rather than to seek for or communicate validity, in a
strict scientific sense (Habermas 1996). Habermas links the former to an
aesthetic mode at the heart of which lies a quest for authenticity. Thus the
quest for authentic knowledge and the desire for authentic communication
of that knowledge becomes an aesthetic work *par excellence*. Habermas
gives an important role to the aesthetic quest for authenticity in the ethics of
life, and this is a significant move because it enables us to bring our aesthetic
awareness to the wider field of politics and society, an engagement which is
missing in many of the post-modern formulations of aesthetics. In such a
calling, the quest for authenticity need not be apologetic; instead a responsible politics and collective action is based on one's authentic being and
one's quest for self-knowledge. As one perceptive commentator writes: '[We
need to replace] the inauthentic notion of the aesthetic under capitalism
with an authentic one. This is Habermas's dream of a new aesthetic of
reconciliation' (Osborne 1997: 133).

In recent times, Charles Taylor was one of the first to put the agenda of
authenticity on the table and not to dismiss it out of hand as narcissistic.
Taylor urges us to realise that there is a 'powerful moral ideal at work' in the
quest for self-fulfillment on the part of the young in a society such as
American society and 'the moral ideal behind self-fulfillment is that of being

true to oneself' (Taylor 1991: 15). Through this quest for being true to oneself, Taylor seeks to establish the connection between self-fulfillment and authenticity. Taylor (1991) also helps us understand the significance of authenticity not only for aesthetics but also for ethics, and ultimately helps us go beyond the limitations of the two through his perspective of self-responsibilisation. For Taylor, 'we ought to be trying to persuade people that self-fulfillment, so far from excluding unconditional relationships and moral demands beyond the self, actually require these in some form' (1991: 72–73). Taylor further argues, 'Authenticity is clearly self referential: this has to be *my* orientations. But this does not mean that on another level the *content* must be self-referential: that my goals must express or fulfill my desires or aspirations, as *against* something that stands beyond these' (1991: 82). For Taylor, 'Authenticity opens an age of self-responsibilization' and 'points us towards a more self-responsible form of life' (1991: 74).

The possibilities and limits of aesthetics

Our engagement with various new ways of understanding the work of aesthetics has important lessons for us in thinking about and relating to the field of development. First, aesthetics as sensitivity to configurations of togetherness without reducing them to an *a priori* plan or teleology of order can help us to look at the field of development as a field of togetherness. But this togetherness is not a product of an ordered plan, nor is it teleologically geared to the production of order. A preoccupation with order has led to dangerous consequences in the field of development where leaders have deliberately tried to put conflict, ambiguity and contradictions under the carpet. It has also led to a denial of the work of contingencies in developmental dynamics, as we have seen in Chapter 1. And with Ankersmit and Welsch we see how an aesthetic awareness helps us to be aware of and sensitive to the role of contingency in society and history. Aesthetics as openness to the contingent also helps us to overcome the creed of certainty, and to better prepare ourselves for appreciating the work of uncertainty in the developmental world and fashion an appropriate mode of action and management which reflects such a concern. For instance, recently Lyla Mehta, Melissa Leach and colleagues at the Institute of Development Studies, Sussex have urged us to explore new directions in natural resource management which take the uncertainty of people's lives – ecological uncertainty, livelihood uncertainty, and knowledge certainties – seriously, and in this engagement an aesthetic awareness compared with a positivist preoccupation with regulation can help us too (Mehta *et al.* 1999). Finally aesthetics as artistic representation rather than mimetic representation can first enable us to understand the mimetic nature of most development interventions and then encourage us to cultivate various alternative ways of coming out of this closed mimetic world. One aspect of the mimetic character of the contemporary world of development interventions is that the representatives of development are self-confident that they can represent the interests of the donor agencies on the one hand and beneficiaries on the other in a transparent and unproblematic manner. But such an assumption condemns them to a world of self-created continuity while the field of development is characterised by lack of fit between intentions and outcome. And with aesthetic sensibility, once the representatives realise the practical and moral untenability of such a mimetic world, they can engage themselves with various modes of aesthetic ethics and politics which enable them to articulate the interests of donors and beneficiaries in a more responsible manner.

While these examples show some potential for renewing development practice with an engagement with aesthetics, unfortunately there are also fundamental limits to the process. One of these, as we shall discuss in greater detail in the subsequent section on development as a narcissistic trap, relates to a narrow valorisation of care of the self in an aesthetic engagement, a valorisation which does not take seriously and is even blissfully oblivious to its responsibility to others (cf. Krishna 1996). In fact, this problem lies at the core of the Foucauldian care of the self. As Gardiner helps us realise:

> In Foucault's ontology of the subjects, there are only scattered and essentially gratuitous references to our relations with others, little real acknowledgement of the centrality of non-repressive solidarity and dialogue for human existence. One must not have the care for others precede the care of the self, he [Foucault] bluntly declares at one point.
>
> (Gardiner 1996: 38)

Critical reflections on Foucault's own scripting of life also point to a preoccupation with sado-masochism in his life which points to the limits of his aesthetic ethics (Miller 1993: 327). In this context, aesthetic ethics in itself cannot help us come out of the impasse the field of development faces, and we need to engage ourselves with development as an embodiment of responsibility.

Ethics as responsibility and the face of the other

In recent times, Emmanuel Levinas has been foremost in redefining the agenda of ethics as responsibility to the other. For Levinas, ethical engagement involves a transcendence where transcendence consists of a 'passing over to being's *other*, otherwise than being' (Levinas 1974: 3). As Levinas tells us, in ethics 'it is no longer a question of the ego, but of me. The subject which is not an ego, but which I am, cannot be generalised, is not a subject in general. ... Here the identity of the subject comes from the impossibility of escaping responsibility' (Levinas 1974: 13–14). Therefore when critics of ethics such as Ankersmit argue that ethics has always involved a hegemonic and prescriptive relationship with the other, they are enunciating only partial truths, since ethical imagination in the works of savants such as Levinas involves a more caring relationship with the other.

Levinas's ethics of the face has an inspiring parallel in the life and thoughts of Gandhi. Gandhi's life embodied a multi-dimensional responsibility with multiple others – especially the suffering, violated and the marginalised – in a non-hegemonic way (Parekh 1997). As Srinivasan writes: 'All his experiments, whether in the realm of caste, communal, race or gender relations, sought to declassify the Untouchable ... harijan, muslim, white or women through a non-violent exchange' and establish solidarity of love with them (Srinivasan 1998: 76). In his ashram at Sevagram, Gandhi had a leprosy-stricken old man as his fellow ashramite, and his daily routine included cleaning his wounds. When Levinas writes that 'the face is the other who asks me not to let him die alone' we find the embodiment of such an awareness in the life of Gandhi. After the partition of India, Gandhi walked in the villages of Bengal, reassuring faces living in the fear of death – though this partly contributed to his later falling to the bullets of an assassin. Gandhi elevates his concrete relationships with others to a heart-touching moral principle:

> I will give you a talisman. Whenever you are in doubt, or when the self becomes too much with you, apply the following test. Recall the face of the poorest and weakest man you have seen, and ask yourself if the step you contemplate is going to be of any use to him; will he gain anything by it? Will it restore him control over his own life and destiny? In other words will it lead to *Swaraj* for the hungry and the spiritually starving millions? Then you will find your doubts and self melting away.
>
> (Gandhi, quoted in Chambers *et al.* 1989: 241)

But the Gandhian embodiment of responsibility is different from working out an *a priori* plan of ameliorating the suffering of the other. Gandhi's walking with others 'was always (at the same time) an interior journey, an exploration of his being, and not just the working out of a preestablished strategy' (Pillai 1984: 77). 'It is this insistent questioning of himself which distinguishes his actions from all self-sanctifying "social service" based on representation. Every decision for Gandhi was simultaneously the laying open of himself' (Pillai 1984: 77). Thus in Gandhi an appropriate response to the face of the other requires appropriate preparation in the self, but such a simultaneous engagement is missing from Levinas. Levinas takes the readiness of self to look up to and die for the other for granted, and does not realise that the self has to develop itself in an appropriate way for such tasks of responsibility and martyrdom.

The call for responsibility in Gandhi and Levinas has an esteemed predecessor in the inspiring reflections of Søren Kierkegaard. For Kierkegaard,
ethics is a 'mode of praxial engagement and life of commitment' (Schrag
1997: 120). Kierkegaard urges us to realise the limits of an aesthetic cultivation of self and understand the significance of ethics in providing a long-term
commitment to the self. In Kierkegaard's formulation, the life of an aesthete
'falls apart into a series of disconnected moments' when he 'becomes sufficiently self-conscious about his socially given identity to stand back from it'
(Rudd 1993: 96). However, the ethicist 'consciously re-engages in the commitments and relationships of social life' (Rudd 1993: 96). For Kierkegaard, a life
of ethical commitment provides a constancy to the self which is achieved
'through the bonding of self with other selves' (Schrag 1997: 19). Here it is
important to realise the difference in emphases in Foucauldian ethics and
Kierkegaardian ethics: 'The integrity that is won through self-constancy is
sustained not only through a proper relation of self to itself but also in and
through self's relations to other selves' (Schrag 1997: 19).

Development as responsibility and coping with contingencies

This passionate call for responsibility has important lessons for us in re-
imagining and re-living development as a transformative practice. It can
help us reconstitute development as a responsibility that can provide a self-
critical and transformative supplement to the contemporary redefinitions of
development as freedom (Sen 1999). In his recent passionate reflection,
Amartya Sen has urged us to reconstitute development as a 'momentous
engagement with freedom's possibilities' (Sen 1999: 298). But Sen does not
take his explorations of freedom's possibilities in a self-critical direction of
responsibility where one's striving for freedom has within itself a space for
criticism of the self-justificatory claims of one's freedom. In this context, a
redefinition of human well-being in terms of 'functioning' and 'capability'
of individuals and of development as freedom needs to be supplemented by
a reconceptualisation and realisation of development as responsibility where
freedom is an object of both ontological and social commitment.
Embodiment of responsibility requires looking up to the face of the other
and the mirrors of desires within oneself, and going beyond the self-justificatory world of freedom itself. This, in turn, is facilitated by appropriate
self-development. Development then means not only enhancing the functioning and capacity of bonded labourers or enhancing the life expectancy
of disadvantaged groups such as the Afro-Americans within an affluent
society such as the USA, as Sen argues,[3] but also self-development on the
part of the free agents where they do not just assert the self-justificatory
logic of their own freedom but are willing to subject it to a self- and mutual
criticism and 'undergo the suffering that would come to [them] from non-

ego' (Levinas 1974: 123). In Sen, development as freedom is an end state but without the self-development of actors and institutions from freedom to responsibility there would be very few resources left to rescue human well-being from the tyranny of freedom.

But development as responsibility for the other is facilitated by appropriate self-development. In the discourse of development as freedom there is little awareness of this. There is also little awareness about this in the pathway of ethical responsibility as charted by Levinas. As we saw briefly in our dialogue with Gandhi, Levinas takes the readiness for self for granted, and thus in our effort to reconstitute development as a shared responsibility we have to go beyond Levinas while holding his very helpful and alchemical hands. In this context, it is helpful to keep in mind the differential inspiration of Gandhi and Levinas. While in the Gandhian path there is a simultaneous work on self-development and attentiveness to the other, Levinas only speaks of one's responsibility to the other and takes the task of self-preparation for granted (Giri 1998c). In this context, the significance of aesthetic ethics lies precisely in stressing the point that attentiveness to and responsibility for the other requires appropriate self-preparation. But then the task here is again to be on our guard, so that our engagement with self-preparation does not degenerate into beautification of the self. So, we deal with a contingent world here, and the task before us is to cope with the contingent challenges of self-development and responsibility to the other in a balanced and transformational manner. Our choice is not one of either or, either the care of the self or the care of the other, between aesthetics and ethics, or between Foucault and Levinas. The task is to be attentive to both – both developing ourselves and taking care of others. But this simultaneous effort may never reach a successful balance and we have to be prepared for the slippery nature of this relationship. As we have argued in the introduction, we are thus, in the fields of both ethics and development, simultaneously confronted with the challenge of being aware of the contingency of the other and the contingency of the self.

Beyond the aesthetic and the ethical and the calling of transcendence

However, on this pathway of simultaneous attentiveness, at one point we have to go beyond the aesthetic and the ethical in a spirit of transcendence. Here it is helpful to remember that Kierkegaard, who is a great votary of the ethical project of the self, does not grant this absolute primacy. While for Kierkegaard the aesthetic project of the self can be transformed by the ethical, the ethical at the same time is not granted absolute primacy. The perennial significance of Kierkegaard lies in urging us to realise the limits of the ethical as well. For Kierkegaard, the ethical has its limit in preparing us for our absolute duty as illustrated in Abraham's sacrifice of his own son at God's command (Derrida 1998).[4] So, the limits of the ethical are supplemented by the transcendental which Kierkegaard calls 'Religiousness B' which is different from religion as an organised way of life and code of ethics, 'Religiousness A'. But it is important to realise that Kierkegaard's three stages of existence – the ethical, the aesthetic and the religious – are not 'successive developments': 'They are to be understood as co-present profiles and interlaced dimensions of selfhood, ways of existing in the world, that inform the odyssey of self as it exists from moment to moment. As the ethical stage does not leave the aesthetical behind but rather refigures it, so also the religious stage does not annul the ethical but rather effects its redescription' (Derrida 1998).

Thus neither the aesthetic nor the ethical in itself is adequate to help us come to terms with the calling of life. Reducing the one to the other is not helpful and a reconciliation between them is always enriched by bringing a view from afar and beyond, by bringing a transcendental perspective. Both Sri Aurobindo and Kierkegaard provide us with a helpful suggestion. For Sri Aurobindo, before forcing a superficial reconciliation between care of the self and care of the other, it is helpful to acknowledge the differences between them. For Sri Aurobindo, 'There is in our mentality a side of will, conduct, character which creates the ethical man; then there is another side of sensibility to the beautiful – understanding beauty in no narrow or hyperartistic sense – which creates the artistic and aesthetic man' (Sri Aurobindo 1962: 87). In an argument similar to Ankersmit's aesthetic critique of the ethical, Sri Aurobindo argues that the self-mastery that is at the heart of the ethical can have an imperialistic implication.[5] Sri Aurobindo here suggests that the cultivation of an aesthetic sensibility can transform this relationship of domination. Thus the limits of the ethical in the field of development – ethical being understood as a will to mastery (self-mastery as well as mastery over the other) and as applying *a priori* principles to improve the lives of others without involving them in the determination of these principles and without simultaneously engaging oneself in a process of self-development – can be overcome by developing an aesthetic dimension in our lives as actors of development. But here aesthetics in itself is not enough. There is a need for a combination of the two. In the words of Sri Aurobindo: 'We can combine them; we can enlarge the sense of ethics by the sense of beauty and delight and introduce into it to correct its tendency of hardness and austerity and self-discipline which will give it endurance and purity' (1962: 92). But this combination is difficult to realise when we start from the primacy of either the ethical or the aesthetic, and Sri Aurobindo urges us to realise that the reconciliation between these two requires the work of a 'higher principle' which is 'capable of understanding and comprehending both equally and of disengaging and combining disinterestedly their purposes and potentialities' (1962: 92). And it is quite interesting that while talking of this higher principle, Sri Aurobindo does not immediately frighten us with the name of God or some other mystical agency. For Sri Aurobindo, 'That higher principle seems to be provided for us by the human faculty for reason and intelligent will' (1962: 92–93).

Sri Aurobindo's appreciation of the role of reason and intelligent will in helping us to realise a reconciliation between the ethical and the aesthetic, the care of the self and the care of the other, can help us look at our relationship with Kant, Foucault and Habermas in a new way. All of them in their own way urge us to continue the emancipatory project of enlightenment. Foucault is of course not as enthusiastic a defender of enlightenment as Habermas, but it is quite interesting that in his dialogue with Kant, Foucault does not abandon him; instead he urges us to find ways of restoring Kant's longing for freedom without making such a longing hegemonic. Foucault writes:

> The critical ontology of ourselves has to be considered not, certainly, as a theory, a doctrine, nor even as a permanent body of knowledge that is accumulating; it has to be conceived as an attitude, an ethos, a philosophical life in which the critique of what we are is at one and the same time the historical analysis of the limits that are imposed on us and an experiment with the possibility of going beyond them.
>
> (Foucault 1984: 50)

But Foucault's critical ontology and the 'experiments of going beyond' can be enriched by spiritual efforts and realisation as suggested by Sri Aurobindo and also hinted at by Foucault in his later works and writings. Sri Aurobindo, while acknowledging the crucial significance of reason in human life and of enlightenment in human history, urges us to understand the limitations of them, and supplement the project of enlightenment with a practice and imagination of spiritual transformation of the bounded and judgemental rational self and society. Such a spiritual supplement to the rational is a crucial help in going beyond the impasse in which we are today (Giri 1998b). But bringing such a spiritual perspective to our throbs of life and acts of reconciliation also goes beyond the imagination of enlightenment and it urges us to acknowledge transcendence as an existence sphere and value sphere of self and society along with 'the standard threesome of science, morality, and art' – an acknowledgement we find insufficiently in Kant and Foucault, and almost altogether missing in Weber and Habermas. In this context, what Schrag argues, building on Kierkegaard, deserves our careful attention:

> Transcendence in its threefold function as a principle of protest against cultural hegemony, as a condition for a transversal unification

[as different from a hegemonic universalistic unification] that effects a convergence without coincidence, and as a power of giving without expectation of return, stands outside the economies of science, morality, art, and religion as culture-spheres. This defines transcendence as a robust alterity. Responding to the beckoning of this otherness of transcendence, the wayfaring self struggles for a self-understanding and a self-constitution within the constraints of an irremovable finitude.

(Schrag 1997: 148)

Transcendence as transversality

For Schrag, 'The self in action is a self in transcendence – moving beyond that which it has become and going over to that which is not yet' (1997: 111). But transcendence does not lie at one side of the bipolar division of transcendence and immanence. It does not lie high above the sky; there is a transcendental dimension within immanence as there is an urge for immanent embodiment within transcendence. For Sri Aurobindo, there is such a creative ongoing dialogue between transcendence and immanence. But despite this dialogue, transcendence for Sri Aurobindo seems to work at a much higher level and has its predominant reading as a vertical process. Schrag brings this much closer to the ground through his concept of *transversality*. In transversality there is a quest for beyond, across many diagonal lines in the lateral and horizontal plane. This quest for beyond in the horizontal plane makes it much more down to earth, and thus transcendence as transversality has a lot of significance for renewing development practice. The work of transversality while going beyond self and categories, at the same time, seeks to establish threads of connection between and among several identities and selves. The post-modern deconstruction of totalitarian functions of unity still faces this task of establishing connection between identities and differences, and here transversal engagement offers us an alternative model of unification, a unification which is not totalitarian. As Schrag helps us to understand:

Radical transcendence operates transversally, and the salient point at issue is that the grammar of transversality replaces that of universality. The dynamics of unification in a transversal play of lying across and extending over surfaces, accelerating forces, fibers, vertebrae, and moments of consciousness is not grounded in a universal telic principle but proceeds rather as an open-textured gathering of expanding possibilities. As such it is a dynamics of unification that is always an 'ing', a process of unifying, rather than an 'ed', a finalised result ... the unity that functions as a coefficient of transversality is very much an open-textured *process of unification*, moving beyond constraints of the metaphysical oppositions of universality versus particularity and identity versus difference. Transversal unity is an achievement of communication as it visits a multiplicity of viewpoints, perspectives, belief systems, and regions of concern.

(Schrag 1997: 129, 133)

Transcendentality and the calling of virtues

A transcendental awareness enables us to understand the limitations of an either/or approach to ethics and development and to realise the contingent nature of this relationship. This transcendental awareness does not refer only to an abstract spirit but also to our day-to-day realisation of a 'beyond' in our lives which does not grant absolute authority to one's position and is open to listening to others. A transcendental awareness makes us much more modest in our claims, respects the contingencies of life but does not treat them as accidentality, and seeks to relate contingencies to a web of connectedness, an experience of a whole – a whole which however is not hegemonic nor totalitarian. Transcendentality is also an aspect of our day-to-day life and embodied experience, which helps us to understand the limitations of any particular location, position, worldview and to be open to another self, worldview, and another world. Transcendality also enables us to live with what Schrag (1997) calls the 'grammar of paradox'.[6] But leading a life of ethics and aesthetics with a 'grammar of paradox' requires cultivation of appropriate virtues in our lives. Virtue ethics here is concerned with the development of appropriate skills of negotiation and relationship with contingencies, a skill which makes the cultivation and work of virtues a public affair. But the skill of negotiation, coping and creativity that is required in contingent locations – of knowledge and action – is not confined to the contingent location itself. It is not just a matter of situational and transactional ethics; it is also trans-contingent and thus a matter of ontological cultivation and not only procedural. At the same time, the actor has to learn that there is no *a priori* principle by reference to which the contradictions between the different imperatives of life, the ethical and the aesthetic, can be resolved. Without our own capacity, we can not resolve these contradictions by a mechanical application of any *a priori* principle (see Harris 1999; Miller 1996). The resolution of this contradiction would always be contextual. Without the cultivation of appropriate virtues which have an ontological anchorage, this contextual resolution may not be a just and adequate one, and respect for paradox can easily degenerate into an excuse for sitting idle in one's home and doing nothing about and in the world. Without the cultivation of appropriate virtues, it is easy to fall into the trap and temptation of either care of the self or care of the other.

Beyond the narcissistic trap of development interventions

The field of development has indeed been caught in such a trap. For a long time, it has been a field for the care of the other. But development as a care of the other without appropriate self-cultivation has led and continues to lead to alienation and domination, the picture of which has been movingly portrayed for us by James Ferguson (1990) and Arturo Escobar (1995). As an alternative to this, it is easy to fall into the trap of care of the self as an exclusive agenda of ethics, development and conduct of life. But an exclusive preoccupation with care of the self makes actors narcissistic and unable to look up to the face of the other. That this is not only a theoretical possibility or a figment of imagination can be realised when we look at the field of development today where actors are more concerned with their own salaries, money and power in the name of development rather than with being engaged in responsible action for altering the condition which has created the need for development intervention in the first place. Here it is helpful to critically observe how a concern of care of the self manifests itself in the field of development. There has now appeared a new 'theology of the market' in the field of development interventions. This theology of the market not only expects development organisations and development interventions to create more market-friendly and market-supportive conditions for people but also pressurises development organisations to behave as profit-maximising market-organisations and corporations. So, there is now a radical change in the self-definition of development organisations and voluntary organisations. Earlier development organisations had the primary self-understanding of themselves as partners in people's struggle against the unequal and unjust systems and for a more dignified life and society. But now more and more development organisations have the self-understanding of themselves as entrepreneurs. They are more concerned with their own survival, their own profit-maximisation rather than with the condition of the suffering of the struggling millions of humanity.

This concern for one's own survival as an entrepreneurial development organisation rather than for the lives of the poor creates the problem of authenticity for development organisations.[7] Development organisations present an image that they are for the people but in reality they are interested in their own survival and success. It is probably in this context that Baudrillard's argument that there is no longer any relationship between representation and reality is applied to the field of development (Baudrillard 1993; Quarles van Ufford 1999). Development organisations now create a hyper-real world which is a world of illusion. People formulate agendas which they do not believe in, and neither do the listeners. Images do not have the role of representation any more. In order to mobilise funds they are more concerned about creating and maintaining an appropriate image about themselves rather than working and struggling with the poor. Development in technologies such as media and computers have here come to their aid.

Many development organisations today are city-based and most of their leaders spend a lot of time in generating appropriate data in the computer rather than working and struggling with people.

The concern for one's own survival and success has also made development organisations erratic and flexible. In order to mobilise more funds, they do not feel reluctant to do anything or utter any *mantra*. In order to succeed and survive, development organisations now multiply their own initial programmes leading to a situation of cancerous multiplication rather than growth. In order to make the most of the opportunities available in the market, development organisations must present themselves as always ready to do anything, so, they must not have any particular purpose or worldview. The question of the identity of development organisations is not relevant anymore. Both funding organisations and development organisations look at the ability to produce results as being more important than their identity of social partnership and the struggle for the realisation of a worthy goal. In fact, in order to be able to succeed and be acceptable in the new market conditions, they think that they must erase the memory of their past as struggling organisations. This erasure of one's past makes the development organisations erratic in a Baudrillardian sense. They move from one agenda to another and strive to be ever young and flexible in the market. And in this moment of triumph of the market, development organisations as well as concerned actors forget that if you lose your past, you also lose your future. This poses probably the most important challenge in our reconstructive initiative in the field of ethics and development. In developing agencies, now, there is a loss of personhood and crisis of authenticity which affects the way they work. So, while the contemporary challenge of reconstruction and renewal calls for a creative interpenetration of consequentialist ethics and an ethics of care of the self, a majority of development organisations are interested in neither, though in their preoccupation with market success they seem to be living under and creating the illusion that they are promoting an ethics of care of the self. Various contributions in this volume provide us many examples of this. In Albert Alejo's chapter, we find how the autonomous people's moblisation is suspicious of the voluntary organisations in the locality, who, they are afraid, would hijack their struggle for their own benefit. In a similar way, David Mosse shows us the narcissism that goes in the name of participatory development, which empowers more the leaders of development organisations rather than the people.

Reconstituting development as a field of acknowledged mutuality

The narcissistic turn in development has been accompanied by a result-oriented, consequentialist approach to morality and a yardstick of judgement. In such an approach, which is the new theology of our times, it is the results of development intervention which count, and especially results of a quick and quantifiable kind. The whole process of realisation of the result and the moral evaluation of the process of arriving at consequences, for instance asking such questions as whether it involved genuine participation or top-down implementation, are out of fashion now (Strathern 2000). The result-oriented morality in contemporary neo-liberal development practice is a variant of utilitarianism, where the moral concern is external to the process of realisation of results and the actors (Mohanty 2000; Thompson 2001). In place of such an externalist morality, we now need a morality and ethics of participation where 'knowledge of' can never be dissociated from the process of 'knowing with' (Sunder Rajan 1998). At the same time, we have to acknowledge that if consequentialism and result-oriented morality cannot take us out of our moral predicament, the answer does not lie in an uncritical reiteration of a Kantian goal-oriented morality. A goal-oriented morality is also an externalist morality, and it also leads to a 'morality of black box', discussed in the first chapter.[8] In its place we now need a morality of participation, a field of participation which has within its very heart the brokenness of the world. MacIntyre (1999) charts such a pathway for us with what he calls 'virtues of acknowledged dependence'.

MacIntyre develops his outline of 'virtues of acknowledged dependence' to help us understand the qualities that are required to participate in a relationship which involves not only an abstract self and an abstract other but a particular self and a particular other, or particular selves and particular others. For MacIntyre to participate in such a relationship, neither the language of self-interest nor the language of benevolence is enough. Instead, it requires a language of giving and receiving in which both the self and the other are giver and receiver at the same time. To participate in such a relationship, there is a need to cultivate both virtues of giving and receiving, the virtues which lie at the intersection of two other virtues, the virtues of generosity and justice. While in the conventional understanding of virtues, these two virtues are looked upon as different from each other, and approached in isolation, for MacIntyre it is important to bring them together in our art of relationship. We shall recall here the arguments of both Welsch and Benhabib about the need for the quest for political justice to be supplemented by an aesthetic sensibility, and here the virtue of generosity provides precisely to her sister, namely to the virtue of justice, such an aesthetic supplement. But these two sisters together make our lives beautiful, just and worth living. While the virtue of justice makes us aware what we owe to both the self and the other, the virtue of generosity helps us to move from conditional care to unconditional obligation, both in our relationship with ourselves and in our relationship to others.

This mode of engagement of acknowledged dependence provides us a way out of the black box of being trapped either in goals or results in coming to moral judgement and evaluation about our conduct of life in the world of development. Rather, it urges us to be attentive to how interdependence is put into place in the practice of development, for example the dialectic between goal and result, the interaction between actors and target groups, others and self. Such a perspective of acknowledged dependence also urges us to realise how meaningful action and evaluation in development depends on our capacity to acknowledge the relative significance and limitations of different modes of engagement such as care of the self and care of the other. This also calls for realising development as responsibility, a responsibility which is aware of the contingent nature of our locations and the need for a transcendental and transversal opening of our vision.

In more concrete terms, we can imagine the field of development as consisting of four important actors of hope, doing, and understanding – state, market, social movements/voluntary organisations, and the creative and transformative self. Overcoming the impasse in which we are today in the field of development requires us to realise the significance of all these actors, but on the part of each of these actors an acknowledgement is needed of the contingency of its action and vision, and a recognition of the significance of the other three in a spirit of mutual learning, dialogue, and conversation. In such a reconstructed field of dialogue and polygonal conversation, none of the actors make an exclusive claim about their significance in the field of development and always look for and facilitate the creative unfoldment of the other. This is facilitated by an opening towards a transcendental and transversal point of view. In our earlier discussion of transcendence we have seen how transcendence helps us to acknowledge the four culture spheres of modernity – science, morality, art and religion – and go beyond the exclusive claim of each of these. Similarly in the field of development, a transcendental and transversal mode of engagement can help us to acknowledge the significance of the four agents of development – state, market, voluntary organisations/social movements, and self – but not to grant absolute primacy to any.

For MacIntyre, any moral relationship between intimate particulars is sustained through such a virtue of acknowledged dependence and this can help us redefine development as a field of relationship which helps us to grow and be engaged in worthwhile activities which are nurturing and life-enhancing both for the self and the other, the other and the self, the agents of development and recipients of development cooperation. But the major challenge we face in this task of reconstruction and reconstitution is that the actors in the field of development rarely behave as participants in a field of acknowledged dependence. Overcoming this distance and establishing an intimacy between and among different categories of actors in the field of development is then the fundamental task needed to overcome the impasse in development in which we currently are. For this, alongside our aesthetic engagement and ethical responsibility, we also need a transcendental inspiration of unconditional love and a quest for delight in each other's fellowship (Kierkegaard 1962).

Notes

1 In a recent discussion with us (8 August 2001) Ankersmit makes the connection between aesthetic autonomy and the quest for freedom and the possibility of renewal in individual and social life clear.

2 But the metaphor of the architect may not be always accompanied by such an arrogant assumption. For Harvey, an architect not only executes *a priori* hegemonic plans, s/he also negotiates with contingencies on the ground. But 'contingency does not imply, however, that, as opposed to the designer's ideal, the actual architecture is secondary and constantly in danger of collapse. Rather, contingency insures that no architect is able to determine a design free from the relationship with the "other" – the client, staff, and other factors relevant to the design process' (Harvey 2000: 230).

3 Amartya Sen writes: 'African Americans in the United States are relatively poor compared with American Whites, though much richer than people in the Third World. It is, however, important to recognise that African Americans have an absolutely lower chance of reaching mature ages than do people in many third world societies, such as China, or Sri Lanka, or parts of India. ... If development analysis is relevant even for richer countries ... the presence of such inter-group contrasts within richer countries can be seen to be an important aspect of the understanding of development and underdevelopment' (Sen 1999: 6).

4 It is interesting that Kierkegaard's interpretation of Abraham's sacrifice of his son has been now interpreted in a new way. In his essay, 'Levinas and the *Akedah*: an alternative to Kierkegaard' (2001), Jeffrey Stolle writes: 'If Abraham's actions throughout this story are really the responses they seem to be, then they are not merely steps along the way in a course of action determined by first command. They are all new instances of going forth. Abraham could not have known Yitzak's question ahead of time, and he certainly could not have predicted how the sacrifice would end. He responds to these interruptions in the moment they appear. Without this responsiveness, Abraham could never have heard the call to sacrifice, a command that contradicted the earlier one. He would have continued on in single-minded obedience to a previous command, which is not really a going forth at all' (Stolle 2001: 134).

5 In this context, Sri Aurobindo writes: 'Rome was the human will oppressing and disciplining the emotional and sensational mind in order to arrive at the self-mastery of a definite ethical type; and it was this self-mastery which enabled the Roman republic to arrive also at the mastery of its environing world and impose its public order and law' (Sri Aurobindo 1962: 89).

6 J.N. Mohanty (in Gupta 2000), building on Edmund Husserl, calls this enigma. What Mohanty writes about the empirical and transcendental in Husserl deserves our careful attention:

> This last distinction [between transcendental and empirical subjectivities] is no doubt enigmatic. In distinguishing between them, and in using the epoch to move from the one to the other, Husserl asserts a difference. He also affirms their identity: the empirical is the transcendental, only when stripped of the naturalising interpretations. More famously, he affirms a parallelism between the two: each numerically selfsame intentional experience of an empirical ego is also a transcendental experience of the 'corresponding' transcendental ego. To think these aspects of the relation – identity, difference, and parallelism – together would appear to be baffling. And yet, we do not understand transcendental phenomenology if we do not understand this enigma.
>
> (Mohanty, in Gupta 2000)

7   In this context, it may be noted what the pre-eminent systems theorist Robert
L. Flood writes about these organisations: 'For non-profit-making organizations purpose and identity often have become increasingly elusive' (Flood
1999: 1).
8   In this context, what J.N. Mohanty writes helps us understand the limits of both
utilitarianism and Kantianism:

> Moral theories still oscillate between utilitarianism insofar as public policy
> decisions of the emerging democracies are concerned, and a Kantianism in
> so far as individual moral life is concerned. On the one hand, public policy
> issues are settled putatively by what brings about maximum utility; on the
> other hand, individuals get moral credit for pursuing moral goodness irre-
> spective of consequences. Both these alternatives, however appealing, are
> now seen to be of limited application, for both of them take a point of view
> external to the moral agent. For utilitarianism, addition of utility value
> takes no account of individual points of view on things, anyone counts no
> more or no less than the other; my only moral obligation to the other is to
> produce social utility. For Kantianism, I have to overcome my inner perspec-
> tive from which I can give meaning to my life in favour of a universal point
> of view, which respects no difference.
>
> (Mohanty 2000: 11)

In his recent work on applied ethics, communication theorist Cees Hamelink also
draws our attention to a similar impasse: 'The application of moral theories of
deontological or utilitarian provides little or no help in the resolution of concrete
moral dilemmas in real-life situations' (Hamelink 2000: 4).

References

Ankersmit, Frank R. (1996) *Aesthetic Politics: Political Philosophy Beyond Fact
and Value*, Stanford: Stanford University Press.
Apel, Karl-Otto (1991) 'A planetary macroethics for humankind: the need,
apparent difficulty, and the eventual possibility', in Eliot Deutch (ed.) *Culture
and Modernity*, Honolulu: University of Hawaii Press.
—— (2000) 'Globalization and the need for universal ethics', *European Journal of
Social Theory* 3 (2): 137–155.
Baudrillard, Jean (1993) *Symbolic Exchange and Death*, London: Sage.
—— (1996) *The Transparency of Evil*, London: Verso.
Bauman, Zygmunt (2001) *The Individualized Society*, Cambridge: Polity Press.
Benhabib, Seyla (1996) 'Critical theory and postmodernism: on the interplay of
ethics, aesthetics and utopia in critical theory', in David M. Rasmussen (ed.)
The Handbook of Critical Theory, Cambridge, MA: Blackwell, pp. 327–339.
Binde, Jerome (2000), 'Toward an ethics of the future', *Public Culture* 12 (1): 55.
Brennan, Teresa (1993) *History After Lacan*, New York: Routledge.
Carmen, Raff (1996) *Autonomous Development*, London: Zed Books.
Chambers, Robert (1997) *Whose Reality Counts? Putting the Last First*, London:
Intermediate Technology Publications.
Chambers, Robert, N.C. Saxena and Tushaar Shah (1989) *To the Hands of the
Poor*, London: Intermediate Technology Publications.

Derrida, Jacques (1998) 'Whom to give to (knowing not to know)', in Jonathan Ree and Jane Chamberlain (eds) *Kierkegaard: A Critical Reader*, Oxford: Basil Blackwell, pp. 151–174.

Escobar, Arturo (1995) *Encountering Development: the Making and Unmaking of the Third World*, Princeton: Princeton University Press.

Ferguson, James (1990) *The Anti-politics Machine*, Cambridge: Cambridge University Press.

Flood, Robert L. (1999) *Rethinking the Fifth Discipline: Learning Within the Unknowable*, London: Routledge.

Foucault, Michel (1984) 'What is enlightenment?', in Paul Rabinow (ed.) *The Foucault Reader*, New York: Penguin Books.

—— (1988) 'An aesthetics of existence', in *Politics, Philosophy, Culture: Interviews and Other Writings, 1977–1984*, London: Routledge.

Gardiner, Michel (1996) 'Foucault, ethics and dialogue', *History of the Human Sciences* 9 (3): 27–46.

Giddens, Anthony (1994) *Beyond Left and Right: the Future of Radical Politics*, Cambridge: Polity Press.

—— (1999) *The Third Way: the Renewal of Social Democracy*, Cambridge: Polity Press.

Giri, Ananta K. (1998a) 'Well-being of institutions: problematic justice and the challenge of transformations', *Sociological Bulletin* 47: 73–95.

—— (1998b) 'The calling of an ethics of servanthood', *Journal of the Indian Council of Philosophical Research* XVI (3): 125–134.

—— (1998c) 'Moral consciousness and communicative action: from discourse ethics to spiritual transformations', *History of the Human Sciences* 11 (3): 87–113.

Gupta, Bina (2000) *The Empirical and Transcendental: a Fusion of Horizons*, Lanham, MD: Rowman and Littlefield.

Habermas, Jürgen (1990) 'What does socialism mean today? Rectifying revolution and the need for new thinking in the left', *New Left Review* 183.

—— (1995) 'Reconciliation through the public use of reason: remarks on John Rawls's "Political Liberalism" ', *Journal of Philosophy* XCII (3): 109–131.

—— (1996) 'Coping with contingencies: the return of historicism', in Jozef Niznik and J.T. Sandes (eds) *Debating the State of Philosophy: Habermas, Rorty, and Kolakowski*, Westport, CT: Praeger, pp. 1–30.

Hamelink, Cees (2000) *The Ethics of Cyberspace*, London: Sage.

Harris, George W. (1999) *Agent-Centered Morality: an Aristotelian Alternative to Kantian Internalism*, Berkeley: University of California Press.

Harvey, David (1989) *The Condition of Postmodernity: an Inquiry into the Origins of Cultural Change*, Cambridge, MA: Basil Blackwell.

—— (2000) *Spaces of Hope*, Edinburgh: Edinburgh University Press.

Kierkegaard, Søren (1962) *Works of Love*, New York: Harper and Row.

Krishna, Daya (1996) *The Problematic and Conceptual Structure of Classical Indian Thought about Man, Society and Polity*, Delhi: Oxford University Press.

Küng, Hans (1993) *Global Responsibility: In Search of a New World Ethic*, New York: Continuum.

Levinas, Emmanuel (1974) *Otherwise Than Being, or Beyond Essence*, Dordrecht: Kluwer Academic Publishers.

MacIntyre, Alasdair (1999) 'The virtues of acknowledged dependence', in *Dependent Rational Animals*, London: Duckworth, pp. 119–128.

Mehta, L., M. Leach, P. Newell, I. Scoones, K. Sivaramakrishnan and S.A. Way (1999) *Exploring Understandings of Institutions and Uncertainty: New Directions in Natural Resource Management*, Discussion Paper 372, Institute of Development Studies, Sussex.

Miller, James (1993) *The Passion of Michel Foucault*, New York: Simon and Schuster.

Miller, Richard B. (1996) *Casuistry and Modern Ethics: a Poetics of Practical Reasoning*, Chicago: University of Chicago Press.

Mohanty, J.N. (2000) *The Self and Its Other: Philosophical Essays*, Delhi: Oxford University Press.

Nederveen Pieterse, Jan (2001) *Development Theory: Deconstructions/Reconstructions*, London: Sage.

Osborne, Thomas (1997) 'The aesthetic problematic', *Economy and Society* 26 (1): 126–147.

Parekh, Bhikhu (1997) *Gandhi*, Oxford: Oxford University Press.

Pillai, P.V. (1984) '*Hind Swaraj* in the light of Heidegger's critique of modernity', in Nageswar Prasad (ed.) *Hind Swaraj: A Fresh Look*, New Delhi: Gandhi Peace Foundation.

Quarles van Ufford, Philip (1988) 'The hidden crisis in development: development bureaucracies in between intentions and outcomes', in Philip Quarles van Ufford, D. Kruyt and Th. Downing (eds) *The Hidden Crisis in Development: Development Bureaucracies*, Amsterdam: Free University Press; Tokyo: United Nations University.

—— (1999) 'The organization of development as an illness: about the metastasis of good intentions', in John R. Campbell and Alan Rew (eds) *Identity and Affect: Experiences of Identity in a Globalising World*, London: Pluto Press.

Rehenema, Majid (1997) 'Towards post-development: searching for signposts, a new language and new paradigm', in *The Post-Development Reader*, compiled and edited by Majid Rehenema with Victoria Bawtree, London: Zed Books, pp. 377–403.

Roy, Ramashray (1993) 'Swadhyaya: values and message', in P. Wignaraja (ed.) *New Social Movements in the South*, New Delhi: Sage.

Rudd, Anthony (1993) *Kierkegaard and the Limits of the Ethical*, Oxford: Clarendon Press.

Scarry, Elaine (1999) *On Beauty and Being Just*, Princeton: Princeton University Press.

Schrag, Calvin O. (1997) *The Self After Postmodernity*, New Haven: Yale University Press.

Sen, Amartya (1999) *Development as Freedom*, Oxford: Oxford University Press.

Sheth, N.R. (1994) *Children of the Same God*, working paper, Gujarat Institute of Development Research, Ahmedabad.

Sri Aurobindo (1962) 'The aesthetic and ethical culture', in *The Human Cycle. The Ideal of Human Unity. War and Self-Determination*, Pondicherry: Sri Aurobindo Ashram.

Srinivasan, Amrit (1998) 'The subject of fieldwork: Malinowski and Gandhi', in Meenakshi Thapan (ed.) *Anthropological Journeys: Reflections on Fieldwork*, Hyderabad: Orient Longman.

Stolle, Jeffrey (2001) 'Levinas and the *Akedah*: an alternative to Kierkegaard', *Philosophy Today* 45 (2): 132–143.

Strathern, Marilyn (2000) 'New accountabilities: anthropological studies in audit, ethics and the academy', introduction to Marilyn Strathern (ed.) *Audit Cultures*, London: Routledge, pp. 1–18.

Sunder Rajan, R. (1998) *Beyond the Crisis of European Sciences*, Shimla: Indian Institute of Advanced Studies.

Taylor, Charles (1991) *The Ethics of Authenticity*, Cambridge, MA: Harvard University Press.

Thompson, Judith Jarvis (2001) *Goodness and Advice*, edited and introduced by Amy Gutman, Princeton: Princeton University Press.

Welsch, Wolfgang (1997) *Undoing Aesthetics*, London: Sage.

Chapter 13

Afterword

The calling of global responsibilities

Ananta Kumar Giri

Kierkegaard saw it better. He said that we are caught up between time and eternity, between finite and infinite. Kant also said that there is no human existence without regulative ideas. The one world – not merely a grand totality, but one infinite horizon – is such a regulative idea. But you cannot just import a regulative idea by fiat. It needs to be shown that such an idea is operative from the beginning.

(Mohanty 2000: 96)

When asked his view of Western civilization, Mahatma Gandhi famously answered: 'It would be a good idea.' His reply reminds us that 'civilization' is not a secure possession but a fragile, ever-renewable endeavour; grammatically it has the character more of a verb than a noun. This is particularly true of the emerging global or 'world civilization' – what sometimes is called the nascent 'cosmopolis'. Here again, caution is imperative. Anyone today who claimed to speak 'in the name of' world civilization would be suspected (with good reason) of harbouring hegemonic or imperialistic designs ... if there is to be a civilizational encounter, participants have to proceed modestly and soberly, by taking their departure, at least initially, from their own distinct perspective or vantage point ... while simultaneously guarding against any form of cultural or ethnic self-enclosure.

(Dallmayr 2001: 64)

A spiritualized society would treat in its sociology the individual, from the saint to the criminal, not as units of social problem to be passed through some skillfully devised machinery and either flattened into the social mould or crushed out of it, but as souls suffering and entangled in a net and to be rescued, souls growing and to be encouraged to grow. ... The aim of its economics would be not to create a huge engine of production, whether of the competitive or the co-operative kind, but to give to men – not only to some but to all men each in his highest possible measure – the joy of work according to their own nature and free leisure to grow inwardly, as well as a simply rich and beautiful life for all. ... And that work would be to find the divine Self in the individual and the collectivity and to realise spiritually, mentally, vitally, materially its greatest, largest, richest and deepest possibilities in the inner life of all and their outer action and nature.

(Sri Aurobindo 1962: 241–242)

The knowledge of ethical issues in development that this volume deals with is the world of development interventions. In this world, international donor agencies play a determinant role, sometimes in 'partnership' with states and local groups. But there is an unease with such an interventionist conceptualisation and realisation of development in this volume which leads one of the contributors, Alan Rew, to speak of this world as a black box. This unease becomes quite vocal in the contribution of Albert Alejo. Alejo is not wedded to an interventionist model of development and presents us with glimpses of a socio-cultural movement fighting against development as an interventionist project. Thus, understanding the contingent nature of this volume as it deals with ethical issues emerging primarily from interventionist development projects calls for broadening our efforts to take part in and study varieties of socio-cultural movements in the field of development – movements which resist the violence of interventionist development projects from the experiential perspective of the violated and the displaced, and movements which aspire for self-development and social transformation in an autonomous manner without the trappings of the interventionist mode. In order to submit this volume as a stepping stone for a truly global conversation on development as a multi-local and multi-sited global responsibility (where responsibility means not only individual and collective responsibility but co-responsibility (cf. Apel 1993; Strydom 1999)), the task for us is to understand the ethical issues of development not only from within the interventionist world but also as they emerge from movements of resistance as well as movements of new aspirations and beginnings. It is probably for this reason that John Clammer writes:

discourses of 'development' in anthropology … still reflect a distinctive and self-limiting frame within which 'development' issues are posed and a distinctive language constituted of an old amalgam of the terminology of development economics, the reportese of development agencies and the currently politically correct. … Yet if development is about social transformation, then indigenous social movements are where it is happening, if at all, in ways outside of the economistic paradigm, critiques that it is surely the responsibility of anthropologists, and anthropologists of development in particular, to pursue.

(Clammer 2000: 3)

In this afterword, I undertake such a journey. In order to open the contingent world of development interventions that the present volume deals with for further conversation, I describe the vision and experiments of both socio-spiritual and socio-political movements. With reference to the latter, I discuss the dynamics of contemporary socio-political movements such as ATTAC in Europe and the anti-mining struggle in Kashipur, India, fighting against corporate globalisation and for globalisation as humanisation; and on the former, I discuss the work of Swadhyaya, the self-study movement in contemporary India. Swadhyaya brings a new cultural and civilisational perspective on development to that offered by the enlightenment model of human development, which interventionist models of development are now striving to globalise with the forces of money and power. The reflections in this afterword describe the violence in such a globalisation of worldview and plead for a trans-civilisational and transcultural dialogue on the telos, meaning and process of development. I submit that such a trans-civilisational dialogue calls for mutual interrogation and open-ended learning where we are concerned not only with issues of application and justification, but prepare ourselves to undertake suffering for peace, justice and renewing development as practices of hope. This I argue is essential to rethinking and reconstituting our responsibilities in and to the world after the violent turbulences of 11 September 2001.

Swadhyaya is a socio-spiritual movement in contemporary India which also works globally in England, the Caribbean, the USA, and Africa (Giri 2000). Swadhyaya means study of the self but both these terms are understood broadly, and here efforts in self-study and self-development are intimately connected with being with others in many experimental ways. Swadhyaya does not believe in an interventionist mode of development. It has varieties of activities which can be called community development projects but that would be an externalist representation of the vision and practice of Swadhyaya. Swadhyaya calls these *prayogas*, which means experiments – experiments which facilitate the self-development of participants in an experimental ground of working and being together where the self is attuned both to the higher self within and the other self standing laterally. *Bhaktipheri* – devotional travel – and *Shramabhakti* – devotional labour – are the foundations of Swadhyaya. Swadhyaya believes that one of the greatest contemporary challenges is to overcome the distance between 'man' and 'man', and for this people should meet with each other without any motivation to profit. In *Bhaktipheri* Swadhyayees go from one place to another and spend time with each other. In *Shramabhakti*, Swadhyayees offer their devotional labour in experimental grounds of self-development and collective well-being. For example, in villages where Swadhyaya is active, there is a *prayoga* called *Yogeswara Krishi*, or Lord's farming, in which Swadhyayees cultivate a piece of land taken on lease on a cooperative basis and through their own labour. The produce of this experiment is treated as impersonal wealth or *apoureshaya laxmi*, and this is utilised for addressing the needs of the community. Through such generation of impersonal wealth from varieties of experiments, some of which exist at a supra-village level (for instance the experiment of Sri Darshanam and Brukha Mandir brings people together from more than twenty villages for the offering of devotional labour), Swadhyayees also learn to overcome the bindings of a narrow economic reason, and learn to relate to wealth in a non-possessive way, a lesson which can transform the contemporary discourse of social capital. In contemporary discourse, social capital is primarily thought of in rational terms, but rationality is not enough to tackle the problems of individualism, atomism and the tendency to free ride in contemporary societies. In Swadhyaya trust is a value in itself, a value which is generated and strengthened in networks of divine relationships, and here a dialogue with Swadhyaya can help us to understand the significance of spirituality, namely practical spirituality, in the generation and renewal of social capital.

For its work, Swadhyaya does not accept any grant, neither from multilateral donor agencies, such as the World Bank or IMF, nor from the state, and not from the philanthropists either. Swadhyaya generates wealth and wellbeing from the time and labour that participants bring to these experimental grounds of mutual nurturance. Here we witness a new attempt to realise value from our own time and labour without passing through the media of money and market and without standing with folded hands in the corridors of international and national donor agencies for starting rural and tribal development work in one's vicinity. Many efforts in the contemporary West such as the LETS network in Netherlands and Canada (cf. Offe and Heinze 1992) and what Ulrich Beck (2000) calls varieties of civil labour where one works for the common good also embody such a spirit of realisation of value from our own free time and free labour, an art which we have lost in the logic of organised modernity. Realising development as a shared global responsibility calls for a new relationship to time and labour – a time which is not just what Heidegger calls a 'clock time' but a lived time and labour which is not teleologically geared only to earning money for oneself but becomes a means of taking part in a shared world of working together for a new hope, for a new beginning (Dallmayr 2000b). We find such a new relationship to time and labour in Swadhyaya which has been made possible by a spiritual mobilisation of tradition. Swadhyaya does not believe in the post-traditional telos of modernity, the telos which guides the discourse of development too, that tradition is necessarily a barrier to be overcome in development; rather there are many spiritual resources in traditions which can be creatively mobilised for alternative development at the contemporary juncture. In such mobilisations, unlike for Giddens (cf. 1999) and Habermas (cf. 1993), justification of faith is carried out not through rational argumentation alone but also through one's participation in concrete projects of practical spirituality which are embodiments of aesthetic and ethical projects of love. Love of God as simultaneously love of self and love of the world is at the heart of such an initiative in development which helps us to understand the calling of a new dialectic of transformation that Roy Bhaskar has recently presented to us: 'The dialectics of de-alienation (of retotalisation) are all essentially dialectics of love, of love of self (Self), of each and all (Totality) and in both inner and outer movements, both as essentially love of God ... and God, we could say, is not essentially love but essentially to be loved' (Bhaskar 2000: 44).

In Swadhyaya, practical work of development and spirituality are not separated from each other but here combining love of God with love of the world is not free from ambiguity, tension and contradiction (cf. Touraine 2001). Followers of Swadhyaya make a distinction between God's work and social work; for them contributing to development of the human mind and heart through various life-elevating projects is an aspect of God's work, while building new roads is an aspect of social work. This distinction has not enabled Swadhyaya to come to terms with the concrete challenge of social development in local communities such as repairing dilapidated roads, building cowsheds, and stopping the encroachments on village common land by influential landlords. But here followers of Swadhyaya appeal to us to rethink the very meaning of development. During one of my fieldwork journeys to Gujarat in Western India, the state where Swadhyaya is most active, I was once asked a question. I was walking with Pappot Bhai, an inspiring leader of Swadhyaya, and his fellow co-walkers in a village near the coastal town of Veraval. Pappot Bhai asked me: 'Is building a road the only meaning of development? Developing the mind, intellect and heart of human beings – is it not development?' This question of Pappot Bhai could be asked to the project of development which, despite its shift from economic development to human development, does not have within itself any striving for development of the human heart.

In fact, Fred Dallmayr, the preeminent philosopher of our times, for whom philosophy is an experiential embodiment of cross-cultural dialogue, asks such a foundational question: should development participate in what he calls 'Enlightenment Blackmail' and globalise modern Western models of economic development and rationality, or be a critical hermeneutic effort in understanding the limitations of such a philosophical and historical starting point, undertaking efforts to create new spaces of self-development and mutual flourishing (Dallmayr 1998)? Dallmayr tells us that in Europe itself there was also another tradition of *Bildung* which emphasised self-cultivation, a cultivation which simultaneously aimed at authentic humanisation and divinisation.[1] The ideal of *Bildung* is not confined only to the classical German period but is found in virtually all cultures of the globe which have stories or mythical-religious narratives that emphasise the 'process of divine human formation', but 'how much of these older stories of formation, culture (*Bildung*), and self-development still lives in contemporary conceptions of social development?' (Dallmayr 1998: 245). Thus cross-cultural dialogue on the meaning of development where we seek to understand the contingency of not only our social locations but also our values is an important task here. Applying the insights of self-cultivation, Dallmayr tells us: 'With specific reference to global development, formation (*Bildung*) postulates an open-ended encounter between societies and cultures, a reciprocal learning process animating a "global village" continuously in the throes of formation' (Dallmayr 1998: 14). And in such an engagement with development as a cross-cultural striving for human flourishing we need to build on alternative traditions of spiritual humanisation, but bringing these voices to the contemporary discourse of development requires a memory-work, an act of courageous remembrance and contemporary restitution. In the words of Dallmayr:

> This path of humanization [as charted by Confucius and Herder] offers the potential for renewal that is never cut loose from historically sedimented moorings and situated vernacular beliefs. To avoid rupture, what is needed along this path is memory-work, attention to the still untapped resources of the past; in our time of rapid globalisation with a bent toward global amnesia such memory-work emerges as a crucial requisite for the preservation of critical humanness.
>
> (Dallmayr 1998: 11)

Thus in order to take part in development as a global conversation we cannot ignore the task of cross-cultural and cross-civilisational dialogue on the telos, process and practice of development. Such a dialogue should not be another exercise in imposing the dominant conception of human development as propagated by contemporary triumphal capitalism, but an engagement in 'mutual interrogation and interpellation' where 'a distinct life-form – a concrete mode of "being-in-the-world" – opens itself up to the challenge of otherness in a manner yielding a deeper, transformative understanding of self and other' (Dallmayr 1998: 6–7). And in this dialogue we should also overcome the tempting contemporary logic of clash of civilisations (cf. Huntington 1996) and take part in various attempts at overcoming their situational, valuational and historical contingencies and arriving at spaces of mutually created co-beings. But in this cross-civilisational dialogue on the meaning, telos and process of development, we should not be confined only to the horizontal dimension of self–other relation, but should be open to the vertical dimension as well. This vertical dimension refers to how a civilisation or culture relates to nature and the divine. For Dallmayr, 'On the level of civilizational discourse, horizontal openness means attentiveness to other civilizations, but also to civilization's corollaries (nature and the divine) … which speak or intervene in human discourse, but do so in recessed and "non-informatic" ways. The question is whether we allow ourselves to be addressed in this fashion' (Dallmayr 2001: 16).

But the enlightenment model of development self-confidently cuts itself off from the world of nature except as an object of domination and the world of transcendence except as an idle superstructure or a collective hallucination. Here a widening of our universe of discourse is urgently called for in both axes. On the first axis, we need to engage ourselves with a much more radical critique of anthropocentrism and go beyond the contemporary rethinking of development as 'anthropocentrism with a human face' (cf. Nederveen Pieterse 2001). Here a cross-cultural experience of nature would be helpful, for example the experience pointed to by the Indian spiritual traditions where all life is sacred and human beings do not have any right to dominate the non-human world. Emergent developments in technology, such as the rise of cyborgs (virtual people with artificial intelligence), may also force us to rethink our anthropocentric models of development as, 'for the first time in their history, human beings would have to cooperate with a different species' which takes all sentient beings, not only humans, seriously (Hamelink 2000: 36). And insofar as the axis of transcendence is concerned, contemporary development discourse is an unreflective participant in the enlightenment dichotomy of the human social world and the world of transcendence, and the task for us here is to realise the harm such a dissociation does to the relationship between humans here on Earth itself. As Jean-Luc Nancy tells us: 'It is precisely the immanence of man to man, or it is man, taken absolutely, considered as the immanent being par excellence, that constitutes the stumbling block to a thinking of community' (quoted in Dallmayr 1998: 281; also Unger 1987).

The introduction to the present volume points to the impasse in which we are in pursuing development as a project in 'applied enlightenment' but neither our introduction nor various other recent critical engagements with enlightenment call for a fundamental transformation in our modes of being and modes of relationship along these two axes – the natural world and the transcendental. Both the critics and defenders of enlightenment leave unproblematic these oppositions, and here Foucault's much drummed about reconstitution of enlightenment along 'people's knowledge' is also part of the same enlightenment privileging of the human social world. The proposal of a third enlightenment or practical enlightenment offered by enthusiastic Anglo-American philosophers such as Hilary Putnam (2001) and Richard Rorty (1999) also seems to be very much a family quarrel rather than a radical, global interrogation of the presuppositions of enlightenment. Here Putnam's proposal of practical enlightenment and Toulmin's call for return to reason via reasonable human practice do not explore the spiritual ontology of human practice.[2] John Dewey is a hero to the American pragmatists and they are now out in the world preaching his virtues everywhere, but unfortunately in a missionary way. Surely all over the world we have a lot to learn from the democratic and educational experiments of Dewey, but in this age of global conversations, while talking about enlightenment can we beat the drums of Dewey in an uncritical manner, without relating the democratic enlightenment of Dewey with the spiritual enlightenment of experimenters such as Gautama Buddha and Mahatma Gandhi? In fact both Buddha and Gandhi combined spiritual seeking with reason and democratic and spiritual enlightenment in their own ways, Buddha spending his post-enlightenment days in teaching the excluded sections of society and exhorting them not to abandon reason in the name of custom (Carrithers 1983). Thus, as we make development a part of global conversation, we need to proceed cautiously *vis-à-vis* the contemporary American proposal about third enlightenment, as there is a one-sided globalisation of John Dewey here which is not delinked from the globalisation of Coca-Cola.[3]

The dualism between universalism and particularism is another legacy of enlightenment which determines our modes of development and embodiment of responsibility. In order to rethink development as an embodiment of global responsibility, we have to transcend the boundaries between the two. Here a critique of universalism, as offered by Foucault and others, is not enough; what is called for here is an understanding of and participation in the work of what Wallerstein and his colleagues call 'particularistic universalism' – a proposal which has close affinity with the one of 'situated universalism' recently submitted by Sheldon Pollock, Homi Bhaba, Carol Appadurai Breckenridge and Dipesh Chakrabarty (Pollock *et al.* 2000; Wallerstein *et al.* 1996).[4] This in turn calls for a multi-valued logic in place of the either/or logic of particularism and universalism and an ethics of non-injury and non-violence. Philosopher J.N. Mohanty (2000) brings a cross-culturally sensitive philosophical reflection to bear on this pathway of multi-valued logic:

> The ethic of non-injury applied to philosophical thinking requires that one does not reject outright the other point of view without first recognising the element of truth in it; it is based on the belief that every point of view is partly true, partly false, and partly undecidable. A simple two-valued logic requiring that a proposition must either be true or false is thereby rejected, and what the Jaina philosopher proposes is a multi-valued logic. To this multi-valued logic, I add the Husserlian idea of overlapping contents. The different perspectives on a thing are not mutually exclusive, but share some contents with each other. The different 'worlds' have shared contents, contrary to the total relativism. *If you represent them by circles, they are intersecting circles, not incommensurable, [and it is this model of] intersecting circles which can get us out of relativism on the one hand and absolutism on the other.*
>
> (Mohanty 2000: 24; emphasis added)

From a philosophical perspective, J.N. Mohanty presents us the picture of intersecting circles to transcend the opposition between universalism and particularism, and David Harvey presents us the picture of multiple theatres from the perspective of emancipatory political practice. Harvey writes: 'The metaphor to which I appeal is one of several different "theatres" of thought and action on some long frontier of "insurgent" political practices. Advances in one theatre get ultimately stymied or even rolled back unless supported by advances elsewhere. No one theatre is particularly privileged' (Harvey 2000a: 234). Harvey's meditations can help us reach a turning point in this reflective journey, and encourage us to combine the widening of the universe of discourse of development with concrete socio-political and spiritual struggles. But as we undertake this task of combination, development as humanisation meets with specific and often violent challenge now in the contemporary effort to turn the world into a global marketplace. True, markets have their own place in enabling continued socio-economic development in the planet but the contemporary marketisation of the globe has no sense of limit, is a narrowing of our conceptions of self and the world, and shrinks our sense of responsibility (Sachs 1999). In this context it is helpful to keep in mind what Jean and John Comaroff write about our contemporary predicament: 'Life under millennial capitalism is neither a game nor a repertoire of rational choices. … Already there are signs of altered configurations, of fresh efforts to challenge the triumphal reign of the market' (Comaroff and Comaroff 2000: 334–335; see also Bourdieu 1999).

There are anti-systemic and alternative movements on the rise everywhere now, and while the advocates of corporate globalisation including their media spokespeople dismiss these anti-globalisation movements, they are in fact striving for an alternative globalisation, for globalisation as humanisation (see Nederveen Pieterse 2000). For these movements marketisation of the globe is not an inevitable destiny, and they strive to shape the unfolding contours of globalisation in favor of primacy of the human rather than the market or corporations. Thus one of the slogans I heard in the demonstrations against the EU summit meeting in Gothenburg in June 2001 was: 'People, not Profit: Our World is not for Sale'. On the final day of this gathering, 25,000 people marched peacefully in the streets of Gothenburg chanting 'International Solidarity, International Solidarity'. The battle of Gothenburg was continued just a month later in Genoa, Italy, where 150,000 people took part.

In both Gothenburg and Genoa there was violence, though the overwhelming majority of protesters were non-violent and did not believe in violence as a mode of contestation. In reflecting on this violence, the mainstream global media, for example CNN, holds protesters responsible. But this is a systematically biased reporting. I had taken part in the Gothenburg summit and I saw how police riding on galloping horses and with dogs first jumped into the marching crowd. In the ensuing confrontation, while police had the most sophisticated weaponry, protesters did not even have stones to throw. But as the confrontation intensified, protesters with black masks started digging stones from the ground and throwing them at the police. So what we see here is a fight between the defenders of the system, who have the most advanced technologies at their command, and the protesters (here referring to only those protesters who do not feel shy to use violence), who have only stone age tools such as stones and chairs. Despite this, police in Gothenburg shot at the volunteers of the Reclaiming the Street group, who were having their anti-corporate street rally in the night, critically wounding three people including a journalist. On the second day of the summit, in the garden near the canal where protesters had set up their tents, I met a young man who showed me his bleeding hand – blood coming out of the bites from the police dog. Despite this, he and his friends were chanting the slogan 'Love, Love' and flying balloons, not stones, towards the police.

But the level of violence during the G8 summit in Genoa was considerably higher, and here police killed one demonstrator. This unnamed man is the first martyr from Europe in the struggle against corporate globalisation but while his martyrdom has recently inspired demonstrations in many parts of Europe especially among the young, he still remains unnamed to most of us. In this contestation, the defenders of the system are engaged in a one-sided condemnation of violent protesters and even use the name of Mahatma Gandhi for this.[5] But Gandhi is not a purist proponent of non-violence, especially non-violence of a cowardly kind, and though he himself would give his life in a truthful non-violent (*satyagrahic*) fight against the oppressive forces of the system, he would never pass an *a priori* moralising judgement on those who use violence to protest against the inhumanity of a system, a system which has shut its doors and windows of perception. A Gandhian engagement with dramas of contestation at both Gothenburg and Genoa also needs to ask this question: what prevents the assembled world leaders from inviting the protesters into a roundtable conversation and listening to them?

Thus as we reconstitute development as a global responsibility there is no way we can dissociate our duties from taking part in this violent confrontation between corporate globalisation and globalisation as humanisation. For students of development studies it calls for an understanding of the emergent new logic of violence, where forces of multinational capital and state power join hands in suppressing the rights of people (see Mohanty *et al.* 1998). Such a development scenario is ethically problematic and morally wrong in the first place, not to mention that it violates the spirit of democratic constitutionalism (cf. Habermas 1996). To understand this, let us acquaint ourselves, albeit briefly, with another struggle. Kashipur in the state of Orissa is one of the most backward tribal areas of India. For the last six years, the people of Kashipur have been waging a fight against multinational mining companies bent on establishing mines in their area. With the might of the state these companies have also acquired land from many people in the affected villages. Neither the multinational companies nor the state government have ever discussed with the local people what they want to do in their area and what is going to be their fate after being evicted from their homelands. Agragamee, a local voluntary organisation, which has not been afraid to support a dialogue between these contending parties, has been subjected to attacks and the State of Orissa under the leadership of a tyrant chief minister even banned it for two years. Local people themselves have been subjected to numerous violent attacks, and in some cases villagers have also kidnapped the functionaries of multinational mining companies. But when all this did not deter the spirit of the local people, a platoon of police descended on the village of Maikanch on 16 December 2000 when people had just completed their communal lunch together, and started firing at them. The police killed in cold blood three people who were running to the hilltop for their lives, and before leaving the village, burnt its own vehicle and told the world that it had resorted to firing in self-defence.

The multinational Hydro company of Norway is one of the parties in this contestation and the voluntary organisation named Norwatch, based in Oslo, has brought the struggle of Kashipur to the public sphere in Norway. Tarjei is one of the activists of Norwatch, and he has provided support to this struggle. Of his own experience about this participation in an emergent movement of global solidarity, Tarjei says: 'I am struck by the fact that our own organization Norwatch is such a small group, we are only two people, but we are able to create a public opinion here against the mining activities of Hydro. I feel that as the system is becoming increasingly more and more powerful, it is also becoming more and more vulnerable where a single individual can challenge and transform it in concrete ways.'

ATTAC is one of the fast-growing transnational social movements at present which is struggling for the embodiment of global responsibilities in concrete ways. Starting in France, it has spread quickly into many parts of Europe and the world, and in countries such as Sweden and Finland it has taken the character of a multi-dimensional grass-roots mobilisation involving both non-violent public protest as well as critical study of the contemporary dynamics of globalisation. It conducts study circles on both the logic of corporate globalisation as well as democratic alternatives in economy and society. Young and old cutting across ideological and party lines are now joining the space of global solidarity that a movement such as ATTAC creates. I had a discussion with Bjorn and Gunnar, two young volunteers of ATTAC, Sweden in Stockholm last June (2001), and they told me that members from the Social Democratic Party of Sweden are leaving their old party and joining ATTAC, because they find in it a democratic space for self-expression that is not available in the party spaces. ATTAC also provides them a space to think about issues of global justice in a more concrete and personal way. One of the demands of ATTAC is that multinational companies should pay a certain amount of tax to the local community where they are working, what is now called the Tobin Tax. The volunteers of ATTAC are responding to the calling of global responsibilities at the contemporary juncture in multiple modes of contestation and creativity, reflection and action. They were at the forefront of the peaceful demonstration on the final day of the EU summit. When one talks to the animating volunteers of ATTAC one realises that the global community is 'not simply an empirical reality or presence, but matter of an advent, a calling' (Dallmayr 1998: 282).

But in this global fight over life and death, the issue of concrete human suffering is an elusive one, and it requires a sensitive development anthropology to record this beyond the representation of movements themselves. In this context, Upendra Baxi, a sensitive scholar of contemporary globalisation and social suffering, writes: 'The "analytic" standpoint fails to see the logic of social movements from the perspective of those violated' (Baxi 2000: 39). But what Baxi does not realise is that leaders of social movements themselves can fail to identify themselves with the suffering faces and bodies of men and women whose lives they represent. Here it is helpful to come back to the story of the anti-mining struggle in Kashipur. Abhilash Jhodia was one of the three people killed in the police firing in Maikanch last year, and he hailed from the village of Maikanch itself. He was a young man, only twenty-five when he was shot dead, leaving behind his pregnant wife, two children and aging parents. During my visit to Maikanch I felt that the leaders of the anti-mining struggle were in a way happy that the firing had taken place, because police fire and the unintentional martyrdom of these three people have provided new momentum to the struggle and have contributed to people's loss of fear. But the experience of Subarna, Abhilash's wife, and his children is different. When I went to the house of Abhilash along with some young people of the village, Subarna was not at home. She had gone to a distant forest, even at this advanced stage of pregnancy, to collect wood which she would sell for her livelihood. Abhilash's father, who was holding his young son, told us: 'In the night it is difficult. The young boy is asking when will his father come home?' And when I was finally able to meet with Subarna, she was silent as a statue. Words and tears have run their course in her life, and her vacant eyes embody a different experience of struggle compared to the leaders for whom Abhilash has quickly become a dead somebody, whose martyrdom has contributed to new energies of the movement. There is an erasure of concrete faces in such a movemental representation as well, and here the calling responsibility calls for a vigilant awareness which refuses to be trapped even in the logic of anti-systemic movements, and in a spirit of continued seeking of solidarity brings the untold suffering of women such as Subarna Jhodia to our consciousness.

Thus there are many more ethical sides to globalisation and global responsibilities than meets the eye, and it is essential for development anthropology to take part in these manifold imaginations, explorations and struggles.

Alongside globalisation, cosmopolitanism is another regnant discourse today with which it is helpful to have a brief encounter as a prelude to our following reconstitution of development as an undertaking in suffering and hope. Here again, we witness two contending forces: cosmopolitanism as an elitist globalism which wants to be cosmopolitan in its lifestyle (not in life-politics) and cosmopolitanism which represents the force of global democratisation – a fight for cosmopolitan democracy from within local societies and nation-states. About the first kind of cosmopolitanism, Sheldon Pollock and his colleagues write: 'The discriminatory perspectives of an older form of globalization – colonization – seem to have revived themselves at the point at which we readily consider ourselves to be worldwide citizens forever "hooked up" (connected) on-line. All the derring-do between the local and the global in the dialectic of worldly thinking should not conceal the fact that neoliberal cosmopolitan thought is founded on a conformist sense of what it means to be a "person" as an abstract unit of cultural exchange' (Pollock et al. 2000: 581). And about the later, Ulrich Beck tells us: 'cosmopolitanism means global interrelationships and a transnational vocabulary of symbols, but it also means a deep engagement in local activities, local consciousness, connection to local people. It means having wings and roots at the same time' (Beck 2001: 2). Beck goes on to argue: 'globalism is a basic enemy of democracy and therefore to be supplemented by the cosmopolitan principle of recognizing the otherness of the other' (2001: 2).

Responding to the calling of global responsibilities at the contemporary juncture requires development to participate in this contested field of cosmopolitanism, the struggle between cosmopolitanism as a global elitism and cosmopolitanism as a yearning for cosmopolitan democracy, which parallels the struggle between globalisation from above and globalisation from below (Appadurai 2000a, 2000b; Das, C. 2001a; Habermas 1998). And here, as David Harvey argues, 'A meaningful cosmopolitanism does not entail some passive contemplation of global citizenship. It is, as Kant himself insisted, a principle of intervention to make the world (and its geography) something other than what it is' (Harvey 2000b: 560).

But Harvey is not alone in invoking the memory of Kant in radical ways to help us come to terms with the contemporary challenge of global responsibilities. Notable here are the passionate reflections of anthropologist Keith Hart, who writes: 'Kant saw that the world was moving towards war between coalitions of nation-states; yet he posed the question of how humanity might construct a "perpetual peace" beyond the boundaries of state, based on principles we all share. ... Kant held that the last and most difficult task facing humanity was the administration of justice worldwide' (Hart 2000: 3). As we have seen with the case of movements such as ATTAC, the Kantian question of a global justice is now at the heart of many movements for a humane globalisation, and has gone beyond the speculative world of Kantian philosophers of justice of our times such as John Rawls (see Rawls 1999, 2001). For Hart, 'In order to pursue this goal, the world has to be imaginatively reduced in scale and our subjectivity expanded so that a meaningful link can be established between the two' (Hart 2000: 3).

In this praxis of establishing meaningful linkage, Hart says: 'We need to feel more at home in the world, to find the means of actively resisting alienation' (2000: 3). The task of resisting alienation can be enriched now by creatively embodying the spirit of both Marx and Heidegger.[6] Marx spoke about the need to overcome social alienation, and Heidegger about the alienation of our authentic self. At the contemporary juncture there is a need to combine these two aspirations of overcoming alienation.[7] But here Heidegger also challenges us to understand the fragile character of our being in the world, and he urges us not to cling to our secured homes and to undertake a journey of homelessness, a travel in the world.[8] We of course have to come home, but the home we come back to is not a secured abode – 'the "home" sought and found in homecoming is not a place located somewhere else in empirical space-time, but rather something like a promise ... – a promise which also does not point simply to a no-place or a place outside of space-time, but rather inhabits the journey from beginning to end' (Dallmayr 2001: 8; see also Gibson-Graham 1997). In our effort to resist alienation in the world at present we need to understand and take part in this dialectic between homelessness and homecoming.

But taking part in this dialectic of homelessness and homecoming is not a smooth affair; it calls for us to be able to undertake suffering for the sake of our journey. Hart forgets this issue of suffering, and here it is helpful to realise that for the sake of embodying a life of justice as 'subjects in history', we have to prepare ourselves to undertake suffering, in fact embody the pains of a groaning humanity. For this we have to go beyond Kant, as in the Kantian world we find little preparation for undertaking suffering for the sake of justice, an inadequacy which continues to haunt us even now despite the glorious chanting of Kant's name by many of us. For this we would have to befriend Gandhi. Gandhi presents us with a passionate call to undertake suffering for the sake of establishing peace and justice. Gandhi urges us to understand the link between morality and martyrdom, as he, following a long line of martyrs – Antigone, Socrates, Jesus Christ – lays down his life for the sake of peace and justice (Giri 2002; Uberoi 1996). Without mentioning the name of Gandhi, Edward Said also provides us a similar path of engagement. For Said, the conflict between entrenched rivals such as Palestinians and Israelis cannot be resolved unless both the parties understand the suffering of each other, rather than inflicting suffering on the other, and through such shared suffering lay the foundations of peace. What Said writes below with reference to Jews and Palestinians provides us with glimpses of the path of shared suffering that is relevant to development imagination in many parts of the world now:

Most Palestinians are indifferent to and often angered by stories of Jewish suffering. ... Conversely most Israelis refuse to concede that Israel is built on the ruins of Palestinian society. ... Yet there can be no possible reconciliation, no possible solution unless these two communities confront each other's experience in the light of the other ... there can be no hope of peace unless the stronger community, the Israeli Jews, acknowledge the most powerful memory for Palestinians, namely the dispossession of an entire people. As the weaker party Palestinians must also face the fact that Israeli Jews see themselves as survivors of the Holocaust, even though that tragedy cannot be allowed to justify Palestinian dispossession.

(Said 2000)

Thus shared suffering is a key challenge now and the challenge for a morally sensitive development anthropology here is not only to describe the suffering of those who are violated by the logic of corporate globalisation but also to share this suffering in an embodied mode.[9] Such embodiment of justice has its own mode of justification as well. Neo-Kantians like Habermas, who are now celebrated heroes of a politics of inclusion of the other, tell us that we must justify our beliefs to others through a process of rational argumentation. But rational argumentation has its limits in convincing the other about the soundness and significance of our moral beliefs and convictions. And here suffering – in fact, suffering undertaken for the sake of love – has the power to unlock the minds and hearts of others (Giri 2001).

The need for such a mode of engagement, that feels identified with the suffering of others and approaches one's own not from a position of valorised strength but from acknowledgement of human vulnerability, has become urgent after the violent turbulences of 11 September 2001. On 11 September 2001, the twin towers of the World Trade Center in New York City were destroyed and thousands killed by so-called terrorists. But what must our response to this be? A key issue here is, as heart-touching Indian anthropologist and philosopher Veena Das tells us: 'Might we be able to mourn with the survivors of September 11 without the needing to appropriate their grief for other grander projects' (Das, V. 2001: 111). And the grand project in the global order now is the war on terrorism, but those who are leading this war do not want to acknowledge that their war on terrorism is itself posing a great threat to human security and global peace. Veena Das helps us understand this:

The point about many terrorisms versus a single grand terrorism that threatens that are seen to embody the force of history is indeed significant. ... While in many other countries the wounds afflicted through such violence are acknowledged as attesting to the vulnerability of human life, American society seems unable to acknowledge this vulnerability ... the theatrical display of sovereign power is only part of the story. There is also the further need to replace the pain of the nagging questions posed to American citizens about what relation their pain bears to the pain of others. What kind of responsibility do they share when successive regimes elected by them have supported military regimes, brutal dictatorships and warlords mired in corruption with no space for the exercise of critical monitoring of politics in the Middle East?

Thus there is a need for a different response to the so-called problem of terrorism. The first thing to realise is that this problem cannot be solved through war, especially when those who are fighting this war on terrorism are themselves terrorists in killing innocent children, women and men whenever they feel like doing it. They are enabled in their terrorism in the now triumphant ideology of just war. As Michael Hardt and Antonio Negri write in *Empire* (2000):

> The traditional concept of just war involves the banalisation of war and the celebration of it as an ethical instrument, both of which were ideas that modern political thought and the international community of nation-states had resolutely refused. These two traditional characteristics have reappeared in our postmodern world: on the one hand, war is reduced to status of police action, and on the other, the new power that can legitimately exercise ethical functions through war is sacralised.
>
> (Hardt and Negri 2000: 12)

Now war has become part of the ideology of an imperial formation, and here 'Just war is no longer in any sense an activity of defense or resistance. It has become rather an activity justified in itself' (Hardt and Negri 2000: 13).

This new imperial mode of justification is now beginning to create new modes of justification for development. Now the emerging new justification for development is: we must have development so that we might eliminate social situations of poverty and underdevelopment which breed terrorism. But development as global responsibility has to go beyond such instrumental and violent justifications. A humanistic development anthropology has to go beyond such instrumental and violent justification for development. A humanistic development anthropology concerned with the pathos of human suffering has a greater role to play in creating self-awareness that the key challenge here is not terrorism but the establishment of peace, and helping us remember what Erasmus urged us to realise in his epochal work, *Querila Pacis* (1516), more than five hundred years ago:

Peace speaks: If it were to their advantage for men to shun, spurn and reject me, although I have done nothing to deserve it, I would only lament the wrong done to me and their injustice; but since in rejecting me they deny themselves the source of all human happiness and bring on themselves a sea of disasters of every kind, I must shed tears rather for the misery they suffer than for any wrong they do me. I should have liked simply to be angry with them, but I am driven to feel pity and sorrow for their plight.

(Erasmus 1986: 293)

By putting forward visions of peace, justice and shared suffering, development can contribute to the reconstitution of hope in a new way, as the global community is now at a turning point parallel to the catastrophic decades of the 1940s, when development emerged as a new hope. In this book too, we have proposed a multi-dimensional field of development as a moral and political undertaking to better the human condition in concrete ways. We have delineated three domains of this undertaking – development as hope, development as critical understanding, and development as politics and administration. All of us concerned do not belong to all the domains in the same intimate way, and may have a more intense involvement with one or other of the domains. But how do we convince those who belong to other domains of development about the significance of our insight, experience and critique for the enrichment of the field of development? How do we enable the flow of insights and learning across domains, cutting across borders? Is the mode of rational argumentation, which proceeds on the hypothetical hope that participants would fall into 'self-contradiction' (cf. Matustik 1997: 29) if they do not open themselves to each other in discourse, enough? Here suffering provides us a mode of justification and mutual persuasion. We convince the other about the significance of our point of view in the development world not solely through the force of our arguments nor through displays of power and money, but by undertaking suffering for the sake of our convictions, and through this we stand as an example in which even our critics and non-involved onlookers start to take an interest. Those of us who belong to the domain of development as critical understanding can undertake suffering for the sake of our critical knowledge and through this open the minds and hearts of actors enmeshed in other domains of development – development as politics and development as hope. And here neither a Foucauldian critique of development nor a Habermasian mode of rational justification is enough; what is helpful here is to radically and transformationally supplement these modes with a Gandhian mode of undertaking suffering for the sake of love, peace and justice.

This preparation to undertake suffering provides a substantive content to development as hope in the present context. At present we talk about development as hope only in an archaeological manner, characterising the history of development in its formative years. But now we have to renew development as multiple practices of hope by undertaking multi-dimensional political and spiritual struggles, all of which call for some amount of undertaking of suffering from all of us concerned. There is an intimate connection between suffering and hope and this is mediated through our concrete activities and relationships in the world.[10] But at the contemporary juncture there is a decline of hope especially as it relates to improving the quality of relationships in the world and in our readiness to undertake suffering for the realisation of social hope. Hope persists, if at all, mainly in our individualistic domains confined to issues of a rising income and one's own security. This dimension of the contemporary situation is beautifully portrayed by Richard Rorty when he writes about our 'increasing inability to believe that things could ever get much better than they are now' (Rorty 1999: 230). For Rorty, 'Specifically, the last few decades have witnessed the increasing inability to believe that someday we shall ever have a classless global society; one in which there are now vast differences open to children in one nation and another, or between those open to children in one section of a city and those in another section of the same city' (Rorty 1999: 230; also see Wilfred 2000).

In this context, to be able to hope requires courage – courage not only of the intellect and will but also of the whole being. But here we have to learn to hope in a new way, different from past modes of certainty (cf. Strathern 2001a; Toulmin 2001). We have to learn to hope in the concrete spaces of our socio-political and spiritual struggles, but at the same time to proceed with an acknowledgement of contingency and a sense of human finitude and fragility. But in coming to terms with the calling of global responsibilities neither contingency nor human finitude should be an excuse for not undertaking concrete activities which contribute to self-development, reduction of human suffering and transformation of the world. As Chittaranjan Das (2001b) urges us: 'One liberates oneself by collaborating with a liberating process and that is perhaps how we collaborate in the march of this world of ours.'

Notes

I am grateful to Dr Philip Quarles van Ufford for his comments and to Professor Fred R. Dallmayr for helping me with many of his unpublished papers.

1   Dallmayr, like Dumont (1994), is sensitive to the elitist bias in the historical manifestation of *Bildung* in Germany, but for Dallmayr reviving the spirit of *Bildung* now is not to perpetuate elite culture or class privilege but to embrace popular culture with openness to learning.
2   Stephen Toulmin is open to such possibilities. Building on the work of the late Wittgenstein, Toulmin writes: 'our imaginations are particularly open to metaphysical yearnings at the point where language "goes on holiday". ... Our yearnings begin at a time when meanings are no longer bounded by the demands of workday disciplines or responsibilities, and language finds its fulfilment in the

High Holy Days. Then we are free to speak in ways that expand outside these boundaries to an unlimited extent: after all, as he [Wittgenstein] put it, *die sprache ist keir kafig* – Language is not a Cage' (Toulmin 2001: 201–202).

3   Dallmayr (1999) has shown this in his critical appreciation of Richard Rorty's programme, 'Achieving Our Country', which has an uncritical US bias. It is probably for this reason that the title of Dallmayr's forthcoming reflections on this issue is 'Achieving Our World'.

4   What Pollock *et al.* (2000) write below *vis-à-vis* their elaboration of what they call cosmofeminism, as an example of situated universalism, deserves our careful attention:

> Any cosmofeminine would have to create a critically engaged space that is not just a screen for globalisation or an antidote to nationalism but is rather a focus on projects of the intimate sphere conceived as a part of the cosmopolitan. Such a critical perspective would also open up a new understanding of the domestic, which would no longer be confined spatially or socially to the private sphere. This perspective would allow us to recognise that domesticity itself is a vital interlocutor and not just an interloper in law, politics and public ethics. From this reconfigured understanding of the public life of domesticity and intimacy it follows that spheres of intimacy generate legitimate pressure on any understanding of cosmopolitan solidarities and networks. The cosmofeminine could thus be seen as subverting those larger networks that refuse to recognise their own nature as specific systems of relations among others. That is, we would no longer have feminism as the voice of the specificity interrogating the claims of other putative universals. Instead we would have the cosmofeminine *as the sign of an argument for a situated universalism that invites broader debate based on a recognition of their own situatedness.* A focus on this extensional understanding of domesticity and intimacy could *generate a different picture of more public univeralisms,* making the domestic sphere subversive of *thin claims to universalism.*
>
> (Pollock *et al.* 2000: 584–585; emphasis added)

5   This was the position of Mr Jim Clancy, the CNN anchor man hosting the discussion on damage caused by violent protest in Genoa: 'Who is Going to Pay for the Loss of Property?'

6   Consider here the following provocative lines of Marilyn Strathern who, even without using the name of Marx or Heidegger, helps us to understand the problematic character of our feeling at home through the media of property relations:

> The manner in which Euro-Americans attach things to themselves makes them at home in the world – whether contained by Technology or by Nature – from which they think of such things as coming. Ownership is a kind of second skin to these two containers, a world through which people are infinitely interconnected through the inclusion or exclusions of property relations, and in which possession is taken to be at once a natural drive and just reward of creativity.
>
> It would I think be an enchanted world, created not least by the magico-purificatory divide at the heart of property relations, the cultural sleight of hand that suggests that just as things are intrinsically separate from persons so things intrinsically separate persons from one another.
>
> (Strathern 2001)

7 David Harvey invites us to such a path. In his *Justice, Nature and the Geography of Difference* (1996), Harvey writes:

> Marx regards experience *within* the fetishism as authentic enough but superficial and misleading, while Heidegger views that the same world of commodity exchange and technological rationality is at the root of an inauthenticity in daily life which has to be repudiated. This common definition of the root of the problem (though specified as particularly capitalist by Marx and modernist – i.e. both capitalist and socialist – by Heidegger) provides a common base from which to reconstruct a better understanding of place.
>
> (Harvey 1996: 315).

8 From the point of view of our concern with cross-civilisational dialogue, it is helpful to keep in mind Heidegger's urging that we should not think of cross-cultural dialogue in a planned manner which resonates his spirit of homelessness. Here, what Halbfass (1988) writes deserves our attention:

> In his own way, Heidegger accepts the Hegelian diagnosis that there is no escape from history and the global presence of European thought; but to him this does not mean that ancient or non-Western traditions are superseded by ... modern Western thought. They may, in fact, reach far beyond our current capacity of comprehension. ... The enigmatic future 'dialogue' with the East, to which Heidegger refers, cannot be planned and organized. What we have to learn above all is 'Gelassenheit', a serene willingness to wait.
>
> (Halbfass 1988: 170)

9 In this context, what Upendra Baxi (2000) writes with reference to the struggle of victims of the Union Carbide gas disaster in Bhopal, India deserves our careful attention:

> the violated of Bhopal through their movement prefigure a wider struggle against the catastrophic politics of cruelty encoded in the contemporary globalisation. ... Karl Marx said more than a century and half ago that the future of humanity depends on the conjuncture of two traditions: when suffering people begin to reflect and those who think begin to suffer. The violated of Bhopal have been deeply reflexive. It is time, perhaps, for the theorists of the 'new social movements' to begin to respond.
>
> (Baxi 2000: 45)

10 As philosopher Jayne M. Waterworth (2001) tells us: 'hope is an anticipatory activity; hoping is primarily something that people do, not something that just happens to them. ... Its significance is shown especially in contexts of suffering ... hope sustains the humanness of human beings.'

References

Appadurai, Arjun (2000a) 'Grassroots globalization and the research imagination', *Public Culture* 12 (1): 1–19.
—— (2000b) 'Spectral housing and urban cleansing: notes on millennial Mumbai', *Public Culture* 12 (3): 627–651.

Apel, Karl-Otto (1993) 'How to ground a universalistic ethics of co-responsibility for the effects of collective actions and activities', *Philosophica* 52 (2): 9–29.

Baxi, Upendra (2000) 'Human rights: suffering between markets and movements', in Robin Cohen and Shirin M. Rai (eds) *Global Social Movements*, London: Athlone Press.

Beck, Ulrich (2000) *The Brave New World of Work*, Cambridge: Polity Press.

—— (2001) *Cosmopolitanism and Risk*, manuscript, University of Munich.

Bhaskar, Roy (2000) *From East to West: the Odyssey of a Soul*, London: Routledge.

Bourdieu, Pierre (1999) *Acts of Resistance*, Cambridge: Polity Press.

Carrithers, Michael (1983) *Buddha*, Oxford: Oxford University Press.

Clammer, John (2000) 'A critique of "cognitive" development anthropology', *Anthropology Today* 16 (5): 1–3.

Comaroff, Jean and John Comaroff (2000) 'Millennial capitalism: first thoughts on a second coming', *Public Culture* 12 (2): 291–343.

Dallmayr, Fred (1998) *Alternative Visions: Pathways in the Global Village*, Lanham, MD: Rowman and Littlefield.

—— (1999) 'Achieving multiple countries: millennial reflections', *Journal of Contemporary Thought* 10: 5–26.

—— (2000a) 'Homelessness/homecoming: Heidegger on the road', manuscript, University of Notre Dame.

—— (2000b) 'Future of tradition', keynote address presented at the International Seminar on 'Future of Tradition', Forum for Contemporary Theory, Aurangabad, December.

—— (2001) 'Dialogue of civilizations: a Gadamerian perspective', manuscript, University of Notre Dame.

Das, Chittaranjan (2001a) 'Jagatikarana: Sanskruitka Atmaparichiti [Globalization: the question of cultural idenity]', the text of a memorial lecture delivered in Sambalpur, India.

—— (2001b) 'Integral education: the vision and the experiment', in Ananta K. Giri (ed.) *Rethinking Social Transformation: Criticism and Creativity at the Turn of the Millennium*, Jaipur: Rawat Publications.

Das, Veena (2001) 'Violence and translation', *Anthropological Quarterly* 75 (1): 105–112.

Dumont, Louis (1994) *German Ideology: from France to Germany and Back*, Chicago: University of Chicago Press.

Erasmus (1986 [1516]) *Querila Pacis: a Complaint of Peace Spurned and Rejected by the Whole World. The Collected Works of Erasmus*, Toronto: University of Toronto Press.

Gibson-Graham, Julie Kathy (1997) 'Postmodern becomings: from the space of form to the space of potentiality', in George Benko and Ulf Strohmayer (eds) *Space and Social Theory: Interpreting Modernity and Postmodernity*, Oxford: Basil Blackwell.

Giddens, Anthony (1999) *A Runaway World: How Globalization is Reshaping our Lives*, London: Profile Books.

Giri, Ananta (2000) 'Globalization of Hinduism: Swadhyaya in England and Sai Baba in Bali', *IIAS Newsletter* (Leiden), October.

—— (2001a) 'Moral commitments and transformations of politics: Kant, Gandhi and beyond', in *Conversations and Transformations: Towards a New Ethics of Self and Society*, Lanham, MD: Lexington Books.

—— (2001b) 'Gandhi, Tagore and a new ethics of argumentation', *Journal of Human Values* 7 (1).

Habermas, Jürgen (1993) *Justification and Application: Remarks on Discourse Ethics*, Cambridge: Polity Press.

—— (1996) *Between Facts and Norms: Contributions towards a Discourse Theory of Law and Democracy*, Cambridge: Polity Press.

—— (1998) *The Inclusion of the Other*, Cambridge: Polity Press.

Halbfass, William (1988) *India and Europe: an Essay in Understanding*, Albany: State University of New York Press.

Hamelink, Cees (2000) *The Ethics of Cyberspace*, London: Sage.

Hardt, Michael and Antonio Negri (2000) *Empire*, Cambridge, MA: Harvard University Press.

Hart, Keith (2000) 'Reflections on a visit to New York', *Anthropology Today* 16 (4): 1–3.

Harvey, David (1996) *Justice, Nature and the Geography of Difference*, Cambridge, MA: Basil Blackwell.

—— (2000a) *Spaces of Hope*, Edinburgh: University of Edinburgh Press.

—— (2000b) 'Cosmopolitanism and the banality of geographical evils', *Public Culture* 12 (2): 529–564.

Huntington, Samuel P. (1996) *The Clash of Civilizations and the Remaking of World Orders*, New York: Simon and Schuster.

Matustik, Martin J. (1997) *Postnational Identity: Critical Theory and Existential Philosophy in Habermas, Kierkegaard, and Havel*, New York: Guilford Press.

Mohanty, J.N. (2000) *Self and Other: Philosophical Essays*, Delhi: Oxford University Press

Mohanty, Manorjan and Partha Nath Mukherji with Olle Tornquist (eds) (1998) *People's Rights: Social Movements and the State in the Third World*, New Delhi: Sage.

Nederveen Pieterse, J. (ed.) (2000) *Global Futures: Shaping Globalization*, London: Zed Books.

—— (2001) *Development Theory: Deconstructions/Reconstructions*, London: Sage.

Offe, Claus and R.G. Heinze (1992) *Beyond Employment*, Cambridge: Polity Press.

Pollock, Sheldon, Homi K. Bhabha, Carol A. Breckenridge and Dipesh Chakrabarty (2000) 'Cosmopolitanisms', *Public Culture* 12 (3): 577–589.

Putnam, Hilary (2001) *The Spinoza Lectures, Lecture 1: Three Enlightenments*, University of Amsterdam.

Rawls, John (1999) *The Laws of Peoples*, Cambridge, MA: Harvard University Press.

—— (2001) *Justice as Fairness: a Restatement*, Cambridge, MA: Harvard University Press.

Rorty, Richard (1999) 'Globalization, the politics of identity and social hope', in *Philosophy and Social Hope*, London: Penguin Books.

Sachs, Wolfgang (1999) *Planet Dialectics: Explorations in Environment and Development*, London: Zed Books.

Said, Edward (2000) 'Invention, memory, and place', *Critical Inquiry* Winter: 175–192.

Sri Aurobindo (1962) *The Human Cycle. The Ideal of Human Unity. War and Self-Determination*, Pondicherry: Sri Aurobindo Ashram.

Strathern, Marilyn (2001a) 'Blowing hot and cold', *Anthropology Today* 17 (1): 1–2.

—— (2001b) 'The patent and the Melanggan', in Christopher Penny and Nicholas Thomas (eds) *Beyond Aesthetics: Art and the Technologies of Enchantment*, Oxford: Berg, pp. 259–286.

Strydom, Piet (1999) 'The challenge of responsibility for sociology', *Current Sociology* 47 (3): 65–82.

Toulmin, Stephen (2001) *Return to Reason*, Cambridge, MA: Harvard University Press.

Touraine, Alain (2001) Foreword to Ananta K. Giri, *Building in the Margins of Shacks: the Vision and Projects of Habitat for Humanity*, Delhi: Orient Longman.

Uberoi, J.P.S. (1996) *Religion, Civil Society and State: a Study of Sikhism*, Delhi: Oxford University Press.

Unger, Roberto M. (1987) *False Necessity: Anti-necessitarian Social Theory in the Service of Radical Democracy*, Cambridge: Cambridge University Press.

Wallerstein, Immanuel *et al.* (1996) *Open the Social Sciences*, Stanford: Stanford University Press.

Waterworth, Jayne M. (2001) *Living in the Light of Hope: an Investigation into Agency and Meaning*, Umea University, Sweden: Department of Philosophy and Linguistics.

Wilfred, Felix (2000) *Asian Dreams and Christian Hopes*, Delhi: ICPCK Publishers.

Index

Page numbers followed by 'n' represent endnotes